Keep this book. You will
need it and use it throughout
your career.

MANAGING CONVENTIONS and GROUP BUSINESS

Educational Institute Books

MANAGING
CONVENTIONS
and
GROUP BUSINESS

Leonard H. Hoyle
David C. Dorf
Thomas J. A. Jones

A nonprofit educational foundation

Disclaimer

This publication is designed to provide accurate and authoritative information in regard to the subject matter covered. It is sold with the understanding that the publisher is not engaged in rendering legal, accounting, or other professional service. If legal advice or other expert assistance is required, the services of a competent professional person should be sought.

—From the Declaration of Principles jointly adopted by the American Bar Association and a Committee of Publishers and Associations

The authors, Leonard H. Hoyle, David C. Dorf, and Thomas J. A. Jones, are solely responsible for the contents of this publication. All views expressed herein are solely those of the authors and do not necessarily reflect the views of the Educational Institute of the American Hotel & Motel Association (the Institute) or the American Hotel & Motel Association (AH&MA).

Nothing contained in this publication shall constitute a standard, an endorsement, or a recommendation of the Institute or AH&MA. The Institute and AH&MA disclaim any liability with respect to the use of any information, procedure, or product, or reliance thereon by any member of the hospitality industry.

©Copyright 1989
By the EDUCATIONAL INSTITUTE of the
AMERICAN HOTEL & MOTEL ASSOCIATION
1407 South Harrison Road
P.O. Box 1240
East Lansing, Michigan 48826

The Educational Institute of the American
Hotel & Motel Association is a nonprofit
educational foundation.

Printed in the United States of America
      10 94 95

658.4562
H867

Library of Congress Cataloging-in-Publication Data
Hoyle, Leonard H.
   Managing conventions and group business.

   Includes index.
   1. Hotels, taverns, etc. 2. Congresses and conventions.
3. Convention facilities. I. Dorf, David C. II. Jones, Thomas J.A. III. Title.
TX911.2.H69 1989 658.4'562'068 88–31096
ISBN 0–86612–042–4

Editor: Daniel T. Davis

Contents

Acknowledgments

The Educational Institute extends its appreciation to the following industry and academic professionals for contributing their time and expertise, in addition to useful illustrative materials, to the development of this valuable resource:

Bill Beggs, Director of Sales, The Sagamore, Bolton Landing, New York; Rudi Frei, CHA, Holiday Inn, Lansing, Michigan; Roger Fries, Special Events Program Manager, Chrysler Corporation, Highland Park, Michigan; Sharon S. Giroux, Instructor, Department of Habitational Resources, University of Wisconsin—Stout; Valerie MacLeod, Manager, Convention Services, Buena Vista Palace, Walt Disney World Village, Lake Buena Vista, Florida; George Palacios, Director of Convention Services, The Grand Kempinski, Dallas, Texas; Keith Patrick, Director of Convention Services, Disneyland Hotel, Anaheim, California; Monica Rafter, Director of Convention Services, The Westin La Paloma, Tucson, Arizona; Rick Rosenau, Banquet Manager, Vanderbilt Plaza Hotel, Nashville, Tennessee; Dr. Peter VanKleek, CHA, Dean, School of Hotel/Restaurant Management, Northern Arizona University; Marc VanWormer, College of Engineering, Michigan State University; Debbie Wardrop, Director of Convention Services, The Arizona Biltmore, Phoenix, Arizona; Ray Waters, Director of Convention Services, Opryland Hotel, Nashville, Tennessee; Doug Weir, Viacom Conference Center, New York City; and Chuck Wrye, Publisher, *Successful Meetings*, New York City.

Preface

"The sale merely consumates the courtship; then the marriage begins."
—Theodore Levitt, Editor, *Harvard Business Review*

Doing business successfully in the meetings market requires building close relationships—perhaps more so than in any other segment of the hospitality industry. There is no other route to success, and this book will make that clear to you if you don't already believe it.

People who plan meetings are frequently at great risk. Many meetings, from large association conventions to small corporate board meetings, are planned by busy executives who have numerous other responsibilities. They seldom understand the magnitude of the job, even for planning the smallest meeting, and the results usually reflect this lack of knowledge. For their meetings to be successful, planners need the help that comes from forming close and mutually beneficial relationships with the staffs of hotels, resorts, conference centers, and convention centers.

That is why this book is so important. No matter which part of the meetings business you're in, this text will give you an essential understanding of how successful meetings are planned and conducted. It was written by three men who know the business well, and they look at the meetings business from every angle.

Leonard "Buck" Hoyle was an association meeting planner for a large part of his professional career. He was director of conventions and expositions for the American Society of Association Executives prior to becoming the executive director of Hotel Sales & Marketing Association International, where he still plans an annual convention. David Dorf has been with Hotel Sales & Marketing Association International since 1955 and is presently the association's director of education and training. His strength is in sales and marketing aspects of the hospitality industry. Tom Jones, assistant professor in the School of Hotel & Restaurant Management at Northern Arizona University, has 15 years experience in various areas of the hospitality industry.

So if you want to plan better meetings, or if you want to get business from meeting planners, this book is for you.

The book is organized in a way that will help you understand the types of meetings business that exist, how to get that business, and how to service the business after you get it.

Chapters 1 through 5 discuss the various market segments and their convention/meeting requirements. Profiles and descriptions of requirements are provided for each segment.

Chapters 6 through 8 tell you how to evaluate a property's ability to get and service meetings, and then how to find customers and make the sale to them.

Chapters 9 through 12 tell you how to execute all aspects of successful meetings, from food functions to trade shows.

Each chapter contributes to what I think should be the maxim for this exciting business: "Marketing is a philosophy, not a department."

May all your meetings be successful meetings.

Charles L. Wrye
Publisher, *Successful Meetings*

1 Overview: Definition and Scope of the Meetings Market

Chapter Objectives

1. To identify the types of meetings that are frequently held at lodging properties

2. To learn the various ways in which a lodging property might be perceived by the public

3. To identify those factors having the greatest impact on the growth of the meetings and convention industry

4. To explain why the hospitality industry has to be viewed as a people business

The meetings and convention market is big business today, but this hasn't always been the case. Although virtually every element in American society has had to meet for business or pleasure, recognition of this activity as a viable industry did not occur until just recently.

The growth of the meetings and convention industry reflects parallel developments in the hospitality industry, especially during the past quarter century. There is a strong interrelationship between the two industries, and each has complemented the other.

This chapter provides a general framework in which to study the interrelationship of both industries. This will aid in obtaining a better understanding of the contributions each industry has made not only to this country's business economy, but to American society as a whole.

Lodging Facilities in the Meeting Environment

Throughout American history, there are few examples of any sociological, political, or economic phenomena as significant as the tandem evolution of the hospitality industry and the meetings and conventions industry. Both industries are significant for several reasons: the amount of money they generate throughout the economies in which they operate; the sociopolitical decisions and positions that result from their activities; and their impact upon the lives of those who participate in them, either as members of groups or as individuals.

Those not associated with our work usually fail to appreciate the important role the hospitality industry plays in the conduct of our society's business, government, and entertainment.

A presumptuous statement? It would be were it not for the evolution the hospitality industry has shared with the meetings industry. In the face of that important alliance, the statement is not presumptuous. It is, instead, a fact clearly understood by those who work in, report on, and benefit from the emerging discipline of convention management and service.

In this context, the convention management and service industry includes those who are either staff members of convention properties (hotels, convention centers, conference centers, etc.) or of organizations that hold meetings (associations and societies, corporations, labor unions, etc.). For, in this association of the hospitality and the convention/meetings industries, each element needs its own convention managers.

We might reflect on our earlier observation that the hospitality industry plays a very important role in our society through its facilitation of the meetings industry. It should not come as a surprise that the authors of this book would make so strong a statement. After all, our democracy was founded in Philadelphia at a meeting called the "Constitutional Convention."

Today, our political parties hold conventions to select candidates, to debate, and eventually to determine policies and platforms that directly influence the quality and direction of our lives. In a more personal vein, if you belong to a fraternal organization, a service organization, or a professional society, bear in mind that the degree to which they benefit you and our society is decided primarily "in convention."

Obviously, without hotels or other entities providing the necessary accommodations and facilities, meetings and conventions as we know them today would not be possible. On the other hand, without the associations, corporations, and other groups we will examine in this text, there would be no meetings and conventions to accommodate.

And so, there is the making of a solid, mutually beneficial union. It is not always a completely harmonious association, and we will learn the reasons for this later. But certainly, a group's need for a controlled, well-managed environment and the development of that environment and those management skills in the hospitality industry have produced not only a multi-billion-dollar industry, but also a new and growing career specialty called "convention management." It is, however, a specialty with its share of growing pains.

Meeting Planners in the Convention Environment

To understand this new industry, we must consider the plight of the convention manager. To begin with, he or she works in an area that is not very well known by the general public. Few persons outside the industry recognize the disciplines and skills needed to manage the affairs of a modern hotel or convention facility. Why? Because the field has developed from a rudimentary one to a highly challenging, well-defined specialty in little more than a quarter of a century.

As late as the 1960s, convention management was a sideline for most of its practitioners. Knowledge about the industry was scant, highly unscientific, and untested. Few groups existed to aid either planners or suppliers of convention products and services in understanding and professionalizing their work.

In those early days, agreements were consummated by a handshake. Legally binding contracts between meeting sponsors and suppliers were novel. Conventions and meetings were often designed out of habit, predicated largely on what had taken place in the past.

Association conventions emphasized political and social activities—not necessarily in that order—and the stereotypical funny hats, bugles, and water balloons were in fact frequently observed in the lobbies of convention properties.

Company meetings, on the other hand, were more oriented toward corporate products and issues because of the greater homogeneity of the attendees. Still, the complexity and demands of their programming (especially in the areas of staging, audio-visual, and special effects) were unsophisticated by today's standards.

In terms of their design and service, lodging properties were highly standardized and relatively uncreative in marketing, production, and implementation techniques. Whether a cause or a result of that fact, meeting and convention planners were undemanding and uncreative as well. A key point here is that most planners had neither the inclination nor the understanding to be creative. Many of them were planning conventions and meetings on the side while also serving as executive directors, membership managers, or government relations directors of associations. In the corporate sphere, planners were office managers or public relations directors.

No one specialized in convention management. Everyone in the field came from another discipline. More traditional work responsibilities assigned to association and corporate meeting planners competed for these individuals' time and energies.

We said earlier that the general public knew little about the real business environment and skills of a lodging property executive. They knew even less about "convention management" as a profession.

Nikolaj M. Petrovic, president of the American Dental Trade Association, began his career in association management as a convention planner. He remembers the environment of the 1960s, and he recounts the feeling of being overwhelmed because of his enormous responsibilities and his clients' lack of knowledge about convention planning.

"There I was," he said, "responsible for the welfare of thousands of people, planning their menus, their accommodations, their education programs, transportation, speakers, security, and communications. I was literally responsible for their very existence and well-being in a foreign environment."

As with all meeting planners, Petrovic was often asked what he did for a living. He remembers one case in particular.

"I was asked, 'What do you do?' I said I was a convention manager for an association. The immediate response was, 'Boy, I wish I had your job. I'd love to throw parties for a living.'"

Petrovic continues, "That is really what people perceived in those days. Come to think of it, that is what they thought of hotels too."

Perhaps those perceptions were logical, the result of a hundred years of public gatherings where the food and drink were the foundation of success, and everything else was more or less secondary.

Perceptions and Growth of the Lodging Industry

For thousands of years, a hotel meant a place of shelter. Since the Gospel account of Bethlehem, an inn was a place to stay for the night and perhaps take sustenance. How things have changed!

Today, the general public no longer perceives hotels as suppliers of only beds and food. Properties are now being seen as centers for community activities—financial magnets that attract outside dollars to local economies. Even more, they are appreciated as status symbols representing a community's prestige, visibility, and growth.

For example, Detroit, Michigan, has designed its major urban renewal projects around the Renaissance Center, a complex of office and retail space surrounding the skyscraping Westin Renaissance Hotel in downtown Detroit.

In the past 20 years, Orlando, Florida, has grown from a small Florida resort community to a vast vacation and convention mecca where the hospitality industry is centered on the Disney World complex. The area's properties contain 60,000 guestrooms and 350,000 square feet of meeting room space.

The same phenomenon also can be observed in Anaheim, California. Years ago, Jack Benny was its only booster when he listed it among train stops equally nondescript, such as Kookamonga and Azusa, California.

Now, since the opening of Disneyland, 35,000 guestrooms, and a convention center, Anaheim and Greater Orange County have gained a reputation as a hub of leisure and convention activity as well as the home of major league baseball (California Angels) and football (Los Angeles Rams) teams. It seems incredible that in the past 30 years Jack Benny's whistlestop has become one of the most prestigious metropolitan areas in the United States. More than any other factor, the hospitality industry and the convention industry put Anaheim on the map—in capital letters.

Numerous other examples exist that show how the lodging property and meetings industries permeate the image of a community and the psyche of its people.

Atlanta, Georgia, often called "the city ten years ahead of itself," boasts of the world's first atrium lobby (the Hyatt Regency Atlanta), one of the world's tallest properties (the Westin Peachtree Plaza), and the nation's largest airport (Hart Field). Its Georgia World Congress Center ranks among the five largest convention centers in the United States.

In Washington, D.C., tourism and hospitality rank second in size only to the Federal government.

Growth of Convention and Conference Centers

Until the 1960s, meetings and conventions were synonymous with hotels. Meeting planners had few alternatives about where to hold meetings, regardless of their size and scope. In general, no other facilities existed that offered the same range of rooms and services that hotels did. The situation, however, changed markedly with the advent of convention centers and conference centers.

The emergence of convention and conference centers allowed planners to concentrate more on the actual meeting environment and less on secondary items and services. The existence and continued growth of these centers are much too important to be ignored in any analysis of the meetings and conventions market.

Convention Centers   Expansion is the one word best describing the status of the convention center industry in the United States since the 1970s. By the 1980s, 145 cities had centers accommodating 20,000 people or more.[1] Some critics maintain that the market is totally saturated and the building boom is over. However, this expansion was necessary to keep pace with the explosive growth of the associations market. This market has almost doubled in 20 years, from about 12,000 in 1975 to more than 21,000 today.

Because these associations must hold conventions each year, their need for meeting facilities has increased markedly. Some even conduct two meetings a year. In addition, many associations hold expositions that can be housed only in convention centers. The number of associations conducting expositions has grown from about 30% of those polled in the early 1980s to almost 50% today. But convention centers have an appeal to other market segments as well.

The corporate meetings market has a natural affinity for convention centers because their size is an important consideration for exhibitions and trade shows. These are activities that do not fit readily into a hotel environment. In addition to space for meetings and conferences, there is more than adequate room for exhibits and booths.

Although presently the demand for new centers may not be increasing significantly, many center managers are renovating their properties to meet the special needs of their clients.

Physical Characteristics. Most convention centers are public facilities owned by city, county, or state agencies. A convention center contains 50,000 to 700,000 square feet of exhibition space and a large number of meeting rooms that range in size from 30% to 50% of the amount of space contained in the exhibition hall. Other space is available for kitchens, banquet facilities, and other specialized areas.[2]

The exhibition space in a typical convention center often can be subdivided. Floors are usually constructed of concrete, and ceilings are 25 feet high or even higher.

When selecting a center, meeting planners usually consider the following factors:

- Access to the city and overall appeal of the area
- The efficiency of the center's management and labor pool
- The layout and location of the center's physical plant
- The quality of such services as food and beverage facilities and audiovisual equipment

Conference
Centers

Conference centers first emerged almost two decades ago as properties whose sole purpose was to provide all the elements of a successful meeting atmosphere. They are a viable alternative to meeting planners who may not want to hold a meeting or conference in a hotel environment.

Modern conference centers are characterized by the following attributes:[3]

- Single-purpose design of meeting rooms
- Ability to service a primary market of 10- to 60-person meetings
- Permanent soundproof walls
- Excellent acoustics and lighting
- Good audiovisual design
- More user orientation (i.e., speaker access to lighting and ventilation controls)
- Superior support staff
- Functional design of off-hours facilities to promote interaction among meeting attendees

The International Association of Conference Centers (IACC) distinguishes six different types of conference centers: executive, resort, corporate, not-for-profit/educational, non-residential, and ancillary. The characteristics of each are shown in Exhibit 1.1, "Conference Center Characteristics."

Size of the Meetings Market

Despite its importance, it is impossible to accurately measure the size of the meetings and convention market. Because of the large number of group events and the growing variety of types of meetings, records are inexact in many areas or non-existent in others. Therefore, it is widely felt that statistics about the industry are actually quite conservative.

In the most recent survey prepared by Murdoch Magazines Research Department for *Meetings & Conventions* magazine (a survey that covered off-premises association and corporate meetings held by subscribers to the magazine), it was determined that those subscribers held 903,740 meetings in 1985.[4]

Further, associations and corporations queried in the survey spent a total of $31.4 billion on meetings in that one-year period.[5] When these figures were projected to the total meetings market as determined by the researchers, that figure reached $34.6 billion. The *Meetings & Conventions* data is shown in Exhibit 1.2.

It is important to note that these expenditures represent only the *direct* expenses incurred to produce the meetings. In terms of the financial impact of this growing industry on hotels, other facilities, and communities as a whole, direct expenses are a relatively *minor* part of the overall financial picture. Even more important is the money spent by delegates for their personal needs and services.

Exhibit 1.1   Conference Center Characteristics

Type of Center	Clientele	Identifying Characteristics
Executive	Specialized meetings for middle- to upper-level management.	Meetings gravitate toward training and strategy/planning sessions, including board meetings. Meetings typically range from 20 to 300 people.
Corporate	Two types: —exclusive for parent company and subsidiaries. —priority bookings for in-house use with facilities available for outside organizations.	Training for supervisory and management personnel for parent company. For outside users, meeting purposes are similar to executive conference centers. Outside organizations increase utilization and offset costs of maintaining centers.
Resort	Group meeting business is primary market.	Meetings for educational as well as training purposes, and incentive or reward programs. Have extensive recreational facilities, which can have a beneficial effect on meeting's outcome. Occupancy generally influenced by seasonal demand. Fastest-growing segment of conference centers.
College/University/Not-for-Profit	Adult education programs, academic and/or scientifically oriented meetings. Large corporate or entry-level meetings geared toward management training or continuing education programs. Mainly selected groups, to maintain tax advantaged status. Center may be for the primary use of parent, not-for-profit organization.	Many of these centers were developed as a result of the information explosion and declining undergraduate enrollment. Advantages include having a recognized, talented faculty. Usually offer full array of facilities, accommodations, services, and recreation found in other types of conference centers.
Non-residential	Same as executive, college/university and not-for-profit.	No guestrooms; therefore majority of conferees are locally oriented. Located in urban and suburban areas where there is a high concentration of corporate headquarters. One reason for these centers is the high cost of air travel.
Ancillary	Conferees are a mixture of executive and resort clientele.	An ancillary conference center is one segment of a larger organization. They are similar in all respects to the other types of centers.

Source: Adapted from Laventhol & Horwath, *The Conference Center Industry: A Statistical and Financial Profile, July 1985-June 1986* (Philadelphia, Pa.: 1986), p. 5.

Exhibit 1.2 Total Meetings and Expenditures

	No. of Mtgs.	Percent
Corporate Meetings	706,100	78
Major Association Conventions	12,240	1
Other Association Meetings	185,400	21
TOTAL MEETINGS	903,740	100
	Total Expenses	
Corporate Meetings	$ 7,527,800,000	
Major Association Conventions	12,675,800,000	
Other Association Meetings	11,213,300,000	
TOTAL EXPENDITURES	$31,416,900,000*	

*This is representative of subscribers to *Meetings & Conventions* magazine only.

Source: "The Meetings Market '85," *Meetings & Conventions*, March 31, 1986, Tables 9 and 42.

According to the International Association of Convention and Visitors Bureaus (IACVB), each delegate to a convention and exposition spent an average of $788 in 1986, an increase of about $70 per person from 1985.[6] This was based on an average stay of four nights. Thus, the individual's average daily expenses were $125.66, and this was *in addition* to per-attendee expenditures by the sponsoring association.

The dynamic growth of the convention industry is illustrated by a simple comparison of figures. We learned earlier that, in 1985, *Meetings & Convention* magazine found that expenditures for corporate and association meetings were more than $34 billion. In 1974, the magazine's research had estimated expenditures for similar meetings to be only $5.5 billion. A key element in the industry's growth is that it provides a rapidly growing market to transportation companies, retailers, service contractors, and virtually every outlet in the vicinity of a convention facility. In the old days, conventioneers were ridiculed and often unwelcome outside of the meeting facility itself. Today, they are sought aggressively by cities, courted by hotels and convention centers, and welcomed with open arms by all who have a product or service to sell.

The *Meetings & Conventions* survey reported that more than 13.5 million persons attended major conventions in 1985. Further, each delegate spent an average of $890 on such items as transportation, meals, entertainment, shopping, and hotels. That amounts to $12.15 billion in delegate expenditures for a one-year period. And these figures do *not* include attendance or expenditures by spouses or children. Spouse attendance alone was estimated at 5.5 million persons.

We can add to the 13.5-million figure another 18,172,700 persons who attended other types of association meetings, such as seminars, board meetings, committee meetings, and special industry professional and technical conferences. Average attendee expenses for these types of meetings were $690. Again, *without* including money spent by spouses (estimated to be an additional 2.2 million people), this totals $12.5 billion in delegate expenditures.

And while these figures may represent a bonanza to the suppliers of goods and services to conventions and meetings, even better news is that they represent only the tip of the financial iceberg.

Delegate expenditures are even greater in the corporate meetings sector. *Meetings & Conventions* reported that 39,788,200 persons attended corporate meetings in the 12 months prior to its 1986 survey.[7]

Individual out-of-pocket expenses for these meetings were not covered in this study because, for corporate meetings, such delegate expenses as transportation, food, entertainment, and accommodations are paid by the sponsoring company. There were 706,100 corporate meetings during the 12-month-period studied, and each meeting cost the sponsoring company an average of $116,710.[8]

We can also assume that attendees at corporate meetings spent money from their own pockets to pay for expenses not covered by the meeting sponsor. And, once again, spouse attendance was not factored into these figures. In the case of corporate meetings, spouse attendance was projected at more than 7 million persons. These projections are particularly important for budget planners in the local communities because it is thought that spouses spend more per person than delegates at the convention site.

Therefore, it is apparent that the convention/hospitality industry has become a relatively recent and very important source of revenue, jobs, and prestige for major cities and resorts. Virtually every dollar spent on meeting activities is added to those normally circulated in the daily economic life of the host community.

Growth of the Meetings and Conventions Industry

The growth of the meetings and conventions industry has been nothing short of phenomenal. The interesting thing is that most of this development has occurred within the past 25 years. Industry experts agree that this growth has been due to several factors: meeting planners associations, the airline industry, the lodging industry, convention centers, convention bureaus, conference centers, meeting technology, and ground handlers.*

Meeting Planners Associations
There was unparalleled development of the associations connected with meeting planners. These organizations not only grew in numbers, even bringing in corporate planners, but they also expanded the list of services they offered their members. The majority of these associations significantly increased their emphasis on education. Other growth factors included the emergence of the independent meeting planner, an increase in the number of women planners, certification and the development of standards, and the integration of travel agents into the profession.

Airline Industry
The maturation of the airline industry made it possible for relatively large numbers of people to travel from one point to another quickly and efficiently. This was made possible by the introduction of the jet airplane, an

*For a detailed description of the factors contributing to the growth of the meetings and convention industry, see "An Industry Comes of Age," *Meetings & Conventions*, June 1986, pp. 34–67.

innovation that revolutionized transportation worldwide. A related factor was the deregulation of the industry. This resulted in the airlines' competing more vigorously for passengers and caused a corresponding reduction in the cost of air travel.

Lodging Industry

The lodging industry recognized the financial significance of conventions and meetings and adapted accordingly. Hotels grew and became convention centers. Hoteliers learned how to adapt their services to a spectrum of different clients. Even smaller properties began searching for groups they were equipped to handle. Property marketing directors learned how to work with meeting planners.

Convention Centers

Convention centers took on new roles. They expanded in terms of exhibition space, accessibility, and storage facilities. They became capable of accommodating all the activities of a convention and trade show under one roof. Traffic flow design was improved, allowing large numbers of people to move quickly from one area to another.

Convention Bureaus

Convention bureaus saw rapid growth both in terms of numbers and size of operations. The number of bureaus has doubled since 1980, from 100 to more than 250, and their operators have become much more professional, participating to a much greater degree in industry and association affairs.

Conference Centers

During the past two decades, conference centers changed their appearances. At one time, they maintained a "business only" facade, but this has been replaced by up-to-date restaurants and recreational facilities. In addition, most contain the latest high-tech audiovisual equipment.

Meeting Technology

Changes in audiovisual equipment, brought about mainly by the electronics revolution, gave meeting planners a degree of flexibility and creativity never before possible. Video projectors, 360-degree projection techniques, multi-image presentations, and unique sound systems have all become commonplace

Ground Handlers

As meetings and conventions became more complex, so did the need for effective ground arrangements. Ground arrangements can include planning tours, transportation, sightseeing, banquets, and even hotel reservations. In the 1970s, convention service companies appeared on the scene to develop creative meeting programs.

A People Business

And yet, as large as the industry has grown economically, the long-term success of its practitioners cannot be quantified solely in terms of dollars. This is because the convention industry, like the hospitality industry, is a "people" business. One cannot demonstrate success or efficiency in a property serving the convention industry only by using such typical barometers of operations as average rate, room nights occupied, or food and beverage revenue.

This is not to say that operational barometers and management controls are not as essential for a lodging or convention property as they are for any other business. However, setting standards and controls for successful and profitable property operations must be done with full knowledge that the ultimate key to continued success and profitability rests primarily with pleasing the people who pay their money, stay at that property, and use its products and services.

In other words, this is not a hard-product industry. Rather, it is an industry with a primary product (guestrooms or meeting facilities) that has no shelf life. Success is made even more precarious because of the alternatives available to the consumer. There are not just a few major competitors with similar products on the market. Rather, there are literally thousands across the country. All are trying to sell a highly perishable primary product—guestrooms or meeting facilities.

Only a few years ago, the competition an individual property faced was restricted to its own geographic region. With the advent of jet air travel and the low fares resulting from airline deregulation, properties now have to compete with distant ones for guests.

This has led not only to greater competition but also to a much more discerning, experienced, and demanding guest. What used to be the trip of a lifetime now is often just a casual break of routine for a businessperson or an entire family.

Today, a property rarely competes for the favor of a traveler enjoying lodging services for the first time. Instead, the typical guest, whether a conventioneer or a transient, has already experienced many levels of lodging property services and environments and is in a good position to judge each against the best. It is against this perception of a property at its best that each hotelier competes.

It stands to reason that being judged favorably can result in repeat business. It is important that individual guests form the right impression of the property, and it is even more important in the case of large groups attending meetings. Conventioneers' favorable experiences at a property can result in lucrative leisure and business travel in the future.

The extent of that business is almost impossible to predict or to quantify. But veterans of the industry attest to its importance.

And even beyond the impact of repeat business is the new business generated by the informal, incredibly influential, word-of-mouth testimonials of those whom the property has served well. This is true of the individual guest as well as the convention attendee. However, the prudent hotelier realizes that a typical meeting or convention presents a unique opportunity for implementing a concept known as *marketing through servicing.*

A group is an entity with similar interests, rather than just a collection of individuals. This group assumes its own set of characteristics and the members will be largely influenced by the experiences they are sharing. If these experiences are positive, they are more efficient and productive in a marketing sense than advertising, exhibiting, or sales blitzes. If, on the other hand, they are negative, the results will be devastating.

A property's failure to effectively service and manage a meeting can undo all its advertising and marketing efforts.

Examples of such failures are chronicled in the lore of meeting managers. In this industry, the network of communications is extraordinarily broad and swift. And memories are long.

Chapter Summary

Over the years, the hospitality industry has facilitated the growth and development of the meetings and convention industry. In addition, several other related factors have also contributed to this growth. This has had an impact felt in all sectors of American society.

As the industry continues to expand, it will become better known in the public's mind. In addition, the role of the professional meeting planner will take on even greater significance and importance.

The hospitality industry will continue to benefit from the meetings and convention market so long as property executives never lose sight of the fact that they must provide the same services and amenities to corporations and associations that they do to the typical guest. Underneath it all, the meetings and convention industry still remains a people business.

Notes

1. *The Convention Liaison Council Manual* (Washington, D.C., 1985), p. 27.
2. Material from a forthcoming publication provided by Laventhol & Horwath, Philadelphia, Pennsylvania.
3. Geoffrey Kirkland, "Small Meetings Explosion Feeds Rapid Conference Center Growth," *Meeting News*, November 15, 1987, pp. 48, 60.
4. "The Meetings Market '85," *Meetings & Conventions*, March 31, 1986, Table 9.
5. Ibid., Table 42.
6. International Association of Convention and Visitors Bureaus, *1986 Convention Income Survey* (Champaign, Illinois, March 1987).
7. "The Meetings Market '85," Table 10.
8. Ibid., Table 9.

2 Associations and the Meetings They Hold

Chapter Objectives

1. To identify the various purposes associations serve

2. To identify the types of meetings most associations conduct

3. To describe the decision-making process within a typical association

4. To identify meetings at other than the national or international levels that associations conduct

In a sense, meetings and conventions have almost become synonymous with associations.

There are numerous types of associations, and they serve many purposes. One element common to all associations is their need to gather their members for business, professional, and social activities. This aspect is particularly important to the hospitality industry, which provides the facilities and services for these gatherings.

This chapter provides an in-depth look at associations—their types and the purposes they serve. It analyzes the types of meetings these groups conduct and how they go about selecting particular sites for their conventions and meetings.

Associations Defined

Although the association industry is almost as old as the hospitality industry itself, relatively little is known about it, even by those who deal with it on a frequent basis.

Individuals who choose to work in association management soon learn that those in other career areas find it difficult to understand the nature and purpose of association work. Yet, virtually everyone belongs to or is affected by one or more associations. There are so many different associations that it is sometimes difficult to define them in simple terms. Perhaps this is why they have remained in low profile over the years.

The dictionary defines an association as "an organization of persons having a common interest."[1] This is a very accurate description of what an association is.

Formal political associations have existed since the days of Caesar Augustus. Modern trade associations can be traced back to the European guild system of the Middle Ages. In the United States, associations have become important political, social, commercial, and professional factors. Thousands of associations exist today, influencing the lives of practically everyone in our society. Examples of how associations play some role in our day-to-day activities are abundant.

To begin with, remember that the sociopolitical-economic framework of society is largely determined by "special interest" groups. These are associations that lobby on the national, state, and local levels for laws and regulations that favor their members' special interests.

For example, contractors specializing in air conditioning and heating systems may belong to the Mechanical Contractors Association of America. This association analyzes contractors' business interests and personal opinions and then expresses them to lawmakers in Washington.

In a similar vein, the owner of a small retail firm in Georgia may belong to the Georgia Business and Industry Association. This association's lobbyist at the statehouse in Atlanta would represent the retailer's interests and desires to lawmakers there.

At the local level, persons may belong to a parent-teacher association or a neighborhood improvement group. The principle is the same in both cases. Individuals' opinions and interests are shared and analyzed, and the consensus is then used to influence the adoption of new elementary school curricula, local zoning ordinances, or programs to improve the quality of life in the community.

But this growing influence of associations in our sociopolitical fortunes is not without its critics. Many people view special-interest groups in a negative light. These critics include even those who participate in associations and actually benefit from them.

Nevertheless, associations perform two important functions. First, they research and analyze opinions and attitudes of their members. Second, they crystallize those opinions to assist lawmakers in developing appropriate legislation.

Some critics maintain that special interest groups wield too much power, influencing politicians to enact laws and regulations favoring only a minority. Associations and lawmakers alike refute that notion.

And so, associations continue to play a major and ever-growing role in the administration of society. Why is this important to hotel sales and convention service executives? Because the deliberations that generate policies for government and legislative affairs most often take place at meetings of members, both in committee and in convention, and the hospitality industry is instrumental in bringing these people together and providing the facilities for their conferences.

Purposes of Associations

It is said that associations have as many purposes as they have members. We can list at least 16 purposes that associations serve:

1. To influence legislation
2. To offer professional education to members
3. To provide opportunities for peer interaction or networking
4. To extend career and professional development
5. To maintain social relationships
6. To disseminate general information
7. To disseminate political information
8. To make available research and statistical data
9. To provide better purchasing power through group discounts
10. To distribute specialized publications
11. To perform public relations activities
12. To handle legal affairs
13. To ensure industry standardization
14. To offer group travel opportunities
15. To perform public service activities
16. To improve employee/employer relations

These items are in no particular order of importance because prioritizing would vary, depending on the association involved.

From the viewpoint of the hospitality industry executive, however, it is obvious that many of these purposes directly or indirectly involve the products and services of hotels, conference centers, transportation companies, and many other industry enterprises.

Types of Associations

It is important that we examine various types of associations. The more suppliers know about major markets, the greater their opportunity for determining needs and then selling products and services that fill those needs.

Managing Membership Societies, published by the American Society of Association Executives, lists a variety of associations, virtually all of which hold meetings and conventions.[2] Exactly where a group falls within these broad categories (which can be subdivided) is sometimes difficult to tell, based only on the name of the organization. Nevertheless, hoteliers should at least be familiar with the following types of associations. They should know that these different types operate under different rules and restrictions, and for different purposes and needs. Hoteliers who understand those differences have a much greater opportunity to position their products to fit those needs and to develop specialized market plans aimed at these groups.

The following are descriptions of some of these groups and the types of meetings they usually hold.

Trade and Professional Associations

Trade and professional associations are organizations composed of companies or individuals who want to improve conditions, efficiency, and profitability within the fields or industries in which they practice.

For example, the Society of Automotive Engineers has members representing many different automobile manufacturers. They have a common interest in the engineering discipline within that general industry. But it often goes further than that.

There are engineers and scientists from other industries, who, beyond the specialized needs of their primary associations, find more general needs affecting them. The Council of Engineering and Scientific Society Executives, for example, is a coalition of associations within the science and engineering field represented by the executives who manage the various engineering associations.

This is not a unique development. A similar coalition exists in the convention industry. The Convention Liaison Council is composed of representatives of 21 associations with direct interest in the convention, meetings, hospitality, and travel industries. Each of the constituent associations holds its own slate of conventions, meetings, and expositions. And the Convention Liaison Council, representing those associations, holds a number of its own meetings each year.

What types of meetings do trade and professional associations hold? Virtually all those listed on pages 20-29. And, especially in the case of national and international organizations, they require the full spectrum of property facilities and services.

Medical and Scientific Societies

The general tone of these organizations' meetings is similar to that of trade and professional associations in many ways. Their conventions usually emphasize serious pursuits, although some attention is paid to relaxation and social events.

Rapid changes in technology and procedures distinguish the scientific and medical communities. Because of this, scientific meetings are often called with little advance notice to consider new discoveries or techniques. The results of these meetings can have an immediate and direct impact on people's health and lives. Scheduling arrangements are quite different from those for trade and professional associations that normally meet on a relatively standard, pre-set schedule.

Presentation of papers, plenary sessions, lectures, and demonstrations of new techniques characterize these meetings. This often means extensive audiovisual requirements, including closed circuit television and videotape facilities for close-up demonstrations of detailed work.

Exhibits are often sophisticated, featuring demonstrations of new devices and equipment developed for the scientific community.

Scientific meetings often carry over into the food and beverage events as well. Luncheons, for example, typically feature a speaker. Here again, one may find the need for modern, high quality audiovisual equipment designed to bring a large group of attendees into close proximity with the speaker.

Religious Organizations

Religious conventions are a rapidly growing factor in the convention industry. There are two major categories of such meetings. The first includes individuals who practice religion as a vocation, such as ministers, rabbis, or executives of religious associations. The second is composed of individuals who practice their religion as an avocation.

The Religious Conference Management Association (RCMA), founded in 1972, has 754 members who are responsible for more than 1,800 meetings and conferences each year. These conferences attract more than 1,100,000 people.[3]

Religious conferences include meetings typical of those found in other associations, along with some that are unique to the religious establishment. For example, there are the requisite board meetings, committee meetings, seminars and workshops, and regional and area meetings. Sectional council meetings are also common, involving 20 to 200 attendees and lasting from one to several days.

The RCMA membership profile shows that 23% of its members plan conferences for 10,000 to 45,000 attendees. While 100-person meetings do exist, it is quite common for 25,000 to attend the Southern Baptist Convention or the Campus Crusade for Christ, or for 45,000 to attend the General Conference of Seventh-Day Adventists. These conferences last from three days to two weeks.

Religious conventions are primarily family affairs. A conference planner might warn a convention bureau executive, "If you can't provide me with 500 cribs, I can't bring my group to your city." In addition, attendees usually finance their own attendance. Because they do, room rates and subsistence costs are paramount considerations in many cases.

Educational Associations

Educational associations are organizations of professional educators whose meetings are very similar to those of religious groups.

Because the attendees are primarily educators or school administrators, convention dates are typically set for times when schools are not in session. For convention organizers and properties, this means that the meetings are often scheduled during soft seasons, times when occupancy rates are traditionally lower. This results in more moderate rates for attendees and higher occupancy for properties.

Educators cannot meet frequently, so their conventions often last longer than those of other groups. Five-day conventions are not unusual (in contrast to the typical three-day conventions of trade and professional associations). And special educational sessions have replaced the more traditional evening receptions, dinners, or parties.

Attendees usually pay their own expenses, so budget considerations are a major factor in the negotiating process.

Charitable Organizations

Charitable organizations include those groups that function in the public interest for such varied goals as the defense of human rights, relief for the poor, and fighting community deterioration.

Foundations often fall within the charitable organization category. Association foundations are considered within this broad category by the Internal Revenue Service, under whose codes tax-exempt associations of all types are categorized. However, association foundations are more commonly dedicated to research, education, and publications than they are to charity.

Labor Unions   Unions are organized to improve the conditions of workers, as well as to improve the quality of their products and the efficiency of their skills and workplaces. With more than 13 million members, labor unions represent one of the largest types of associations.

Because large attendance is usually the norm, union conventions are held in major cities. Large general assemblies characterize these conventions, but there are numerous smaller meetings like caucuses and committee meetings as well. Convention expenses usually are borne by a local union or the parent organization. Conventions are held during the summer months.

Business Leagues   Business leagues include trade associations, chambers of commerce, boards of trade, real estate boards, and other groups that are not primarily religious, charitable, scientific, literary, or educational in nature.

A business league is an association of people or companies whose purpose is to promote a common business interest. The majority of associations to which properties sell their products or services fall within this category.

Avocational Associations   Thousands of avocational associations exist on the international, national, regional, state, and local levels in the following categories:

- Recreational
- Hobby
- Cultural/Ethnic
- Civic
- Patriotic
- Fraternal

Participants at meetings of these groups differ from members of other associations in that they come from various vocational backgrounds to share a common avocational interest. In the United States alone, some 2,500 associations support a vast range of avocations,[4] including such disparate groups and specific interests as the Postcard History Society, National Pigeon Association, American Philatelic Society, National Puzzlers League, and Civil War Round Table Associates.

The number and variety of avocational organizations typify the variety and richness of American life. The groups encompass such interests as sports, hobbies, literature, history, patriotism, art, and music. Also included in this category are civic associations, such as the American Legion and Rotary International.

Ethnic or cultural associations are composed of individuals who share a special interest in their places of origin. Meetings are largely social, although speakers and audiovisuals related to those common interests may be a part of the programming.

Much the same can be said for fraternal organizations, civic and patriotic associations, hobby groups, and other avocational societies.

Because convention attendees normally pursue an avocation, meetings tend to be scheduled during weekends, holidays, or during summer months when children are out of school. Many hold annual meetings, special seminars, exhibits, auctions, and other group events. Some are quite substantial. For example, the American Philatelic Society has 53,000 members, a staff of 45, an annual budget of $2 million, and an annual meeting that attracts 5,000 members.[5]

Attendees at these conventions usually travel at their own expense, often in family units. Their main motivation for participating is usually fellowship, relaxation, pursuit of philanthropic works, participating in rituals of the organization, peer exchanges, and identification with a community sharing common and sometimes unusual interests.

Government Organizations

Government associations and agencies at the federal, state, and municipal levels provide yet another significant market for meetings.

The meeting planner for government conferences often faces many regulations and restrictions not found in the association meeting field in general. Although government planners enjoy an increasing degree of freedom and flexibility in site selection, suppliers of convention facilities and services must recognize certain considerations inherent in government meetings.

For example, the United States General Services Administration (GSA) establishes guidelines and regulations to administer government meetings at the federal level. In addition, individual agencies and bureaus generally have their own regulations. There are restrictions for air travel, per diem allocations for government travelers, and guidelines for negotiating with and securing lodging properties and other facilities.

An important consideration for the government meeting planner is to take into account the price of room and food in order to remain within the per diem limits established by the GSA for 410 municipalities within the United States. The per diem is the set dollar amount at which the traveler will be reimbursed for lodging, food, and incidentals.

Moreover, regulations require that attendees be reimbursed only half the daily per diem rate for meals and incidental expenses on the day of departure and day of return. And, the per diem is also reduced when food functions are part of the meeting program itself.

The amount allowed for food must cover gratuities. Meeting planners are extremely sensitive to the need to hold meetings at properties where the guestroom rate will not have to be subsidized from attendees' food and incidentals allocations.[6]

Selecting a site also can be tricky. For example, if the overall cost of a meeting exceeds the monetary parameters allowed by agency regulations, the meeting planner must show proof that bids were offered and that the lowest was accepted.

Selection of a site may also be determined by the location itself, because many government agencies have contracts with airlines that provide discounted air fares to certain destinations.

Lead times for booking government meetings can be considerably shorter than for association meetings. Therefore, it is not unusual for government organizations to maintain extensive files of properties categorized by price, location, and facilities. This allows them to book meetings at a property in short order, and within the applicable guidelines.

Another important restriction applies to liquor service. Government agencies usually will not pay for cocktail parties for traveling employees. Cash bars, however, are allowed and are frequently used at government meetings.

So, even though the rules for government meetings are different and even somewhat restrictive, these conferences now make up a multi-billion dollar portion of the convention industry.

The founding of the Society of Government Meeting Planners (SGMP) in 1981 reflects the growth and influence of this market. It is an association of full- and part-time government meeting planners and suppliers to that segment of the convention community. SGMP serves more than 900 government meeting specialists.

Types of Association Meetings

Suppliers to the association meeting market appear to make a common mistake when they plan their marketing strategies: They often think solely in terms of just a convention or annual meeting.

The truth is, however, that conventions or annual meetings represent a minority of all meetings held by trade associations and professional societies.

Conventions or annual meetings of associations are usually defined as those meetings that are held each year either through tradition or to fulfill bylaws requirements. They typically involve large numbers of participants and attendees, and perhaps include expositions, political elections, and a mix of general sessions, breakout sessions, social events, recreational events, and other features designed to answer the needs of a wide variety of registrants. But there are other types of meetings as well, all of which represent potential markets.

Annual Conventions and Expositions

Regardless of their size, scope, and purposes, most associations are required by their bylaws to hold at least one convention each year.

All of the types of meetings discussed previously are actually microcosms of the annual convention; that is, elements of those meetings are often incorporated in the overall programming for an annual convention.

There are as many purposes for holding conventions as there are for associations themselves. Some of the more traditional objectives convention planners try to accomplish through their annual convention programming and planning include the following:

- Educate
- Inform
- Introduce innovations
- Unite members in common goals
- Perpetuate the organization
- Advance the image of the organization
- Provide a forum for debate
- Entertain
- Provide for peer interaction

- Determine member needs and attitudes
- Re-emphasize the value of membership and belonging
- Evaluate the past and forecast the future

Besides being familiar with these elements of annual convention programming, suppliers to this industry should study the economic significance of these meetings to the associations.

Both trade publications as well as associations publish research results. One such study, published by the American Society of Association Executives (ASAE), analyzes the operating ratios of all major association activities.[7]

According to the ASAE study, all types of associations received 14.5% of their income from conventions and expositions. They spent 10.8% of their funds to produce their conventions and expositions. The 602 respondents to the survey reported incomes of $177.4 million and expenses of $109.8 million.

The financial importance of such meetings to associations is apparent. So, too, is the economic potential for the lodging industry as it strives to effectively sell to and service this market.

Associations find that when they can accurately define purposes to be served by their convention programs and then fulfill them, conventions grow—and so do the dollars they generate. That is an important consideration for properties.

The *Association Meeting Trends* study cited earlier showed that 85% of all associations surveyed held one or more conventions in the previous three years, with 50% of those also holding expositions, usually in conjunction with the convention.[8] Interestingly, the number of associations holding more than one convention during that period increased from 20% in 1982 to 27% in 1986.[9] This is explained not only by the greater need for members to interact and learn but also by the financial advantages these meetings offer associations.

When are these meetings held? The *Association Meeting Trends* Survey showed the following results:[10]

January	14%	July	11%
February	17%	August	11%
March	16%	September	28%
April	21%	October	29%
May	28%	November	19%
June	26%	December	7%

Meeting planners were also asked which day of the week their associations held the first general session of their annual conventions. According to the following data, Monday seems to be the favorite day:[11]

Sunday	16%	Thursday	17%
Monday	28%	Friday	12%
Tuesday	8%	Saturday	3%
Wednesday	12%		

(4% failed to respond.)

We will discuss site inspection and selection criteria later in this text. At this point, however, it is interesting to note those factors that site selectors felt were most important in this process.

The *Association Meeting Trends* study asked respondents to rank various factors from 1 (very important) to 6 (not very important) in their evaluations. The following 12 items were considered:[12]

	Ratings
Meeting room facilities	1.4
Guestroom facilities	1.5
Overall appeal	1.7
Air transportation	2.1
Membership appeal (city image)	2.1
Affordability	2.2
Dining/Entertainment	2.3
Climate	2.6
Recreational facilities	2.7
Exhibit facilities	2.7
Geographic rotation policies	2.8
Accessibility by highway	2.9

It is important to note that the two major products sold by a lodging property rank first and second in the list of priorities: meeting rooms and guestrooms. Further, the property's image and appeal follow closely behind. Overall affordability (for both the meeting planners and their delegates) is less important than overall appeal.

These statistics give credence to our earlier observation that price alone is not the fundamental issue in site selection. Rather, the price-quality ratio ("Are we getting our money's worth?") has become primary.

What number of attendees does the typical annual convention draw? According to the Meetings Market Study by *Meetings & Conventions* magazine, attendance at the average convention is usually much smaller than the huge gatherings depicted in newspapers and the trade press.[13]

Delegate Attendance	% of Associations
Fewer than 50	3
100–149	8
150–199	18
200–299	9
300–399	10
400–499	7
500–999	12
1,000–1,999	8
2,000 or more	14

Still, many observers categorize conventions as the "big" meetings of national and international associations, drawing thousands of delegates. Consequently, many smaller properties (particularly resorts, downtown properties, and suburban hotels) eliminate themselves from competing for this market segment.

They should note that 67% of all association annual conventions draw fewer than 1,000 persons. Even more significantly, 55% attract fewer than 500 attendees. And nearly 4 out of 10 conventions host fewer than 300 delegates.[14] This lucrative market, then, is obviously attainable for properties having 300 to 400 rooms or fewer, as long as adequate meeting and function room space is available. These properties can make working arrangements with neighboring properties for overflow space if the need arises.

Typically, national and international association conventions last three to four days, while local, state, and regional annual meetings are one to two days in duration. These are only averages and should not be taken at face value, however.

How do these figures translate into income for the property? First, bear in mind that a three-day, 300-room convention does not mean that the property will realize a neat 900-room-night package spread over three days. Typically, some rooms will be picked up in advance for board and committee meetings; most associations take advantage of the convention draw to hold leadership meetings before the arrival of the larger body. Further, not all delegates will arrive for the first day or stay for the duration. This leads to a key consideration for maximizing room occupancy.

When holding a block of rooms for a convention, your determination of the number of rooms blocked should reflect the peak night or nights. Therefore, the room flowchart for a 300-room convention beginning on Sunday and concluding on Tuesday might resemble the following:

Day	Rooms	Events
Wednesday	3	Staff pre-planning meeting
Thursday	18	Executive committee, staff
Friday	55	Board of directors meeting
Saturday	280	Early arrivals, convention
Sunday	300	Convention
Monday	280	Early departures, convention
Tuesday	20	Convention ends, extended stays

This example shows that the three-day, 300-room convention is not really three days in duration, nor does it involve a total of 900 room nights. Instead, the account actually covers seven nights of guestroom accommodations, with only one night projected for the peak 300 rooms. Nevertheless, the number of room nights booked is 956.

A flowchart is essential for booking any type of business—association, corporate, union, or others. The property needs it to fill empty rooms resulting from the natural ebb and flow of meeting attendance. Assuming that a 300-room convention will actually fill 300 guestrooms each night of the convention has cost many properties countless dollars in lost room revenue.

Board and Committee Meetings

Virtually all associations rely on the services of volunteer workers. Many members volunteer their time and expertise to serve in leadership positions with their associations. To lead, they must meet to discuss strategies, tactics, budgets, and all of the reasons for which an association exists. These meetings are often called leadership meetings, and they usually include board meetings, executive committee meetings, and committee meetings. Of these, board meetings (meetings of the board of directors) and executive committee meetings represent significant markets for properties.

There are a number of major reasons that leadership meetings are of unique importance to properties.[15]

First, and perhaps most important, leadership meetings are made up of just that: leaders. These individuals are the "movers and shakers" of our professions and industries. This means that they very likely serve on additional association leadership panels. They are very likely to be influential in the decision-making process of a number of other groups, including associations or the very corporations for which they work or serve on the boards of directors.

In other words, there is a ripple effect here. These individuals serve on association panels because they are leaders in their industries and professions. As such, they influence others. And that represents potential new business from markets perhaps as yet undefined by the property sales executive.

According to the 1986 ASAE/IACVB study of association meeting trends, 77% of associations responding to the survey held both executive committee and board of directors meetings.[16]

There are no significant differences in the months these meetings are conducted because they are held primarily for business or professional reasons that have no relation to seasons or locations.

However, it is significant that 66% of associations hold these meetings at downtown properties, while 60% also book resort properties.[17] This is logical because leaders of industry and the professions usually seek two things: expedience in their work lives (e.g., meeting at downtown properties to permit easy access to other duties) and a chance to mix business with pleasure (e.g., going to resort facilities).[18]

This study also showed that 77% of the associations responding reported that attendance at these smaller leadership meetings was between 11 and 50 individuals.[19]

Fifty-four percent said the meetings lasted one day, with 25% citing two days, and 11% reporting a total of three days for these meetings.[20]

These statistics show that these meetings are significant for reasons other than just the status and influence of those who attend them. The meetings are also important economically.

According to a March 1986 study by *Meetings & Conventions* magazine, 18,172,700 persons attended off-premises meetings for other than major conventions in 1985. Association direct budget expenditures were $764 million. In addition, delegate expenditures at these leadership meetings were $10.5 billion. This means that meetings in hotels and conference facilities, not including annual conventions, generated some $11.2 billion in revenue in the United States in 1985.[21]

Who books these meetings? The ASAE/IACVB study clearly reveals the predominant role of the salaried staff in this process.[22] For example, 58% of the time the association's chief paid executive makes the site inspections for board or executive committee meetings; 28% of the time it is done by meeting planners (paid staff); and 8% it is done by volunteer members. When it comes time to make the final site selection, the chief paid executive is involved 57% of the time; meeting planners, 15%; and volunteer members, 25%. (NOTE: the percentages in each case do not equal 100% because of additional answers.)

The implications of this study are obvious. Board and committee meetings represent a significant market for properties. And the primary influence in site inspection and selection is that of the salaried staff.

But, there are other types of meetings common to associations besides those for committees and boards of directors.

Seminars and Workshops

Many associations report education programs to be the fastest-growing association activity. There are two reasons for this. First, the body of knowledge in most fields is changing and growing so rapidly that members look to their associations for help in maintaining and improving their levels of competence and competitiveness. Second, these conferences have become important revenue sources for associations because most charge a registration fee.

These seminars and workshops normally do not contain the variety of activities that a convention does, such as political campaigning, business sessions, and socializing. Instead, they concentrate mainly on a specific educational subject or subjects, with attendees listening to speakers, panelists, and each other in a classroom format.

However, sellers to this market should be aware that a significant trend has begun to develop. Attendees are becoming less satisfied with educational programs in which they play solely a passive role (being "taught at"). They also want the opportunity to teach and share some experiences.

Meeting planners are now allowing time for self-teaching and peer interaction. This has become an integral part of the phenomenon known as networking. Although networking has become a popular label, it is not new. It defines the peer interaction that, we learned earlier, is a major reason people belong to various groups in the first place. For example, a significant part of education programs of the Hotel Sales and Marketing Association International is a "Topic Table" format. Here, participants have an unstructured opportunity to informally discuss topics of interest with no formal presenter attending.

The astute property sales executive can use this trend as an effective sales tool. For example, opportunities for self-teaching in workshops and seminars can be effectively programmed. Planners can provide areas for small, informal discussions where various groups can meet to deal with specific pre-assigned issues. Each table will be assigned a discussion leader to keep the conversation on track. The groups note major points made in their deliberations and report either verbally or in writing to their peers.

The hotelier who is familiar with trends in education meetings can suggest these new approaches to meeting planners who may not have this knowledge. For example, planners can be shown how "topic tables" or discussion groups can be set up and conducted virtually anywhere in a property's public space—foyers, corridors, and even lobbies. They do not have to be confined only to meeting rooms. They require no audiovisual capabilities or sophisticated room-sets. Basically, these sessions are nothing more than a place for people to sit and discuss a mutually interesting subject.

Suggesting such an approach to a meeting planner as a means of rounding out a program while taking full advantage of limited meeting space is an example of how a hotelier can act as a problem-solver for the client. Property sales executives who are perceived as problem-solvers for their clients are usually highly successful sales executives!

As we said earlier, meeting planners prefer to deal with sales executives who not only have a product to sell but who also understand how to plan an effective meeting. Knowing current trends in education-session planning and how to set up the proper environment are valuable tools to help the salesperson sell facilities and services to this rapidly growing sector of the association market.

What types of facilities are meeting planners booking for their educational seminars? According to the ASAE/IACVB survey, there are seven:[23]

Downtown City Hotel 75%
Airport Hotel 46%
Suburban Hotel. 52%
Resort Hotel 44%
Conference Center 24%
College/University Campus 28%
Association Headquarters 21%
(Note: Multiple answers were permitted.)

Although education is regarded by many association executives as an increasingly important service to members, note that cost factors are forcing a trend toward fewer seminars with larger attendance.

About 57% of the associations surveyed reported that seminars had become more expensive to conduct between 1984 and 1986.[24] Only 43% reported increases in income from these seminars.[25] Because most associations are reluctant to subsidize seminars through meeting dues, it would appear that the alternatives for containing expenses are to raise registration fees (which usually must be done in small increments) or hold fewer seminars with more participants at each—or both. The data for 1984-1986 substantiates this.

In 1986, 83% of associations conducted educational seminars for members.[26] This figure was up from 73% in 1982. However, they averaged only three such programs per year, as compared to five in 1982. But attendance during that period increased by 11.6%.[27]

Part of this trend may be explained by the regionalization of more meetings, primarily among chapters of parent associations. We will discuss this in greater detail later.

Issues Briefings

As associations become more involved with issues about their professions and industries, they often find it necessary to invite members to attend briefings on these matters. This is particularly true during crises involving government relations and legislative or regulatory matters.

These briefings typically involve only a few speakers, or perhaps a panel, with considerable audience involvement. The briefing sponsor usually provides coffee breaks and sometimes even a full meal. Advance scheduling is normally very short because of the nature of the meeting. Properties are finding these special, one-time-only meetings an emerging and lucrative field.

Fund-Raisers   Still another trend in the association community is the establishment of both specialized corporate entities and membership activities. These are designed to generate revenues over and above those normally obtained from such traditional sources as membership dues, registration fees, and subscriptions to publications.

An example of such a revenue source is a foundation, a separate but related corporate unit usually incorporated under the Internal Revenue Service tax code 501(c)(3). A foundation is set up to produce educational benefits, conduct research, and publish data of benefit to its parent industry and the general public. Foundations depend on grants, contributions, gifts, and "services in kind" to raise the funds necessary for such work.

As the numbers of foundations increase, one of the most popular methods of funding them is through a major social event called a fund-raiser. It is not unusual for an association to charge $100 or more per seat to an event like a black-tie banquet, complete with dancing and entertainment. Because the benefactor (the foundation) has tax-exempt status, the cost of each ticket is tax-deductible.

Properties pursuing this type of business realize not only the revenue from the dinner itself but also from the sale of guestrooms to participants who do not wish to drive home after a late night of celebrating. Additionally, properties can make special breakfast arrangements the following morning.

Similar formats can often be suggested and sold to an association to celebrate holidays, special events, or anniversaries of interest to that particular organization.

Exhibitions   Many associations often produce exhibitions to raise funds. They invite companies that normally sell products or services to their industries to display their wares in an exhibition (often called a trade show). These companies then pay a fee for the opportunity to show their products or distribute information about their services.

In some cases, properties charge the associations a rental fee for the space they allocate to the trade show. In others, they provide the space for free. The latter arrangement allows associations to retain more of the revenue generated by the exposition—provided the properties realize some revenue from other activities related to the show (e.g., guestrooms or food and beverage sales).

Association annual conventions often include an exposition. Because expositions are becoming more lucrative to associations, they are being added to other types of association meetings as well. "Mid-year" meetings (as contrasted with annual meetings or conventions) that once were mainly educational in nature now often feature trade shows, too. And some associations have found that expositions can be successful without secondary programs—if the shows are properly planned and promoted.

Earlier, we discussed the popularity of networking at association meetings. This activity has become common in the trade show environment as well. Here, buyer and supplier operations are often coordinated through computerized "appointments" schedules. These produce an office-like atmosphere among hundreds of participants in hotel ballrooms. Because this is becoming an increasingly popular activity in the association environment, it represents a potentially lucrative market for any property selling to associations.

Trade shows, however, are not without hazards. A show often requires exhibit booths (sometimes referred to as "rack and drape" or "pipe and drape") along with pegboard, easels, corkboard, foamcore, signs, carpeting, and other types of staging devices or special decorations. If these items are brought into the property, they first must be approved by the local fire marshall or public health authorities for their fire-retardant qualities and to ensure they present no safety hazards.

A trade show, probably more than any other activity, offers the chance for products and materials to be brought in by exhibitors and outside suppliers. These items are unfamiliar to the property staff and thus outside the control and maintenance of the property. The property must take great care in determining the degree of risk presented to its guests by those materials and products in addition to identifying the persons responsible for their proper security and maintenance. The facility must establish a close working relationship with the local fire marshall and a reputable security firm if it plans to target the trade show market.

In the past, hoteliers have not always liked exhibitions, especially when large amounts of space had to be "donated." However, these events can still turn a profit. Creative hoteliers can suggest incorporating food and beverage activities as part of the exposition. For example, exhibit hours can encompass breakfast or lunch periods, with buffets arranged to provide a "picnic" atmosphere where attendees can remain mobile while enjoying hand foods. (Mobility of attendees is important to exhibitors.) Or, the exhibit sponsor can be asked to reopen the exhibits for an after-dinner or late-evening hospitality center. At this type of event attendees and exhibitors can end the day together (an important group dynamics principle for any meeting), perhaps with exhibitors providing specialty desserts or cordials at their booths. Music and some special features such as door prizes can turn an empty evening into a special occasion—and generate additional food and beverage revenue for the property.

The point is that exhibits or trade shows do not have to be "necessary evils" for which a property must commit large amounts of space just to land a meeting. Instead, they may provide an additional source of revenue for both the meeting sponsor and the property. Some creative planning is all that is required.

According to the 1986 ASAE/IACVB survey, 50% of the associations surveyed hold expositions, an increase of 13% over the 1982 figure. These shows are not always held in conjunction with the associations' annual meetings. The survey also showed that 34% of those associations hold 3 expositions per year.[28]

Because income from expositions has increased by 19.4% and expenses only by 12.7% during that period, it is likely that the number and size of association expositions will continue to grow.[29] As we pointed out earlier, expositions are supported by suppliers' participation and funding. This works to the advantage of the associations because they find that source of revenue more easily obtainable and politically feasible than increased dues and registration fees charged to members.

The 1986 study by *Meetings & Conventions* magazine showed that hotels accommodated 52% of expositions held in conjunction with conventions, while convention centers attracted 42%. Other facilities housed the remaining 6%.[30]

Exhibit 2.1   Exhibition/Trade Show Space Requirements

Square Feet/Exhibit Space	Exhibits
10,000 or less	24%
10,000–20,000	16%
20,001–30,000	12%
30,001–40,000	5%
40,001–50,000	3%
50,001–100,000	9%
More than 100,000	15%
No response	17%

Mean: 95,400 square feet
Median: 25,000 square feet

Source: Adapted from International Association of Convention & Visitor Bureaus and American Society of Association Executives, *Association Meeting Trends* (Washington, D.C., 1986), p. B23.

According to the data in Exhibit 2.1, these shows occupied from 10,000 square feet or less of exhibit space to more than 100,000 square feet:[31]

Because 40% of expositions required 20,000 square feet or less of space, hotels may find this growing activity deserving of special marketing attention.

Professional and Technical Meetings

Yet another type of association meeting is the technical or professional meeting. This meeting is normally educational in nature, but it may require a large amount of meeting space as well as technical equipment and materials. These are needed for "breakout" sessions, small meetings in which segments of the entire attendance can deal with specific issues.

For example, the development of new computer technology has generated countless special meetings for demonstrating the applicability of hardware and software to a certain industry or profession. These meetings may be sponsored by the association serving that industry or by manufacturers of technology who want to market their products or services to that industry. In the latter case, the association may be a secondary partner in the initiative, perhaps providing promotional assistance as well as the special interest community for attendance.

In addition to providing adequate meeting space, properties must have access to audiovisual equipment, versatile electrical service, and staging materials needed for the elaborate displays and exhibits associated with these types of meetings.

Types of Association Membership

Associations typically have several categories of membership. The majority of an association's members are usually companies or individuals whose occupations or avocations directly relate to the stated purposes and objectives of that association. These persons or groups are usually called "regular" members.

Many associations also have a category for members who do not practice directly within the industry, trade, or profession represented by the association. Still, these individuals have a vital interest in the organization because they sell products or services to the members of that group. These members are often called "associate" or "allied" members.

Those terms are often interchanged with a third class of membership. This class includes persons who neither practice directly in the field nor sell products and services to members of the group. Instead, these individuals work in a related field and only have some peripheral interest in keeping abreast of developments in the group's major area. They may be called allied members, associate members, or even participating or supporting members.

These membership categories are exemplified in the case of the Hotel Sales & Marketing Association International:

Regular Members: These individuals work more than 50% of the time in an executive capacity with a hotel, motor inn, cruise ship, or other entity providing accommodations to the traveling public. A specific example would be the director of sales at a large property.

Allied Members: This category includes individuals or companies who sell products or services to regular members of Hotel Sales & Marketing Association International. An example might be a designer and producer of promotional literature for hotel companies. Although this person may be interested in some of the more vital interests of the association and its members, he or she participates only to sell a product.

Associate Members: Included in this category are individuals or companies with a continuing interest in developments within the hospitality industry, as represented by the Hotel Sales & Marketing Association International. Persons who teach industry-related courses in an academic setting would be typical associate members. Because they teach the disciplines represented by the association, they are interested in the publications, research, and education provided by the association.

There are several important reasons that property executives should be familiar with these classes of membership.

Knowing that regular members are the people who actually attend conventions, seminars, and leadership meetings of associations helps in soliciting their business and servicing them properly.

It is also important to know that allied or associate members who sell products and services to an association usually participate in expositions and entertain association members as part of their sales approach. They are interested in such property amenities as hospitality suites, rental of floor space for exhibits, deliveries of gifts, food, and beverage trays to rooms of association VIPs, and plans for entertaining business clients in the property's restaurants and lounges.

In other words, even though they are only allied or associate members, they can still represent large profits—if you are willing to study them and learn their convention or meeting needs.

Exhibit 2.2 summarizes the key aspects of association membership categories.

Typically, an association will invite members from all three categories to register for an annual meeting or convention. Usually, regular members will pay only a standard registration fee, while allied members will be charged a premium fee (and often be required to purchase an exhibit booth). The latter are charged this extra fee because the association is providing them with a market for their services and supplies.

Exhibit 2.2 Association Membership Categories

> *REGULAR MEMBER:*
>   **Key Interest:** Business or professional advancement
>
> *ALLIED MEMBER:*
>   **Key Interest:** Marketing to regular members (May also be called "Associate" members)
>
> *ASSOCIATE MEMBER:*
>   **Key Interest:** Secondary relationship but keen interest in work of regular members (May also be called "Allied" members)

On the other hand, the associate member who only has a peripheral interest in the association (such as continuing education) may be charged a discounted fee to participate.

Association Staff and the Decision-Making Process

Just as there are no standardized terms for the various membership categories of associations, neither are there standardized titles for association executives. Because the association movement has grown so rapidly, the types and duties of executives have overlapped. Therefore, as the industry's body of knowledge and maturity are evolving, so, too, is its nomenclature. The astute property sales executive will disregard titles and deal with functions instead.

As associations grow in size, scope, and sophistication, they tend to turn to a professional staff for administration. Twenty years ago, volunteer members administered many associations and societies. Paid staffs, when they existed, were much smaller than they are today. The hotelier who dealt with these early staffs often found that such functions as site inspections and selection, convention programming, and even negotiations were still handled by volunteer workers.

Today, the typical international or national association has a salaried staff of adequate size to provide sufficient specialization in the organization's functional activities. Therefore, the property executive now usually deals with an experienced, salaried official who is not merely "moonlighting" as a convention planner or negotiator. Instead, this person is a career specialist. This poses a greater challenge to the property executive, who must be equally knowledgeable about conventions and meetings management.

The transition from volunteerism to professionalism among association staffs, while inevitable, is not complete. There still are some exceptions. Although it is rare, volunteers with little or no association management experience still run a few international associations. But in the structure of most associations—beginning at the national level, through regional and state levels, and finally down to the multitude of local associations—the number of volunteers increases.

This is not to imply that volunteer leaders cannot make politically binding or consequential decisions. To the contrary! Because they are volunteers (and therefore have little vested responsibility toward the organization) these leaders are relatively immune to criticism from colleagues and are protected from political and legal prosecution.

This discussion points out a very important principle for the property executive who must deal with both the volunteer leader and the professional association staff executive: When the time comes to deal with either, remember the following four major differences between them. These distinctions directly affect the hotelier as a supplier of products and services to the meetings market.

First, the staff member is paid. This means the person's career depends upon his or her knowledge of the industry and ability to make correct decisions. The volunteer is not paid and therefore has probably spent little time studying the industry for career progression purposes.

Second, the staff member has a permanent position. Therefore, he or she presumably will be around to answer for the success or failure of his or her actions. Volunteers, on the other hand, are typically placed in or elected to leadership positions for a year or two at most. There is little accountability involved.

Third, the professional staff executive probably is receiving formal training in convention and meetings management from the growing number of associations serving meeting planners.* Among these groups are the Professional Convention Management Association, the National Association of Exposition Managers, and Meeting Planners International. On the other hand, it is highly unlikely that a volunteer member negotiating or planning a convention for an association has had prior experience in this activity.

Fourth, the professional staff executive is in frequent contact with colleagues who have similar careers and common experiences. As a result, their "grapevine" is intense and effective. It stands to reason, then, that their shared experiences about properties and their facilities are critical in making or breaking the reputation of any property and its executives. This is not normally the case with the volunteer members, who, after the meeting or convention ends, return to their careers in unrelated fields.

So, prepared with all this knowledge about associations and their officers, the property sales executive or convention service manager now must begin selling or servicing conventions. Several questions come to mind. Whom do you contact? To whom do you listen? Where should your allegiance be?

Again, there are no ready answers. Probably the most important thing to remember is that when dealing with a salaried staff member, *obtain your primary guidance from that person.* The reason for this is simple. Paid staff members usually have the greatest in-depth knowledge of the meeting, the people, the needs, and the group's ability to pay. They also have the most to lose if anything goes wrong.

In the case of a small association staff consisting of only one or two persons, you may be referred *by staff* to a volunteer with whom you will deal.

---

*The Convention Liaison Council, an organization representing associations dealing in the convention and meeting industry from both the supplier and buyer categories, now lists 21 associations among its membership.

On the other hand, if there is no paid staff, you will have to direct your efforts to the association volunteers responsible for selection, negotiation, and execution of the convention. This information is usually available from the chief elected officer (the president or chairman of the board).

Beyond a doubt, the organizational structure and politics of associations are variable and complex. Thus, it is very important that property executives make an effort to understand them.

Communication Channels

What is an association's organizational structure? Who reports to whom? Exhibit 2.3 shows the organization of a typical trade association that has primary activities in the areas of government relations, education, standardization, and conventions and meetings.

First, note that the group's membership sits at the top of the organization chart. In every association they are presumed to be the final authority on all matters, and the elected leadership and the paid staff serve at their pleasure. It is apparent that if a property does a good job of satisfying these members, it can reap large future rewards in the form of positive references and repeat business.

But also note that the members are not typically involved in the day-to-day work of policy-making, planning, and executing programs. Essentially, the members are merely the judges of that work. In the example shown in Exhibit 2.3, committees are formed to carry out the main purposes of the organization.

These committees *coordinate* their assignments with the staff personnel responsible for the various activities. But they *answer* (report the results of their work) to the executive committee and the board of directors.

Committees also communicate with each other on matters of common interest. This is especially true in the case of the convention committee because a convention usually incorporates all association activities.

You will see another interesting element in Exhibit 2.3. The staff communicates with and is answerable to the president or executive director, who, in turn, reports to a relatively small executive committee.

The executive committee typically considers issues and opportunities and then makes recommendations to the larger board of directors. The board then reviews these executive committee recommendations and, acting on behalf of the association membership, votes on these issues. This brings us back to the top of the organizational chart.

This discussion points to three key factors property executives should be aware of:

1. The critical person to please is the president, the chief staff executive. He or she is responsible to the association's leadership. A job is on the line.

2. Although the president usually makes the final decision on convention site selection, the staff person responsible for conventions and meetings has great influence in most cases. Remember, too, that the

Exhibit 2.3 Typical Trade Association Organization

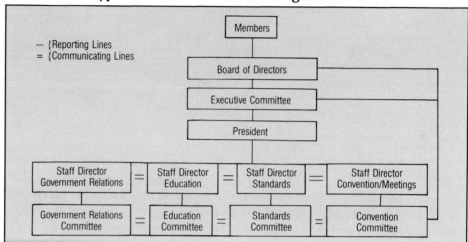

staff director in charge of conventions communicates with the staff director in charge of education. If that person runs seminars and workshops, another market emerges. The same may be true of other staff directors. This "ripple effect" is the property sales and convention service executive's greatest potential ally—and enemy.

3. Typically, volunteers "create" ideas, policies, and organizational direction through their committees and boards. The paid professional staff actually executes the result of that creativity. It is important that the property executive understand these organizational relationships within the association.

Therefore, prudent hoteliers should remember this essential principle of marketing to associations: volunteer leaders come and go, but the paid staff represents continuity. A property must nurture its relationship with the association on a permanent basis, not with the volunteer leadership whose involvement is only temporary. This means that a relationship must be established with the salaried staff on a primary basis and with the leadership volunteers secondarily.

Why is knowledge of staff composition important to the property sales executive, the director of food and beverage operations, the convention service manager, and others who must help plan conventions or meetings with association planners? They must know the makeup of the association's staff to determine who is responsible for policy consideration, negotiation, and implementation of conventions and meetings.

Another important consideration for the property executive is the political environment of the association, especially when it comes to selecting a convention site.

Consider the mind-frame of the staff executive of any association. He or she must constantly balance the narrow interests of those members interested in hosting a convention. There are few things more emotional, or ego gratifying, than to host a convention.

Yet, for many reasons, there are sites where an association's convention should not be held. The location may be in the wrong geographic area; it may demand too high a price; or it may offer the wrong demographic makeup.

The hotelier who exerts uninvited and unwelcome pressure on the association executive by going through members and volunteer leaders has likely alienated that executive for many years to come. This executive in turn may create significant ill will for that property and its sales executive through the grapevine of association communications to which we referred earlier.

At all costs, avoid the political arena of any association. If there is conflict within the group, the protagonists are fighting over issues much more complex than a facility or convention site. In this type of struggle, the property or its executive could easily be dragged in as a "cause célèbre." The association members involved in the struggle have little to lose from the political infighting because their engagement is a relatively temporary one. Much more important in this situation is the salaried staff, especially if they lose a battle—political or pragmatic—because they will never forget who joined the other side.

So, your plan of action should be quite clear. The relationships you establish to market and service associations should begin with the salaried staff, if one exists. The advice they give you—about the players, the decision-making process, and the needs of the association—must be analyzed carefully before you develop a marketing approach for that organization. Make certain you are dealing with the right person within the association. If you are successful, you probably can anticipate years of profitable repeat business and extraordinary referral sales.

The market is complex, difficult to define, and unpredictable. But given the investments associations are making in conventions and meetings, it would be well worth your efforts to study them in order to approach their many entities with precision and expertise.

Lower-Level Meetings

Throughout this chapter we have referred to other types of associations and association meetings besides those we have discussed. The major characteristic of these additional groups is that they are formed at levels other than national and international. Nevertheless, they represent a very lucrative market to the hospitality industry.

Regional/Local Chapter Meetings

Many associations have units, chapters, or allied associations at the regional, state, or local levels. Each of these chapters is an association unto itself, possessing many of the same characteristics as its parent association. These "micro-associations" are an excellent market for conventions, board and committee meetings, expositions, and periodic social events. For example, the American Hotel & Motel Association is a federation with related associations in every state. The Printing Industries of America has affiliated groups at the local, state, and regional levels.

National and international associations are the main sources of information about their chapters, including the nature of their operations.

Increasingly, local and state chapters are joining together in regional meetings. With a larger number of attendees, these groups are better able to conduct educational programs, discuss industry affairs, and hold social events.

Regional/State Meetings

We have observed that associations operate at various geographic levels: international, national, regional, state, local, and, in some cases, even at the neighborhood level.

Many of these groups hold meetings and expositions similar to those examined earlier in this chapter. However, as the geographic scope of the associations decreases and the size of their meetings becomes smaller, data becomes increasingly difficult to obtain. Nevertheless, industry statistics are researched periodically for regional and state association conventions, and they reveal significant expenditures and growth trends in this segment of the market as well.

For example, a 1986 study by the International Association of Convention & Visitor Bureaus found that between 1979 and 1985, association expenditures for conventions of all types increased 65%.[32]

What did regional and state conventions mean to the host properties and cities? According to the IACVB study, delegates to these conventions each spent $84.65 per day, or a total of $274.10 for the entire average convention. Those expenditures are broken down by expense category in Exhibit 2.4.

These figures show that almost 61% of every dollar spent is for direct property services (guestrooms and incidentals, hotel restaurants, and hospitality suites). In addition, we can assume that at least some of the other expenditures are property-related (such as entertainment or retail stores).

In the six years before the 1986 IACVB study, the lodging share of the convention dollar increased by 8.3%. This was due to large increases in average guestroom rates during that period as well as to an increase in the average length of stay.

Although regional and state meetings are smaller in scope than national or international conventions and attract fewer attendees, they still feature many of the same program elements, logistical challenges, and principles of planning and execution that characterize larger conventions. However, they also have several significant characteristics of their own.

First, attendance is likely to be heavily "commuter" generated. Therefore, adequate parking for delegates is an important planning consideration.

Second, planning lead time will often be shorter than for the national or international convention because the regional or state association's convention planning staff is usually smaller, though responsible for more general duties than the larger, more specialized association staffs. Again, the smaller the geographic region the meeting serves, the greater the likelihood that the association staff representative with whom the property executive deals will be distracted by many unrelated duties. Another consideration when dealing with smaller associations is that there is no permanent association staff person who is responsible for convention planning. In this case, the property will have to work with one or more volunteer workers to plan and execute the convention. Because this volunteer is responsible for only one particular meeting, it is often booked and planned less than a year before it is actually held.

It also stands to reason, then, that site selection visits and decisions will

Exhibit 2.4   Delegate Expenditures by Expense Category

	Total Expenditures Per Delegate	Daily Expenditures Per Delegate
Guestroom and incidentals	$122.98	$ 38.32
Hotel restaurants	29.39	9.32
Other restaurants	36.61	11.48
Hospitality suites	13.85	3.83
Entertainment	15.98	4.77
Retail stores	31.81	10.03
Local transportation	12.29	3.56
Other	11.19	3.34
TOTAL	$274.10	$84.65

Source: Laventhol & Horwath, *Convention Income Survey* (Champaign, Illinois, July 1986), p. 15.

often be made by volunteers who are untrained in convention planning and staging skills.

Because the success of the meeting is as important to the property as it is to the convening group, the hotelier who works with the volunteers during the site selection process and during the convention itself must understand the disciplines of convention management. Only then will the proper decisions be made and the correct strategies implemented. It is obvious that in these cases the hotelier must also wear the hat of the meeting planner—and do so without appearing to take over the prerogatives and authority of the client.

A third characteristic of the state or regional meeting is that usually more delegates will pay for their convention expenses from their own pockets. In contrast to expense-account purchases, this practice often results in more discriminating buying decisions by guests. It can also mean more delay or difficulty in collecting billed accounts after the meeting. It is easier to collect master accounts billed to the sponsoring association or to obtain money from attendees when their corporations provide them with expense accounts.

Further, because many delegates pay their own way, they tend to purchase smaller, less expensive guestrooms. The IACVB survey noted that daily expenditures per delegate averaged $38.32 for guestrooms and incidentals at state and local conventions. At national and international conventions, where the use of corporate expense accounts is higher, the average was $55.89 for guestroom and incidental expenses.[33]

A fourth characteristic of the state or regional meetings is that the potential for return business is greatest at these levels. There are fewer potential sites to consider because of the more restricted geographic area involved. Although there is a trend among state and regional associations to liberalize their bylaws and policies concerning geographic restrictions of meeting sites, they will still select facilities that are relatively accessible to their members. This is due to the personal time and expenses members must commit to attend the meeting. Tighter budgets tend to make the meeting planners and their delegates highly sensitive to price-value relationships.

There is often a rotation of convention sites from year to year (such as city to city, or resort versus downtown site), but the alternatives normally exist within a certain state or region.

Therefore, it becomes very apparent that when a state or regional convention is serviced well, the host association can provide a property with repeat business for many years to come.

Chapter Summary

The association field is so varied that it is sometimes difficult to analyze and understand.

Associations range from religious groups and trade associations to government organizations and medical societies. Their purposes are broad and wide-ranging, from influencing legislation and maintaining social relationships to ensuring industry standardization and performing public service activities.

Typically, associations meet for a number of reasons. Besides conducting annual conventions, they also hold board and committee meetings, seminars and workshops, issues briefings, fund-raisers, expositions, and technical meetings.

Associations are complex entities, and their decision-making process reflects their organizational structure. Anyone seeking to do business with an association must learn who wields power and how business decisions are made.

Notes

1. *Webster's Ninth New Collegiate Dictionary* (1986), s.v. "Association."
2. Joseph Greif, ed., *Managing Membership Societies* (Washington, D.C.: Foundation of the American Society of Association Executives, 1979).
3. *Religious Conference Management Association Market Report* (Bayard Publications, December 1986). No pagination.
4. *National Avocational Organizations,* 7th ed. (Columbia Books, Inc., 1987).
5. Ibid., p. 46.
6. *Convention World,* March/April 1987.
7. *Association Operating Ratio Report, 1985-86* (Washington, D.C.: American Society of Association Executives, July 1986).
8. *Association Meeting Trends* (Washington, D.C.: International Association of Convention & Visitor Bureaus and American Society of Association Executives, 1986), p. A3.
9. Ibid., p. A4.
10. Ibid., p. B2. (Note: Total will exceed 100% because multiple answers were permitted.)
11. Ibid., p. B8.
12. Ibid., p. B15.
13. "The Meetings Market '85," *Meetings & Conventions,* March 1986, Table 48.
14. Ibid.
15. *Association Meeting Trends,* information extrapolated from data on leadership meetings.
16. Ibid., p. B38.
17. The *Association Meeting Trends* survey of 1986 regarding location of leadership meetings permitted multiple answers, resulting in total responses exceeding 100%.
18. *Association Meeting Trends,* p. B40.

19. Ibid., p. B42.

20. Ibid.

21. Data extrapolated from "The Meetings Market '85," *Meetings & Conventions*, March 31, 1986.

22. *Association Meeting Trends*, p. B43.

23. Ibid., p. B30.

24. Ibid., p. B31.

25. Ibid.

26. Ibid., p. B26.

27. Ibid., p. B30.

28. Ibid., p. B17.

29. Ibid., p. B21.

30. "The Meetings Market '85," Table 53.

31. *Association Meeting Trends*, p. B23.

32. *1985 Convention Income Survey* (Champaign, Illinois: International Association of Convention & Visitor Bureaus, July 1986), p. 15.

33. Ibid., pp. 11-13.

3 Corporations and the Meetings They Hold

Chapter Objectives

1. To explain the evolution of the corporate meeting market

2. To identify and describe the major differences between corporate and association meetings

3. To identify and describe the types of meetings corporations conduct

4. To explain the emerging role of the independent meeting planner

Like their association counterparts, corporations also represent a major user of meetings and convention services and facilities.

Perhaps the easiest way to understand the corporate meeting market is to note the differences between it and the association meeting market. The major thrust of this chapter is to contrast the corporate and association meeting markets, noting in detail aspects ranging from the authority to conduct meetings to factors associated with booking lead time.

In addition, the reasons corporations hold meetings will also be discussed.

The Corporate Meeting Market

A 1974 survey by *Successful Meetings* magazine reported that U.S. corporations held 573,000 meetings in all types of hotels, resorts, and motor inns. In a 1986 *Meetings & Conventions* magazine survey, the total number of meetings held by corporations had increased to 706,100. These meetings and conventions produced direct expenditures totaling $7.6 billion.

It is important to note that the corporate meetings field is less precisely defined than the association meetings field. This is largely because of the more recent evolution of corporate meetings as a force influencing hospitality and travel. It is also the result of the very nature of the meeting sponsors. Companies are individualistic and competitive by their nature, often reflecting the policies of private, entrepreneurial ownership and management.

Therefore, plans and strategies for corporate meetings and conventions are less publicized. The responsibility for booking and planning these events often falls upon that employee who appears to have the talent or abilities to do the job.

As the field grows, the attention it draws increases. Research firms and trade publications are becoming more interested in studying and reporting on the corporate meetings segment of this industry. As the coverage increases, the perception of corporate meeting planning as a discipline grows, creating greater recognition of those who practice it.

Like their association counterparts, corporate meeting planners are joining organizations such as Meeting Planners International to learn how to do their jobs better. Even more significant is the formation of associations serving the needs of planners in specific industries, such as the Insurance Conference Planners Association that serves those who are involved with meetings and group travel for insurance company employees.

Still, while there is a trend toward full-time convention managers in the corporate sector, most of those doing this type of planning actually hold titles and responsibilities that may be totally unrelated to the conference planning function. This can make it difficult for property sales executives to identify corporate conference buyers.

According to a *Meetings & Conventions* magazine study,[1] meeting planners usually come from administration or sales and marketing positions. Exhibit 3.1 shows a more complete breakdown of the results of this study.

Before examining corporate meetings and conferences more closely, it is important to compare and contrast them with those of associations.

To begin with, most of the differences arise from the principal distinctions between the organizations themselves. Associations are voluntary in nature. Therefore, participation cannot be delegated or demanded. Rather, it must be promoted and even requested. This elective atmosphere, however, does not exist in corporations.

Corporations are business entities designed to make a profit. They do this by developing and selling products, concepts, and services. In contrast, the vast majority of associations are non-profit, tax-exempt organizations.

Advances in manufacturing technology, increased worldwide competition for markets, and improvements in communications and transportation systems have set the stage for an enormous and growing corporate meetings market.

Automation has created a need for workers to understand and practice production techniques that seem to change every day. In addition, new concepts and adaptations of foreign management principles require an unprecedented degree of continuing education in American business and industry.

Employees must learn product development and marketing techniques as well as how to handle sudden fluctuations and changes within their industries. This applies to those persons responsible for development, testing, production, distribution, sales, and marketing of products and services.

Government relations and legislative affairs are priority issues from boardrooms to production lines. New developments and changes in these areas also create a need for continuing education and other types of formal meetings within the corporate sector.

Exhibit 3.1 Meeting Planners' Corporate Positions

Job Title/Position	Corporate Planners
Sales/marketing	37%
Corporate administration	35%
Advertising, public relations	13%
Meeting/exhibit planning	7%
Personnel/training & development	5%
Travel/traffic	1%
Manufacturing/operations	1%
Other	1%
Total	100%

Differences Between Corporate and Association Meetings

While many of the principles of meeting management are the same for corporate and association meetings, fundamental differences exist in meeting planning techniques for the two. These distinctions are very important to those who sell and service conferences of all types. Property sales executives can be quite successful if they understand the unique requirements of corporate meeting planners and can gear their sales approaches, the packages being sold, and the delivery of the products to match those specific needs. Exhibit 3.2 illustrates some of the basic differences between corporate and association meetings. An examination of these elements in relation to the two major meetings markets will illustrate some of the primary concerns of meeting planners representing both disciplines.

Reasons for Holding Meetings

Corporations and associations have different reasons for holding meetings.

In contrast with associations, corporations do not conduct as many meetings of the type that a property would normally host. Certainly, many corporations are required to have board meetings and stockholders' meetings, but these are often held in the organizations' corporate offices.

As we noted in Chapter 2, associations' bylaws or constitutions usually require them to have certain types of meetings each year. Specifically, the elected leadership should convene for meetings of the boards of directors and the executive committees. In addition, certain other committees should meet and there should be at least one annual membership meeting each year. These meetings are mandatory.

Therefore, there is a certain predictability in an association's annual meeting and leadership meetings. They are normally held at the same times each year, with roughly the same configurations and number of attendees. These types of meetings represent a potential source of business to the hospitality industry.

A major factor influencing a corporation or association's decision to schedule a meeting is the state of the nation's economy.

During periods of economic decline, corporations are likely to economize by eliminating or cutting back a certain number of sales meetings, product introductions, and incentive programs. This is seen as a cost-cutting measure. For example, during the recession of the early 1980s, a large number of corporate meetings were canceled.

Exhibit 3.2 Differences Between Corporate and Association Meetings

	Corporate	Association
Reasons for holding meetings	Discretionary	Mandatory
Decision-making authority	Centralized	Decentralized
Budget considerations	Established	Flexible
Attendance	Mandatory	Voluntary
Participation	Mandatory	Voluntary
Guarantees	Established	Flexible
Attendee homogeneity	Consistent	Variable
Finance/Master Account billing	Centralized	Individual
Booking lead time	Relatively Short	Relatively Long

On the other hand, association meeting attendance usually increases when times are tough. The very reasons for belonging to an association encourage many members to turn to these groups for help when confronted by crises or challenges.

Decision-Making Authority

The decision-making process for planning and conducting meetings illustrates another major distinction between corporations and associations.

In a corporation, one individual is usually responsible for site selection and programming. This person may be a corporate meeting planner, a corporate travel executive, or the manager of a company's branch office in the vicinity of where the meeting will be held. A committee is seldom involved in the decision-making process. Therefore, the decision-making process is normally *centralized.*

In many associations, however, committees are intimately involved in this process. All decisions relating to planning and execution may fall completely upon volunteers. Even if the salaried staff is involved, it may be working under the direction of committees that direct site selection, programming, promotion, and perhaps much more. It is very likely, however, that staff input and advice has great influence on the committees. This leads to a classic situation encountered by many suppliers of association meetings.

Although these committees may or may not have actual decision-making authority, they frequently become scapegoats for unfavorable decisions or when decisions are delayed.

It is not unusual for the property executive to be told by the association meeting planner that "the committee has not made a decision yet" or "I'll have to take your proposal for room rates and menu prices before my committee."

Regardless of the consequences, it is normal in the archetypal association to have a decision/authority base that is *decentralized.*

Budget Considerations

Budgets for corporate conferences are routinely developed as part of the larger overall corporate financial operating plan.

Because no revenue is obtained from attendees, the corporation determines the acceptable expense level in light of the meeting's purpose and develops a budget accordingly. This process dictates clear financial parameters that both the property sales executive and the meeting planner must use to plan for the best possible conference for a predetermined price. Unless there are subsequent budget changes, the financial plan for the meeting is relatively stable and established.

This contrasts with the typical association meeting budget, which normally must be predicated on anticipated income from registration fees, exhibit fees, sponsorships, and the like.

It stands to reason that associations do not plan to run conventions at a net loss. Rather, they typically budget to generate income over expense, or at the very least to break even. Their management philosophy is that, in those cases where conventions cost more than revenue will cover, other funds (possibly from dues) will be used to make up the difference. Thus, monies intended for other uses must be set aside to subsidize a convention that may be attended by only a small fraction of the overall membership.

During the budgeting process, anticipating shortfalls in income can produce necessary reductions in the expense budget. On the other hand, if income is greater than anticipated, the convention program can be upgraded, perhaps through last-minute changes in decorations, entertainment, or food and beverage functions.

In other words, the association budget is often dynamic rather than static. That is, the budget is often highly flexible because of the unpredictability that is inherent in voluntary attendance. The property sales executive or convention service manager who realizes this will stay in close contact with the client to make certain that services being offered are still compatible with the cost of services expected.

Attendance   Individuals attending corporate meetings go because their presence there is mandatory; it is part of their jobs. Unlike association attendees who must pay to attend, corporate attendees are paid to participate.

Association members attend conventions, seminars, and workshops at their own expense. Because registration fees are not considered an account receivable, association officials do not consider attendance mandatory. Rather, there is a conscious decision by the delegates themselves to voluntarily spend their time and money to attend a meeting.

This presents the association meeting planner with numerous challenges and considerations that do not confront the corporate meeting planner. Budgeting is an example we have already discussed. Other challenges include designing a program with interesting economic and political issues, promoting and marketing the meeting itself, taking members' demographics into account, and obtaining local support in the convention host's area. Many facilities have sold conventions by promising help in these activities.

For example, a property can help solve some of the promotional challenges facing a meeting planner by assisting with promotion. The property can make available pre-printed advertisements in which the group can add its own copy.

Or, rallying local support by contacting local chapters, city fathers, and related associations, a facility can significantly improve the convention's chances for success. These activities should assure a foundation of attendance and participation that may not otherwise exist.

In addition, obtaining local sponsorships of receptions, programs, or luncheons will be very helpful in eliminating many of the meeting planner's budget concerns. Often, such sponsorships can be arranged through suppliers to the industry or profession that the association represents. The property, usually perceived as an important community leadership entity, may be able to help solicit such sponsorships.

A basic principle comes into play here. When a property is successful in booking a convention or meeting, the entire community benefits financially and psychologically. Too often, this message is not communicated.

Participation

Corporate meeting attendees come to a meeting or convention as part of their job responsibility or as a reward. Thus, they have a responsibility to their employers to attend the sessions and events planned for them. Usually, they will attend all events sponsored by the convening organization. In other words, it could be justly claimed that actual participation at official corporate events is mandatory.

The property's convention service and banquet departments, therefore, can assume that the preliminary counts provided by corporate meeting planners will be very close to the actual number of participants for an event. Guarantees are more probable and can be more precise. Again, budget projections can be more realistic. Commitments are more easily predicted and fulfilled.

Association meetings, on the other hand, present much more of a challenge to both the facility and the meeting planner. Association meeting attendees are there only because they want to be, not because they have to attend.

Simply because 1,000 people registered for a convention and have actually arrived at the host property does not mean all 1,000 will attend every event. Association meeting attendees participate in convention events on a voluntary basis. As a result, the "no show" factor becomes a major element in planning the number of seats in a meeting room, the number of tables for a luncheon, and the number of meals ordered for a food and beverage event. The guarantee, upon which most of the meeting's financial success or failure can rest, becomes critical.

The novice meeting planner should remember the industry rule of thumb that 15% of registered attendees will not actually attend every function. The more experienced planners, however, will not risk this rather casual approach.

Seasoned meeting planners have their guarantee procedures down to as much of a science as is practicable. They keep detailed and accurate records of previous activities so that they can plan for future events. They note all special conditions.

The reason for this meticulousness is simple. No meeting planner wants to guarantee more than the actual number of meals consumed. Neither does the planner want to underguarantee, forcing the property's kitchen staff to prepare additional meals that were not anticipated.

This issue of actual participation—whether for food functions, meeting rooms, or guestrooms—presents probably the greatest single element influencing the artistic and financial success of a meeting. Miscalculating the number of actual participants in an association meeting can have negative effects for years to come.

Association management lore is filled with examples of practitioners who did not master this management skill and who consequently paid the ultimate price—their jobs.

Guarantees   Establishing guarantees for food functions and anticipating attendance at all other events is a challenge for meeting planners. Miscalculating guarantees creates any number of problems, like too many people waiting for too few meals.

How can the process of establishing attendance estimates or food and beverage guarantees be formalized? Most meeting planners have their own methods of arriving at a guarantee. Here is a typical example:

1. Determine the total number of people registered.

2. Add to that the number of "locals" expected to attend.

3. Next, add in the number of invited guests (speakers, VIPs, etc.).

4. Determine the number of beds being occupied by your attendees in participating properties (number of rooms doesn't count; you are counting *people*, not rooms). Notify properties in advance that you will need this information periodically for guarantee purposes.

5. Add in the number of expected arrivals prior to the event (East-West Coast flight schedules are vital in this exercise).

6. Subtract cancellations and "no-shows" (your registration desk personnel must know you will need this information periodically).

7. Determine in advance any competing events that will draw attendance away from your event. For example, major-league athletics or top-name entertainers in town may result in "no shows." If this is the case, subtract a numerical factor to reflect this.

8. Finally, taking all these factors into account, the planner then makes the guarantee—and hopes for the best!

Here are some additional considerations concerning guarantees. Most properties ask for guarantees 48 hours prior to the event, with 72 hours notice on weekends. However, this requirement can often be modified based on the menu selected and the number of people to be served. Often, the "labor call" for servers, bartenders, and other service personnel is a bigger problem for the property than ordering the raw menu items from suppliers.

If the meeting planner and the property food and beverage staff work together in this critical area of guarantees, menu selection and scheduling can often result in a guarantee timetable of 24 hours in advance of the event, and sometimes even less.

Other potential problems with guarantees can occur when the meeting planner's program fails to take into account *all* aspects of a scheduled activity. For example, if spouses are with the main group throughout the meeting *except for one period* when a tour is planned, the planner must remember to deduct the number of spouses from the guarantee for that time frame only. While this might appear to be obvious, all too often it is forgotten. And the results can be as embarrassing as they are expensive.

Also disconcerting is the failure to consider head table or reserved-table guests when determining the overall count for a guarantee. As often as they are forgotten when the guarantee is placed, they are also added twice, thereby overstating attendance. Either way, someone loses.

The key to effective guarantees for the association meeting planner is *knowledge of the attendance pattern of participants.* Nothing compares to knowing your audience. This is done by maintaining accurate records and then analyzing them over time. Behavioral patterns of participants can be established, and these trends can assist planners in predicting actual participation in events. Association meeting planners need this kind of assistance more than their counterparts running corporate conventions whose participants will usually be at the appointed place on time.

Attendee Homogeneity

People who attend association and corporate meetings do so for different reasons. Additionally, their backgrounds, interests, and personal goals often differ.

Participants at association meetings attend for a variety of reasons. Their objectives and aspirations may be significantly disparate.

Those who attend corporate meetings do so to fulfill specific company objectives and responsibilities. They may have to learn about a new product line at an annual sales meeting or they may be able to relax and have fun at an annual company outing.

Regardless, participants at the typical corporate function will likely have a much greater degree of homogeneity in their professional lives than those attending association meetings.

This is a fundamental consideration for the planner in developing program emphasis and structure. The hotelier who understands these differences and can apply that knowledge will have a significant edge on the competition.

A critical ingredient of any proposal is tailoring the plan to the unique needs of the client.

Understanding the variety of purposes for which people attend association conventions, for example, will enable the property executive to solicit those in the community who can provide the products and services needed to serve those purposes. This could include outside speakers with specific expertise; sports and recreation facilities and events; house and garden tours; study sessions utilizing local businesses or institutions; or an endless list of creative approaches to help the meeting planner fulfill attendee needs.

Determining those needs in the corporate meeting realm is considerably easier but still not without a challenge. Again, the prospective client will welcome suggestions, local contacts, and direct assistance in achieving meeting purposes. Ironically, as helpful as this consideration might be to closing a sale, the issue is rarely raised.

Most sales approaches deal with dates, room availability, food and beverage requirements, room rates, and so forth. Seldom is the primary question asked: What are the objectives of the meeting and the goals of the meeting organizer? If the potential buyer is asked this question, he or she will likely feel that the hotelier has an interest in the meeting greater than simply selling rooms.

**Finance/Master
Account
Billing**
There are fundamental differences in financial management procedures for corporate and association meetings. These differences are important considerations for the property's accounting department and for the projection of cash flow.

For corporate meetings, billings are typically *centralized.* That means one master account is compiled and then billed to a central authority in the corporation. That account will cover all direct expenses related to the execution of the meeting.

Included in the account are billings for guestrooms (plus incidental expenses and taxes), official food functions, audiovisual and staging costs, ground transportation fees, and any other charges related to the program.

In many cases, the meeting may be negotiated at an all-inclusive package price, which can simplify the master account process even more.

Association meetings, however, often involve multiple billings. Guestroom accounts, for example, are normally the responsibility of individual guests and must be billed accordingly. The master account for the association's meeting will likely be billed to the association, but it may have to be reviewed by a convention committee or finance committee before payment is made.

Additionally, many associations invite outside interests to sponsor certain events. Those sponsors may have to be billed separately as well. This procedure introduces even greater potential for confusion or delay because several authorities may have to approve expenditures.

Therefore, while corporate master account approval and payment procedures are typically centralized, association billings could be classified as more *individual.* This does not mean association master account payments are less reliable. However, because of the number of entities that may be involved in association meetings, approval and payment of charges may be less expedient than those for the corporate meeting.

Property executives should have some idea of the variety of expenses faced by both corporate and association meeting planners, including those costs that might not appear on the property's master account. Items that would be included in a typical convention expense budget are shown in Exhibit 3.3. These are typical cost factors for a convention or meeting budget. Some are less extensive or detailed, some much more.

The list shown in Exhibit 3.3 is not intended to enumerate every possible expense item related to a convention, but rather is an example of typical items encountered. Our point is that most conventions generate costs that may remain hidden to planners unless the budget is comprehensive and accurate. The hotel or facility expecting prompt payment for its convention or meeting services should understand the client's full range of financial obligations.

Sensitivity to these cost factors will help suppliers of convention facilities and services, as well as the meeting planners themselves. Suppliers must keep requests or offers for services within the financial capacities of the sponsoring organization.

**Booking
Lead Time**
In general, association meetings follow more established patterns than corporate meetings. As a result, association conferences are often booked with a *relatively* long lead time. Conventions and leadership meetings, such

Exhibit 3.3 Typical Convention Budget Elements

1. **Administrative**
   a. Office overhead/allocations
   b. Temporary help
   c. Staff travel (pre-convention)
   d. Staff travel (at meetings)
   e. Staff rooms (in excess of complimentary rooms)
   f. Telephone (at convention)
   g. Shipping
   h. Insurance
   i. Office equipment (at convention)
   j. Administrative printing
   k. Board/committee events
   l. Property gratuities

2. **Food & beverage events**
   a. Opening night theme party
   b. "Breakfast of Champions"
   c. Leadership luncheon
   d. Exhibitor refreshments
   e. Formal dinner/dance
   f. Coffee breaks

3. **Registration expenses**
   a. Registration forms
   b. Badges (printing)
   c. Badge holders
   d. Ticket books
   e. Registration kits
   f. Registration desk
   g. Desk supplies
   h. Registration personnel
   i. Message center

4. **Attendance promotion**
   a. Printing
   b. Postage
   c. Mailing house
   d. Envelopes

5. **Exposition promotion**
   a. Prospectus
   b. Rules & regulations
   c. Floor plans
   d. Cover letter
   e. Envelopes

6. **Theme and artwork**
   a. Convention theme art
   b. Repro proofs
   c. Meeting/expo promotion

7. **Exposition administration**
   a. Traffic builders/prizes
   b. Market research books
   c. Decoration/staging
   d. Booth installation
   e. Booth equipment
      (1) Table
      (2) Chairs (2)
      (3) Wastebasket
      (4) Smoker
      (5) Sign
   f. Labor
   g. Guard service
   h. Exhibit hall rental
   i. Exhibit hall cleaning
   j. Exhibitor briefing/lounge
   k. Exhibitor lists/printing
   l. Directional signs

8. **Program participants/speakers**
   a. Speakers/performers fees
   b. Speakers/performers expenses
      (1) Transportation
      (2) Per diem/subsistence
      (3) Accommodations
   c. Rehearsals
   d. Speakers lounge
      (1) Food and beverage requirements
      (2) Audiovisual test equipment
   e. Speakers gifts

9. **Audiovisuals**
   a. Audiovisual requirements for each session (equip. rental)
   b. Preparation of visuals
   c. Generic film rentals
   d. Rehearsals
   e. Labor/technicians
   f. Insurance/security for audiovisual equipment on site
   g. Microphone rental
   h. Audio recording
   i. Video recording
   j. Flipcharts/easels
   k. Simultaneous interpretation
   l. Teleconferencing
   m. In-house sound system rental
   n. Other accessory equipment (projection stands, screens, rear-screen staging, loudspeakers, etc.)

10. **Staging/special decorations**
    a. Drapes to cover wall lights, mirrors, distractions behind speakers
    b. Props, scenery
    c. Special lighting (tree lights, spots, lichos, troupers, dimmers, etc.)
    d. Lectern signs
    e. Corporate logo/signs on stage, property marquee, etc.
    f. Party favors
    g. Labor/installation
    h. Hospitality center decorations

11. **Spouse, youth events**
    a. Spouse, youth center
       (1) Decorations
       (2) Food and beverage requirements
    b. Tours/buses
    c. Tickets to ball games
    d. Counselors
    e. Special insurance riders

12. **Music and entertainment**
    a. Organist (opening session)
    b. Organ rental
    c. High school band contribution
    d. Harpist (president's party)
    e. Orchestra (dinner/dance)

13. **Signs**
    a. Silk screening on sign stock
    b. Labor (sign painters)
    c. Identification signs
    d. Directional signs
    e. Registration desk headers
    f. Sponsor acknowledgment signs
    g. Bus signs

Exhibit 3.3 *(continued)*

14. Flowers
    a. President's suite
    b. VIPs
    c. Ribbon cutting bouquet
    d. Centerpieces at banquet tables
    e. Centerpieces at buffet and hors d'oeuvres tables
15. Press/publicity
    a. Typewriter or computer rentals for press room
    b. Telephones for press room
    c. Food and beverage items for press room
    d. Press credentials
    e. Press releases/photos
	16. Miscellaneous printing
	    a. Menus for dinner/dance
	    b. Special notices
	    c. Rehearsal schedules
	    d. Staging guides
	    e. Special event invitations
	    f. Seminar sign-up sheets
	    g. Directory of sponsors
	    h. Directory of local restaurants
	    i. Certificates for property staff
	    j. Message center cards
	    k. General session scripts
	    l. Thank-you letters

as board of directors and nominating committees, are often required to be held at certain times of year and at certain frequencies.

Corporations, on the other hand, have greater latitude in conceiving, planning, and booking their meetings. As a result, their lead time for booking meetings is *relatively short* in comparison.

It is not uncommon for corporate meetings to be booked in a facility with only two or three weeks notice. The reason for this is that corporations can require attendance. Associations, on the other hand, may require the meeting, but they must promote attendance.

Types of Corporate Meetings

What types of meetings are most common in the realm of corporate conferences? The *Meetings & Conventions* magazine's survey referenced above lists nine categories reported by its subscribers.[2] This list is shown in Exhibit 3.4.

Management Meetings

There are two major types of management meetings in the corporate sector: executive conferences and management development and training programs.

The number of attendees at executive conferences will vary greatly, based upon the subject of the meeting and the scope of interest throughout the corporate ladder. The average length of such conferences is two days.

Management development and training conferences, on the other hand, tend to offer greater complexity of programming and are longer in duration—often lasting up to six days and containing a mixture of educational sessions, motivational speakers, and management training.

According to Berkeley Rice, senior editor of *Psychology Today*, most types of meetings are designed for an exchange of ideas and information about buying and selling and motivation. Management development and training sessions, however, are generally designed to change behavior and attitudes.[3]

At these meetings, relaxation and recreation are often blended with intensive training in corporate philosophies and management skills. For this

Exhibit 3.4   Numbers and Types of Corporate Meetings Planned

Type of Meeting	Number per Year	% of Total
Management meetings	178,000	25%
Training seminars	163,500	23%
Regional sales meetings	113,100	16%
New product introductions	67,750	10%
Professional/technical meetings	63,900	9%
National sales meetings	44,300	6%
Incentive trips	27,600	4%
Stockholder meetings	21,900	3%
Other meetings	26,050	4%
Total Meetings	706,100	100%

Source: "The Meetings Market '85," *Meetings & Conventions*, March 31, 1986, Table 9.

reason, resort hotels are often selected for management meetings—particularly conferences of higher ranking executives.

Training Seminars

Training seminars are similar to management meetings in that both usually include some recreation to offset the fatigue of intensive training sessions. However, attendance at training seminars often will be larger (as many as 50 persons is not uncommon) because companies bring in segments of their work forces to learn new techniques, new product applications, or new industry trends that affect their work.

When larger numbers of attendees are involved, the corporations may look for facilities convenient to the home office or manufacturing center in order to economize and to expedite travel. *Meetings & Conventions* magazine statistics indicate that the average attendance at each such meeting in 1986 was 42. The average duration of these training seminars was just under three days.[4]

It is also noteworthy that the majority of training sessions are planned and managed by persons other than corporate meeting executives. Instead, this responsibility often falls upon a division head or training executive who may have little experience in meeting planning.

Suppliers who realize this and can compensate for the client's inexperience by taking time to learn the meeting's objectives and the client's needs will enjoy repeat business from that client.

Training seminars typically require extensive meeting room space, although the food and beverage business, recreational activities, and guestrooms involved will likely provide an equitable offset in terms of revenue.

The meeting probably will require a considerable amount of audiovisual equipment and teaching aids. Consequently, it is necessary to have access to the type of equipment shown in Exhibit 3.5.

The key point is that corporate training seminars are designed primarily to facilitate learning through the spoken word and visual imagery. This is why effective audiovisual presentations are so important.

Properties wishing to pursue this lucrative market must be prepared to fulfill these needs by providing audiovisual services and equipment internally or from outside suppliers at a competitive price.

Exhibit 3.5   Audiovisual Equipment Used in Training Seminars

- 35mm slide projectors
- Overhead projectors
- Opaque projectors
- 16mm and 35mm motion picture projectors
- 35mm filmstrip projectors
- Projection screens
- Projection stands

- Flipcharts and easels
- Videotape equipment
- Electric and laser pointers
- Lectern microphones
- Gooseneck microphone stands
- Unidirectional microphones
- Floor microphones for audience use
- Sound mixers

Regional/ National Sales Meetings

These types of corporate meetings form perhaps the oldest and best known category. They encompass the learning requirements of the training seminars but also bear many of the characteristics of product introduction conferences and incentive trips.

The primary goals of the sales meeting are to hone selling skills, ensure that salespeople are familiar with current product lines, and reaffirm corporate philosophies about the markets being served. Also important are motivating those who market the product, re-instilling pride in the company and the products being sold, and sending the attendees home in an enthusiastic mood.

Thus, the typical sales meeting emphasizes education and training, with generous side orders of color, music, theme development, and peer interaction.

The emergence of the sales meeting bearing all these elements has grown with the realization that marketing and sales are skills positions. That is, they are disciplines that require professionalism and continuously updated knowledge and awareness. For many companies, to accept less in the marketing function has been to accept failure. As a result, sales meetings are growing rapidly both in number and in the complexity of their design.

There are several differences to note between regional (or local) sales meetings and those national in scope.

First, regional, state, and local meetings are often the responsibility of the respective area's sales office or administrative team. Therefore, meeting planners will probably not have extensive experience and may require significant consultative assistance by the property executive and staff to ensure that the meeting's objectives are fulfilled.

Second, the audiovisual equipment, staging requirements, and physical plant facilities may be less complex for the regional or local sales meeting than for those of the national sales meeting. Corporations are more inclined to use regional meetings for sales training and product orientations, while reserving national meetings for inspirational, motivational, and educational productions designed to reunify the entire sales force.

There is no clear-cut pattern to the type of facility selected. A market exists for virtually all kinds of facilities.

New Product Introductions

New product introductions are multidimensional meetings. They are often educational in nature, prime opportunities to teach salespeople and others about the features that make new product lines unique and marketable. These meetings are also often celebrations. They can be designed to motivate employees to become more enthusiastic about the value of the company and its products.

Additionally, new product introductions will likely involve not just employees of the sponsoring company but also wholesalers, distributors, and perhaps even retailers of the product line.

At other times, company "distributor meetings" will include only distributors and those involved in the product delivery system. Distributor and dealer meetings, however, will bear many of the same characteristics of new product introduction events. However, there is an important difference between the two.

Product introduction meetings involve salespersons and company representatives. Distributor meetings, on the other hand, involve distributors, wholesalers, and perhaps even retailers of the company's products. The primary difference between these meetings is the same as one of the essential dissimilarities between corporate and association meetings: employees attend product introduction meetings on the command of the sponsoring company. Attendees at distributors meetings, however, are usually not so beholden to the company sponsoring the meeting. Consequently, product introduction meetings can be somewhat predictable. As we noted in our discussion on the differences between association and corporate meetings, this rationale for attending a meeting has a direct impact on both participation and food and beverage guarantees.

Still another dimension of new product introductions is the invitation to diverse publics to take part in the event. These may include the press, government or agency officials, industry observers, and even consumers in general.

Broadening the scope of participation, however, creates new factors for consideration, such as security and crowd control, logistics, press facilities, VIP suites or lounges, issuing credentials, and attendee identification.

The broader the spectrum of attendees for any event, the less control the property or its clients have over the efficient execution of that event. Because many corporate meetings are planned and managed by individuals with little formal training in convention management, the property executive must determine precisely who will be included in the client's meeting activities. Not knowing this information can have disastrous consequences.

Product introduction meetings include elements of other types of meetings, and they may involve at various times groups ranging from a handful of executives to scores of people bearing everything from television cameras to checkbooks. The implications for the property, in terms of planning, security, and even law and liability, are clear.

Finally, product introductions are often accompanied by elaborate and sophisticated audiovisuals, staging devices, and exhibits. In other words, this can be the annual "show-time" for the meeting sponsor. While site selection will vary depending on the nature of the audiences being invited, the availability of the elements needed for dramatic productions may play an important role in the selection process.

Professional/
Technical
Meetings

Professional and technical meetings may have some of the characteristics of management meetings and training seminars. Because of rapidly escalating technologies, changing laws, and evolving competition, the number of these meetings ranks just under that of product introduction meetings.

Participants at these meetings will likely have similar areas of interest and reasons for attending. Small conferences may be combined with larger group lectures for discussions about highly technological, scientific, or even philosophic issues such as industry ethics.

Incentive Trips/Meetings

Incentive travel programs are rapidly becoming a lucrative market for the lodging industry. As enormous as the income potential has become, however, the market remains a primary target for only a limited number of properties, inns, and other facilities.

Because of the nature of an incentive trip, location becomes a more important consideration than the property itself. Therefore, properties in exotic locations, resort properties, and overseas venues are primary choices for incentive business.

Another important difference between the incentive trip and other types of corporate meetings is the amount of promotion involved. The corporation's promotion of incentive programs becomes a major planning activity. This aspect is unique among all types of corporate meetings.

These programs are designed to reward sales and management personnel who have achieved certain measures of excellence in their work. Establishing corporate goals and holding out a glamorous trip as a reward for those achievers (and often their spouses) require skillful promotion to eligible employees if the production goals are to be fulfilled.

The *primary* objective of incentive programming is to fulfill corporate goals and objectives. Thus, the term *incentive* is quite literal in its description of this type of corporate activity.

There are other unique attributes to be considered. For example, emphasis is on luxury, first-class travel arrangements, recreation, relaxation, and savoring the fruits of exotic places and outstanding facilities.

Because such events often involve group travel, transfers, sightseeing, entertainment, show productions, meals, gifts, and special amenities, the market has given rise to a growing, relatively new industry entity: incentive travel planners and companies.

Proof of the growing importance of this field is the formation and growth of a professional society representing this discipline: the Society of Incentive Travel Executives, headquartered in New York City.[5]

It should also be noted that incentive planning trips are often promoted among distributors, dealers, and even customers as an inducement to sell and use the company's product.

According to the Hotel Sales & Marketing Association International, incentive travel exceeded $3 billion in 1985, with most incentive trips lasting from five to seven days. However, longer trips, often to Europe, are not unusual, nor are short weekend getaways. It is also important to note that incentive trips can involve groups as large as 1,400 persons and as few as 2.[6]

Because the event is a reward, entertainment is primary. However, this is not to say that business meetings are not a part of many incentive trips. They are, and this leads to another characteristic of incentive travel that is important for hoteliers to understand.

Reporting on a survey of the incentive market, *Successful Meetings* magazine announced that only 21% of the respondents said they never hold business meetings as part of an incentive trip. Twelve percent answered that they hold such meetings rarely, while 33% reported that they hold meetings some of the time, and 32% reported that they always include business meetings as part of the incentive trip agenda.[7]

Some 53% of the respondents said they hold "token" business meetings. A major reason to hold such meetings is so that the participants can avoid having to report the value of the trip as taxable income.

Further, it is not unusual for the sponsoring company to list the business meetings as part of the overall incentive program and then cancel them after the trip begins.

Some companies, however, use incentive trips as opportunities to hold meaningful sessions to introduce new products, distribute new marketing tools, and reaffirm the loyalty of the participants. They capitalize on their "captive audiences."

It becomes obvious, then, that incentive trips and meetings can take on many of the attributes of other types of corporate meetings. Thus, there is some confusion over whether the trip is an actual incentive, a prize trip, a business trip, a group tour, or some combination of all these. This disorientation points to the need to develop a better definition of incentive travel.

Regardless of the confusion that exists as the market grows, certain needs of the meeting planners are apparent. Properties that try to fulfill those needs will enjoy significant returns on their investments.

According to Margaret Shaw, an effective plan for reaching corporate meeting planners and incentive houses includes the following four elements:[8]

1. Making certain that advertising, direct mail, and other marketing devices create an "image" and an awareness. Hard selling of the property itself is secondary.

2. Ensuring that the property's management philosophy embraces individuality and flexibility in treatment of guests. Incentive travel participants want to be treated like vacationers, not conventioneers.

3. Maintaining high standards of product and service, especially during site visits by corporate and incentive meeting executives.

4. Appointing one person from the property to deal exclusively with incentive planners and clients. This person should have a high level of authority and flexibility in deciding on pricing and operations.

This is one of the few cases of property marketing where it is difficult to obtain repeat business. Because corporations must continue to motivate their people to reach goals, the rewards must continually be fresh and different. As a result, new destinations are usually part of the incentive planning process.

An interesting sidebar to the incentive meetings activity consists of the role cruise ships are playing in this market. Cruise ship lines are offering an increasingly viable alternative to properties for incentive travel and meetings. Cruises can be customized for a company's specific needs. The ships concentrate on customizing shore excursions for ports of call, reflecting the specific requirements of the incentive group on board.

Stockholder
Meetings

We have already discussed how association boards and committees govern voluntary membership organizations. In a sense, the same could be said of a corporation's stockholders.

At least once a year, most companies are required by law to invite their stockholders to a meeting to discuss the previous year's financial operations and overall status. Although many of these meetings are held at hotels, they generally represent the lowest income source for properties.

While there are exceptions, most meetings last one day or less and are held in the home city of the corporation. There is rarely any food and beverage service, except for perhaps coffee and soft drinks.

Therefore, unless the property trades off the event for future revenue-generating business, the only direct revenue often realized is rental of the meeting room itself.

The audiovisual requirements for these meetings might include projection equipment, floor microphones, and a sound mixer. It is not a bad idea to have a sound technician on hand to make certain that only the microphone being used is "live" at a given time. It is not unusual for lively debates to develop, and a roomful of "live" microphones can turn debate into total confusion.

There is usually no financial benefit for the property holding a stockholders meeting. Instead, it has the opportunity to service a company when the company's top executives are present. These persons likely serve on boards of directors of other companies and also have leadership roles in associations and societies related to their industries and professions.

For this reason, serving the stockholders' meeting well can result in lucrative future business from the other companies and associations with which those executives in the meeting room are involved.

The Independent Meeting Planner

The growth of corporate meetings has given rise to yet another definable segment of the overall industry: the independent meeting planner.

Some ten years ago, there existed only a handful of independent firms that contracted with sponsors to help with, or entirely manage, their meetings. Today, more than 700 independent meeting planner firms operate in the United States, and the number continues to grow.

For economic reasons, corporate meeting planners are often the first to be laid off during periods of recession. These positions are usually not considered essential. Independent meeting planners, therefore, can be brought in to conceive, plan, and execute an entire meeting on a turnkey basis. Or, the independent may be asked to be responsible for only one or for several meeting elements. It is quite common for an independent to be hired to handle the administrative tasks, including negotiations and planning with suppliers, in order for the corporate meeting planner to be able to concentrate on program content. Creative staging of special events is also a widely-sought service of independents.

On other occasions, an independent planner may be retained as a consultant, to observe and to recommend procedures and strategies for improving future meetings.

Independent planners usually are former association or corporate conference planners who, for entrepreneurial reasons, have decided to offer their experience and skills at large in this growing field.

Chapter Summary

The number of meetings held by corporations has increased significantly in recent years, and this trend shows no sign of falling off in the foreseeable future. This is good news for the hospitality and convention services industries that are the recipients of much of this business.

Like associations, corporations hold meetings for very well-defined reasons. These range from management meetings and training seminars to sales meetings and incentive trips.

Although there are many similarities between corporations and associations with respect to their holding meetings and conventions, they differ on nine key points. These items must be understood by those wishing to provide convention and meetings services to the corporate market.

An interesting sidelight to the growth of the corporate meeting market has been the emergence of the independent meeting planner. These individuals are becoming more prominent in arranging and managing meetings and conventions.

Notes

1. "The Meetings Market '85," *Meetings & Convention*, March 31, 1986, Table 33.
2. Ibid., Table 9.
3. Berkeley Rice, "Do Management Development Meetings Change Attitudes and Behavior?" *Successful Meetings*, June 1987, p. 32.
4. Ibid., Table 7.
5. Society of Incentive Travel Executives (SITE), 271 Madison Ave., New York, NY 10016. Tel. (212) 889-9340.
6. Margaret Shaw, "A Look At the Lucrative Incentive Travel Market," *HSMAI Marketing Review* (Spring 1986):24–27.
7. Ann E. LaForge, "Survey Reveals Confusion Over the Nature of Incentive Travel," *Successful Meetings*, February 1987, pp. 40–43.
8. Shaw, *HSMAI Marketing Review*, pp. 24–27.

4 Miscellaneous Markets

Chapter Objectives

1. To list the factors that athletic teams consider important when selecting a property

2. To identify the criteria properties must meet to pursue the trade unions market

3. To learn why the tour group market is becoming increasingly popular

4. To identify the types of senior citizen travelers

5. To list the reasons why properties pursue the theater market

In Chapters 2 and 3 we examined association and corporate meetings, respectively. We learned that the groups described in those chapters were the most typical ones, the easiest to identify.

Yet, there are many other groups. Some would qualify as associations by certain definitions, others perhaps as corporations. But all have certain unique characteristics that require them to be examined separately.

The Sports Market

The athletic environment can produce a surprisingly consistent and lucrative market for the hospitality industry in cities where professional sports exist, or where collegiate or even high school sports are an important part of community life.

The teams themselves are only part of that market. There are also visiting fans and members of the press to accommodate, team meetings, pre-game meals, awards banquets, booster meetings, and rallies.

When we analyze the sports market, we tend to think of it in terms of professional or major college athletics. These segments, however, constitute only part of the overall market.

Club, recreational, and tournament sports are growing rapidly throughout the United States. Track and field events, soccer, volleyball, bowling, softball, and swimming, as well as other typically amateur sports, are evolving into a major lodging industry market.

As leisure time, ease of travel, and interest in sports of all types increase, more teams and individual sports participants travel extensively to various events. For example, many high school teams that used to compete against teams only from a very limited geographic area now are invited to tournaments or play regularly scheduled games out-of-state.

The most useful sources of information about these events are local convention and visitors bureaus, local colleges and universities, school boards, and athletic clubs. All can be found in phone books.

The Lodging Industry's Services

What do teams at any level expect in terms of lodging industry services? There are at least 10 things property executives should keep in mind when they seek to expand their share of the sports market:

1. Teams look for properties that are accessible to the closest airport and to the athletic facility where they are to compete. This is especially true of major league professional teams.

2. Many top athletes are public figures, so security and privacy are important considerations.

3. Price considerations are more important for minor-league professional, college, high school, and amateur teams than for major league teams.

4. If food service must be provided for a visiting team, the property chef probably will have to design team meals around nutritionally balanced menus as specified by team policy.

5. In those sports where the physical size of the athlete is a factor (e.g., basketball or football), the size of the room is not as important as the size of the bed. Two king-size beds per room would be ideal, although this arrangement is rarely found. Two queen-size beds are the next preference, but two double beds are normally acceptable. In order to economize, most teams prefer to house players two to a room. Professional basketball is often an exception to this limitation because a player's size—and superstar status—earns him single-room accommodations and other amenities.

6. Many innovative hoteliers negotiate with colleges and universities, or with travel agencies, to arrange team and fan accommodations for away games. Besides accommodations, the package may even include a welcome party, pep rally, and post-game party for the fans.

7. Many teams prefer to negotiate a package price for the trip. Included in the price are pre-registration (no coach wants his or her team standing in the lobby while rooms are processed), accommodations, team meals, and the use of meeting rooms. A complimentary suite with a parlor (for private meetings) for the coach or coaching staff is an effective negotiating tool regardless of the

number of guestrooms involved in the package.

8. For reasons of security and privacy, team events should not be listed on the property's events schedule.

9. Special telephone service should be arranged by the property to direct all calls to a team official instead of the players themselves.

10. Innovative properties have created sports markets by producing, promoting, and administering athletic events that did not previously exist. This is especially true for amateur sports and individual sports like tennis and golf, where tournaments can be created to attract athletes and spectators. In this way, a property seeking new business can virtually create a new market.

The Indianapolis Example

Indianapolis, Indiana, is a prime example of a community that has targeted the sports market as a major objective for its hospitality industry. This was brought about only through the cooperation of the city's convention bureau, convention center/stadium complex, and city government.

The emphasis there in serving the sports market began with a concerted effort to attract sports-related association meetings. The city hosted such groups as the American College of Sports Medicine, the U.S. Olympic Council House of Delegates, the Golf Course Superintendents Association, the Professional Golfers Association, the National Conference of High School Directors of Athletics, and the National High School Athletic Coaches Association. Another group, the Pan American Economic Leadership Conference, had a powerful influence on the city's hosting the prestigious Pan American Games in 1987.

For Indianapolis, the Pan American Games meant occupancy of some 6,000 guestrooms for 21 nights. The 6,000 rooms multiplied by 21 nights translated into revenue for 126,000 room nights. And that did not include the other direct and indirect expenses budgeted by the organizers of the games nor the out-of-pocket expenses of the athletes and spectators.

Booking Considerations

Lead times for booking team accommodations will vary, depending on the sport involved and the level of competition. Soliciting business from team boosters usually can begin as soon as schedules are announced. However, scheduling is not the same for all sports.

In Division I college football, most games and locations are contracted for between the competing schools and approved by the National Collegiate Athletic Association (NCAA) four or five years in advance. On the other hand, professional football schedules are set less than a year before the current season begins.

The time of year a sport is played dictates the lead time for the booking process. Hockey and basketball are winter sports, so arrangements are made in the spring and summer. Football is a fall-winter sport, so arrangements are made the preceding winter and spring. Baseball, a spring-summer sport, has its travel and accommodation schedules set in the fall and early winter.

Who makes the decision to book a property for a team? While general managers, traveling secretaries, and even trainers may be involved, the head coach will most likely be the final arbiter.

Several factors will be considered. Price is an important consideration for all teams below the major-league professional level. The distance from the property to the airport, arena, or stadium is another. And the property should be able to work with the team trainer in providing specially planned meals at precise times before the games.

Meeting facilities that have audiovisual capabilities (including videotape equipment) will have an advantage.

Room service will not matter to most teams below the major league level, but major league teams prefer 24-hour service.

A property's ability to pre-register its team guests, and to be prepared to welcome them with full service including registration and bell personnel when they arrive at 3:00 a.m., is an important consideration.

The most important local contact for securing business from visiting teams is the local coach. At the college and high school levels, coaches tend to seek the advice of their colleagues in securing accommodations that are suitable and affordable. Therefore, developing rapport with local coaching staffs at all levels and in all sports is a prudent step for hoteliers who wish to seriously pursue this growing market.

Remember that accommodations are important to athletes and athletic teams. These groups want expeditious convenience first, comfort second, affordability next, and security fourth. Their only reason for visiting your city is the game or event in which they are to participate.

The Trade Unions Market

Industrial and professional trade unions are among the most politicized organizations in America. As such, they rely heavily on meetings to perpetuate their causes, to refine their policies and doctrines, and to elect their leadership. To accomplish their goals, unions hold three types of meetings:

1. National conventions
2. Regional meetings/conferences
3. Executive councils/committees

National Conventions

Union conventions are colorful affairs, complete with campaigns and elections, membership recruitment, and heated debate over policy issues, union bylaws, and endorsements of political candidates at all levels.

A Hotel Sales & Marketing Association International study of group markets notes four major criteria that must be met if a property is to seriously compete for the union market:[1]

1. The property employees must be unionized. Newer facilities should have been constructed by union labor.

2. The property must be able to accommodate large numbers of attendees in general session. Union meetings of 2,000 delegates or more are not uncommon.

3. The property must be accessible to and able to provide service for large numbers of media representatives.

4. Sophisticated audiovisual equipment is a requisite for most union meetings.

Union conventions are often held at East and West Coast properties located in resort areas. It is important to note that many of the national conventions are held every two years, rather than annually.

Because of the absence of a convention every other year, many unions hold regional meetings to conduct interim business.

Regional Meetings

Attendance at regional meetings will be in the 200- to 500-person range, with meetings lasting two to three days. Many of the meeting criteria and characteristics are the same as those of the larger national meetings. Again, the property must be unionized in order to even be considered to host the meeting.

Executive Council and Committee Meetings

Council and committees hold small but high-level meetings. They are similar to association leadership council meetings because they are normally composed of the most influential members of the organization's hierarchy.

While only 15 or 20 persons may be in attendance, they are in a strong position to influence decisions about future national convention sites. Successfully servicing these smaller meetings is critical to the property that hopes to compete for larger union meetings.

In many unions, the final decision to select the site for the national convention rests with the general secretary. Regional meetings are often the responsibility of the district vice president. Smaller leadership meetings, however, will often fall within the purview of the union's secretary-treasurer.

As a general rule, union executives do not belong to convention and hospitality industry associations such as Meeting Planners International, Hotel Sales & Marketing Association International, the American Hotel & Motel Association, or the American Society of Association Executives. Rather, union meeting planners tend to work more unilaterally. This does not imply lack of attention to detail or limited knowledge of the industry. On the contrary, general secretaries and other decision-makers demand detailed reports on property qualifications prior to the decision-making process.

Additionally, hoteliers will likely find union planners with extensive experience in planning and managing meetings with very similar requirements year after year. Also noteworthy is the tendency of many unions to stay with a property they like. Repeat business, in other words, is a reasonable expectation for the property that effectively services the union market.

The union market has become so important that a number of individual properties and chains now employ sales executives to specifically nurture contacts within the union community and to sell property facilities to that market. The selling process is often a result of long, continuing, and essential personal relationships that generate a sense of trust between the individuals involved.

The Tour Group Market

Group tour and travel is another market that does not fall neatly within the association or corporate meetings markets. Yet, because of its size and importance to the hospitality industry, it bears examination here.

More people than ever are benefiting from the discounts available through group purchases of tour packages. This is due to an increase in the amount of leisure time available, improvements in all types of transportation systems that make more destinations accessible than ever before, and the availability of more money to spend on travel.

Transportation is a very important factor because it can include the means to arrive at a destination (airlines, motor coaches, railroads, or limousines) or it can be the final destination itself (such as cruise ships). Moreover, transportation conveyances can be used at the destination for group movement and entertainment (e.g., deep-sea fishing boats or special excursion trains).

How is the tour group business marketed? To begin with, it is important to understand the partners in the marketing and sales chain.

The first to be considered is the travel wholesaler. This individual or company contracts with properties, transportation companies, and other suppliers to create a variety of travel packages. These are then made available to travel agents for retail sales to the public.

It is incorrect to assume that travel wholesalers never sell their products directly to the public, because they do. They make that decision with great care, however, in order to avoid alienating travel agents upon whom they rely for delivery of the majority of their products to travel-oriented consumers.

Travel agents, therefore, are the largest source of group tour business for properties. Through brochures, manuals, and personal advice, they interest groups in specific travel packages. They do this by matching customers' time availability, monetary resources, and personal interests with the types of travel packages available.

Some agencies are more resourceful than others in working directly with properties to develop and market group travel packages. These agencies' relationships with wholesalers and the properties are vital to their success. Therefore, decisions to work directly with one property over another or to omit the wholesaler must be made with great discretion.

An easy way to remember the difference between the travel wholesaler and the travel agent is that the wholesaler will sometimes negotiate packages for larger groups of customers, such as travel clubs, associations, or corporations. This service is important because large volume allows for greater purchasing power and therefore lower prices for the groups involved.

The travel agent, on the other hand, sometimes deals with individuals as well as groups, selling pre-packaged, full service, travel programs that were probably negotiated and prepared by wholesalers.

In addition to the travel wholesalers and travel agencies, the variety of suppliers is made even more complex by the involvement of tour operators who provide one or more group travel services (e.g., sightseeing, entertainment, or group ground movement).

While tour operators generally sell their products directly to the public, it is not unusual for them to also function as tour wholesalers. In this role they serve as both retailers and wholesalers, depending on the products or services being sold. Many tour bus companies, for example, offer their services on both a retail and wholesale basis. And if this were not confusing enough, facilities often sell their packages directly to clients or guests as well as through wholesalers and travel agents.

The point to remember, however, is that while some properties have clear preferences about the channel of distribution they use (wholesaler, travel agent, tour operator, or direct to the consumer), most use a combination.

How do properties promote their packages to their customers? Most use direct mail, advertising in trade publications serving the tour and travel industry, and distributing brochures and collateral materials to the traveling public. In addition, they can offer familiarization trips (also known as "fam" trips) to travel agents.

"Fam" trips are designed to give agents a favorable impression of the property or facility that they can then relate to their customers. Usually, most of the expenses for such visits are picked up by the sponsoring property. For the facility seriously pursuing the group tour market, the investment could produce major dividends.

There are several associations actively serving various segments of this market. The four most important are:

American Bus Association
1025 Connecticut Ave., N.W.
Suite 308
Washington, DC 20036

American Society of Travel Agents
4400 MacArthur Blvd., N.W.
Washington, DC 20007

National Tour Association
120 Kentucky Ave., Bldg. A
Lexington, KY 40502

Travel Industry Association of America
1899 L Street, N.W., Ste. 600
Washington, DC 20036

The Ethnic Organizations Market

Ethnic organizations (sometimes called cultural organizations) include members who share the same place of national origin. We touched on ethnic organizations as a market in Chapter 2 while looking at avocational associations in a larger context. Because of the breadth of this subdivision and its potential as a market for hospitality suppliers, it deserves separate treatment here.

Property executives should understand that ethnic organizations often cut across the lines of other avocational groups, such as hobby organizations or social welfare societies. Thus, while a listing of purely ethnic organizations dedicated to the perpetuation of a certain culture may be hard to find, an examination of other types of avocational organizations may reveal them.

For example, these ethnic organizations emphasize nationality of family origin, but they are categorized by a more immediate common interest:

1. American French Genealogical Society

2. Polish Singers Alliance of America

3. Federation of Alpine and Schuplattler Clubs in North America

4. Belgian American Educational Foundation

The ethnic or cultural meetings market remains one of the most viable for hospitality properties, especially in low-demand seasons and in the so-called "second-tier" cities.

Although the organization may be gathered around some avocational interest, the group's *real* interest is cultural. Social and cultural contact is the goal.

It stands to reason, then, that a property can do well servicing and selling to ethnic markets if it is sensitive to and has a basic understanding of these markets' particular cultures.

Ethnic organizations lean heavily toward family participation. This means a preference for meeting on weekends, during holidays when schools are not in session, and at times of the year when property rates are most affordable. Social, entertainment, and recreational facilities must be available, or at least convenient, for these groups.

Ethnic groups categorized by race are becoming increasingly important in this category. These meetings differ from those described above in that they may be more political than cultural/avocational or cultural/heritage types of gatherings.

Therefore, the hotelier should be alert to the purpose of the organization before soliciting its business.

For example, the ethnic meeting designed to call attention to equal rights or to seek social reform will usually meet in urban areas that are within easy access of the press as well as those interested in the cause.

Also, the purpose of a meeting often will determine where it will be held. The cultural/family ethnic meeting with no political or economic overtones will gravitate toward a location where accessibility and price are right, and it will be held at a time when the participants are free to attend.

Again, these types of meetings are described here because they are not often found among the meetings listed under many established volunteer groups.

The Senior Citizens Market

The lodging industry has long viewed the senior citizens market as having "last resort" business potential. With some notable exceptions, few properties include senior citizens in their primary market mix because of the assumption that people over the age of 60 simply sit at home and do not travel.[2]

U.S. Census Bureau statistics provide important background

information about these people. At the present time, one person out of ten in the United States is 65 years of age or older. By 1990, however, 31.1 million persons (12.7% of the population) will be over 65. By the year 2000, that figure will reach 35 million. And, by 2030, it is projected that more than 20% of the population (about 64.6 million persons) will be over the age of 65.

Hospitality sales executives who feel they can ignore more than 20% of the population in marketing a product are actively courting failure.

Further, the argument that this market segment does not have to be solicited today because it represents only some 10% to 12% is erroneous. The astute property sales executive realizes that the senior citizens of 2030, or even 2000, are today's active travelers. The attitudes and opinions they form today will influence their future behavior.

Senior citizens are rapidly becoming the mass market of the leisure class. The image of the elderly as being a sedentary and uninterested element of the population is fallacious.

Canadian marketing executives view senior citizens as "affluent free-spending retirees." Their figures show that in Canada 13.4% of the population will be 65 or older by the year 2000.[3] In France, studies show that the number of citizens over the age of 60 there will increase by *2 million* between the years 1985 and 2000, and by another *5 million* just 5 years later.[4] Throughout Europe, 17% of all people will be 65 or older by the turn of the century.

Will they travel? Industry observers and statisticians are proving that they already do, and in increasingly substantial numbers.

Will they have the discretionary dollars to spend for hospitality products and services? That is, will they have money left after fixed-cost expenses and other obligations are paid?

There seems to be little doubt that they will have the money to spend for travel. Despite the debate over the social security system and the economic well-being of U.S. senior citizens in general, in 1986 this group enjoyed the largest discretionary dollar per-capita balance of any age group. The yearly disposable income figure for persons 65 and older was $5,633—almost twice that of any other group under age 40.[5]

According to James Murray, CHSE, director of marketing at Grossinger's in New York State, hoteliers must consider the following two questions when pursuing this market:[6]

First, is this a desirable market for the property? Are there "off periods" that could be filled by other types of groups that may not require possible physical changes in the property?

Second, can the property afford mixing this market with its other markets? Large numbers of senior citizens may alter the image of the property in the eyes of the other markets being served.

This last consideration is a major one for all properties. Regardless of their improved physical health, interest in travel, and disposable income, many senior citizens seek the company of others who share demographic similarities. The property that seeks their business must balance their presence with the interests of other markets being served.

To properly serve this market, the facility must make a judgment as to whether or not the physical plant is designed to serve the unique needs of senior citizens and whether or not capital improvements are economically justifiable. Quality of staff attitude and training are important because many employees may not identify with the values and psychographic interests of this guest market.

In addition to being aware of the interests, opinions, and attitudes of senior citizens, the entire property staff must be sensitive to the fact that this group now seeks new adventures. Previously, the sales efforts to attract this market centered on the "3-S" comfort syndrome: safety, security, and shelter. This no longer does the trick. Instead, many seniors are seeking excursions, culinary adventures—something different, more social, more daring. Destinations being promoted to this group by the travel community include Alaska, China, the Soviet Union, India, and other exotic and adventuresome places.

In general, there are four types of senior citizen travelers:

1. Independent self-sufficients—those who travel as individuals and who require no extraordinary assistance

2. Group self-sufficients—those who are self-sufficient but prefer to travel as part of a larger group

3. Social dependents—those who enjoy programming that provides for social activities with others having similar interests

4. Physical dependents—those who require special facilities, services, or equipment to function because of physical handicaps

As senior citizens become more knowledgeable about travel, more economically stable, and more physically vigorous in the years ahead, the growth opportunity of the first two categories will continue to increase.

Time, money, and desire are three essential ingredients that lead to a discretionary travel experience. Statistics show that senior citizens have both the time and the money. Properties seeing this group as a viable market will develop the marketing plans to create the desire.

The Theater Market

There is little reliable data to accurately describe the very individualized theater market. Still, anyone who reads newspapers or magazines or who watches television will note striking increases in theatrical productions.

Decades ago, other than in cities such as New York, Chicago, and Los Angeles, there was very little for people to do for entertainment. Because there was no television then, visual entertainment was often a product of personal or family creativity. Communities hungered for visual diversion and amusement. In order to fill that need and to enjoy the financial rewards of so doing, entrepreneurs brought "live" entertainment to the people.

Theater became a community activity. Chautauquas, touring vaudeville shows, traveling evangelists, and barnstormers of all types flourished.

Then came television. For a period it replaced live entertainment, but it also meant disaster for a large segment of the motion picture industry, including neighborhood theaters and drive-ins.

But trends are reversing. Live entertainment is back.

Throughout the country, innovative properties and restaurants have recognized the trend toward community theaters, summer theater performances, and productions by theater schools at the secondary school and collegiate levels. Communities that barely knew they had high school bands now boast of symphony orchestras. Local comedy clubs, often inviting unknowns to do routines or to participate in improvisational comedy, are proliferating.

There are four important reasons why some properties aggressively target this market in their strategic and tactical planning:

1. It is easier to sell to and service a group that is already gathered than to have to go out and somehow bring that group together.

2. Theaters provide a group, already gathered.

3. Theater-goers, by the nature of the activity, are out to celebrate. They have left their homes for the sole purpose of having some fun. This might include dining, dancing, and socializing before the end of the evening.

4. Local theaters and production companies are usually sources of pride in a community. Therefore, relating any promotion to that source of pride is a positive marketing tactic.

There are a number of ways a property can tap this market. The steps shown in Exhibit 4.1 show how a profitable relationship can be established.

Quite obviously, the entertainment does not have to be Broadway quality. Rather, the mood of the public today is to support theater and the arts and to take pride in local products.

That interest and that pride present a good opportunity for properties to provide a service as well as to sell a product.

The Arts Market

Exhibiting and selling the works of local artists is another market that cannot be ignored.

Exhibiting the works of local or unknown artists in the public spaces of a property serves several worthwhile purposes: it provides an exhibit area for these artists to display their works; it provides interesting decorative ambience to the facility itself; and it indicates to guests that the property is interested in supporting the arts, especially at the local level.

The art pieces can contain a sticker indicating the name of the work, the name of the artist, and the price. The work can be sold by the property, which may or may not have agreed upon a commission for the transaction. Arrangements for such exhibits can be made through a local art gallery or directly with the artists.

A relatively new, but increasingly popular, device for attracting new customers is the "starving artists" exhibit. The source of the art is the unknown artist. Through art distributors or retailers, a property may arrange for an exhibit of a large number of pieces from various artists (possibly including a sprinkling of works from well-known contemporary artists) and then promote the show to the public.

Exhibit 4.1   Steps for Garnering the Theater Market

1. Sponsoring some aspect of the theater group's production, such as the playbill or intermission refreshments
2. Advertising in the playbill, perhaps to promote a special theater-goers' "after-theater supper" menu
3. Sponsoring appearances by performers or celebrities
4. Catering refreshments before, during, and after the show
5. Advertising special after-performance entertainment or menus with the advertising for the performance itself
6. Opening performance areas in the property itself, taking advantage of the interest in live theater to attract patrons, not only to see the show but also to enjoy the food and beverage services of the facility (Dinner theaters, which are becoming extremely popular throughout the United States, can be housed with relative ease by many hotels.)
7. Holding "talent contests" in the property's food and beverage outlet, inviting local performers to entertain clients, with prizes ranging from cash to scholarships

Using the same sources for obtaining artwork, properties may also attract customers by holding art auctions. For a percentage of the gross receipts, many art distribution houses will supply the auctioneers and administer the evening's activities.

For the sponsoring property, however, the revenue from the sale or exhibition of art is not relevant. The real value is in those who attend, people who otherwise may never have come to the facility. After the art show, they may very likely stop by the lounge, eat in the restaurant, and possibly make repeat visits to the food and beverage outlets.

Social/Public Service Organizations

Many communities boast of locally based chapters of national and international social and service organizations, such as the Lions Club, Rotary, and Kiwanis.

These organizations typically have weekly or monthly meetings, which often include luncheons or dinners. Because of the number of meetings held over the course of a year and the need to develop a sense of familiarity and continuity among their members, these organizations often will contract with a facility to reserve a room and arrange a series of set menus for all scheduled meetings. This arrangement provides a constant and predictable patronage for the property hosting such meetings.

In addition, who has not driven past the highway markers showing the limits of a city and not seen the signs of these organizations? They show not only the logo of the society but also the day of the week and the location—at a local hospitality property—of the organizations' regularly scheduled meetings.

This is a clear indication that the property is a positive and well-accepted force in community affairs.

Further, the attraction of these members and their guests on a continuing basis increases the chances that they will return on their own to enjoy a restaurant meal or to hold a special family event such as a wedding reception, Christmas party, anniversary celebration, or Bar Mitzvah.

There is no question that any facility can position itself to become a part of family celebrations and to be regarded as an integral, and in some cases indispensable, member of the community. This is true, regardless of whether the property is a downtown property in a major metropolitan area or a small property located on the outskirts of a rural community.

We said earlier that people tend to deal with people they trust. That principle is a vital element in this particular market segment.

Chapter Summary

In addition to associations and corporations, there are other groups fitting neither definition that also hold meetings and are thus important customers of convention and meetings services and facilities. These organizations range from athletic teams and trade unions to tour groups and senior citizens.

In all cases, these groups represent an important part of the overall meetings and convention market and the hospitality industry cannot afford to ignore them.

Notes

1. Margaret Shaw, *The Group Market: What It Is and How to Sell It* (Washington, D.C.: The Foundation of the Hotel Sales & Marketing Association International, 1986), p. 71.
2. David Dorf, "Don't Overlook the Buying Power of Senior Citizens," *HSMAI Marketing Review,* Spring 1986, pp. 19–21.
3. Ibid.
4. Ibid.
5. Ibid.
6. Ibid.

5 Planning and Managing the Meeting: the Planner's Perspective

Chapter Objectives

1. To identify and describe the general considerations of a site inspection

2. To identify those individuals who should attend pre-conference meetings

3. To learn how to negotiate prices for food and beverage functions

4. To understand the legal considerations inherent in conference activities

5. To identify those items the meeting planner should negotiate with speakers

6. To learn those control devices the meeting planner can use to successfully manage a meeting

To better understand and meet the needs of conference and meeting clients, it is important that we cover some of the more fundamental considerations of planning a conference. In this chapter we will discuss site selection, transportation arrangements, marketing the conference, and planning rehearsals.

Overview of Site Inspection

The elements of a site inspection are as varied as the groups seeking conference locations. Obviously, the issues to which the potential customer pays most attention are those directly related to the particular needs of that meeting.

However, virtually all site inspectors should consider the upkeep and appearance of the facility, staff attitudes, accessibility and ease of transportation, and the community's perception of the facility.

Overall Upkeep and Appearance

From the front marquee to the lobby, from the meeting and guestrooms to the restaurants and outlets, the general condition and appearance of the facility impose an overall impression that lasts for the duration of the site inspection. And the key to that impression is cleanliness.

Litter in the hallways, dirty ashtrays in the lobby, and other signs of untidiness should be danger signals. They imply a certain staff attitude, a lackadaisical management style, and suggest an unacceptable work ethic that may permeate all operational divisions of the property. These can destroy the facility's efforts to make the sale and please the customer.

Staff Attitude

Many meeting planners make their first site inspection trip without advance notice. One of the reasons for this is to observe property staff attitudes and the type of service received by typical guests.

Enterprising hoteliers impress upon their staffs that anyone on the premises could be a meeting planner, who at that very moment is debating whether or not to bring a million-dollar-meeting to the property.

Accessibility: Ease of Transportation

For meetings at sites where transportation is an important consideration, site inspectors should obtain as much information as possible about transportation facilities in the area.

This information should include route maps for commuters, airline schedules for the meeting planner's promotion campaign, shuttle bus arrangements for airport transfers, and free parking at the facility. All of these are important for eliminating some of the inconvenience inherent in getting to the site.

Community Standing

The property that supports community causes and is a member of local organizations such as the convention and visitors bureau and the board of trade has earned a positive image that is important to a potential client.

There are two reasons this has a direct bearing on the decisions clients make. First, community involvement is directly related to the attitudinal considerations discussed earlier in this chapter. It suggests a positive, supportive philosophy of management.

Second, community involvement also means local contacts can be used to support the meeting itself. Influence with the convention bureau, the mayor's office, police and fire departments, and other local bureaus and service organizations can be of immense help to the meeting planner before and during the conference.

Site inspectors can learn about a property's community standing by talking to civic leaders and local businesspersons.

Specific Factors Considered Important by Meeting Planners

Meetings & Conventions magazine asked corporate and association meeting planners to indicate those factors most important in selecting a facility or hotel.[1] The corporate responses are shown in Exhibit 5.1.

It is interesting to compare the data in Exhibit 5.1 with that derived from the same questionnaire given to association meeting planners. The latter were asked the same questions about their major conventions, and the results are shown in Exhibit 5.2.

In both cases, meeting room factors, guestroom factors, and quality of food service rank high in site selection considerations. Further, the degree of

Exhibit 5.1   Factors Considered Important by Corporate Planners

Factors Considered Very Important	Pct. of Planners
Quality of food service	79%
Number, size, caliber of meeting rooms	64%
Efficiency of billing procedures	52%
Number, size, caliber of guestrooms	49%
Efficiency of check-in, check-out procedures	48%
Assignment of one staff person to handle meeting	46%
Availability of support services, such as AV	44%
Previous experience in dealing with facility/staff	39%
On-site recreational facilities, e.g., golf, tennis	27%
Convenience to other modes of transportation	26%
Proximity to airport	24%
Provision of special services, e.g., pre-registration	18%
Availability of exhibit space	16%
Number, size, caliber of suites	12%
Proximity to shopping, restaurants, entertainment	12%
Newness of facility	8%

Source: "The Meetings Market '85," *Meetings & Conventions*, March 31, 1986.

overall property service and efficiency also ranks high. Apparently, if these factors receive high grades, the facility's age is not important.

Other Considerations   Many considerations go into the selection of a conference site and the hotel(s), convention center, or conference center to accommodate it. A major failing of many meeting planners is their inability to analyze their own and competitive sites from the perspective of the attendee.

Some of the more fundamental considerations of conference site selection include geographic and demographic elements, the conference's previous location, and how the delegates will perceive the site.

Geographic/Demographic Elements. These elements are primary in the decision-making process because an organization's policies may require that certain restrictions be observed. For example, government and state association groups may be restricted to meeting within their state borders. On the other hand, certain religious organizations may have a policy excluding potential sites in those areas that have legalized gambling.

A company may require that all sales and training meetings be held in resort areas, or, for different reasons, require that sales meetings be held in a business setting near the home office.

Additionally, in those cases where attendance is voluntary (e.g., for association meetings), the site selection process should consider the degree to which the potential sites are convenient, accessible, and affordable to the majority of those persons encouraged to attend. In other words, the site should be consistent with the demographics of the attendance market.

It is important to know where organizations have held their meetings in previous years. Many associations, for example, must rotate conference sites to make the meeting equitably accessible to all members and to satisfy local chapters' desires to host the conference.

When considering geographic/demographic elements, the planner

Exhibit 5.2   Factors Considered Important by Association Planners

Factors Considered Very Important	Pct. of Planners
Number, size, caliber of meeting rooms	88%
Number, size, caliber of guestrooms	74%
Quality of food service	72%
Efficiency of check-in, check-out	56%
Assignment of one staff person	52%
Availability of meeting support service	50%
Previous experience with facility/staff	44%
Availability of exhibit space	44%
Number, size, caliber of suites	24%
Convenience to other transportation	22%
On-site recreational facilities	22%
Proximity to shopping, restaurants, etc.	20%
Proximity to airport	17%
Provision of special meeting services	14%
Newness of facility	6%

Source: "The Meetings Market '85," *Meetings & Conventions*, March 31, 1986.

should ask the following questions: Is the group restricted only to selecting certain areas? Are the sites under consideration accessible to large numbers of members or potential attendees? Are the sites affordable for attendees and their sponsors?

Perception of Site by Potential Attendees. In the final analysis, a meeting planner's knowledge of a site is not nearly as important as what the potential attendees think of the site. Through word of mouth, the press, or from their own personal experiences, people can form unfavorable impressions about cities and facilities that may or may not be valid. It is important that the executive who represents the city or the facility learn and then candidly evaluate these perceptions.

The next step is to work toward altering negative impressions. These impressions may center on crime, cost of living, convenience, quality of service, attractiveness, climate, or other considerations. Meeting planners must work with site officials to overcome those negative perceptions that may result in a site's not being selected to host a meeting or conference.

Meeting Facilities Checklist

Meeting planners and property sales executives alike would do well to use a checklist to assess the meeting rooms and services required for a successful conference. Obviously, separate checklists should be developed for each area. A typical checklist resembles that found in Exhibit 5.3.

Transportation Arrangements

Meeting planners are responsible for making air and ground transportation arrangements for attendees. Earlier in this chapter, we noted that the more a hotelier can do for a client in this area, the greater the chance of a successful sale.

Exhibit 5.3 Meeting Facilities Checklist

1. Number of meeting rooms required
2. Names and capacities of meeting rooms reserved for use
3. Rental charges for meeting rooms
4. Room soundproofing
5. Availability of special lighting
6. Availability of special staging, such as theatrical stage
7. Availability of house sound or efficient portable system
8. Availability of risers (platforms) to build staging
9. Distractions, columns, mirrors, wall decorations, sightlines, chandeliers, ceiling heights with which to deal in planning effective speaking areas, audio-visual productions, and other productions
10. Availability of adequate electrical outlets and voltage for special requirements
11. Ease of access and egress
12. Proximity to public areas of the facility (important in terms of security, noise, and general confidentiality)
13. Availability of rooms for staff offices, storage, and conferences, as well as speaker's lounge and other special-requirement space
14. Teleconferencing equipment and facilities, if required
15. Climate control, lighting, and sound controls accessible to meeting planner
16. Availability of basic visual equipment such as easels, flipcharts, blackboards, electric or manual pointers, overhead projectors, 35mm slide projectors, 16mm projectors, and screens
17. Availability of smoking section, no-smoking section signs, and ashtrays
18. Availability of closed-circuit television equipment
19. Availability of flowers and plants for decorations
20. Gavel (perhaps the smallest, and most often forgotten, item for business meetings)
21. Availability of notepads and pencils for attendees
22. Identification signs

A planner is generally responsible for arranging the following services:

- Air transportation
- Airport shuttle service
- Multiple-property shuttles
- VIP transportation
- Pre- and post-conference tours
- Local tours
- Staff transportation

Air Transportation   In some cases, meeting planners leave airline arrangements entirely up to the attendees. In others, a planner may negotiate with one or more airlines to select an official carrier or co-carriers to handle the majority of traffic heading to and from the conference. This arrangement may or may not include the naming of an official travel agent for the meeting.

In return for naming an official air carrier, the sponsoring organization will usually receive reduced air fares and other amenities for travelers. These may include any or all of the following: free tickets (typically, one free ticket for each 50 sold to conference delegates or for corporate meeting attendees); assistance in promoting the meeting; a travel assistance desk at the meeting; and a complimentary freight shipment, usually meeting materials and supplies. Other benefits might include beverage coupons for the attendees, personalized itineraries, upgraded tickets for VIPs, personalized items like luggage tags, and mementos for delegates.

The conference planner should not select the carrier solely on the basis of the benefits to be received but rather on the strengths of that carrier's service to the conference area.

Deregulation has thrown airlines into intense competition, creating an interesting situation for meeting planners. Deregulation has meant not only lower air fares but also frequent route changes as feeder airlines join with major carriers to service areas not covered before by either one.

Planners should investigate the safety record and dependability of all carriers involved. The more plane changes involved, the greater the chances of delays, misplaced luggage, and cancellations that can seriously affect the meeting.

The meeting schedule itself should be a major consideration when selecting the official carrier. Arrival times for the majority of flights are primary factors in determining the beginning of the program and the blocking of guestrooms.

West Coast delegates attending a meeting on the East Coast must plan on arriving at the site a day earlier than the opening of the meeting (unless they opt for the overnight "red-eye," which can deliver them to East Coast designations around 7:00 a.m.).

Conversely, a traveler flying east to west actually gains several hours. Because there is no red-eye currently scheduled between major East Coast hubs to West Coast designations, delegates should arrive the day before a 9:00 a.m. meeting start. However, attendees could make a 2:00 p.m. opener if they take a flight in the morning from the East Coast.

The same scheduling conditions should be reviewed before arranging the close of the meeting. One of the most common problems in conference planning is the early departure of delegates who wish to catch more convenient return flights. They usually skip the final session, and this results in a sea of empty seats before the closing speaker.

Airport Shuttle Service

Realizing the need to make attendees feel "at home" as soon as possible upon arrival, many meeting planners arrange transportation from the airport to the conference properties. An airport shuttle ensures that delegates will arrive at the right place and time, and in the right mood. These arrangements are important for both association and corporate meetings as well as tour groups.

Some properties, especially those that consider air travelers a major market (i.e., airport properties or facilities located within easy driving distance from an airport), have a limited number of courtesy vans available. These provide an airport shuttle service, or at least augment one.

Multiple Property Shuttles

Meetings held at more than one facility often use shuttle service to provide easy access to various events. This is important for two reasons. First, those persons who do not have accommodations in the immediate vicinity may feel that they are not an integral part of the program. Thus, they are more difficult to please. Second, to ensure that conference events begin and end on time with a full complement of attendees, the planner must facilitate movement to those meetings.

A shuttle service between the properties and the facility where the conference is taking place is often the answer. There are several sources that can provide this service:

- A franchised motor coach company

- Local bus company

- Local taxi company

- School district school buses

- Local limousine company

Price, comfort, convenience in scheduling, and availability should be major considerations when selecting a service. In addition, at least 12 other factors must be weighed:

1. Are the vehicles adequately heated and air-conditioned?

2. Is the carrier properly licensed and insured?

3. Is the carrier experienced in providing shuttle service for similar groups?

4. Are there sufficient vehicles and operators in the fleet to provide the extent of service required?

5. Will the carrier provide copies of the schedule to the meeting planner?

6. Can the carrier add vehicles and operators if needed, and what is the penalty for cancellation?

7. What is the per-hour cost and minimum number of hours required per vehicle?

8. Will the carrier provide dispatchers at key points when group movement is heaviest and most critical?

9. Will dispatchers have radio communications with the drivers and the headquarters depot?

10. Will the carrier provide identification signs for vehicles serving the attendees, as well as destination and lobby signs if needed?

11. Are the operators unionized, and, if so, when does the union contract expire?

12. Are there specific routes within the city, or areas outside the immediate vicinity, that are off-limits to the vehicles being used? This includes parking, standing, and holding areas for the vehicles.

The property sales executive should be familiar with any restrictions imposed by the property with respect to public transportation vehicles. For example, what are the traffic patterns around the property? Are entrance overhangs designed to accommodate large vehicles? Where should service signs be placed for best use? And, what other properties are most convenient to the host property via serviceable bus routes?

VIP Transportation

Most meeting planners would like to provide efficient and luxurious transportation from the airport to the conference scene for their very important guests.

Limousine service provides this type of service regularly. Some larger properties have their own limousines or contract with limousine companies to offer VIP transportation to favored clients.

Offering such service as an inducement to landing a meeting can be quite effective. This goes a long way toward helping the conference planner or manager look good.

Local Tours

Tours of local areas can be an important part of a conference, especially when spouse and youth programs are included.

In many cases, the same company that provides airport shuttle service or multiple property shuttles may be selected to handle local tours. Tour packages also can be coordinated through a tour agency, a convention bureau, or even the convention service department of the property itself.

Because of the requirement for hiring buses for a minimum number of hours, tours often can be scheduled during off-peak hours of shuttle service requirements for the convention.

In making such arrangements, the meeting planner should take into account many of the elements of shuttle service selection indicated above, including questions of insurance, experience, penalties for cancellation, routes, timing, and costs.

In addition, the planner must determine what admission fees are required for tours, who will provide qualified guides, the minimum and maximum number of participants required, and what alternatives are available in the event that primary choice of tour activities must be canceled for any reason.

Staff Transportation

One of the most effective inducements for booking a conference is a property's offer to meeting planners of a limousine or complimentary vehicle for their use during the convention.

A planner may have business throughout the area, as well as VIPs to meet and take to the airport. Access to a limousine, or even a rental car placed at his or her disposal, is a welcome amenity. It simply makes the planner's job easier, and that is nothing more than good selling.

Meeting/Function Rooms

In Chapters 2 and 3 we discussed the growing importance of educational sessions, general sessions, and other business meetings to both association and corporate meetings.

With this in mind, the knowledgeable meeting planner will carefully consider a number of factors related to the meeting and function rooms offered by a facility. These criteria will vary depending on the purposes for which the rooms will be used. However, virtually all these observations should be made for meetings where function rooms are used for typical convention events. Additional information about meeting/function room requirements is found in Chapter 9.

Number of Rooms Available

It is not enough just to know the total number of meeting rooms available at the site. Instead, the meeting planner must know the number of rooms that will be available at the time of the convention.

Although the hotel or convention center may claim to have a large amount of meeting space, rooms from that inventory often must be set aside for other groups that meet regularly at the property.

Are Rooms Soundproof?

It is very difficult to conduct an important meeting when sounds from another room provide a constant distraction. While compromises often can be made with regard to many inconveniences, noise distractions are not one of them. Many meeting planners now soundtest meeting rooms during the selection visit to ensure that movable walls dividing larger rooms are in fact capable of lowering sound between the rooms to an acceptable level.

Availability of Sound Systems

Many potential meetings are lost because the meeting rooms (especially in older and smaller properties) do not have built-in sound systems balanced for them.

The audience must be able to hear the speakers. A portable sound system, which may be a part of the lectern itself, is not always the answer. Very often, it is inadequate for the size and configuration of the meeting room. Audio requirements for the meeting must be carefully determined in advance and then compared with what is available at the site. A detailed description of audiovisual equipment is contained in Chapter 11.

Location of Rooms

Meeting rooms located on various levels of the property, or at distant areas on the same level, will present difficult logistical challenges when participants move from session to session. While this is not normally an insurmountable problem, it does affect the length of individual sessions, the amount of time between sessions, and the number of signs that will be required to show locations and other meeting information.

Potential for Conflicting or Distracting Activities

An element that is often overlooked when selecting a meeting room is the potential for noise or distractions from nearby activities to disrupt meeting activities. For example, a meeting room that is located adjacent to a lounge or showroom may be subject to the annoying spillover of loud music, laughter, or considerable foot traffic. Once the meeting begins, there may be little or no control over these distractions. This problem can be aggravated by the high decibel levels of much of today's popular music.

Meeting planners should even consider the view from meeting room windows. It is difficult for many attendees to concentrate on the work at hand when a full view of a crowded swimming pool, for example, is available through the windows.

Access to Rooms

The ease of access to meeting rooms poses another logistical consideration. Are some of the rooms accessible by elevator only? Is the large general session room served by one escalator? Again, the movement of large numbers of people in a relatively short time is the issue when reviewing access.

In some older facilities where additions to the physical plant have been made at different times, it is not unusual to find that access to a function area is available only through another function area.

Problems may also arise when the facility's service staff require access to meeting rooms during the course of a session. For example, one may encounter a situation in which, because of the location of the kitchen, food must be delivered through or immediately next to meeting rooms.

The perceptive meeting planner will carefully evaluate the potential for such problems of access.

Capacities of Rooms by Type of Setup

The property should provide accurate charts showing room capacity. However, very often the number of people who can fit comfortably into a room will vary depending on the room setup selected. When determining capacity, take into account the amount of space needed for a typical speaker's area, water stations, and, for food and beverage functions, service lanes and food holding areas.

A property providing inaccurate or inflated capacities virtually ensures serious problems at times when they can be least afforded.

Room Design

The experienced convention planner will carefully examine function rooms for potential obstructions or distractions that may affect the nature or conduct of activities planned for that room.

Columns, ceiling heights, low-hanging chandeliers, and the corners found in "L-shaped" or "T-shaped" rooms limit sight-lines and projection-lines. Elaborate wall sconces and wall lighting fixtures behind speakers are distracting if audiences can see them.

Proximity of Rooms to Kitchen

The degree to which food will be served hot and fresh is often a product of its distance from the kitchen. Having to transport food a great distance means that certain types of menu items may be presented to diners in an unappealing condition. In addition, food carts being pushed down service corridors (or even through public space in some properties) can become serious noise distractions for meetings in progress along the route.

Special Features, Services, and Equipment

Still another site inspection consideration is the availability of special features of the physical plant that may enhance a meeting. A list of these features includes the following items:

- Sound/projection booth
- Full stage
- Teleconference equipment
- Track lighting for speaker's area
- Freight elevators serving meeting rooms
- Conference room with permanent tiered seating

- Tape recording facilities and equipment
- On-site availability of theatrical lighting

In addition, rental or use charges for any of the special services, equipment, or features described above must be taken into account.

Guestrooms

For virtually all meetings, a careful evaluation of guestrooms at the facility must be made in light of the client's needs. Certainly, the site inspector will have observed the condition of the guestrooms as well as variations in levels of luxury, location, accessibility, and cleanliness. But there are other important considerations. Additional information about guestroom requirements is found in Chapter 9.

Number of Rooms Available

The meeting planner should understand that virtually all properties have contractual and policy obligations that require them to make available a certain number of guestrooms on a continual basis. This means the facility can provide only a portion of its total guestroom inventory to one particular conference.

The exact number of rooms made available to a conference will often vary, depending on the value of that conference to the facility. Airlines personnel, corporation staffs, and attendees of other conferences usually constitute the markets for which guestrooms are committed by the facility.

Important aspects when booking guestrooms at the time of the site inspection are the number and mix of the rooms. For example, how many rooms must be singles, doubles, queens, kings, double-doubles, or suites? Also, it must be determined if any differences in quality among rooms at all sub-categories are acceptable. These differences might include physical appearance, view, or proximity to the facility's public areas.

Complimentary Room Rate

The site inspector will make the first query about complimentary (comp) rooms. Usually, the typical allotment is one complimentary room for each 50 rooms sold. However, the exact figure can become a negotiable item in many cases.

The discussion about comp rooms needs to include not only the number of rooms but also the *types* of rooms, the *cost* of these rooms, and whether a certain number of comp rooms can be traded for complimentary suites. For example, it is not unusual for three regular rooms to be traded for a two-bedroom suite with a parlor.

In addition, the exact length of time the complimentary rooms will be available should be discussed at the site inspection. This becomes quite important if the comp rooms are assigned to the convention staff, because many staff members will probably arrive well before the meeting begins and stay a day or two afterward to wrap up convention business.

A common practice is to determine complimentary rooms on a room night basis. For example, here is how you calculate the number of rooms for a three-day corporate meeting with 200 singles:

$$3 \text{ Days} \times 200 \text{ Single Rooms} = 600 \text{ Room Nights}$$

Then:

$$\frac{600 \text{ Room Nights}}{50 \text{ (one comp room per each 50 sold)}} = 12 \text{ Complimentary Room Nights}$$

Therefore, the meeting manager could assign the complimentary rooms to two staffers staying six nights each, or three staffers staying four nights each, or perhaps 12 speakers staying only one night each.

It is important that the meeting planner be flexible when allocating complimentary rooms. The comp room factor is a major concern of the planner and an effective selling tool for the property.

Duration of Room Rates

Special guestroom rates usually are in effect during a convention or conference. These prices are lower than the published "rack rates" of the property. This is a type of quantity purchasing that is routine throughout the hospitality industry. Problems, however, will arise unless it is determined ahead of time exactly how long the convention rates will remain in effect.

Because many attendees arrive before the official convention dates and stay after the close of the convention, questions will arise concerning room rates. Unless a policy is agreed upon and communicated to the attendees, guests who find at check-out that they were charged the convention rate of $79 for three days, and for two additional days they were charged $120, will likely argue the issue at the check-out desk. They will delay the check-out process for others and have a legitimate reason for expressing displeasure to everyone within earshot, as well as to the meeting planner and property staff.

The duration of the convention rate is thus another negotiable item. But it must be discussed and agreed upon, preferably at the time of the site inspection.

Release Date for Unused Rooms

This is more pertinent to association meetings than to corporate conferences because the exact number of attendees at the latter is known much earlier than those for the former. Associations usually must wait for their promotional efforts to take effect before they can arrive at an accurate headcount.

The property's policies about releasing the room block held for a meeting should be determined during the site inspection. Normally, this is specified as percentages of the block that will be sold to other guests a certain number of days or months in advance of the opening date of the meeting. For example, 50% of a room block may be released for sale to other guests 60 days before the meeting. The remainder of the room block still unsold 30 days before the meeting will then be released for sale to others.

As with the majority of items considered during the site inspection, the release date is often an important matter of negotiation between the client and the facility.

Reservations Procedures

Both the property and client should review and thoroughly understand each other's reservations policies and procedures. This will ensure that each party can accommodate the other's requests.

For example, will the client use the property's reservation cards, and if so, in what number? Will the client collect these reservation cards at the association or corporation and then forward them to the property, thus controlling where attendees will stay? If so, how can the property make certain there will be no delay in forwarding the cards to the facility? And in what form will they be sent (e.g., a housing list or copies of the forms themselves, or both)?

On the other hand, how will the property report reservations to the meeting planner? How often will reservations lists be sent? Will the facility provide a toll-free number for telephone reservations? Will telephone reservations be prohibited by the sponsoring organization?

There are no right or wrong answers to these questions. They require discussion and agreement during the site inspection.

Check-out Procedures

The same types of questions that were asked about reservations policies should also be asked concerning the property's check-out policies and procedures.

For example, a corporate meeting planner may want all room accounts billed to the corporation's master account. Conversely, an association meeting planner may want the room charges for staff members, speakers, and VIPs billed to the master account, and ask the facility to bill all other attendees separately.

The following list contains other items that should be agreed upon by the facility representative and the meeting planner:

1. Does the property accept personal checks?

2. Does the property accept credit cards? Which ones?

3. Is there a credit limit imposed on convention attendees?

4. Will the property bill convention delegates directly?

5. Will the convention sponsor be responsible for attendees who fail to pay their hotel bills?

6. If attendees do not check out by the posted check-out time, will they be charged for an extra night's stay? This point can have a direct impact on the convention schedule itself. Often, the issue of late check-outs arises too late to change the schedule, and last-minute adjustments must be made to allow guests to check out before the program is over. This can be a major distraction and a prime cause of early departures.

7. Can guests avoid the cashier's desk by an express check-out system whereby they drop off the room key and perhaps a signed room-account tabulation, and then be billed direct?

Once again, the opportunity for serious consideration of these issues begins with the site inspection visit.

Exhibits

Exhibits are an integral part of many meetings. They are designed to place the right buyers with the right suppliers, and they are often a major source of revenue for the sponsoring organization. In many cases, exhibits provide the funds that make the overall meeting possible in the first place. As a consequence, the facility that understands the nature of expositions and the needs of the exhibit sponsor will do much to ensure the meeting's success.

When the planner decides to hold an exhibit in conjunction with a meeting in a hotel or conference center, it is important that both the meeting planner and the property services personnel understand their responsibilities.

The *Convention Liaison Council Manual* provides a comprehensive chapter on exposition management, including a checklist covering virtually all aspects of an effective exposition production.[2] The major areas described in the *Convention Liaison Manual* are shown in Exhibit 5.4. In addition to the specific items shown in this exhibit, it is important that the exhibitors themselves understand the rules under which they must operate.

These rules would include the following items: registration of exhibit personnel; codes of conduct within the exhibit area; policies covering hand-out materials; rules about dress and conduct of booth participants; local or state laws governing games and contests; and precise instructions on times and conditions of move-in, move-out, and shipments of exhibit materials.

Negotiating with a Convention Center

Because of their unique nature, convention centers contain facilities and offer services that are particularly important to many meeting planners. When it comes to negotiating with a center, the planner must be prepared, know what is involved, and have a thorough understanding of how costs are determined.

Convention center managers will insist that space rental fees are fixed and remain non-negotiable. These costs are based on cost per net square foot, the number of free move-in/move-out days, and free meeting rooms. While in most cases these costs will not be changed, meeting planners should be aware that under certain conditions center managers will sometimes make concessions in these and other areas. For example, food and beverage functions represent an area in which the center's management will maintain some flexibility.

Timing is another important aspect in negotiating. If a meeting planner can schedule a meeting for a slack period, the convention center might reduce rental fees and other charges. Repeat business is as important to a convention center as it is to any other hospitality entity. If you are returning to a center for a second or third year, you might even be able to induce the center management to show some flexibility in rental fees.

Meeting planners should realize that they have an important ally in convention and visitors bureaus. If a bureau feels a meeting or convention is particularly important to its city, it may be able to help the planner by obtaining lower rental rates from the center, getting the center to throw in extras, or by resolving conflicts between parties.

Items Included in Contracts   There are 21 items which should be specified in contracts with convention centers, and all parties should fully understand their responsibilities.

Exhibit 5.4   Considerations for Exhibitions

I.   Exhibit Area, General
   A.   Total square footage
   B.   Obstructions: columns, vents, ducts, etc.
   C.   Floor loads (for heavy equipment shows)
   D.   Ceiling height
   E.   Maintenance and housekeeping
   F.   Restroom locations
       (In this category, it is important that agreement be reached regarding whose responsibility it is to clean aisleways, booth areas, and public areas including restrooms and lounges.)

II.   Access to Exhibit Area
   A.   Streets
   B.   Doorways
   C.   Corridors
   D.   Elevators
   E.   Freight loading and unloading areas
   F.   Freight loading limitations, like weight, dimensions, delivery schedules, and traffic patterns
       (These considerations are important, not only in logistical terms but also in security maintenance.)

III.   Utilities
   A.   Limitations and accessibility
   B.   Electricity
   C.   Special lighting
   D.   Gas
   E.   Compressed air
   F.   Steam
   G.   Water
   H.   Drainage
   I.   Telephone connections

IV.   Labor Considerations, Including Union and Non-union Contracts
   A.   Carpenters
   B.   Electricians
   C.   Plumbers
   D.   Riggers
   E.   Stagehands
   F.   Other skilled labor
   G.   Unskilled labor

V.   Signs
   A.   Booth identification signs
   B.   Aisle identification signs
   C.   Directional signs
   D.   Exhibitor listings
   E.   Registration signs
   F.   Specialty signs
       (Because of last-minute needs for signs by the exhibit manager, as well as exhibitors themselves, it is often necessary to have a sign production facility on-site during the exhibit.)

VI.   Booth Decorations
   A.   Selection of backwall and sidewall drapes (colors)
   B.   Carpets
   C.   Furnishings
       1.   Tables
       2.   Chairs
       3.   Wastebaskets
       4.   Easels
       5.   Ashtrays
       6.   Other
   D.   Entranceways and archways
   E.   Specialty decorations and exhibit design and construction
       (Here, it is important to note that many of the items ordered, from additional furnishings to exhibit design and construction, are made available to exhibitors at their expense.)

Exhibit 5.4 *(continued)*

VII. Additional Services
  A. Exhibit manager's desk
  B. Decorating contractor service desk
  C. Transportation and haulage
  D. Crate storage
  E. Food and beverage facilities
  F. Florist (decorations)
  G. Public address system
  H. Telephone (for show manager)
  I. Parking (for attendees and trucks awaiting outshipments)
  J. Press facilities
  K. Models, mimes, and actors (for hiring by exhibitors to promote products)
  L. Photographer

VIII. Shipping Details
  A. Shipping address
  B. Local drayage
  C. Check-in and check-out procedures at exhibit area (requires credentials for delivering and removing materials by exhibitors for security purposes)
  D. Schedule for set-up and teardown of booths and display materials
  E. Limitations of storage facilities
  F. Instructions for consignment shipping of materials after close of show
  G. Instructions for disposition of materials without consignment left by exhibitors

IX. Insurance/Liability
  A. "Hold Harmless" clauses to protect facilities from damage and liability
  B. Accident
  C. Damage
  D. Fire
  E. Theft

X. Facility Regulations
  A. Alcohol
  B. Licenses
  C. Construction
  D. Fire
  E. Personal/general liability
  F. Cleanup responsibilities

Source: *The Convention Liaison Council Manual* (Washington, D.C., 1985).

1. Exhibit hall rates
2. Cancellation policy clauses
3. Move-in costs
4. Number of days for move-in activities
5. Deposit clauses
6. Insurance requirements
7. Utilities costs
8. Property damages
9. Hiring labor
10. Sharing the center with other events

11. Holdovers

12. Abandoned property

13. Parking facilities

14. Room setup charges

15. Catering services

16. Notification of center remodeling

17. Late payments

18. Ownership of concession sales

19. Approval for advertising

20. Limit on outside guests

21. Audiovisual equipment rental

Items to Check Ahead of Time

The beginning of a convention is not the time to learn that certain items or services provided for in the contract with the center are unavailable. People move to new jobs and conditions can change. Checking on contract provisions ahead of time can save you many problems later.

Several months before your convention is scheduled to begin, review the following items with the convention center management:

- Meeting room and exhibit requirements

- Setup and move-in days for offices and contractors

- Events scheduled for the center the same time as your convention

- Events scheduled for the center immediately before and after your convention

- Provision of custodial services

- Changes in parking facilities

- Improvements in center facilities

- Frequency of restroom cleaning

- Items to be provided in meeting rooms (e.g., water, ashtrays, skirting, etc.)

Pre-Conference Meetings

At the pre-conference meeting, the property must provide the meeting planner with easy and meaningful access to key department heads. These key people would include the sales executive responsible for the selection of that property for the event, the convention service manager, the catering or food and beverage director, and any others whose departments are deeply involved in the successful production of the conference.

The most important formal meeting is the "tie-down" or pre-convention meeting, a conference of all who have a direct hand in the convention. This session is normally conducted a day or two before the opening of the event and, depending on the size and organization of the property, should include the following individuals (or representatives from their departments):

1. The client (meeting planner) and his or her key staff personnel
2. The property general manager
3. The property director of marketing, director of sales, and/or salesperson responsible for securing the meeting
4. The director of food and beverage, banquet manager, and/or restaurant manager, depending on the food and beverage requirements
5. The convention service manager and a supervisor from the following departments:
   a. Housekeeping
   b. Reservations
   c. Front desk
   d. Uniformed service
   e. Telephone
   f. Accounting/comptroller
   g. Garage and car rental
   h. Security
   i. Recreational facilities
   j. Retail outlets
   k. Audiovisual
   l. Setup
   m. Executive steward

Finally, one individual who should be invited to this critical meeting, but frequently is not, is the chef. Undoubtedly, many meeting plans have been made that will involve the kitchen. This will require the chef's commitment and enthusiasm. Too often, however, these plans are made by the meeting planner and the food and beverage department, with no input from the person most directly affected by those plans.

Preferably, the chef should be included in all initial planning sessions. At the very least, the chef should be asked to sit in on the "tie-down" meeting. The chef's understanding of the nature of the attendees, the purpose and importance of the meeting to the property, and the functions the kitchen will serve in contributing to the success of the convention, require his or her involvement in this process. The chef may very well be the most creative member of the property staff, and that creativity will be wasted if it is not brought into the planning process.

Food and Beverage Service

Food and beverage functions form the core of many meetings. Social events, ceremonies, and speeches revolve around these functions, and attendees often remember more about the food and beverage activities than the program elements of the meeting itself. Obviously, this can work to the advantage or the detriment of both the meeting planner and the host property.

Property sales and marketing executives, convention service managers, and other executives with direct client contact are not expected to have expertise in all phases of food and beverage management. Nevertheless, these individuals should have some understanding of the principles of food and beverage service as well as the different and identifiable needs of various groups of people.

In many cases, meeting planners will consider the property sales executive as the first person to consult for help in deciding on food and beverage options. Obviously, sales executives must know what their facilities can or cannot do so they can provide their clients with the best possible service.

Even though capabilities and needs might not always match, both parties must know enough about them so they can successfully negotiate prices for the food and beverage functions. Additional information about food and beverage functions is found in Chapter 10.

Food and Beverage Prices

Because of the fluctuations in food prices, it is difficult for facilities to quote fixed prices more than six months before an event. However, it is possible to agree upon price ranges that will not exceed a certain percentage of current prices.

Because larger meetings are often planned 12 to 18 months ahead of time, price-range quotes and budgeting may have to be executed that far in advance of the function. However, these budgets must be tentative and should be adjusted as food and beverage prices fluctuate.

Close attention to costs and prices is critical to the hotelier. Food and beverage operations typically represent the second greatest source of revenue for a property (after room revenues). They are frequently the leading expense category for group meeting budgets. For these reasons negotiations for food and beverage events often are very competitive. Typically, the following questions will be raised during the negotiations.

1. **What records will be used to determine payment? Ticket count? Head count? Plate count? Or quantities consumed?**

Ticket counts are the most acceptable form of determining attendance at food and beverage functions. The meeting sponsor provides tickets to the attendees, and the tickets can be collected at the door as people enter the function, or by servers at the tables.

Tickets should contain the name or number of the event. This arrangement provides for easy identification and avoids mixing tickets from one event with those from another. Tickets are often color-coded for easier and quicker identification upon collection.

When deciding on ticket counts, both supplier and buyer should determine who will collect the tickets (meeting planner, staff, servers, or maitre d') and collaborate in the count. Counted tickets should be packaged and presented by the property to the meeting planner for verification if necessary and for historical documentation.

If tickets are not used, other procedures can be used to determine the number of guests served. Head counts are often used, and it is not unusual for the meeting planner and the facility to designate one or more individuals with hand counters to keep track of guests as they pass through the entrance.

For smaller functions, the property may keep a count of the number of plates of food served. However, the meeting planner should agree to this procedure in advance. Finally, charges may be based on the quantity of consumption, especially when determining charges for beverage service.

2. When will guarantees be required?

Most properties require guarantees at least 24 hours in advance. Some require 48 hours, and 72 hours is not unusual for a weekend meeting.

The length of the guarantee advance will also depend to a great extent on the complexity of the menu selected. Exotic foods usually must be ordered far in advance of more standard items. Certain menu items take more time to prepare than others. Thus, menu selection will be a major factor in guarantee flexibility.

3. If the guarantee is exceeded, what additional percentage can be served?

Again, different facilities have different policies. However, typically a facility will prepare for 10% above the guarantee for groups of 50 or fewer, and 5% above the guarantee with larger groups. This is a major item of negotiation during the pre-convention meeting, particularly for association conventions or conferences in which attendance and actual participation are more speculative than for corporate meetings.

4. How many servers will be provided?

The number of servers is often prescribed by union regulations. The minimum number, however, may not be sufficient for some events. Certain food functions are more functional than social, and service must be provided quickly enough to feed the diners and allow them to return to important sessions.

Determining the number of bartenders presents a similar problem. Typically, one bartender can serve 100 guests with relative efficiency during a cocktail reception. This calculation assumes a relative consistency in traffic flow.

Many experienced meeting planners know that the first half-hour of a reception is the most critical. In most cases, the heaviest traffic flow during an evening reception occurs in the first half-hour to one hour. Sometimes, guests may actually be waiting for the doors to open. At that point, they descend immediately upon the bar. It is also during this period that many guests decide whether to stay.

Guests waiting in line to get a drink probably are not enjoying themselves. That means the client should have negotiated for one bartender for each 50 guests during the first hour. This arrangement has saved many receptions.

5. How should beverages be charged?

It is critical that there be a clear understanding by the property and the meeting planner about the method of charging for beverage consumption. The risk of "blowing the budget" is greatest in this area for both the facility and the meeting planner.

Costs are a product of the number of guests, the pace of service, the degree of consumption, the quality of the products selected, the length of time of the function, the degree of accessibility to the service areas and bars, and, in general, the nature of the event.

The last consideration can be quite subtle. Nevertheless, common sense indicates that an evening reception celebrating a 50th wedding anniversary will generate brisker consumption than a noon reception preceding a business luncheon.

The following considerations should be observed when trying to reach an agreement about billing procedures for receptions.

Drinks may be charged several ways: by the person (package rate), by the drink served, by the hour, or by the bottle. The best method depends entirely upon the nature of the group and the meeting planner's knowledge about its consumption patterns. There should be clear agreement on the method chosen.

Paying the package rate (a set amount per person) means that the planner would prefer to have a set expense to deal with in the budget. The property gambles that the set price agreed upon will cover consumption as well as service charges and profit.

The meeting planner, who probably has better knowledge of the attendees' consumption patterns, instead may elect to pay by the drink poured (specifying the size of each drink, i.e., 1 oz., 1 1/2 oz., or 2 oz. drinks).

Many meeting planners prefer to pay by the bottle at larger receptions, especially when they know the drinking habits of attendees. They can control the size of drinks poured (again, the ounce size of drinks must be specified in advance). It is also important to remember that when clients pay by the bottle, they have in fact purchased any bottle that has been opened (the seal has been broken). Therefore, these bottles are the property of the meeting sponsor. They may be removed to a storage location or shipped home for later use without additional charge.

The hotelier and the meeting planner must agree that, when the client pays for the reception by the bottle, the tab will include any bottle opened or "broken," regardless of whether it is empty or whether only one ounce of liquor has been served from it.

As the reception wears down and the crowd thins out, the planner may ask the facility to close certain bars sequentially (usually from the back of the room toward the front in order to maneuver the group toward the exit). At the same time, they can consolidate "broken" bottles and remove those that have not been opened. This tactic often leaves few partially empty bottles at the end of the function.

Regardless of how liquor is purchased by the client, it can be sold or provided free to the guests. In many cases, the meeting planner may wish to provide a cash bar rather than an open bar, stipulating that the attendees will pay for their drinks themselves. The hotelier must remind clients that cashiers will be required to sell drink tickets, and that a cost is incurred. However, most facilities will not charge for the cashier if a predetermined minimum revenue is collected at the cash bars. Other items that will have to be determined and/or negotiated include:

- Whether mixers are included in the negotiated liquor prices
- Specifications for pre-mixed drinks
- Liquor liability coverage
- Amounts of and prices for beer, wine, and soft drinks

- Procedures for auditing number of bottles consumed

- Procedures for auditing number of drinks served

- Closing times of bars

- Individuals authorized to continue bar service beyond scheduled closing time

6. How should hors d'oeuvres be charged?

Paying for hors d'oeuvres can also be a very expensive operation for the meeting planner. It is a risky business for the property as well.

As with liquor service, there are several ways clients can pay for hors d'oeuvres: by the person per hour (package price), by the table or tray, or by the piece.

A client with a large budget can purchase hors d'oeuvres by the table or tray, although this option does not preclude early and rapid consumption.

In most cases, however, clients will choose to pay a flat price per person (to stabilize budget considerations) or to purchase by the piece and have the hors d'oeuvres served. If the latter option is selected, the facility must add labor costs for the servers to the overall price. Service can be paced to make certain that the supply lasts as long as possible.

As with any convention or conference event, service and cost factors are determined by the purpose of the function and the environment the client wishes to create. Once the purpose is established, the planner can make intelligent choices between opulence and economy.

The rule of thumb is that each attendee will consume six hors d'oeuvres per hour. But, as is the case with all rules of thumb, this can be misleading. When in doubt, the facility will encourage the selection of certain stretchable (and easily prepared) hors d'oeuvres, such as cheeses, vegetables, and dips.

Meeting planners also should keep in mind the following three guidelines concerning hors d'oeuvres:

- The saltier the snacks (e.g., potato chips, pretzels, and salted nuts), the greater the consumption of beverages. This is an important consideration for those who wish to economize on beverage consumption, as well as the health and welfare of guests and those with whom they come in contact later.

- The facility and the meeting planner share equal responsibility for monitoring the guests' consumption.

- The more crowded the room, the less consumption there will be. For example, 10 square feet per person will provide ample room for guests to move about, permitting easy access to hors d'oeuvres tables and bars. A room where the ratio is 7 1/2 square feet per person will prove to be comfortably crowded (the ideal for most receptions). However, when the figure drops to five square feet per person at a reception, guests will feel crowded. While certain groups enjoy this intimate feeling, consumption of food and beverages will decline because people will find it difficult to move easily to tables and bars.

Certainly, one of the major considerations with hors d'oeuvres is keeping consumption under control. Meeting planners who want hors d'oeuvres displayed elegantly on tables dread having to pay for the heavy consumption that often occurs with such a setup. An effective solution to that problem is to station a server at the hors d'oeuvres table. The server's real purpose is to monitor the replenishing of the trays and to continually bus the table, cleaning discarded napkins and utensils. But, there is a psychological advantage as well. The fact that another person is standing there will deter many guests from overloading a plate or from returning too often. This can reduce overconsumption significantly.

The critical requirement for both the meeting planner and the property executive is control over the function.

7. How much thought should go into planning refreshment breaks?

Coffee and refreshment breaks should be designed to provide attendees an opportunity to refresh themselves and to discuss the programs and issues of the day. Enterprising food and beverage staffs are departing from traditional coffee breaks. They are now creating refreshment breaks complete with health and energy foods, themes, and entertainment.

Many meeting planners will budget a bit more for a break that includes not only the standard coffee, tea, and soft drinks, but also items like frozen chocolate-covered bananas provided by a server dressed as a gorilla, or a sherbet and frozen yogurt break, complete with aerobics instructors.

8. How are labor costs determined?

Roughly 60% of the cost of a plate of food served by a property is for labor. Therefore, the number of servers becomes important in pricing food and beverage activities for meeting planner clients.

The most functional and routinely used style of service for the conference group meal is plated service. Here, the meal is arranged on plates in the kitchen and served in that manner to the diners. While this is the most economical and controllable style of service, it is subject to menu selection. Some foods do not mix very well; i.e., they may discolor or run together if plated too soon before actual service begins.

Still another style of service, often seen in European properties, requires that servers carve the entree and then assemble the plates in full view of the diners. This, combined with white glove service, can be extraordinarily elegant (and fun for the diners to watch), but it requires an inordinate number of servers. It should be considered only for VIP groups.

Finally, buffets offer an alternative to the traditional meal service. However, they are not necessarily more economical than other methods; quite often, buffets become more expensive than plated meals. Nevertheless, they should be considered for breakfasts and brunches, especially when the property may lack adequate coffee shop capacity, or for utilitarian lunches or dinners.

When planning buffets, it is absolutely critical that adequate food lines be established to prevent long backups of guests waiting to eat. Remember, buffets are considered utilitarian, unless they are tied into a specific theme such as a luau. Therefore, any delays in getting to the food line become frustrating for the attendee, inasmuch as time is often important. To further speed service, beverages and desserts may be served at the tables rather than from the buffet line.

The major factors controlling the cost of a buffet service include labor, the number of items on the buffet tables, and the complications added to the guarantee process. Frequently, planners add too many items to the menu to ensure that it does not appear skimpy. This adds to the cost and increases the time of self-service.

9. **What other costs should be considered?**

Additional costs that must be covered in the final arrangements include the following items: taxes (which vary depending on location); gratuities; surcharges for specialty items; and corkage (charges for food and beverages brought into the property by the meeting planner and served by the facility).

Tips for Successful Food and Beverage Service

The following eight tips are offered by the American Society of Association Executives for successfully managing food and beverage operations at a meeting or convention.[3]

1. The banquet manager must know in advance whether or not tickets will be collected and where (at the door or from the tables). Will tickets be collected from guests at the head table? Further, the property must have instructions from the meeting planner about what to do if a guest should arrive without a ticket.

2. Control must be established for the arrival of attendees, placement of the head table, and seating arrangements for the crowd.

3. It is the meeting manager's responsibility to control entry credentials.

4. It is important that head table guests be assembled in a separate room and ushered into the dining room promptly with the proper fanfare.

5. Meeting planners should specify linens, china, and silver service (if there is a choice). Linen colors can coincide with colors selected for the meeting itself or carry out a function theme.

6. The property should attempt to provide, at a charge, floral arrangements for centerpieces. Often these arrangements can be reworked and reused for more than one event.

7. Candles and other flammable devices may be restricted by local ordinances. The meeting planner should be made aware of these restrictions.

8. All too often, proper lighting effects are overlooked. Wall-washers, with subdued lighting on the main floor and candles on the tables, can provide an elegant setting that may exceed funds available for special theme decorations, props, and other staging devices.

Inter-Continental Hotels provide other considerations for properties and meeting planners in checklist form.[4] Included among the items cited are:

- Number to be seated
- Type of seating (rounds, ovals, cabaret)
- Seating at the head table or dais

- Specific seating (place cards)
- Reserved tables for VIPs
- Printed menus at place settings
- Ice carvings and other decorations

Finally, the meeting planner should ask the convention service manager to consider such logistical requirements as a staging area where head table guests can gather, space for registration, coat check facilities, an area for the receiving line if one is planned, and a communication link from the meeting planner to the captain or banquet manager to ensure that service continues as scheduled or that changes in plans can be communicated quickly to the property.

Legal Considerations

Legal considerations now permeate the convention and meetings industry. Monetary awards to those injured through the negligence of others has created a highly litigious society, and the convention/hospitality industry is affected by this problem.

It is important that both the hotelier and the meeting planner seek qualified legal help in assessing risk. This may require both an attorney competent in the unique risks of the convention industry as well as insurance agents who understand the potential liabilities and losses faced by meeting sponsors and host facilities.

Regardless of pre-existing coverage, it is important that each meeting program be reviewed with respect to its potential liabilities, and that both the host facility and the sponsoring organization determine limits of liability and responsibilities for insurance coverage and obtaining legal opinions.

Hold Harmless Agreements

The hold harmless agreement has become standard in many contracts between convention and exposition planners and the facilities and service contractors that provide their on-site products.

Hold harmless agreements are stipulations in the contract whereby one party agrees that the other party will not be responsible for damages arising out of the transaction. For example, a convention contract may absolve the property from any responsibility for injuries or damage claimed to have resulted from attendance at a meeting.

Liability Insurance for Meeting Sponsors and Properties

Many facilities, primarily convention centers, require from meeting sponsors proof that their organizations carry an amount of liability insurance commensurate with the liability protection requirements of that particular facility.

Professional liability insurance is common in the industry. This policy generally covers suits brought because of alleged "wrongful acts" by the meeting planner.

To complete the cycle, many meeting sponsors require in contracts that they be indemnified from damages caused by negligence on the part of the convention center, the property, the decorating contractor, and others. This indemnification may extend even to the issuance of workers' compensation.

Insurance underwriters and carriers offer a range of insurance products designed to cover policy holders in the event of damages, including cancellation insurance and liquor liability.

Cancellation Insurance

Convention cancellation insurance is designed to compensate an organization for loss of revenue as a result of conditions beyond the control of the organization. Acts of God, strikes, or failure of key participants to appear may be covered by this type of policy. As is the case with any policy, there are liability limits, exclusions, and different kinds of indemnification with convention cancellation coverage.

Liquor Liability

Another major insurance issue is liquor liability. Many states have dram shop laws, which set parameters of responsibility and liability in the event of injury or death by or of an intoxicated person. Because state laws vary, it is important for hoteliers to understand the laws in effect where their properties are located. Meeting planners may require a certificate proving that the facility has host liquor liability coverage. They can also ask that the facility be named as a secondary insured party. Additionally, meeting planners often carry insurance for dram shop liability as part of the organization's overall liability coverage.

Antitrust Issues

A second major legal consideration concerns antitrust issues. Convention and exposition planners, whose meetings provide a forum for competition (e.g., expositions, product demonstrations, and promotional/public relations opportunities), must be careful to provide equal opportunity for all competing parties to have access to these markets on a fair and equitable basis. This is one reason that non-members of an association also are invited to a convention (although they usually are charged a premium registration fee because they do not support the organization through dues).

In some cases, denial of access to the convention (even for a premium registration fee or exhibit rental charge) could be considered an unfair restraint of trade. This is a complicated legal issue, and it should be investigated only with the assistance of competent legal counsel. Nevertheless, the principle of restraint of trade is an important one in convention and exposition planning.

The content of convention programming also must be analyzed very carefully. This is done to ensure that productions, seminars, and presentations of papers or convention publications carry no implications that could be construed as defamation of character or product, or that are slanderous or libelous to an individual or company. Properties must be vigilant to ascertain that policies and practices avoid even the possibility of antitrust violations.

The greatest danger of violating U.S. antitrust laws may exist when facilities pursue city-wide conventions or multi-property meetings. In these cases, there is a tendency to provide a package that is not only affordable to the prospective client, but also understandable to the client's prospective attendees.

Therefore, it is vital that hoteliers avoid any situations in which there may be discussion of the following seven elements:

1. Any prices, terms, and conditions of agreements for services or facilities of properties, including but not limited to prices to be

charged to convention groups, tour groups, tour operators, or any other customers. This also applies to off-season prices and discounts.

2. Changes or proposed changes in the rental prices of guestrooms.

3. Formulas or other procedures for the establishment and determination of prices, discounts, and other terms and conditions of rental.

4. Price cutting, pricing too low, or any discussion of prices by individual properties.

5. Activities that could be construed to constitute a boycott of any property, competitor, or other business.

6. Activities that could be construed to constitute an agreement or understanding to fix prices.

7. Activities that could be construed to constitute a division among competitors of geographic markets, customers, or services.

Arrangements with Speakers

Because the planner's arrangements with speakers often require services provided by the facility hosting the meeting, it is important that the property be aware of these agreements.

Before a contract is signed and the speaker is promoted as part of the program, the meeting planner should negotiate with the speaker the amount of the presentation fee and other expenses to be covered by the sponsoring organization, including out-of-pocket expenses, per diem expenses, and all others incurred while attending the convention.

The facility's accounting department must know which, if any, charges applied to the speaker's guestroom should be entered on the master account of the sponsoring organization. It may be all charges, room and taxes only, or room, taxes, and incidentals. This should be determined in advance by the conference planner.

The meeting planner also must be aware of the speaker's transportation arrangements and requirements. For example, transportation expenses must be negotiated, including airfare (first class vs. coach or economy). Ground requirements such as airport transfers and local commuting must be satisfied. The facility may be able to assist with airport pickups and make a limousine available to the speakers. This may be done without charge to the meeting planner. Nevertheless, it is important for the facility to be prepared to handle this request. Often, it may come at the last minute.

Another important consideration is how the speaker wants the meeting room set up. The facility is responsible for having the room set properly and on schedule.

Audiovisual requirements represent another important consideration. If this information is not volunteered by the meeting planner, the property executive must press for details regarding speakers' audiovisual needs. It is possible that the equipment exists on-site. It is also possible that the equipment and technicians must be secured from outside the property. Although satisfying speakers' requirements is technically the responsibility of the client, frequently the problem is placed in the lap of the property executive allowing little time to respond.

Finally, any special requests by the speaker must be complied with. Many speakers require special arrangements when traveling. A large suite, meetings with community VIPs, secretarial assistance, and special diets are not uncommon requests. It is no secret that the more famous a speaker is, the greater the likelihood that he or she will expect extraordinary treatment. It is simply a part of the price paid for successfully serving today's convention market.

Marketing the Convention

While most corporate meetings do not require promotion to guarantee attendance, most association meeting planners must effectively market their conventions to their membership. They must determine the needs of the members and the degree to which the program meets those needs.

Consequently, convention promotional efforts usually emphasize the theme of the convention, its educational programs, key speakers, social events, and achievements of individual members and chapters in awards ceremonies.

However, as we noted earlier in this chapter, the location of the convention often provides a valid inducement for increasing attendance. The property or city selected for the meeting can assist the meeting planner's promotional efforts by supplying photographs and editorial copy highlighting the unique attractions of the convention site. If possible, meeting planners should request the following materials from properties or communities for developing promotional material:

1. Black and white photographs depicting the properties, distinctive features of the city, airport facilities, and notable community activities such as special celebrations and local sports teams in action

2. Color separations for color reproduction

3. Fact sheets containing demographic and economic statistics, information about climate, and special features of the locality

4. Fact sheets covering the history and special characteristics of the convention property

5. Preprinted brochures containing details of the facility or location, designed to allow the insertion of personalized copy by the sponsor

6. Audiovisual items showing features relevant to the convention site, preferably 1/2-inch videotape productions

Managing the Meeting

If both the property and client are to combine their resources to successfully execute the meeting, they must first communicate purposes, strategies, and tactics. All too often, however, communication is inadequate. This is one of the most frequent reasons a meeting fails to fulfill its objectives.

Communication is essential to create the **control devices** necessary to ensure a smooth and successful meeting. One such control device is the events schedule.

Events Schedule   The events schedule is a listing of conference events, prepared by the meeting planner and delivered to the facility from three months to a year before the meeting (depending on the extent of hotel facilities required). This document allows the property to reserve meeting rooms and other space based on advance details concerning numbers of events, dates, times, and locations.

The meeting planner must remember that the property has the right (and the sales executive has the responsibility) to sell unused space to other groups and individuals. Therefore, the events schedule must be carefully prepared by the meeting planner in order to protect both parties.

A typical events schedule may be formatted in the manner shown in Exhibit 5.5. The events schedule should include both definite and contemplated activities until such time as the property requires that all events be made definite.

The schedules should be broken down by date and day of the week. It is not unusual for some conferences to host 200 or more separate events over the course of a 3- or 4-day meeting. It becomes apparent, then, why such a preliminary listing of space requirements is essential at the earliest possible lead time. This advance guide provides sufficient time to spot problems, avoid duplications, and discover conflicts between needs and the amount of space available.

It also provides the basis upon which a much more detailed and expanded guide can be developed.

Conference Worksheet   No communication between the meeting planner and the property is more important than the conference worksheet, often called the "staging guide" or, in its narrative form, the "convention résumé." The information contained in it is critical for the property to do its job effectively.

The format of the worksheet is relatively unimportant. The most important characteristic of any conference worksheet is that it contain all data that the meeting planner wants to give to the facility and its staff. The following items should be included:

1. Event number
2. Event name
3. Location
4. Date
5. Time of room setup
6. Time of room teardown
7. Time doors open to guests
8. Time event begins
9. Time event ends
10. Names of key participants
11. Name of staff contact

Exhibit 5.5   Events Schedule

	EVENT DESCRIPTION	ROOM	TIME SPAN
1	Staff Meeting	Crystal	8 to 9 a.m.
2	Speakers Lounge	North	9 a.m. to 5 p.m.
3	Coffee Break	Foyer	9 a.m. to Noon
4	General Session	Ballroom	9:30 to 11 a.m.
5	VIP Reception	Congress	11:30 a.m. to Noon
6	Leadership Lunch	Esplanade	Noon to 1:30 p.m.

12. Expected attendance

13. Actual attendance

14. Whether tickets are used

15. Who collects tickets

16. Signs to be displayed

17. Room setup required

18. Equipment needs

    a. Audiovisual

    b. Props and scenery

    c. Miscellaneous

19. Food and beverage needs

    a. Menu number

    b. Water stations

    c. Times of refreshment breaks

20. Comments

21. Post-meeting comments

The worksheet becomes a detailed record of the entire conference. It will be valuable in planning the next similar conference, because many room setups and other details will be relatively standard and thus repeated.

You will see that items #13 and #21 on the worksheet require post-meeting comments. These should be noted directly on the worksheet as soon as the event is concluded. Item #13, actual attendance, is an important entry when preparing guarantees and room setups for a similar meeting in the future. Post-meeting comments provide an opportunity for the meeting planner to note what was especially good or bad about the event as it was planned and delivered.

Also note that the times listed on the worksheet include more than the starting time of the event. They also show the time the doors will be opened to the attendees (it is at this point, not the starting time of the performance, that the facility must have the room ready), and the setup/teardown period (the time the room will be committed to this particular function, which actually begins before and extends after the event).

The worksheet can be designed in any format that seems logical for the user. Some require only one page. Others are assembled in notebook form with a separate worksheet for each event number.

The following guidelines should be used when completing the worksheet:

1. The meeting planner must complete the worksheet in as much detail as possible. This document is the most critical vehicle for transmitting information from the planner to the facility.

2. The worksheet should be delivered to the property at least two weeks before the meeting (and earlier for more complicated conferences). This is necessary to allow time for the property to translate the planner's worksheet into the facility's own work orders.

3. The property's work orders must accurately reproduce the planner's staging guide or worksheet requirements. To ensure that nothing is lost in translation, the facility must make its work orders available to the planner before the meeting to reconcile any differences or omissions. This is a step often overlooked.

Each meeting planner has a favorite style of staging guide or worksheet format. The only important consideration is that it be logical, and that it contain the necessary data. Exhibit 5.6 shows a format that includes practically all the elements discussed.

This leads to yet another important meeting management control device, the event script.

Event Script   The event script contains the most intricate details of the event. It not only guides meeting planners and property staff with respect to the exact timing of meeting elements, but also helps direct speakers and other program participants to their proper places at the proper times.

The meeting planner should produce a script and then send it to all parties responsible for elements of the event. The distribution list should include the following:

- Meeting management staff
- Property convention service staff
- Sound, lighting technician
- Banquet captain
- Show producer
- Speaker(s)
- Audiovisual technician
- Spotlight operator

A typical script is shown in Exhibit 5.7. Note that those parts of the script to be read verbatim by the speakers are printed in very short lines. These parts are written as phonetically as possible, including dots (. . .) to

Exhibit 5.6   Staging Guide Worksheet Example

EVENT #_____NAME OF EVENT_____

DATE_____ROOM/LOCATION_____

SET UP FROM/TO _____DOORS OPEN_____

EVENT BEGINS_____ENDS_____

ATTENDANCE: EXPECTED_____ACTUAL_____TIX: ☐ YES   ☐ NO

AUDIO/VISUAL: FOOD AND BEVERAGE:

ITEM: QTY: WATER STATIONS_____

_____   ON TABLES_____

_____   _____

_____   _____

ROOM SETUP:_____

(ALLOW SPACE FOR DIAGRAM IF NEEDED)

_____

KEY SPEAKER_____STAFF CONTACT_____

SIGN(S)_____SMOKING ☐ (Y)   ☐ (N)   ☐ MIX

SPECIAL INSTRUCTIONS_____

_____

POST MEETING NOTES_____

_____

_____

indicate the natural pauses that are essential in relaxed and natural public speaking. Names can even be spelled phonetically if necessary.

The short lines are designed to minimize the speaker's risk of getting lost in the narrative—an embarrassing occurrence that is not uncommon when someone speaks from a lengthy script written in small type.

The script should also be typed in upper case (capital) letters. There are two reasons for doing this. First, lighting is often dim in a theatrical setting, or too bright if spotlights are used, and consequently the script is difficult to see. Second, the speaker's eyesight may be deficient. Many veteran meeting planners prepare their scripts not only with all capital letters but also on a bulletin typewriter or a similar machine that can use large type fonts.

The script is one of the most critical control tools available to the meeting planner. It provides guidance to keep events on target in terms of content

Exhibit 5.7   Event Script

				SCRIPT
LEADERSHIP LUNCHEON	**EVENT #143**		**JULY 7**	**BALLROOM**
PAGE 1	**DOORS OPEN: 11:50 A.M.**			

STAGE SETTING:	THREE SCREEN REAR PROJECTION, FIVE 35MM. PROJECTOR SETUP ORDERED FROM AAA AUDIO VISUAL, INC., (WORKORDER #5). "PROFESSIONAL EDGE" LOGO ON SCREENS STAGE RIGHT AND LEFT WHEN DOORS OPEN. CORPORATE LOGO ON CENTER SCREEN. LECTERNS WITH "PROFESSIONAL EDGE" LECTERN SIGNS, LOCATED STAGE RIGHT AND LEFT. LECTERNS ILLUMINATED WITH ONE LICHO EACH. FOLLOW SPOT IN PLACE ON REAR RISER, TURNED OFF.
HOUSE SOUND:	TAPE OF SOUSA MARCHES (PROVIDED BY AAA AUDIO VISUAL, INC.) PLAYING THROUGH HOUSE SOUND WHEN DOORS OPEN.
	LECTERN MICS, BACKSTAGE MIC, DEAD.
HOUSE LIGHTS:	AT 60%
ROOM SET:	SEE STAGING GUIDE EVENT #143

12:05 p.m.	(LUNCHEON SERVICE BEGINS)
HOUSE SOUND:	FADE SOUSA MARCH, BRING UP "MEDLEY" TAPE THROUGH LUNCH
12:55 P.M.	(LUNCHEON SERVICE CONCLUDES) WAITERS TO LEAVE FRESH POTS OF COFFEE ON TABLES, BUS TABLES.
1:05 P.M.	WAITERS TO BE CLEAR FROM ROOM
1:06 P.M.	
SOUND:	FADE "MEDLEY" TAPE. LECTERN, BACKSTAGE MICS GO TO "LIVE"
HOUSE LIGHTS:	DOWN TO 15%.
AAA A/V:	WHEN HOUSELIGHTS ARE DOWN, DISSOLVE LOGOS ON ALL THREE SCREENS. BEGIN "PROFESSIONAL EDGE" SLIDE MODULE.
1:09 P.M.	"PROFESSIONAL EDGE" MODULE ENDS.
AAA A/V:	CENTER SCREEN ONLY: "PROFESSIONAL EDGE" LOGO. SCREENS STAGE RIGHT AND LEFT TO REMAIN DARK.
HOUSE LIGHTS:	UP TO 60%.
SPOT OPERATOR:	CUE FOR OFFSTAGE INTRODUCTION . . . **"JOHN R. DOE!"** PICK UP JOHN DOE AS HE EMERGES FROM BACKSTAGE LEFT . . . FOLLOW HIM TO LECTERN STAGE RIGHT . . . KILL SPOT WHEN APPLAUSE ENDS.
OFFSTAGE VOICE:	GOOD AFTERNOON, LADIES AND GENTLEMEN . . . PLEASE WELCOME . . . THE PRESIDENT OF OUR SOCIETY, FROM BOSTON, MASS . . . JOHN R. DOE!
SPOT OPERATOR:	PICK UP JOHN DOE. KILL SPOT WHEN APPLAUSE ENDS.
JOHN DOE:	GOOD AFTERNOON, LADIES AND GENTLEMEN . . . AND WELCOME TO A PROGRAM WHICH EXEMPLIFIES THE PROFESSIONAL EDGE.
	OUR ANNUAL LUNCHEON IS DEDICATED TO THE CELEBRATION OF PROFESSIONALISM.

(This format is then followed throughout the program, with as many spoken words as possible scripted, and with precise times indicated for cues. A typical close to our Leadership Luncheon script might be. . .)

Exhibit 5.7 *(continued)*

	...AND, SO, MY FRIENDS, IT WILL BE MY PLEASURE TO SERVE YOU DURING THE COMING MONTHS. I APPRECIATE YOUR CONFIDENCE, AND WILL DO EVERYTHING IN MY POWER TO FULFILL IT. THANKS, ... AND THANK YOU, JOHN.
1:58 P.M.	
JOHN DOE:	RETURNS FROM STAGE LEFT TO SHAKE HANDS WITH SPEAKER. HE THEN CONCLUDES THE PROGRAM:
	THANKS, FRANK, FOR THOSE ENLIGHTENING WORDS ...
	LADIES AND GENTLEMEN ... THIS AFTERNOON IS DEDICATED TO EDUCATION. BE SURE TO CHECK YOUR PROGRAM BOOK FOR THE SEMINAR YOU WISH TO ATTEND .... THEY ALL BEGIN AT 2:15, SO DON'T DELAY ... AND ... DON'T FORGET THAT OUR GENERAL SESSION TOMORROW MORNING IS AN EARLY ONE ... IT STARTS IN THIS ROOM AT 8 A.M.
	YOU WON'T WANT TO MISS OUR GUEST SPEAKER.
	AND NOW ... I'LL SEE YOU AT THE SEMINARS!
2:00 P.M.	
HOUSE SOUND:	SOUSA MARCH TAPE THROUGH HOUSE SOUND. KILL ALL MICS.
HOUSE LIGHTS:	UP TO 90%
	(CONCLUSION OF PROGRAM)

and timing. Often, meeting planners will complain, "I can't get away with using a script because my people won't follow it. They like to wing it." However, the planner should insist that the script be used. Once the precedent is established, program participants will see the results and will become much more comfortable with scripts.

Overall, there are five benefits from using scripts:

1. They ensure that events begin and end on time.

2. They provide the instructions necessary for professional theatrical effects like lighting, sound, music, and special staging.

3. They ensure that important messages will be delivered, such as starting times of succeeding events, political statements required by regulation or bylaws, and changes in scheduling or programming.

4. They prevent mispronunciations of names or titles, and remind the speaker to make important introductions or citations.

5. They ensure that everyone is working together, eliminating the possibility of surprises or last-minute shortages.

Rehearsals   Many conference planners now schedule rehearsals for major sessions and stage events, just as a theatrical show is rehearsed. In convention management, rehearsals are even more critical, because in a theatrical show there is time to modify scripts, performances, cues, and lighting. With a convention, however, there is only one performance. It has to be right the first time.

Thus, rehearsals are becoming important convention planning events. They may be only read-throughs of scripts by the speakers or full rehearsals utilizing audiovisual equipment, technicians, and all participants.

Rehearsals are especially important for larger, more complicated events, such as leadership changes where many persons must be introduced in a certain order, must move to certain spots on the stage, or must be quickly targeted in different parts of a room by a spotlight operator.

In addition, rehearsals are necessary to make certain that speakers can see their notes at the lectern under actual show lighting; to ensure that last-minute instructions can be given to participants; to test microphone levels for various speakers; to pre-set sound and lighting requirements; and to determine that all props, trophies, or certificates are in place for the actual ceremony.

Therefore, rehearsals must be scheduled in the convention résumé or staging guide just as any other event. Doing so will ensure that the room is available, that technicians and other personnel and their equipment are on hand, and that the show will be right—the first time.

Rehearsals, however, are not without cost. Property personnel and the convention manager must be aware of all additional costs that may be levied because of rehearsals. Time of technicians, equipment rental, and perhaps even room rental may be added expenses. In certain union facilities, labor calls for stagehands or other technicians, and user charges for theatrical stages, can be significant expenses. Such expenses must be negotiated, noted, and budgeted for.

Chapter Summary

Planning and managing a meeting is a complex process, one filled with opportunities for disaster for the careless or unwary planner. The task is easier when the planner carefully evaluates all the factors associated with selecting a site, including reserving and negotiating for guestrooms and food and beverage services, meeting rooms, and exhibition space. In addition, all arrangements with speakers must be worked out ahead of time.

Pre-meeting contacts are particularly important for the planner. These meetings are a good opportunity to become acquainted with the facility's staff and to arrange last-minute details.

All arrangements must be carefully reviewed by competent legal counsel to ensure that laws and ordinances at all levels are complied with and that there is no hint of violating U.S. antitrust laws.

Finally, the planner must exercise care in managing the meeting by determining the events schedule, preparing the necessary conference staging guide and event script, and arranging for rehearsals as required.

Notes

1. "The Meetings Market '85," *Meetings & Conventions*, March 31, 1986, Table 20.
2. *The Convention Liaison Council Manual* (Washington, D.C., 1985), pp. 45–46.
3. *Making Your Convention More Effective* (Washington, D.C.: American Society of Association Executives), pp. 41–55.
4. *Inter-Continental Hotels Meeting Planners Guide* (Inter-Continental Hotels Corporation, 1987), p. 31.

6 Marketing: Preparing to Sell and Service

Chapter Objectives

1. To define the marketing concept
2. To identify those elements of the convention business that constitute a marketing mix
3. To learn how to develop a marketing plan for a convention property

All too often, sales representatives try to sell without first doing their homework. They fail to approach their jobs from the marketing perspective. A thorough understanding of the marketing approach is necessary to maximize both service to the customer and profit for the property.

A marketing approach is especially critical in competitive times because of the complexities of satisfying the increasingly sophisticated needs of the many different forms of the meeting market. And to this must be added the increasing knowledgeability and professionalism of group business buyers.

This chapter concentrates on how to use marketing principles to develop the proper product line to meet the needs and wants of the convention and meetings market.

Marketing Defined

The primary distinction between marketing and selling relates to the user or customer. This emphasis on the customer or user as it relates to the hospitality industry is a key to the overall marketing concept.

In ordinary selling, a salesperson must persuade prospects that a product's features are desirable or meaningful. The product is made before users or markets are identified.

Under the marketing concept, the potential users of a product are first researched and analyzed—and their requirements are pinpointed. Then, products are made to satisfy these specific needs and wants. The salesperson persuades and convinces by stressing benefits.

In effect, the distinction between selling and marketing relates to the direction of the flow of goods and services, as shown in Exhibit 6.1.

From the basic marketing concept, five additional definitions of marketing have evolved.

First, marketing involves the flow of the product (goods or services) from the manufacturer to the user (conception to consumption). However, in the hospitality industry the flow is usually in the reverse direction: user to product. With the exception of outside catering and take-out service, potential users must be motivated to physically leave their environment and enter that of the property.

A second definition notes that marketing is distinguished from selling in that the goal of selling is to promote the features of a product or service. Marketing's goal, however, is to motivate specific prospects to purchase benefits based on their individual wants and needs.

A third definition is functional. Marketing encompasses all of the activities undertaken to selectively attract and service all types of business, combined with all activities aimed at getting business to keep returning—at a profit.

Attitudinal concerns characterize the fourth definition. Marketing is the process of solving the seller's problems by solving those of the buyer—for mutual benefit and gain.

The marketing concept has a very direct impact on the seller—particularly as it relates to a company's organizational structure.

Before the marketing concept became prevalent in the hospitality industry, the various sales-related functions such as advertising, direct mail, public relations, publicity, and direct contact selling too often were done independently. There was no coordination or integration.

Thus, you could have had a situation where the "on the road" salesperson was selling conventions on the basis of low guestroom rates and "give away" food and beverage prices, while the advertising director was preparing elaborate four-color advertising showing the facility as a luxury property. This could lead only to total customer confusion. In such a situation, the operating departments such as front office, reservations, and catering also would have operated independently of the sales function.

A structural definition of marketing is this: Marketing is the "umbrella" function that incorporates, integrates, and coordinates all means of producing revenue. This includes sales promotion, personal selling, media advertising, direct mail advertising, collateral, publicity, and public relations. It also includes servicing.

There are many additional definitions of marketing, but the one that is best adapted to the hospitality field is the functional one. It can be reworded to indicate its all-encompassing nature: Marketing consists of all the activities undertaken on a selective basis to **secure** the best possible business mix, to then **service** this business, and to ultimately provide maximum **satisfaction**—at a profit.

Of the three main steps in the functional definition, only **securing** relates directly to the sales/marketing department. The others are usually considered the direct responsibilities of the various operating departments, over which the sales/marketing department has little authority.

Exhibit 6.1 Flow of Goods and Services

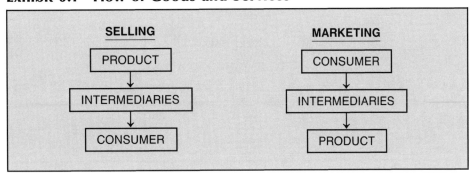

The Marketing Mix

There are two similar-sounding terms used throughout the hospitality industry: market mix and marketing mix.

Market mix refers to the relative ranking of business segments for a particular property, city, or area—based on common segment classifications. This process can be done daily, weekly, monthly, and annually. It is often used to compare figures of comparable time periods in the past. This can be used as a measurement of how well a property is doing in achieving its goal of increasing room nights or revenue from a particular market segment.

Market mix percentages for occupied rooms on a specific date might look like the following:

Individual business travel	35%
Individual leisure travel	10%
Association meetings	30%
Group leisure (tour and travel)	10%

These figures could also show total room revenue and total folio charges (which would include food and beverage and other income) to obtain useful information for forecasting, future goal setting, and the overall financial management of the marketing function.

Marketing mix refers to the key factors that influence the salability of a product or service.

Industries that manufacture consumable "hard good" products can use a marketing mix checklist containing several hundred different items. In the hospitality industry, the following 13 classifications can be used:

1. Price
2. Packaging
3. Label
4. Quality
5. Shape
6. Size
7. Decor

8. Methods of distribution

9. Methods of sale

10. Advertising

11. Sales promotion

12. Publicity and public relations

13. Government regulations

These major factors are essential in ensuring that the product is positioned to best accommodate the needs and wants of the market segments a property has focused upon.

So, there is a direct relationship between the two concepts. The marketing mix must be considered when determining the best possible market mix for a specific property.

A broad look at the marketing mix as it relates to convention and group business could be taken in the form of a self-evaluation questionnaire:

1. **Price.** What is the customary range of guestroom rates, banquet and reception prices, meeting room rentals, and audiovisual equipment charges? What flexibilities are considered with respect to the size of the group, length of stay, volume of food and beverage consumption, time of the year, cost of servicing, and repeat business potential? How are complimentary guestroom arrangements and function room rental waivers determined (especially for negotiating purposes)? What effects do competitive rates have on pricing strategies? What means are used to attractively package and merchandise rates and prices to meeting planners as well as to the attendees?

2. **Packaging.** Nearly every property has the same three main product categories: accommodations, services, and space. How can the various features within each of the categories be **distinctively** combined, packaged, and merchandised to potential convention and other group business prospects? Can the property develop one or more unique selling propositions (USP) that will effectively package the product in new, attractive, and attention-getting ways?

    Who else in the community (other properties, transportation carriers, sightseeing companies, attractions, and theme parks) can the property work with to offer all-inclusive, total package, or total experience programs?

3. **Label.** If it is an independent, does the property position its name properly within the meetings market? A name like Dew Drop Inn does not make the most positive initial impression on a group looking for a high-level board of directors meeting site.

    On the other hand, a name such as Grand Palace Excelsior Deluxe would not, at least on the surface, be too attractive to a price-conscious group.

    Properties carrying a chain or franchise system name may find they have either an added advantage or a potential disadvantage, depending on the prospect's image of and prior experience with other units within the system. Because of this potential liability, some properties prefer to carry their own name first, followed by the system name (e.g., The Center City Conference Center, an XYZ System Hotel).

Another consideration is whether the property should be called a hotel, motel, resort, lodge, spa, or conference center. Some of the more upscale properties have even eliminated this designation from their names (e.g., The Grand, The Plaza, The Imperial, etc.).

4. **Quality.** Different people will have different perceptions of what constitutes quality. But there are some common considerations that are equally important to both buyer and seller:
   a.   Need for renovation or rehabilitation
   b.   Need for replacement of furnishings and equipment
   c.   Overall standards of housekeeping and maintenance
   d.   Updating of physical services and amenities
   e.   Consistency and quality of staff, including upgrading and training
   f.   Ongoing programs of quality assurance
   g.   General reputation among customers, peers, the community, the public at large, and the industry in general

5. **Shape.** Is the property's shape and configuration such that it stands out from its surroundings? Does its shape allow for physical separation of various market segments? Can unusual shapes and other architectural distinctions be merchandised to enhance market visibility and recognition?

6. **Size.** Are the number of floors, guestrooms, suites, function rooms, exhibit areas, and other public areas compatible with the needs of specific markets? Are they related to the requirements of prospects who may hold many different types of meetings having a variety of different requirements? Is there sufficient flexibility to allow for expansion or division, based on changing meeting requirements?

7. **Decor.** Are the overall exterior and interior design and decor compatible with the image of the property? Will the majority of customers feel comfortable with them? How would you describe the overall atmosphere and ambience? Will the color scheme and lighting in the lobby, guestrooms, and especially the meeting space make meeting attendees feel easy and comfortable?

8. **Methods of Distribution.** How extensive and how diverse are the various channels for the distribution of the product line to the convention and group business markets?

   If it is an independent operation, does the property have its own sales or reservations offices in key target cities or use the services of a property representation firm? How effective are such intermediaries as travel agents, wholesalers, tour operators, etc., for reaching the group leisure market? Are others in the travel field (e.g., airlines and bus companies) used cooperatively to create and promote packaged offerings within the marketplace?

If it is part of a chain, how well does the property use the system's resources, such as national and regional sales/reservations offices, to generate both leads and specific sales?

9. **Methods of Sale.** Within the distribution channels, how well are communication tools used to generate business from the convention and group business decision makers? Are personal sales calls, telemarketing, media and broadcast advertising, video sales presentations, and internal promotions coordinated and integrated within specific programs directed at specific markets? Are they designed to achieve specific objectives and goals?

10. **Advertising.** Does advertising try to stand on its own, or is it more effectively coordinated with other promotional efforts? Is it properly placed in those media that best reach the decision makers within specific group business target markets? Does it speak the "language" of the reader? Is the budget allocation for advertising realistic in terms of objectives and goals? Does the overall advertising concept reflect the image the property wishes to instill and maintain within the meetings and group business marketplace?

11. **Sales Promotion.** Is enough attention devoted to the "image and influence" function of sales promotion? What is being done on a continuing basis to promote the property's visibility, such as attendance and participation at customer trade shows, conventions, and meetings? What is the sales/marketing department's role in developing and implementing internal promotional programs to extend sales to in-house guests? What incentives and premiums are offered to encourage maximum product use and reuse?

12. **Publicity and Public Relations.** In what ways are the soft-sell approaches of publicity and public relations integrated with the more hard-sell tactics of personal selling and advertising? What is done creatively to keep the name of the property before the general public? Are publicity and public relations activities coordinated within the marketing plan? What are the property's relationships with the community-at-large, local community leaders, civic and service organizations, educational institutions, local press, trade press, suppliers, the competition, the hospitality industry in general, and the organizations and groups that make up the convention and meetings market?

13. **Government Regulations.** The previous marketing mix factors are variables because they can be expanded and altered depending on changes in the marketplace, changes in product development, and increases or decreases within the competitive arena. However, federal, state, and local laws and regulations cannot be easily or quickly changed to meet marketing challenges. Hoteliers have little if any direct control over those legal regulations that affect the salability of the product. It is therefore imperative that the sales/marketing executive be aware of all laws that can influence the buyer/seller relationship, such as the following: host-guest

relationship and innkeepers liability; room and public space occupancy regulations; fire and safety codes; dram shop laws; third party liability; and anti-trust, price-fixing, and conspiracy.

In addition, such considerations as room/occupancy taxes, food and beverage taxes, and such municipal charges as airport departure taxes can have an impact on competitive pricing strategies.

This initial evaluation of the salability of the product is just a foundation, a starting point on which to build a comprehensive, structured promotion plan. The marketing mix checklist should also be rechecked for each of the property's other market mix components, such as the individual leisure traveler and the commercial or business traveler.

There are four considerations to keep in mind when using this checklist.

First, the checklist should be re-evaluated and updated periodically, especially during times of significant market activity, adjustment, or high competitive growth.

Second, the checklist could be used as the starting point for newly-appointed sales or marketing directors to familiarize themselves with their properties or companies.

Third, it also can be used as the basis for orientation and training new sales and marketing personnel.

Finally, the checklist can be reviewed periodically in department head or operating committee meetings to ensure consistency and teamwork between the sales/marketing function and the operations functions.

Once this product salability overview has been completed, a marketing plan can be developed.

Developing the Marketing Plan

Throughout most of its history, the hospitality industry "flew by the seat of its pants." Until the 1950s, very little was done to prepare structured business development programs to maximize profits. Image advertising, usually by luxury properties, was done to some extent and was primarily directed at a small portion of the public.

But two developments occurred in the mid-1950s: (1) the rapid growth of new properties, both in quantity and in style and concept; and (2) the emergence of the convention and meetings market as a primary business potential.

A corresponding change in operating philosophy began to evolve. One could no longer open the doors and expect business to flock in. In fact, the definition of what constituted a "sale" was re-evaluated. The early sales managers were basically order-takers; they cruised the marketplace and booked business. Volume was what counted, and little thought was given to what constituted a **profitable** sale.

To bring it into modern marketing perspective, the term "sale" can now be defined as "the securing of the right type of business at the right time, into the right space, at the right price."

Since the four key elements—sale, type, space, and price—are suited to all types of business, they readily form the basis for developing an ongoing program of business management.

A marketing plan can be viewed as "a systematic, structured, on-paper program of actions to be undertaken within a specific period to maximize profits."

But the marketing plan, which is usually prepared about six months ahead of the working year it will cover, must be able to reflect ever-changing market conditions. Therefore, it must also be a **flexible** working guide.

Objectives and Characteristics of a Marketing Plan

Before getting into the details of actually writing a convention and group business development program, it is best to review the marketing plan terminology presented in Exhibit 6.2 and the objectives and characteristics of a marketing plan.

A marketing plan defines precise responsibilities over a given period of time. However, it is important that sufficient authority be given to those implementing the plan if it is to be meaningful.

First, the plan must be "sold" to the owner, operator, or general manager and then re-sold to the heads of the operating departments and their staffs who are responsible for both servicing follow-through and internal selling.

Second, the plan must be realistic in terms of the property's delivery system. In short, don't promise what you can't deliver. Product capacity and staff capability must be tied into the objectives and goals.

Third, contingency plans are a must. They are back-ups. The market does not always react as forecasted, or new competition may develop faster than predicted (which can have a serious impact on both market share and fair share), or unexpected and uncontrollable circumstances can come into play (e.g., adverse economic, monetary, or political conditions).

Finally, it must be remembered that the marketing plan is not just a working tool for the sales/marketing department. It is intended to be used by the entire property, and specific responsibilities of the operating departments should be included within the applicable action plans.

Needs and Benefits

The term needs and benefits is continuously stressed as it relates to group business customers. This term can also be used in justifying the marketing plan approach.

In today's highly competitive buyer's market climate, it is essential to have an on-paper marketing plan that will accomplish four objectives.

First, the plan must accurately forecast conditions that can result in achieving realistic, profitable fiscal goals.

Next, it can be used to prepare sales/marketing budgets based on what is realistically needed to reach these goals—rather than blindly following so-called industry averages that have no relationship to what you are trying to achieve.

The plan's third objective is to effectively and productively manage accounts, time, staff, territory, and resources to solicit and secure business on a cost-effective basis.

Finally, the plan must be able to meet challenges from several different directions.

It must take into consideration more knowledgeable, sophisticated, and

Exhibit 6.2 Marketing Plan Terminology

Mission Statement. This is an **internal** declaration of what you are trying to accomplish within the framework of the marketing plan. It is often the first page of the detailed plan.

Example: "To make our property the first choice of the smaller meeting planner working within a 300-mile radius of the property by offering a variety of the most modern meeting room facilities specifically tailored for training sessions and other groups of fewer than 50 persons. To supplement our physical advantage with emphasis on providing the highest quality service that is constantly upgraded through a quality assurance program and attention to sales-minded training."

Position Statement. This is an **external** declaration to the public or to a particular market segment pinpointing what you are or what you would like to be, in terms of the public's perceptions of the benefits you are offering.

Position statements must be related to mission statements and often form the basis for preparing advertising copy, direct mail, and other communications.

Example: "Offering the smaller meeting planner the greatest possible choice of high quality meeting facilities specifically designed to the needs of serious, educationally-oriented groups of less than 50 persons."

Forecasting. Forecasting consists of a series of soundly-based projections indicating where you should be at the end of a specified period, usually the end of the next fiscal year. These projections are generally determined by a thorough analysis of market and competitive activities and their effects on "fair share" and "market share."

Example: At the end of Fiscal Year 19___, we have projected annual gross revenue at $1,500,000. This would break down to $1,000,000 from guestroom sales, $400,000 from food and beverage sales, and $100,000 from other income. Of the total gross volume, $700,000 will be derived from the individual business travel market, $200,000 from the individual leisure market, $100,000 from the group tour and travel market, and $500,000 from the group business market."

Fair Share. This is the ratio of your total available rooms for a fiscal year divided by the annual room inventory composed of yourself and your competitors.

Example: You have a 200-room property, and your four primary competitors have a total of 800 rooms. Thus, there are 1,000 rooms in the daily "inventory bank" of the five competitive properties. Multiplying this by 365 days (and for ease of illustration not deducting rooms unavailable for sale), you derive the following formula:

$$\text{FAIR SHARE} = \frac{\text{YOUR PROPERTY Available Rooms}}{\text{TOTAL Available Rooms}} = \frac{73,000}{365,000} = 20\%$$

Market Share. This is a ratio derived by dividing your annual occupied rooms by a figure arrived at by totaling your occupied rooms plus those of your competitors.

Example: You had a 70% annual occupancy rate, so your 200-room property had 51,000 occupied rooms (200 rooms × 365 days × .7). Your four competitors averaged a 65% occupancy rate for the year, so their total of 292,000 available rooms/year comes to 189,800 **occupied** rooms. To this is added your occupied rooms (51,000), resulting in a total of 240,800 occupied rooms among the five competitive operations. The formula for determining market share in this example would be as follows:

$$\text{MARKET SHARE} = \frac{\text{YOUR PROPERTY Occupied Rooms}}{\text{TOTAL Occupied Rooms}} = \frac{51,000}{240,800} = 21.2\%$$

Fair Share Variance. This is the difference between market share and fair share. It is used as an indicator of how well a property has penetrated the marketplace. Zero variance means you are doing as well as your aggregate competition; a positive variance means you have achieved primary positioning.

Example: Market Share (21.2%) – Fair Share (20.0%) = a Fair Share Variance of +1.2%

In addition to calculating fair share and market share for **total** occupied rooms, it is also essential to break this down according to market segment. Some properties may not be equally competitive for all segments—or you may not be as aggressive in seeking business from one sector as from another. So fair share variances should also be calculated for all the other markets. This is important because forecasting and virtually all other elements of the marketing plan are structured on a segmentation basis.

Exhibit 6.2 *(continued)*

Objectives. These are broad-based ends and general targets that are determined for purposes of forecasting. They are usually based on observations and implications of market activity, and they must be directly correlated to your mission and position statements. They are generally indicated as overall **changes** to be effected in occupancy mix, market penetration, occupancy percentages, average daily rates, average daily folio charges, average total expenditures per guest, food and beverage income, and meeting room use.

Example: "To concentrate on increasing the percentage of business derived from the meetings market so that it becomes our primary business source during the spring and fall seasons, and to increase the value of this business by upgrading food and beverage service to increase F&B revenue."

Goals. Goals are the further refinements of objectives, in terms of specific quantities, units, percentages, and dollar amounts. They are also percentage increases in the market share of specific market segments.

Example: "To increase the number of room nights represented by the meetings market from 20,000 to 25,000, to increase the average daily rate from $60 to $65, and to increase the average daily food, beverage, and other income expenditure from $25 to $30—resulting in a projected total increase in revenue from all sources of $675,000."

Strategies. These constitute the overall method or approach to be used in reaching objectives and goals.

Example: In the hospitality industry, strategies can be initially grouped under one of three major classifications: (1) **Segmentation** (concentration on developing a reputation among specifically targeted segments as being best able to offer benefits that will satisfy their specific needs); (2) **Differentiation** (development of a product or service line that is different or unique); and (3) **Combination** (development of a unique product or service line that will be applicable to the needs of specific selected market segments).

Tactics. If strategies can be looked upon as the "how" of reaching the marketplace, then tactics could be viewed as the "when," "what," "where," "why," and "who."

Example: "To uncover new corporate meeting business leads during the month of January by 'blitzing' six designated target cities using vacationing students of hotel administration from _____ University."

Action Plan. This is the compilation of all of the foregoing items into a chronologically organized system of on-paper "game plans" directed at fulfilling the forecasts and goals for each market segment. They include timing, staff assignments, territory management, and sales tools selection.

Budgeting. This is the determination of what it will cost to fulfill your action plans, according to a task-basis financial analysis of the proper expenditures required to do the job.

professional buyers, especially meeting planners and other group business decision-makers.

It must address ever-changing needs and wants of property guests, especially from those customers who have become accustomed and acclimated to the hotel experience and are therefore more discerning and demanding.

It must consider new competition, especially as chains and franchise systems increasingly become more "multi-tiered" and offer a variety of different hotel types under the same "brand name."

It must take into account the growth of specialized competition such as conference centers, executive retreats, and convention cruise ships.

Finally, it must take into consideration repositioned competition from hotels and hotel systems that are changing their image and often upgrading their product to gain a greater share of the opportunity potentials offered by growth market segments.

Exhibit 6.3   Conception to Consumption Cycle

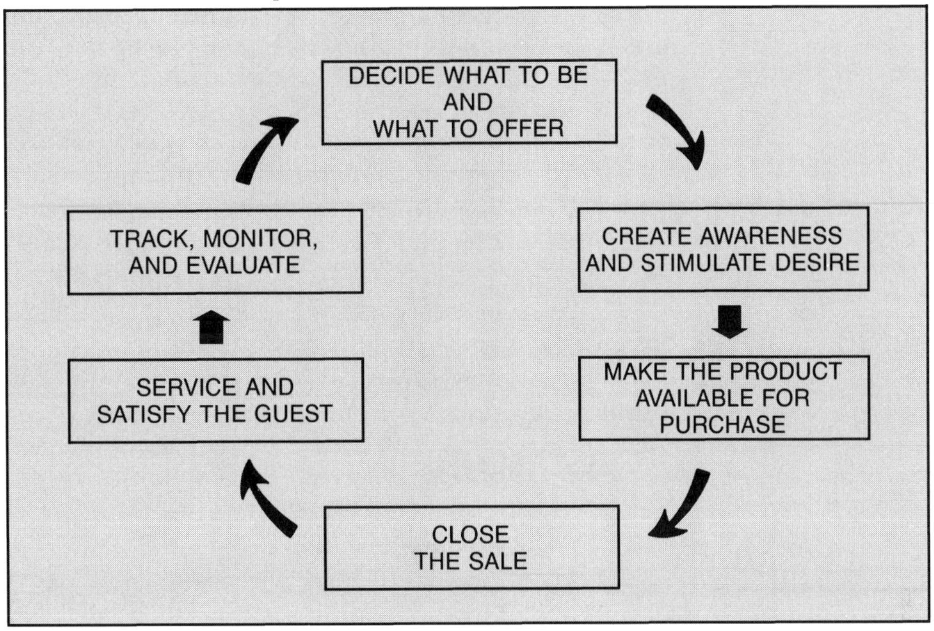

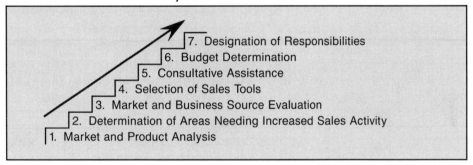

Exhibit 6.4   Checklist Cycle

7. Designation of Responsibilities
6. Budget Determination
5. Consultative Assistance
4. Selection of Sales Tools
3. Market and Business Source Evaluation
2. Determination of Areas Needing Increased Sales Activity
1. Market and Product Analysis

Source: David C. Dorf, *Marketing for the Hospitality Industry* (Ottawa, Canada: Management Development Unit of the Department of Manpower and Immigration, 1967).

Marketing Plan Cycles

An effective plan is built around the concept of the marketing cycle, which takes into account all the forces and actions that lead from conception to consumption. A model of this concept is shown in Exhibit 6.3.

Adaptation and use of this model in the hospitality industry began in the late 1960s. The checklist cycle shown in Exhibit 6.4 was prepared for a group study program course developed for the Canadian Government.[1]

The key distinction in the checklist cycle is the positioning of the budget in relation to the other elements. Traditionally, the budget for sales expenditures was determined **first**, based largely on an arbitrary percentage (usually 3 to 5%) of the previous year's gross sales.

Another key innovation in the transition stages leading to the marketing cycle is the emphasis placed on research. Prior to the general acceptance and use of the marketing plan cycle as a management tool for effective marketing, research was generally limited and often a hit-or-miss situation. The few properties that performed customer analysis usually concentrated on tracking changes about point of origin (where customers came from), transportation (how they came), and time (when they came).

It wasn't until the end of the 1970s that the now popular four-step cycle, with research as its foundation, became an accepted guide for developing an annual marketing plan.[2]

These four key steps are shown in Exhibit 6.5. As the arrow indicates, they form a repeating cycle, with each component dependent on the data and information gained from its predecessors.

The initial expansion of this cycle for use in a specific marketing plan can then be drawn up along the following lines:

RESEARCH

1. Property (Product) Analysis
   a. Product profiling
   b. External features analysis
   c. Internal features analysis
   d. Features to benefits conversions

2. Market Profiling
   a. Present guest analysis
   b. Analysis of potential growth markets
   c. Demographic segmentation
   d. Psychographic segmentation
   e. Behavioral studies
   f. Attitude, interest, and opinion analyses
   g. Market segment preference analysis

3. Competition Analysis
   a. Differential comparison
   b. Non-industry competition

4. Situation Analysis
   a. Current positioning
   b. SWOT listing (strengths, weaknesses, opportunities, and threats)
   c. Market change potentials

5. Property Needs Analysis
   a. Immediate, short-term overview
   b. Long-range objectives and goals
   c. Departmental profit center analysis

PLANNING

1. Strategic and Tactical Planning
   a. Preparing the forecast
   b. Image and positioning
   c. Unique selling (and servicing) propositions (USPs)

Exhibit 6.5 Four-Step Cycle

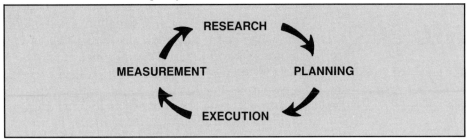

Source: Peter C. Yesawich, "How to Develop a Marketing Program," *The Cornell Hotel & Restaurant Quarterly* (November 1978 and May 1979).

     d. Differentiation, segmentation, and combination strategy approaches

     e. Tactical implementation

2. Business Source Determination

     a. Local markets

     b. Feeder markets

     c. In-house potentials

3. Action Plan Development

     a. Mission statement

     b. Position statement

     c. Action planning by market segments

4. Communications Management

     a. Sales tools analysis

     b. Selection and utilization of sales and promotional media

5. Administrative Management

     a. Time management

     b. Staff management

     c. Resources management

6. Financial Management

     a. Budgeting by percentage

     b. Task or zero-based budgeting

     c. Other marketing cost considerations

EXECUTION

Program Execution

     a. Responsibility versus authority

     b. Negotiating and closing techniques

     c. Contracts

MEASUREMENT

Program Measurement

     a. Methods of monitoring and evaluation

     b. Contingency programming

These cycles serve as a guide to establishing the structure of a formal marketing plan. This plan is usually developed and conducted annually.

There are some operations, usually resort properties, that may prepare more than one marketing plan per year. This is because the property, in essence, has two or more distinct product lines, available at different times, to offer to different markets.

For example, the "Center Mountain Resort and Spa" may direct its primary attention during the summer and winter months to promoting itself to both individual and group leisure markets. However, during the "shoulder seasons" of autumn and spring, it refocuses its positioning to appeal to mainly conventions and meetings. For advertising and other promotional purposes, the property may even alter its name during these latter periods to the "Center Mountain Conference Center."

In this situation, there are very definite distinctions between the image and operation of the property from one time frame to another. And these usually occur within a regularly established pattern from one year to the next.

Thus, there could be sound marketing reasons for developing two sets of marketing plans—as though the property were two separate entities. But in most operations, a single, cohesive program of business activity is prepared **annually**, based on a continuous marketing plan cycle approach.

How big and how detailed should a marketing plan be? Big enough to properly do the job. There are plans that contain no more than 20 or 30 pages, and others are 10 to 15 times that size. It depends on the property's size, its market mix, and the quantity and detail of the supporting documentation needed to implement and execute the program. Exhibit 6.6 shows a table of contents for a typical marketing plan.

Product Analysis

Product analysis answers the question, "What is the nature of the product I have to sell, particularly as it relates to the market segments I will be soliciting and servicing?" The checklist shown in Exhibit 6.7 helps provide the answer.

The items in this exhibit constitute the major areas of property analysis from the functional viewpoint. There are also key areas of product study that relate more directly to a variety of operational considerations.

Guestroom and Function Room Allocation. One of the first management decisions that must be made concerning the product is determining the maximum number of guestrooms that will be allocated for convention and group business. This is usually a twofold consideration.

First, from an operating standpoint, what is the number of guestrooms that at any given time the property could commit for group business and still have sufficient accommodations available to protect its transient base?

This figure is often determined in terms of percentages. For example, on Mondays and Tuesdays the property might commit no more than 70% of the house for conventions (except for unusual circumstances). The remaining 30% will be reserved for the individual business traveler, contract business (airline crews or athletic teams), the leisure traveler, etc. For the remainder of the week, up to 80% of the house can be committed; for Friday and Saturday night stays, the figure can rise to 90%.

Exhibit 6.6   Marketing Plan Table of Contents

1. Statement of Mission and General Objectives
2. Positioning Statement
3. Historical Overview
4. Areas and Community Profiles
   a. Location
   b. Historical Background
   c. Geophysical Factors
   d. Economic and Industrial Overview
   e. Population Studies and Projections
   f. Business Sector Profiles
   g. Educational, Recreational, Social, and Institutional Profiles
   h. Economic Projections
5. Hospitality Industry Overviews
   a. Hotels and Other Lodging Establishments
   b. Outside Meeting Facilities: Convention Halls and Public Arenas
   c. Independent Food Service Establishments
   d. Lounges and Other Entertainment
   e. Theme, Amusement, and Other Recreational Parks
   f. Airlines and Other Transportation Carriers
6. Property Analysis
   a. Physical Description
   b. Floor Plans and Other Schematics
   c. Tariffs and F&B Price Schedules
   d. Organizational Charts and Job Descriptions
   e. Current Market Mix Contribution Analysis
      (1) Type of Guest
      (2) Point of Origin
      (3) Arrival/Departure Patterns
      (4) Demographic Profiles
      (5) Psychographic Profiles
      (6) Segment Preference Profiles

7. Competitive Analysis
8. Market Activity Analysis
   a. Current Situation
   b. Growth/Decline Forecast
9. Fiscal Forecasts
   a. Commercial Travel Market
   b. Contract Business
   c. Individual Leisure Travel Market
   d. Group Business Markets
      (1) Associations
      (2) Corporate Meetings
      (3) Incentive Groups
10. Current Situation Analysis
11. General Statement of Objectives and Goals
12. Strategies and Tactics
    a. Sales
    b. Sales Promotions
    c. Advertising
    d. Public Relations and Publicity
13. Market Segment Strategy Development
    a. Individual Business (Commercial) Markets
       (1) Rooms
       (2) Food & Beverage
       (3) Other Income
    b. Contract & Concession Business
       (1) Rooms
       (2) Food & Beverage
       (3) Other Income
    c. Group Meetings Market
       (1) Associations
       (2) Corporate Meetings
       (3) Incentive Groups
       (4) Local Food & Beverage Functions
    d. Group Leisure (Travel & Tour)
14. Consolidated Action Plan

These percentages are not necessarily fixed for any particular operation. At any given property, there are other variables such as month, season, holiday, or special events.

Second, from a functional standpoint, what is the maximum number of guestrooms that can be committed in relation to the total square footage of function space?

One industry rule of thumb is that the maximum space needed to service a meeting is 40 square feet (about 4 square meters) per attendee. This is calculated on the basis of allocating 10 square feet (1 square meter) per person for meeting space, food/reception, exhibit space and registration, office, and storage space.

Exhibit 6.7 Product Analysis Checklist

1. *Location.* Is the property in the heart of the city? On the outskirts? In the suburbs? In a rural area? On water?
   Is it in a major industrial, agricultural, or political area (which might appeal to both company and corporate accounts representing the applicable professions or trades)?
   Is it in a gateway (or the opposite, a feeder location) from the point of association membership?
   How accessible is the property, not only in terms of highway location and airport distance but also from the point of major carrier schedules?
   Are other facilities (convention halls, exhibit centers, conference centers, and hotels) close by that might be used for sharing convention business or taking care of overflow?
   What attractions are there in the vicinity that will be inviting to convention attendees, especially during their free time?

2. *Guestroom Accommodations.* What is the **total** number of guestrooms available? The maximum number that can be committed at any one time for conventions? When can they be committed? What is the breakdown of types of rooms? Are there special types of rooms or floors (e.g., VIP, executive club, no-smoking, handicapped)? Are there special in-room furnishings, facilities, and amenities?
   Have guestroom rates been posted or published? Are there special convention or group rates? Seasonal rates? Are there complimentary and upgrading room policies?

3. *General Facilities and Services.* Are there public dining and lounge outlets?
   Are there room service, laundry and valet, beauty and barber shops, flower and gift shops, and other concessions? Do entertainment, recreation, and fitness facilities exist? Are business services available?

4. *Convention and Meeting Facilities.* What is the total number of meeting rooms available? What are their dimensions and capacities under various setups?
   Are there special rooms like tiered auditoriums and specially equipped conference rooms?
   Are there separate exhibit areas? Where are they located? What are their dimensions (especially height) and maximum floor load capacities? Are there special entrances?
   Is adequate functional equipment available? Are there sufficient tables, platforms and risers, lecterns and podiums, chalkboards, flip charts, easels, and PA systems?
   Is audiovisual equipment available? Are there sufficient 35mm slide projectors, 16mm movie projectors, and videocassette projectors? Is this equipment available on site or must it be rented? How much are rental charges?
   Are sufficient banquet rooms and reception areas available?

5. *Outside Facilities and Services.* Are off-premise products, facilities, and services (e.g., recreational outlets and business services) an integral part of what you offer both the meeting planner and the attendees?

6. *Transportation.* Does sufficient quantity and quality of transportation exist? Have all major transportation systems between key feeder cities and the property been analyzed? Has the availability of fly-drive packages, rent-a-car agencies, and charter bus companies been examined?

This, of course, represents the maximum requirements in a situation where there is no dual use of space such as a luncheon held in the same room between morning and afternoon meetings.

Using these criteria, a property with 20,000 square foot of function space could accommodate groups containing as many as 500 persons (20,000/40). Guestroom allocation would depend on the group's need or desire to double up. Certain types of corporate meetings, where the company pays for lodging, might require that nearly all attendees double up. Thus a group of 500 persons might need only 250 to 260 guestrooms.

On the other hand, an association convention of 500 delegates could use as many as 350 to 400 rooms. In this situation, there might be a strong drive to encourage spouses and families to attend.

This rough-guide formula is subject to other variables, including the amount of double occupancy desired by a group and the type or purpose of the meeting.

Exhibit 6.8 Convention Floor Plan of the Quebec Hilton

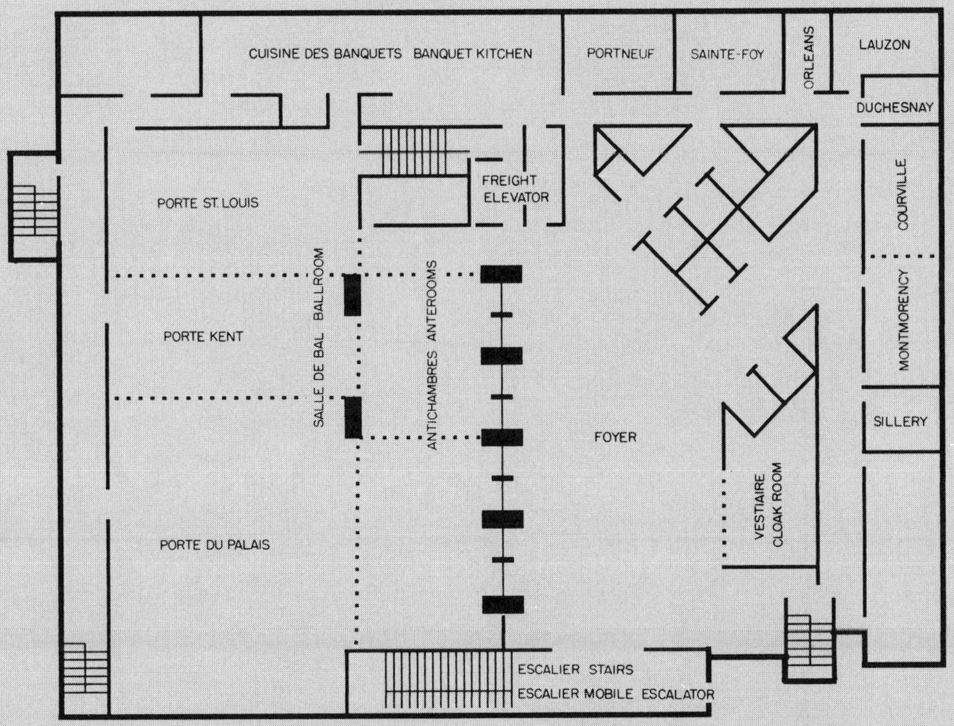

Part of the convention floor plan of the Quebec Hilton illustrates (by the dotted lines) the wide flexibility of both the ballroom and smaller "breakout" rooms.

Source: Bill Bard Associates, Monticello, N.Y.

Some meetings, such as those involving intensive technical training, might require a large number of breakout rooms for discussions and presentations. There would also probably be a demand for exhibit space.

Product launchings might not require as much meeting space, but they would require more exhibit and demonstration areas.

A "work and play" group, or one that is primarily social in nature, might need less space because many of its programs will be devoted to outdoor and other free time activities. Similarly, a hobby or avocational group may spend a large portion of its program time off-property on visitation and field trips.

Another important consideration affecting group space and room commitments is the number of groups being handled at one time. For example, 10 groups averaging 50 persons each usually require more aggregate space than one group of 500.

Other factors include the number and capacities of the various function and meeting rooms, as well as the flexibility of the space; i.e., can rooms be divided or opened up? See Exhibit 6.8, Floor Plan of Quebec Hilton.

Capacities also must be correlated with the **type** of room setup. Auditorium or theater style seating (chairs only) generally takes up less space per

Exhibit 6.9 Room Capacity Chart

CONVENTION CENTRE	Dimensions	Ceiling Height	Sq. Ft.	Sq. Meters	Reception	Theatre	Classroom	Banquet
Metropolitan Grand Ballroom	147' × 170'	24'	24,990	2,321	3,500	3,500	1,300	2,500
Metro West	147' × 56'	24'	8,232	765	1,200	1,100	450	800
Metro Centre	147' × 60'	24'	8,820	819	1,300	1,200	450	850
Metro East	147' × 56'	24'	8,232	765	1,200	1,100	450	800
Frontenac Ballroom	104' × 96'	17'	9,984	928	1,200	1,100	500	800
Queens Quay	46' × 35'	12'	1,610	150	200	180	75	120
— 1	23' × 35'	12'	805	75	100	75	36	60
— 2	23' × 35'	12'	805	75	100	75	36	60
Bay Room	23' × 36'	12'	828	77	100	75	36	60
Richmond	30' × 20'	12'	600	56	50	55	20	50
— 1	15' × 20'	12'	300	28	25	25	—	20
— 2	15' × 20'	12'	300	28	25	25	—	20
Yonge Room	30' × 20'	12'	600	56	50	55	20	50
— 1	15' × 20'	12'	300	28	25	25	—	20
— 2	15' × 20'	12'	300	28	25	25	—	20
Wellington	30' × 20'	12'	600	56	50	55	20	50
— 1	15' × 20'	12'	300	28	25	25	—	20
— 2	15' × 20'	12'	300	28	25	25	—	20

HOTEL	Dimensions	Ceiling	Sq. Ft.	Sq. Meters	Reception	Theatre	Classroom	Banquet
Harbour Ballroom	139' × 58'	12'	6,991	649	900	900	400	550
— Salon A	58' × 45'	12'	2,075	193	250	225	100	150
— Salon B	58' × 49'	12'	2,842	264	350	300	150	200
— Salon C	58' × 45'	12'	2,075	193	250	225	100	150
Pier 2	44' × 26'	9'	1,144	106	100	100	30	60
Pier 3	44' × 26'	9'	1,144	106	100	100	30	60
Piers 2 & 3 combined	44' × 52'	9'	2,288	213	200	200	90	120
Pier 4	44' × 51'	9'	2,144	199	200	180	96	130
Pier 5	44' × 41'	9'	1,804	168	150	130	84	100
Piers 4 & 5 combined	44' × 92'	9'	3,948	367	350	325	190	240
Pier 6	18' × 30'	9'	540	50	30	30	20	30
Pier 7	27' × 25'	9'	675	63	50	45	24	40
Pier 8	27' × 25'	9'	675	63	50	45	24	40
Piers 7 & 8 combined	27' × 50'	9'	1,350	125	100	100	57	80
Pier 9	27' × 32'	9'	978	91	80	75	30	60

A detailed room capacity chart from the Toronto Harbour Castle Hilton Hotel and Convention Centre shows capacities of each room under various types of room setups, and room dimensions in both the English and metric systems.

Source: Bill Bard Associates, Monticello, N.Y.

Exhibit 6.10   Function Room Model

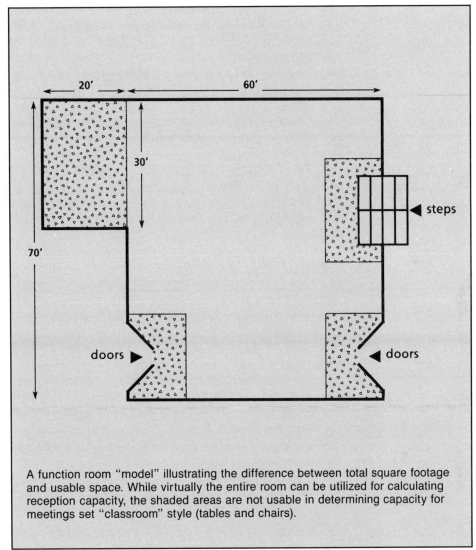

A function room "model" illustrating the difference between total square footage and usable space. While virtually the entire room can be utilized for calculating reception capacity, the shaded areas are not usable in determining capacity for meetings set "classroom" style (tables and chairs).

person than does schoolroom or classroom seating (chairs and tables). A hollow square or a horseshoe (U-style) arrangement, traditionally used for board meetings, takes up the most space. A room capacity chart detailing the capacities under the most common setup styles is essential for both the property sales executive and the meeting planner (see Exhibit 6.9).

Usable Function Space. Rooms with unusual shapes or configurations, as well as space in front of stairs or doors, can alter the effective use of space under various types of setups.

For example, Exhibit 6.10 illustrates a room with main dimensions of 60 by 70 feet with an alcove 20 by 30 feet. The total area is 4,800 square feet. For all practical purposes, this entire space could be used for a reception. In fact, the alcove is particularly suitable because people tend to form cluster groups and congregate in corners or separated areas. However, if the room is to be used for a training session with a classroom setup, the alcove would be useless (except perhaps for displays or exhibits) and the areas near the doorways and stairs could not be set up with tables. Therefore, some 800 to 1,000 square feet of the total 4,800 would not be usable—and this must be taken into account when calculating certain capacities. Additional allowances for non-usable space must be made for rooms with pillars and posts.

The preceding discussion has been a basic overview of the fundamentals of product analysis—primarily as they are viewed from the seller's point of view. Ideally, the product must also be viewed from the buyer's or user's perspective.

Market Analysis

The analysis of the property should be followed by an examination of the facility's current business mix. Various profiles can be developed from studying current records, and analyses can be made of the relative volume and value of each type of business during specific periods of the year, month, and week.

Profile Questionnaire. A sound market analysis addresses who, what, where, when, why, and how, and these elements can be incorporated in a questionnaire:

Who are our guests at designated periods? What is the market mix as represented by the corporate meetings market and by the association meetings market—in general as well as local, state, regional, national, and international segments? How does this mix compare with the business provided by other customers, such as individual business travelers, individual leisure travelers, and the group travel market?

What are the characteristics of the people who make up our various markets? These include such demographic items as age, sex, marital status, income, and education, in addition to psychographic considerations like lifestyles, interests, behaviors, and attitudes.

Where do our guests come from? This is commonly known as a geographic or point of origin analysis. Again, this should be done for each major market segment.

When do they come? This is a chronological analysis of the arrival and departure patterns of various market segments, based on time of week, month, and year. This analysis should be studied as it relates to peak, shoulder, and value-season periods, as well as the property's traditional peaks and valleys in occupancy patterns.

Why do our guests come here? What are the major attractions and inducements of the area, the community, and the property as they relate to each of the market segments and their specific needs, wants, objectives, and goals?

How do they arrive? This form of transportation analysis should include not only a percentage breakdown by general modes (i.e., car, bus, plane, and train) but also identification of transportation carriers and rental car agencies.

This questionnaire should be constantly reviewed and updated. It is especially useful for new sales/marketing executives who may want to discover changes that have occurred during the last five years. Such trend analysis can be very helpful in preparing forecasts as well as for determining sales and advertising strategies and activities for future periods.

Sources of Information. The sources of information for answering the items in the questionnaire are easy to locate. In most cases, they are readily available from the sales office as well as from data and records maintained in operating departments like the front office, reservations, and accounting. Specific sources include the following:

- Reservation inquiry log
- Guest registration cards
- Guest history records
- Convention history records
- Rooming lists
- Guest folios
- Reservation department records
- Accounting department reports
- Sales/marketing department records and files (booking report forms, convention master cards, trace cards, contracts, etc.)

Long-term property employees who have contact with guests are another important source. Room clerks, bell personnel, servers, housekeepers, and other guest-contact employees very often can provide practical, first-hand information about changes and trends that have occurred within the various guest classifications.

Competition Analysis

Once a preliminary survey has been made of both the product and its current users, a similar study should be made of each competitor.

Initial competition comes from other destination areas. In the case of international and large national organizations, the competition comes from other parts of the world. Too many inexperienced sales representatives try to book meetings for their properties and eventually learn that their country, state, or city should not have even been considered as a potential location.

It is essential to determine which areas and cities are competitive with your location for various types of convention and meetings business.

Obviously, a group whose history indicates a pattern of meeting only in "sun and sand" resort locations would be hard pressed to even consider holding a function at your property if it is located in the middle of a large northern city. And, a company that, because of budgetary considerations, traditionally holds its annual sales meeting no more than 100 miles from its home offices would not be too likely to consider your property if you are located 2,000 miles away. In such situations, the locations these groups would choose would not be competitive with yours.

Competitive Criteria. The more direct, everyday competition comes from properties that are similar to yours and that meet the following criteria:

1. They are located in areas or cities that, along with yours, are normally considered in an association's or company's site selection process.

2. They are in the same general category as your property (i.e., luxury, economy, mid-market, all-suites, etc.).

3. They are aggressively soliciting the same general types (and the same specific organizations) as you are.

4. They have comparable guestrooms, meeting and function space, food and beverage outlets, and recreational facilities.

5. They have a fairly equivalent rate and price structure for the above facilities.

6. They have a service and support staff similar to yours in terms of experience, attitudes, and abilities.

Thus, a property the same size as yours, whose market mix is 60% individual business travel, 30% individual leisure travel, and 10% meetings, would not be considered your competition if your ideal mix is 65% meetings, 30% group tour, and 5% individual business travel.

Nevertheless, competitive similarity among properties in the same general category presents a real marketing challenge. Each property must find some unique or outstanding set of attributes that are meaningful to customers and that will position the property favorably in the minds of potential users.

Such a USP often forms the basis of a sales or advertising campaign.

New Competition. Because of the ever-increasing emphasis on convention and group business at all types of properties, the competitive environment becomes more challenging every day. Some of the new competition includes the following:

1. Limited-facility properties, built strictly for conventions and meetings

2. All-suite properties, which offer the attendee larger, upgrade accommodations at competitive prices

3. Conference centers, many of which provide meeting space only and lease guestrooms and food service from nearby properties

4. Smaller properties, which seek out specific types of meetings where the customer wants an informal setting and to be the only group in the house

5. Properties employing new construction (modular) methods that can significantly reduce the time needed for building or expansion

Competitive properties should be studied on a segmentation basis: association conventions, company sales meetings, board of director meetings, etc. In this analysis, you should answer five basic questions as they relate to each segment:

First, what features, services, and benefits do I have that each of my competitors do not?

Second, what features, services, and benefits do my competitors have that I do not?

Next, in what common features, services, and benefits do I appear to have an advantage in either quantity or quality?

Fourth, in what common features, services, and benefits do certain of my competitors appear to have an advantage in either quantity or quality?

Finally, with which of my competitors can I best work for overflow or shared housing or for joint sales presentations at trade shows?

As was the case with the product and the markets using the product, knowing your competition and analyzing changes and trends within the competitive picture is essential in preparing to sell and service the convention and group business markets.

Property Needs Analysis

The final element in the preliminary analysis process relates to determining where business activity is most needed and the types of business that would most likely satisfy the property's goal of maximizing profit.

As a starting point for this type of analysis, it is often helpful to first identify need areas according to a property's major profit centers: rooms, food and beverage, and other income potentials.

The following format is one needs analysis method of identifying the key areas requiring concentrated sales attention:

Guestroom Accommodation Needs

1. Increased occupancy year-round

2. Improved occupancy during specific periods of the year (seasonal fluctuations)

3. Increased occupancy during specific days of the week (weekends, mid-week, etc.)

4. Combination of the previous two items: greater occupancy for specific days of the week during certain seasons or periods of the year

5. Higher average room rate

6. Longer length of stay

7. Increased multiple occupancy ratio

Food and Beverage Needs (Group Functions)

1. Increased total annual volume

2. Increased sales during specific periods of the year (seasonal fluctuations)

3. Increased sales during certain days of the week

4. Combination of the last two items: increased volume during specific days within specified periods of the year

5. Increased volume from specific food and beverage functions: breakfasts, luncheons, receptions, dinners, mid-morning and mid-afternoon breaks, and other events associated with association and corporate meetings

6. Similar volume increases for functions other than those related to the meetings market, such as wedding receptions, or local civic and social club luncheons

7. Higher per-cover income from each or any of the types of functions indicated above

Food and Beverage Needs (Individual)

The same considerations used in analyzing food and beverage group function needs can be applied to those food and beverage outlets available to the general public. At properties having multiple and varied types of outlets, the analysis is often done on both an overall and an individual room or outlet basis.

Other Income Needs

1. Increased volume in other departmental areas such as telephone, room service, laundry and valet.

2. Increased volume in leased stores and concessions such as barber and beauty shops, newsstands, gift shops and boutiques, sightseeing and transportation desks, and similar rental outlets, especially where the property may receive a share of the gross volume in addition to a fixed rental or lease charge.

Where applicable, two additional overriding considerations should be tied into the above need areas.

In many instances, additional volume is not necessarily the actual need. **Net profit** is what the business is all about, so a possible need would relate to increasing the profit factor from existing business without necessarily increasing volume. This would heavily involve such operational considerations as control of the labor and materials costs of preparing and servicing, as well as the sales/marketing executives' knowledge of what constitutes high profit items.

Also, when doing a follow-up analysis relating needs areas to specific market segments, you will often find that a combination of needs (rather than one specific need) will be involved. For example, if you analyze local and state association business (where attendees have to travel only short distances), you might find a combination of challenges: (1) increasing the average length of stay; (2) increasing multiple occupancy (spouse and family); (3) increasing use of food and beverage facilities during free time or open evenings; and (4) moving the entire group into a time period where the business is most needed and could possibly prove more profitable without having to increase rates and charges.

Forecasting   The research and analysis techniques discussed thus far basically revolve around what **was** and what **is**. However, sales and marketing executives are more concerned about the future. This is especially true with conventions and other forms of meeting business, where decisions are made concerning events up to five years in advance.

In addition, the top sales or marketing executive for each property is responsible for submitting for approval by top management a business plan to cover at least the next complete fiscal year.

For many properties, such a plan is developed during the first part of a particular year. The plan is based largely on information from the previous year, and it is submitted in August or September to cover the upcoming calendar year.

This marketing plan defines what the property hopes to accomplish during the coming year in terms of both general objectives and specific goals for each type or segment of business. At the same time, this plan must be correlated with departmental objectives and goals within the property as they relate to each of the main profit centers (rooms, food and beverage, and other income).

Thus, the next area of preparation involves forecasting what the marketplace will offer in terms of business potentials, how the marketplace will act, and what the property can do to gain its fair share of those market segments it has designated as the main components of its business mix.

Forecast Components. While there are some variations, there is a fairly consistent format for preparing a fiscal forecast. In general, forecasting involves collecting documentation relating to the following processes:

- Total annual room inventory
- Market mix analysis
- Fair share analysis
- Market share analysis
- Market penetration
- Area room demand analysis
- Market segment objectives and goals
- Room occupancy forecast
- Annual revenue forecast

In order to fulfill the main goal of the sales/marketing department, all sales planning, all direct selling, and all servicing efforts must relate to the forecast. The goal is to secure and service business that will maximize profit production and return on investment.

Although our concentration in this book is on convention and group business, the forecast initially must be made on a total business potential basis. After that aspect is satisfied, subsequent promotional activities will then be undertaken by appropriate market segments.

Sample Forecast for the Center City Conference Hotel. For the sake of clarity, it might prove helpful to present a sample forecast using a hypothetical 300-room property called the "Center City Conference Hotel" (CCCH). Figures and percentages will be rounded off, and we will assume that, to varying degrees, all competing properties are fully competitive for all major market segments (depending upon how each has determined its best market mix for its particular type of operation).

The rates and prices shown were selected for ease of computation. They do not reflect the prevailing industry rate/price structure.

Exhibit 6.11   Total Annual Room Inventory

TOTAL ANNUAL ROOM INVENTORY			For the Year_____	
PROPERTY	# ROOMS	TOTAL ANNUAL ROOMS AVAILABLE	TOTAL ANNUAL OCCUPIED ROOMS	ANNUAL PERCENTAGE OF OCCUPANCY
Outlaw Inn	149	54,385	38,613	71%
Last Resort	326	118,990	74,964	63%
Action Hotel	198	72,270	52,034	72%
Empty Arms	317	115,705	68,266	59%
CCCH	300	109,500	74,460	68%
TOTALS:	1,290	470,850	308,337	66%

Exhibit 6.12   Market Mix Analysis

MKT SEG	Outlaw Inn OR	%	Last Resort OR	%	Action Hotel OR	%	Empty Arms OR	%	CCCH OR	%	Totals OR	%
					Occupied Rooms (OR) For the Year_____							
GBM	13,514	35%	14,993	20%	10,407	20%	10,240	15%	29,784	40%	78,938	26%
ILT	9,653	25%	18,741	25%	15,610	30%	10,240	15%	14,892	20%	69,136	22%
IBT	7,723	20%	18,741	25%	20,814	40%	30,720	45%	14,892	20%	92,890	30%
GLM	7,723	20%	22,489	30%	5,203	10%	17,066	25%	14,892	20%	67,373	22%
TL:	38,613	100%	74,964	100%	52,034	100%	68,266	100%	74,460	100%	308,337	100%

KEY: GBM = Group Business Market (both association and corporate meetings)
ILT = Individual Leisure Traveler (including family)
IBT = Individual Business Traveler (Commercial Traveler)
GLM = Group Leisure Market (organized tour, including incentive travel)
% = Market Segment "Mix" percentages for each property, calculated by dividing the total number of occupied rooms into the number occupied by each segment.

Step 1. The first step is to inventory both available and occupied rooms for CCCH and those of its competition for the last full 12-month period. This is shown in Exhibit 6.11.

The annual rooms available figures are the number of salable rooms at each property multiplied by 365 (366 in leap years). Determining occupied rooms is a bit more difficult. Very often, annual occupancy figures are published in local newspapers, reported by accounting firms, or related by local convention and visitors bureaus or the chamber of commerce. Each competitive property's total annual occupied rooms figure can then be determined by multiplying the total annual available rooms figure by the occupancy percentage.

Once these procedures have been accomplished, the figures should then be broken down by major market segment, as shown in Exhibit 6.12. In this case, estimating the competition's figures requires more accurate calculations. Exchanging information for mutual benefit is traditional throughout the hospitality industry, but care must be exercised that such exchanges do not violate any federal regulations, especially those involving anti-trust and restraint of trade laws.

Step 2. The next step in this example is to calculate fair share and fair share variance (the difference between market share and fair share). These terms are percentage guidelines that show how CCCH compares with its competition in terms of room availability and occupancy.

$$\text{FAIR SHARE} = \frac{\text{Center City Conference Hotel}}{\text{Total Available Rooms}} = \frac{109,500}{470,850} = 23.3\%$$

$$\text{MARKET SHARE} = \frac{\text{Center City Conference Hotel}}{\text{Total Occupied Rooms}} = \frac{74,460}{308,337} = 24.2\%$$

FAIR SHARE VARIANCE = Market Share (24.2%) minus Fair Share (23.3%) = +0.9%

Note that the variance is positive. Although it is not very large in this case, any positive variance between total availability and occupancy indicates the property is in a top demand position.

This is an overall indicator that takes into account all business market segments. However, properties that share all business potentials generally do so in varying degrees. This becomes evident as we continue our example.

One of the properties is the corporate meetings market's first choice among three properties in a given area because it has the latest state-of-the-art training facilities and audiovisual equipment. But a different property is the first choice for large working association meetings because it has the largest number of breakout rooms conveniently located in one specific area. And a third property gets most of the incentive market and group tours because it is situated within a large theme park complex. There may be considerable positioning variations with the other non-group forms of business such as the individual business market.

Step 3. So, the next step in this example is to examine market share as it is broken down by key market segments. This is shown in Exhibit 6.13.

This compilation provides an overview of how well a property "stacks up" against each of its major competitors for each main market segment. By using the fair share variance principle, you can also determine where you stand as far as measuring your ability to obtain business from each segment, as contrasted with total occupancy from all properties within the competitive arena.

For our hypothetical example, we can chart market penetration as shown in Exhibit 6.14.

Up to this point, we have illustrated "what has been." Now, we enter a stage where sales and marketing executives must use their resources to study the current conditions of the marketplace and use indicator information to anticipate changes in demand for the coming year.

The first source of information on potential demand changes would be the property's present guests. In the case of group business or contract individual business, the people who make decisions for the various market

Exhibit 6.13   Market Share Analysis

	GBM OR	%	ILT OR	%	IBT OR	%	GLM OR	%	TOTALS OR	%
									For the Year_____	
Outlaw Inn	13,514	17%	9,653	14%	7,723	8%	7,723	12%	38,613	13%
Last Resort	14,993	19%	18,741	27%	18,741	20%	22,489	33%	74,964	24%
Action Hotel	10,407	13%	15,610	22%	20,814	23%	5,203	8%	52,034	17%
Empty Arms	10,240	13%	10,240	15%	30,720	33%	17,066	25%	68,266	22%
CCCH	29,784	38%	14,892	22%	14,892	16%	14,892	22%	74,460	24%
Totals:	78,938	100%	69,136	100%	92,890	100%	67,373	100%	308,337	100%

NOTE: Percentage figures rounded off to nearest whole number.
OR = Occupied Rooms

Exhibit 6.14   Market Penetration

For the Year_____

MARKET SEGMENT	Occupied Rooms ALL Properties	Occupied Rooms CCCH	MARKET SHARE	FAIR SHARE VARIANCE
GBM	78,938	29,784	37.7%	+14.4%
ILT	69,136	14,892	21.5%	−1.8%
BT	92,890	14,892	16.0%	−7.3%
GLM	67,373	14,892	22.1%	−1.2%
TOTALS:	308,337	74,460	24.2%	+0.9%

NOTES: 1. MARKET SHARE is calculated by dividing total occupied rooms of the CENTER CITY CONFERENCE HOTEL by the total occupied rooms of all properties—for both the total number of rooms as well as for each segment.

2. FAIR SHARE VARIANCE is calculated by subtracting the CENTER CITY CONFERENCE HOTEL'S overall fair share (23.3%) from its Market Share of each segment.

3. For this illustration, it is assumed that all properties are equally AGGRESSIVE in going after all market segments. In practice this *may*—or in many instances, *may not*—be necessarily the case, depending on how each property evaluates the comparative value and the net profit potential of each segment.

segments are the specific sources. These include corporate meeting planners, association executives, travel agents, tour operators, transportation carrier officials, etc.

Sources in your own community are another excellent source of information. They can provide local economic indicator data to help you determine if there will be increases or decreases in future traffic into your area. Some of these indicators include the following 15 items:

1. New office building construction or renovation (downtown or suburban)

2. Housing demand

3. Highway development

4. Highway traffic reports

5. Airline traffic reports

6. Overall population changes

7. Population shifts (geographical)

8. Retail sales figures

9. Sales tax receipts

10. Food and beverage tax receipts (especially from "freestanding" operations)

11. Occupancy tax reports

12. Help wanted ads in local newspapers

13. The amount of advertising bought by your competitors in key feeder cities

14. Projections and surveys by local convention and visitors bureaus, chambers of commerce, city governments, and independent hotel accounting firms

15. Independent marketing firms commissioned to study local conditions

The preceding list is not all-inclusive. The key consideration is how you interpret the information and translate it into projected room nights.

Continuing with our hypothetical example, the information shown in Exhibit 6.15 is one format that can be used to plot changes in room demand.

Step 4. The fourth step is to calculate how much of the increase in demand you can realistically obtain and how well you can confine losses within decreasing market segments where loss of rooms is anticipated.

First, this involves preparing objectives and goals for each market segment.

For example, your objectives for the next year would relate to your perception of the group business market as a growth segment. You might feel that you can better your positioning within this segment by raising your share of current demand by 7% and obtaining 50% of the anticipated increase in room demand.

Based on these objectives, your goals would be to show an increase of 5,226 occupied rooms from current "carryover" demand (which means you will divert current business from your competition) and obtain 3,946 additional room nights represented by the anticipated increase in demand. As Exhibit 6.16, "Market Segment Objectives and Goals," shows, this results in a specific goal of 9,172 more room nights next year from the convention and meetings market.

Achievement of these goals depends on how well you perceived future changes in the marketplace and how effectively you carried out the best possible strategies and tactics.

Next, you must return to your current figures for occupied rooms by

Exhibit 6.15 Area Room Demand Change Forecast

	ANTICIPATED % OF CHANGE	ANTICIPATED ROOM DEMAND CHANGE	REASONS
Growth Segments			
GBM	+ 10%	+ 7,893	• Industrial Park expansion. • Airport expansion. • Opening of new family-oriented theme park. • Strong new leadership in local convention & visitors bureau. • Municipal Convention Hall renovation completed.
GLM	+ 3%	+ 2,021	• Increase in Social Security benefits. • Decline in annual inflation rate. • International political situation spurs domestic travel.
Stable Segments			
IBT	—	—	• Corporate travel budgets cut from many companies headquartered in key feeder cities to help defray costs of new satellite offices in local industrial park. • New tax legislation on corporate travel and entertainment may temporarily cause some travel cutbacks. • Rising gasoline prices may cause some cutbacks on highway business travel. • Above situations possibly offset by combining meeting attendance with business trips.
Loss Segments			
ILT	– 5%	–3,457	• Lack of creative packaging and merchandising by all area hotels; especially for family business. • Lack of city and area promotional support. • Growth of trailer park and camping facilities.
NET CHANGE IN ROOM DEMAND:		**+ 6,457**	

market segment and add or subtract the applicable changes as determined by your room goals. This produces a room occupancy forecast for the coming year. It is based on demand for accommodations by market segment. An example is shown in Exhibit 6.17.

This analysis takes care of the rooms forecast. However, because the sales/marketing department is responsible for securing business of all types for all revenue-producing departments, food, beverage, and other income also must be incorporated in the total forecast.

It is relatively easy for properties that have been in business a long time to calculate an average market segment ratio between room expenditures on the one hand, and food, beverage, and other income on the other. This "F&B/OI Factor" is often indicated as a percentage of room revenue and is easily converted to its decimal equivalent.

For illustrative purposes, assume that for every $100 a convention delegate spends for guestrooms, he or she might spend an additional $50 (.5 or

Exhibit 6.16 Market Segment Objectives and Goals

		Year Ending_____	
MARKET SEGMENT	GENERAL OBJECTIVES	ANTICIPATED CHANGES IN OCCUPIED ROOMS	(GOALS)
Growth Segments GBM	Raise our share of current "carry-over" demand by an additional 7% (from 38% to 45%).	+5,526	
	Obtain 50% of the anticipated segment increase.	+3,946	
			+9,472
GLM	Maintain current demand.		—
	Obtain 1/3 of anticipated increase.		+673
Stable Segments IBT	Maintain current demand.		—
Loss Segments ILT	Confine our share of the potential decline to 20% of the demand loss.		−691
NET PROJECTED CHANGE			**+9,454**

Exhibit 6.17 Room Occupancy Forecast

	For the Year_____				
MARKET SEGMENT	CURRENT MIX OR	%	FORECASTED ROOM DEMAND CHANGE	FORECASTED MIX OR	%
GBM	29,784	40%	+9,472	39,256	47%
ILT	14,892	20%	−691	14,201	17%
IBT	14,892	20%	—	14,892	18%
GLM	14,892	20%	+673	15,565	18%
TOTALS:	**74,460**	**100%**	**+9,454**	**83,914**	**100%**

NOTES: 1. The forecast projections not only change the room occupancy goals but will also cause an "automatic" adjustment of the Market Mix.

2. The new room occupancy goals will also effect an adjustment in the percentage of occupancy:

$$\frac{83,914 \text{ forecasted occupied rooms}}{109,500 \text{ annual rooms available}} = 77\% \text{ projected percentage of occupancy . . . (compared with current 68\%).}$$

50%) for food, beverage, and other services. Alternatively, because the tour groups your property attracts arrive at midnight, eat an early breakfast, and then leave, the F&B/OI Factor might only be .1 ($10 for every $100 of room revenue).

Adding to room night projections, with anticipated outside income that does not involve room nights, results in a total projected annual revenue from all outlets—the fiscal forecast (see Exhibit 6.18).

Key Planning Steps

The preceding exercise was simplified to highlight the main points. Obviously, there are other variables in addition to those shown that can add to or subtract from the sales department's analysis of future market activity.

The key to the forecast is "doing your homework" on both your property and your competition. You must know how to maintain and increase any competitive edge and to enhance the positioning of the property in the minds of its key customer groups.

Keep in mind, however, that changes can occur quite suddenly and unexpectedly—especially those resulting from changing economic, political, and social conditions.

So, it is essential that you constantly monitor the marketplace and the competition to make any necessary adjustments to the forecasts or to prepare contingency programs in case forecasted increases do not materialize.

It is also possible that in order to maintain a competitive advantage your property will have to make some capital expenditures for renovation, modernization, and overall product upgrading. This is particularly true with certain segments of the meetings market where greater sophistication in presentation methods and the demands of the audience require the latest meeting room environment and audiovisual equipment.

Finally, bear in mind that a fiscal forecast is only a working guide. It is subject to constant re-evaluation. Average room rate goals may have to be changed or greater emphasis placed on creative packaging—especially where there are several properties pursuing the same markets without any appreciable differences in products and services.

In this age of product line diversification, competition may suddenly appear from chains and franchise systems that formerly were not competitive with you for certain types of business potentials. This, coupled with modern construction methods, can result in a sudden and significant increase in room inventory, without an appreciable offsetting growth in demand.

Keeping all this in mind, your next major steps after completing the fiscal forecast involve:

1. Expanding on the objectives and goals that relate to fulfilling the forecast
2. Preparing strategies and tactics to accomplish the objectives and goals
3. Preparing specific action plans for each major goal
4. Determining the key decision-makers, those who "move the market"
5. Selecting the appropriate communications tools to cost-effectively reach and persuade the decision-makers
6. Managing the marketing function in terms of personnel, time, and resources

Exhibit 6.18   Annual Revenue Forecast

For the Year_____

IN-HOUSE SEGMENTS	ROOM NIGHTS	AV. RATE	ROOM REVENUE	F&B/OI FACTOR	F&B/OI REVENUE	TOTAL REVENUES
GBM	39,256	$50	$1,962,800	.5	$ 981,400	$2,944,200
ILT	14,201	$55	781,055	.2	156,211	937,266
IBT	14,892	$60	893,520	.3	268,056	1,161,576
GLM	15,565	$45	700,425	.1	70,042	770,467
IN-HOUSE TOTALS:	83,914		$4,337,800		$1,475,709	$5,813,509

OUTSIDE INCOME:

FOOD SALES	(Local civic and service clubs, company parties, weddings, local diners, tour bus meal stops, outside catering, etc.)	800,000
BEVERAGE SALES	(Basically, the same as above)	300,000
OTHER INCOME	(Store rentals/leases, office rentals, retail sales, etc.)	100,000
TOTAL PROJECTED ANNUAL REVENUE FROM ALL OUTLETS		$7,013,509

NOTES: 1. Room Nights × Average Rate = Room Revenue.
2. Room Revenue × F&B/OI Factor = F&B/OI Income.
3. Room Revenue + F&B/OI Revenue = Total Revenue.
4. Other Income for in-house segments includes laundry/valet, phone, recreational equipment rentals, and other miscellaneous sources.

7. Determining on a task basis the costs of achieving objectives and goals and relating them to short-term and long-term anticipated returns (financial management)
8. Securing the necessary funds to properly carry out the activities necessary to reach the forecast (budgeting)
9. Monitoring and evaluating how well you are doing in terms of reaching the goals

Planning Flowchart

Because there is a definite sequence to the activities listed above, a planning flowchart can be helpful in relating each element to the others (see Exhibit 6.19).

Classifications of Strategies

There are three main classifications of strategies used in the hospitality industry: differentiation, segmentation, and combination. Deciding which to employ depends on the characteristics of your property and your target markets.

Differentiation is best used when there is a perceptible, meaningful difference between yourself and your direct competitors. Usually, this difference is physically observable and measurable. You should be able to say that you are the only facility that has a specific feature or service—and it must be useful to the user. For example, "The only conference property with 20 meeting rooms on one floor" is meaningful and points out specific features.

This type of strategy is often employed by newer properties where certain features were built in because the current markets had indicated they were specifically looking for the benefits derived from such features.

Exhibit 6.19 Planning Flowchart

FORECASTING ⟶	OBJECTIVES ⟶	GOALS ⟶	STRATEGIES ⟶
A sound projection of what your business position should be at the end of a specific period.	General aims and targets to reach your forecasts generally indicated as a change in occupancy mix, occupancy percentage, meal covers, public & meeting space utilization, average room rates, percentage of multiple occupancy, etc.	Specific and quantifiable aims and objectives, usually indicated in terms of specific numbers of room nights, meal covers, and corresponding dollar amounts.	The "hows" of the ways you plan to reach goals & objectives. Often grouped within three main categories: 1. Differentiation 2. Segmentation 3. Combination

TACTICS ⟶	ACTION PLANS ⟶	BUDGETING ⟶	MONITORING
The specific "What," "When," "Where," "Why," and "Who" of your strategies.	Timing, assigning, and controlling the strategy and tactics steps which lead to fulfilling each goal & objective.	What it will cost to successfully fulfill your action plans.	How well you are doing at a given time as far as reaching your goals and objectives in relation to your forecasts.

Segmentation strategies relate more directly to characteristics of the user. Older, more established properties that have a reputation within certain market segments are more likely to employ these strategies. The emphasis is on selective, target marketing that is directed at more narrow demographic groupings such as senior citizens, women business travelers, or meetings of international corporations and associations.

Combination strategies seem to be the most prevalent in the present marketing era. They directly relate specific types of properties to the needs of specific types of market segments. The all-suite hotel (differentiation) catering to the woman business traveler (segmentation) is an example of using combination strategies. These strategies are suitable for properties that are either brand new or that have undergone significant rehabilitation and renovation. They also work well for properties that are trying to reposition themselves.

The determination of which type of strategies to employ becomes highly consequential in the selection of sales tools and in determining what to say in sales literature, advertising, and the personal selling activities of the property.

Action Plans

An action plan is the step-by-step, on-paper guide detailing in chronological sequence what is to be done, by whom, when, where, and with what resources. These details relate to the fulfillment of specific goals directed at specified target markets.

Exhibit 6.20 shows a sample format for an action plan. All the plans directed at all the given markets for a given period form the heart of the marketing plan—which in turn is focused on achieving the fiscal forecast.

Exhibit 6.20   Sample Action Plan

TARGET MARKET: TRAINING MEETINGS	OBJECTIVES & GOALS: Build up July & August business by concentrating on securing training meetings business. Increase number of room nights from this market from 4,500 to 6,000.

ACTION STEPS	Responsibility	Jan	Feb	Mar	Apr	May	Jun	Jul	Aug	Sep	Oct	Nov	Dec
Take out membership in CHART	Dir. of Marketing	✔											
Take out membership in ASTD	Dir. of Marketing	✔											
Place 1/2 page ads in "Training & Development Journal"	Dir. of Advertising	✔		✔		✔		✔		✔		✔	
Initial mailing to Corp. Training Directors (purchased list)	Sales Manager		✔										
Follow up mailing to Corp. Training Directors (from responses to first mailing)	Sales Manager				✔								
Attend ASTD Convention	Dir. of Sales						✔						
Develop and initially promote "Training Directors Networking Retreat"	Dir. of Marketing								✔				

Where appropriate, each line item will have a set of "backup" pages detailing the activities and presenting samples of the applicable direct mail pieces and media ads.

One of the critical aspects of marketing relates to the ability to physically "work the plan." Too many inexperienced executives develop too many programs aimed at unrealistically high goals. They have insufficient resources to accomplish even half the objectives and goals in the action plan.

Bear in mind that the previous illustration only showed one sample directed at one market segment. Imagine a property having 20 or 30 such sets of plans directed at securing not only group business but also individual business as well.

Budgeting

The final consideration in the planning sequence is establishing a budget. This is the financial investment that must be made to properly ensure the best implementation of the program.

Budget Methods. The following three budget methods are described because all are used to varying degrees within the industry:

Budgeting by percentage. There are three ways to budget by percentage. In the first, an arbitrary percentage of the previous year's gross income (in some cases, guestrooms income) is set aside for some function. This is probably the easiest way (and the worst, from the marketing standpoint) because it has no relationship whatsoever to the cost of fulfilling your objectives and goals.

Exhibit 6.21 Task Basis Budgeting

TARGET MARKET: TRAINING MEETINGS **OBJECTIVES & GOALS:** Build up July & August business by concentrating on securing training meetings business. Increase number of room nights from this market from 4,500 to 6,000.

ACTION STEPS	Responsibility	Jan	Feb	SALES/ADV. SUPPORT	BUDGET
Take out membership in CHART	Dir. of Marketing	✓		N/A	$ 100.00
Take out membership in ASTD	Dir. of Marketing	✓		N/A	$ 150.00
Place 1/2 page ads in "Training & Development Journal"	Dir. of Advertising	✓		Development and placement of ads with Center City Advertising Agency	$9,000.00
Initial mailing to Corp. Training Directors (purchased list)	Sales Manager			List Purchase: 3,000 names Brochure and cover letter/postage	$ 120.00 $2,300.00
Follow up mailing to Corp. Training Director (from responses to first mailing)	Sales Manager			Special follow-up letter/postage	$ 500.00
Attend ASTD Convention	Dir. of Sales			Registration, travel/rooms/misc. meals Brochures & give-aways	$1,500.00 $ 500.00
Develop and initially promote "Training Directors Networking Retreat"	Dir. of Marketing			Special folder & collateral materials Sales call expenses, 5 key cities	$3,000.00 $2,000.00

NOTE: The figures included in the budget column in the above example are for illustrative purposes only, and are not to be considered reflective of any particular pricing structures.

In the second, an arbitrary percentage is set aside, and this is based on the forecast of total revenue from all outlets for the coming year. This is somewhat better because it is at least related to goals, but it still has no relationship to the actual costs of reaching these goals.

The third way of budgeting by percentage is called the "7%-5.7% Syndrome." This is the most arbitrary of all because you merely take last year's total income and add 7% (or some other figure) to it to derive a new forecast. You then use the average "Marketing and Guest Entertainment" industry percentage as reported by property accounting firms.*

Direct Spending Budgeting. Parity is one type of direct spending budgeting in which you match or exceed what your competitors are doing. Another type consists of allocating funds left over after all operating expenses have been determined.

*The 1986 edition of *Trends in the Hotel Industry* by Pannell Kerr Forster reported that the average marketing percentage of total revenue for 1,000 hotels was 5.7%. However, this is only a report of what actually took place. It should not be used as the sole determinant of what a particular operation should do for a future period—especially since this average was computed on revenue from different size properties in different competitive situations. Each property must determine what is best for it.

The problem with both types is that they have nothing to do with what you are trying to accomplish.

Task Basis Budgeting. This method is based on what it will cost to develop, implement, and evaluate the cost of securing business. It is also called "zero-based" budgeting because it is not based on arbitrary percentages or on figures relating to past activities.*

The starting point for calculating a budget using the task basis method is to expand the various sales action plans by adding two additional columns (or by developing a sales cost analysis addendum to each action plan) that list the sales tools and promotional activities for each action step along with the projected costs. Exhibit 6.21 shows an example of this based on the previous sample action plan.

The total amount of all promotional expenditures for all action plans forms the basis for calculating a task-basis budget. However, it is not "cast in stone" and should retain some flexibility.

There are several key areas that must be considered if flexibility is to be maintained.

You must consider the costs of developing contingency programs. Consider, for example, the case of a severe economic recession during which most companies cut back or eliminate their outside training programs. The property must find alternative types of business to help fill the 6,000-room-night goal it has set for the training market—and for which promotional funds have already been spent. Now, the property must incur additional, non-budgeted promotional costs.

You must know the costs of conversion (also known as fulfillment costs). In the example shown in Exhibit 6.20, $500 was set aside for a follow-up mailing to the initial direct mail program. But what if the property receives twice the anticipated return from the initial mailing to which it must now send out follow-up letters? From where will an additional $500 come?

Finally, you must take into account advertising wearout. This is a relatively new consideration. It relates to the concept that advertising themes and campaigns may have to be changed after several years because the audience becomes so used to them that they lose their attention-getting impact. Thus, additional costs might be unexpectedly incurred, particularly those for the creative expenses of developing a new theme and campaign.

To compensate for these and other similar variables, it is advisable to include a contingency reserve in the sales/marketing budget that will vary percentage-wise according to the amount of advertising done (in contrast with direct selling methods) and the volatility of the primary market segments.

To complete the budget, it will be necessary to add the administrative costs of running the sales/marketing department.

The Hotel Sales & Marketing Association International (HSMAI) has devised the following budget classification system with its associated sales and marketing department expense items:

---

*This method does not totally ignore the use of percentages. Under task basis budgeting, industry-wide percentages can be helpful *guides* in evaluating the budget to determine if it is out of line—whether too little or too much has been allocated.

Any costs associated with media usage and merchandising should be charged to Advertising and Merchandising.

Advertising and Merchandising

Direct Mail

Fees for Outside Service (Public Relations and Advertising firms)

In-House Graphics

Outdoor (Billboards, etc.)

Point-of-Sale Material

Printing:
Magazine—Group and Travel
Magazine—Other
Newspapers

Production

Radio and TV

Other_____

Total Advertising and Merchandising: $_____

Other marketing activities including convention bureau costs, convention funds, and costs for research should be charged to Other Marketing Activities.

Other Marketing Activities

Civic and Community Projects

Guest History/Research

Outside Services (Consulting or Market Research Firms)

Photography

Other_____

Total Other Marketing Activities: $_____

The following fees are associated with franchise companies and other fees paid for outside marketing services:

Fees and Commissions

Franchise Fees/Royalty Fees

Marketing Fees (National Fees Paid to Parent Company or Franchise Company)

Representative Firms

Trade-Outs/Due Bills/Barter

Other_____

Total Fees and Commission: $_____

Costs relating to reservations in many properties are accounted for in the rooms department. However, more and more properties recognize these functions as sales/marketing responsibilities and charge the following to the sales/marketing department:

Reservations

    Supplies/Forms

    Postage

    Reservation Fees

    Telephone

    Training

    Travel Agency Commission

    Other_____

       Total Reservations: $_____

The following items are associated with the functional management of the sales/marketing department and also include "charge backs" for complimentary rooms:

Sales and Marketing Functions

    Complimentary Rooms

    Dues and Subscriptions

    Operating Supplies

    Postage

    Telephone

    Trade Show

    Travel and Entertainment
        In-House
        In the Field

    Sales Training/Seminars

    Other_____

       Total Sales and Marketing: $_____

The organization chart and reporting structure of the property will affect the departmental allocations of salaries and wages. At some properties, convention servicing is a separate department; at others it may be included under catering; and in still others convention servicing falls directly under the responsibility of the sales/marketing department.

Payroll

    Salaries and Wages

    Employee Benefits and Payroll Taxes

      Total Payroll: $_____

      TOTAL MARKETING EXPENSES: $_____

Remember, the figures for the budget breakdown classification just illustrated are not filled in ahead of time (as is done in some other methods of budgeting). They are calculated from the line items in the various action plans, to which are then added the administrative costs of operating the sales/marketing department.

Chapter Summary

We have completed the initial stage of preparing to sell and service convention and group business.

Up to this point, we have described the nature of the hospitality industry and shown how marketing applies to the industry. We have looked at the development of the marketing plan and discussed the basic principles of analysis as applied to the product, the market, and the competition. We analyzed property needs and examined the principles of forecasting. Finally, we defined the key planning steps necessary to formulate a workable program of business development.

Our next step is make certain we have the right administrative environment, including organization, procedures, systems, and other management considerations essential to proper departmental functioning.

Notes

1. David C. Dorf, *Marketing for the Hospitality Industry* (Ottawa, Canada: Management Development Unit of the Department of Manpower and Immigration, 1967), pp. R23-R31.
2. Peter C. Yesawich, "How to Develop a Marketing Program," *The Cornell Hotel & Restaurant Quarterly* (November 1978 and May 1979).

7 Organizing to Sell and Service

Chapter Objectives

1. To understand marketing as a management function
2. To learn staffing considerations for a sales/marketing department
3. To understand the responsibilities inherent in job descriptions
4. To understand how to use various filing systems
5. To identify work forms
6. To learn how computerization affects administrative aspects of the sales/marketing department

After a marketing approach has been developed, the property sales executive can begin the more structured process of organizing to sell and service.

Administratively, the organization process consists of developing well-defined job descriptions, setting up an effective files and records system, and taking full advantage of computerized systems.

This chapter concludes with a comprehensive checklist that examines all administrative and operational aspects of the sales and marketing department.

Marketing as a Management Function

The term "management" is one of the most widely used words in our industry. Management has been described as the process of getting things done through others. In career areas like hospital administration, managers may not necessarily be experts in any particular area of specialization. Rather, these persons are facilitators, drawing on, integrating, and directing the combined talents of departmental specialists.

As the complexities of property sales and marketing grow and as customers become more specialized, we are finding that in the larger convention properties the vice president of marketing now must also be a facilitator—an administrative generalist. The remainder of the staff can be specialists working within specifically designated customer groups, but the department head must be able to direct them.

The main management responsibilities of the top sales/marketing executive generally fall within four key areas:

1. *Planning*
   a. Forecasting (analysis management)
   b. Programming (systems management)
   c. Scheduling (time/staff management)
   d. Budgeting (financial management)

2. *Organizing*
   a. Delegating (transferring responsibility and authority)
   b. Developing organizational structure (creating the "winning team" spirit)
   c. Developing organizational relationships (interdepartmental cooperation)

3. *Leading*
   a. Communicating
   b. Motivating
   c. Staff development (training and human resources development)

4. *Controlling*
   a. Developing performance standards
   b. Measuring and evaluating
   c. Retraining
   d. Time and stress management

Many of the above responsibilities have a direct relationship with the four key steps of the marketing plan cycle: research, planning, execution, and management. Thus, there exists a strong connection between two major components of management: operations and marketing.

About 25 years ago, it would have been unthinkable for sales executives at most properties to have direct operational responsibilities. Today, it is not uncommon for a sales or marketing executive to serve in any of the following capacities: acting manager when the general manager is off the property; manager on duty or manager of the day on a regularly scheduled basis; and night manager or weekend manager on an assigned rotation.

One of the major benefits of this realignment is that the sales/marketing executive quickly learns what the property can or cannot produce. It also helps this person establish visibility and rapport with guest-contact employees in the operating departments.

Marketing Responsibilities

In recent years, the duties and responsibilities of a modern marketing executive have broadened considerably. Today's executive wears three hats: department head, personal salesperson, and sales trainer.

HSMAI's career booklet, *Career Tips in Hotel Sales and Marketing*, emphasizes this three-hat concept, as shown in Exhibit 7.1.

Staffing Considerations

Can one person perform all the duties listed in Exhibit 7.1?

In a smaller property of 100 rooms or less, the answer is usually a qualified "yes." Many of the functions shown would not apply to any great extent in the smaller property, and many of the secretarial and filing duties could be delegated to staff members in other departments.

Could one person perform all these duties in a 1,000-room property? Yes, if he or she used the managerial principle known as delegation. In a 1,000-room property that concentrates heavily on convention and group business, as many as 15 to 20 other executives might staff the sales/marketing department. The top executive in the department actually becomes a generalist, a facilitator. He or she manages the skills and efforts of the specialists within the department. These specialists would have been hired (or subsequently trained) because they possessed the skills and knowledge to solicit and book the types of business that fulfill the objectives and goals of the property.

There are some rules of thumb that apply to the number of people that should staff a sales/marketing department. One is to hire one person for every 100 rooms at the property, up to and including 500 rooms. After that, hire 1 1/2 persons for every 100 rooms. However, this is only a rough guideline. There are other factors that influence the validity of this formula:

1. The market mix—the ratio of convention and group business to individual business and leisure travel

2. The type of convention and group business and the relative size of the average group booked (large association conventions or a multitude of small group bookings)

3. The amount and relative stability of contract business

4. The ratio of repeat and referral business

5. The department's scope of activity

6. The company's sales and service philosophy

The last item is particularly important if sales or account executives service the accounts they book. If this is the case, the department may require additional sales or account executives because a large part of their time is necessarily spent on in-house activities relating to the booking. Thus, each is responsible for fewer accounts than those who only solicit bookings and then turn them over to the property's convention service staff.

It is very difficult to come up with any ideal staffing formula that will work for all properties.

Exhibit 7.1 Typical Duties and Responsibilities of a Hotel/Motel Marketing Executive

1. **A DEPARTMENT HEAD:**

   General
   a. Recruits, hires, and trains staff.
   b. Prepares job descriptions for each departmental position.
   c. Sets standards, supervises, evaluates, and reviews staff performance.
   d. Coordinates and cooperates with other department heads to provide maximum service.
   e. Participates in industry meetings, seminars, and conventions.
   f. Develops departmental incentive programs.

   Specific
   a. Carries out the marketing policy and sales "philosophy" of the property or company.
   b. Establishes sales goals and objectives.
   c. Develops strategies, tactics, and action plans for each goal and objective.
   d. Determines marketing budget, allocates funds, and evaluates results.
   e. Sets up records, filing systems, trace, and follow-up procedures.
   f. Selects appropriate media for use in specific programs.
   g. Works with advertising agency in preparation of advertising material.
   h. Sets up direct mail advertising programs; establishes and maintains mailing lists.
   i. Develops publicity and public relations programs.
   j. Prepares internal selling programs.
   k. Continually evaluates markets and their needs, comparing them with present products and services.
   l. Creatively develops programs for merchandising rooms, food & beverages.
   m. Develops package programs, tour packages, holiday and special event promotions, off-season ("value" season) programs, etc.
   n. Maintains awareness of competition ("shopping the competition").

2. **A PERSONAL SALESMAN:**
   a. Maintains contacts with existing customers.
   b. Solicits new business.
   c. Assists subordinates in closing sales.
   d. Explores potentials for additional business from existing accounts.

3. **A SALES TRAINER:**
   a. Prepares job specifications for various sales department positions.
   b. Trains new sales staff members.
   c. Conducts sales training meetings for own staff—and for members of other departments.
   d. Trains guest-contact employees in techniques of providing "sales-minded service."
   e. Trains guest-contact employees to be both "customer oriented" and "product oriented" through proper use of the techniques of "suggestive selling."

Source: HSMA International, *Career Tips in Hotel Sales and Marketing.*

Organization Charts

One of the key considerations in the sales/marketing departmental organization is the composition of the staff. There is no ideal table of organization. Many of the same considerations concerning the number of staff members also apply to the type of staff members and their duties and responsibilities.

Exhibit 7.2 shows a sample organization chart for a large property concentrating on a variety of different convention and group business markets. Note that each major segment has an account executive (a specialist) specifically assigned to it.

There are many modifications of this basic organization chart. For example, some operations now include the reservations office within the sales/marketing department. In others, the rooms division manager reports directly to the vice president of marketing. In effect, the front office becomes an integral part of the sales/marketing department. This arrangement is particularly suited to properties that are very convention and meetings oriented.

At larger properties where the association market is national or international in scope, there may be a further breakdown within the association meetings division. You might find a separate account executive for national associations, another who concentrates on regional organizations, and still another who works the state and local associations field.

These arrangements must be correlated with the action plans in the overall marketing plan.

In order for an organization chart to be meaningful and functional, it is necessary to define in writing the responsibilities and duties of each position. It is helpful to have both a condensed position description and a more detailed job description.

The following position descriptions are taken from the HSMAI publication referred to earlier in this chapter and reflect the general responsibilities of the key positions within the sales/marketing structure as shown on the chart in Exhibit 7.2.

Vice President of Marketing

The vice president of marketing establishes annual marketing programs aimed at developing maximum business volume and profits for rooms, food, beverage, and other department outlets; undertakes both product and market research, analysis, and planning; formulates fiscal goals and objectives; prepares sales forecasts, strategies, action plans, and promotional budgets; trains and develops sales and servicing personnel; and supervises and coordinates all related promotional activities such as direct selling, advertising, publicity, and public relations.

Director of Sales

The director of sales administers, coordinates, and supervises the activities of sales department executives who are responsible for soliciting and servicing conventions, sales meetings, tours, and other groups requiring public space and room accommodations. He or she also helps create and implement programs aimed at developing room, food, and beverage business from the individual business and leisure traveler.

Director of Advertising

The director of advertising develops coordinated advertising programs and campaigns involving newspapers, magazines, radio and TV, outdoor advertising, and direct mail. This person works closely with advertising agencies to create and produce advertising and promotional literature.

Exhibit 7.2 Sample Sales/Marketing Organization Chart

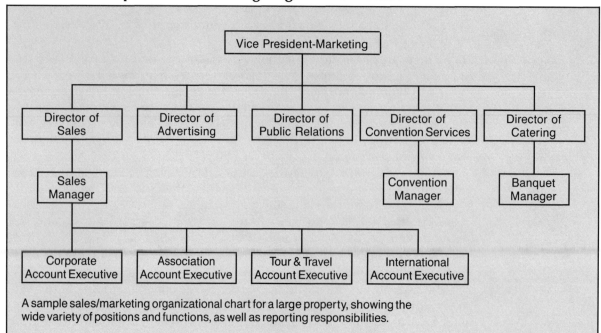

A sample sales/marketing organizational chart for a large property, showing the wide variety of positions and functions, as well as reporting responsibilities.

Director of Public Relations	The director of public relations is responsible for developing positive programs directed at maximizing the property's "image" and its relations with the community, its employees, its guests, the industry, and the general public.
International Sales Manager	The international sales manager coordinates activities specifically aimed at stimulating and developing individual and group business from areas outside the country.
Regional Director of Sales	The regional director of sales is responsible for soliciting accounts within a specific geographic region, generally (though not always) working within a chain or franchise system. This individual may also coordinate promotional activities for the properties within that region, and supplies input relating to advertising, sales promotion, and publicity.
Tour and Agency Manager	The tour and agency manager is responsible for developing both group and individual business through personal contacts with travel wholesalers, travel agents, tour operators, transportation companies, and carrier representatives.
Convention Service Manager	The convention service manager coordinates the activities of all property departments to ensure maximum service to conventions and other groups once they are in the property. The service manager is also responsible for supervising all "in house" activities of the groups that involve property services.
Account or Sales Executive	The account or sales executive contacts both repeat and new business prospects on a regularly established basis through personal visits, telephone calls, and direct mail, for the specific purpose of booking a continuous flow of profitable business.

Each of these basic position descriptions would be expanded into a more detailed job description.

Job Descriptions

One of the challenges in the hospitality industry with respect to job descriptions is that there is no uniformity of titles and even less uniformity in the descriptions themselves.

The example in Exhibit 7.3 is shown mainly for its format rather than to suggest any standardized content. It provides a detailed description of the duties of the convention service manager. You may want to keep this job description in mind when reading Chapter 9, because it directly relates to many of the topics covered in that chapter on servicing a meeting or conference.

Job descriptions are more than just delineations of the responsibilities associated with each position or title. They can also serve as training tools, as employee upgrading and promotion programs, as a means of review and evaluation, and as "backup" during Equal Employment Opportunity Commission (EEOC) audits.

Formal job descriptions also help define the types of records, forms, and filing systems each sales/marketing executive needs to fulfill the functions and responsibilities of the specific job title.

Files and Records

The heart of all marketing activity is found in the records and files systems.* These systems can be manual, computerized, or both.

Because the marketing concept is so critical to both soliciting and servicing convention and group business, detailed accounts are required. These include such information as the past history of group prospects, where and when they hold meetings, who makes decisions, and how and when decisions are made. These historical accounts of past dealings with your property make it essential that you have sophisticated but practical systems and procedures.

It is important that a large convention property have the means to quickly access and retrieve information for planning sales and promotion activities as they relate to the goals and objectives of the marketing plan. This may involve as many as 10,000 account files. And, it is apparent that systemized tracing or follow-up procedures are even more important.

So, the first consideration is determining the type of information you need to record for each prospect or client. Exhibit 7.4 depicts the type of information that is needed for both corporate and association groups.

All this information is recorded and maintained on a variety of work forms and records within various types of filing systems.

---

*Although there is a tendency to use both terms interchangeably, for our purposes a "record" is a document of past history or future commitments. A "file" can be both the device in which records are maintained or a collection of records relating to a specific person or group.

Exhibit 7.3   Sample Job Description: Convention Service Manager

Primary Duties

The convention service manager or director of convention services is in charge of and responsible for representing the property to the convention and corporate meeting officials, their organizations' staffs and leadership, and to their meeting attendees, once the booking has been made and confirmed.

This person's basic responsibilities are to ensure that schedules are maintained and that services are rendered to the customer by the facility in accordance with the written and signed agreements or contracts made with the buyer at the time the convention or meeting was booked.

This position involves continuous coordination with the various operating departments to make certain that quality service standards are maintained. It also ensures that all elements of the convention or meeting, from the time of attendee arrival through the setup to billing and departures, run smoothly and efficiently.

The director of convention services is the chief liaison between the property and the convention or meeting group. In addition to these public relations and service roles, the director of convention services has a sales responsibility to the facility for re-booking the group by providing the best service and follow-through.

In addition to these primary functions, the director of convention services has tasks in the following areas:

Administrative Responsibilities

1. Develop objectives, goals, and policies relating to the group business servicing philosophy and procedures of the property, for approval by the director of marketing and the property's management committee.

2. Develop administrative procedures relating to the daily servicing operations of the facility; establish a procedure for daily review of each convention or group in the house.

3. Maintain the necessary records and filing systems to provide detailed information about the servicing requirements of each group.

4. Maintain inventory of necessary equipment and supplies for the setup of meeting and function rooms; ensure that proper maintenance and replacement programs are followed.

5. Work with outside audiovisual companies for the securing of special equipment not carried by the property.

6. Work with the local convention bureau and with counterparts in other properties in situations where multiple housing or use of outside meeting facilities are needed.

Working Relations with Sales/Marketing Department

1. Work with the director of marketing and the sales/marketing staff to develop and implement sales and servicing programs relating to the development, servicing, and retention of conventions and group business.

2. Coordinate directly with the account executive responsible for each booking to ensure the smooth transition of the handling of the account between the time of the booking and the arrival of the group.

Inter-Departmental Relations

1. Work with the rooms division manager concerning the allocation and assignment of guestrooms, especially VIP and hospitality suites.

2. Work with the catering manager on allocating function space and ensure proper entries in the function book.

3. Work with the food and beverage manager on matters relating to food production, theme parties, and other meal functions.

4. Work with the housekeeping department to handle special housekeeping requirements, such as servicing VIP accommodations and hospitality suites.

5. Work with maintenance and engineering to ensure proper meeting and function room climate control, special utility requests for meeting rooms and exhibit areas, and general maintenance operations.

6. Work with security to ensure proper procedures are followed for securing the registration desk, exhibit areas, and storage space used by each group.

Exhibit 7.3 *(continued)*

7. Work with the accounting department to ensure proper billing procedures are followed and that a system is established for a daily review of the group's master account.

8. Coordinate the activities of all property departments participating in the servicing of each convention and meeting, and ensure on an event-by-event basis that all servicing details by all departments are carried out.

9. Prepare and distribute detailed requirements memoranda to all department heads well in advance of each convention or meeting.

Customer Service Responsibilities

1. Take over each account after confirmation of booking and contact the group's meeting planner or other representative to establish a schedule of communications.

2. Meet with association executives, corporate meeting planners, and other convention officials to finalize plans concerning details of meetings, food and beverage functions, and recreational/entertainment activities that are part of the program; offer assistance, ideas, and creative input to help showcase the program activities.

3. Maintain a checklist of services available from both the property and outside local firms, including audiovisual equipment, exhibit management services, security, printing, registration desk personnel, photography, and entertainment.

4. Inform convention representatives of local fire regulations, room occupancy limitations, exhibit area floor load allowances, drinking age and beverage servicing restrictions, and other legal requirements.

5. Check on behalf of convention or meeting representatives with the property's operating departments to ensure that rooms, food, reception, meeting, and exhibit space have been blocked and that servicing requirements are understood in accordance with the contract or letters of agreement.

6. Periodically inform the operating departments of any changes, additions, or deletions concerning meeting requirements.

7. Working with the meeting planner, prepare a detailed servicing memorandum on a daily, event-by-event basis.

8. Schedule a pre-convention briefing session with the convention and meeting representatives and the property department heads the day prior to the opening session to review all details and record any last-minute changes.

9. Greet convention representatives upon arrival and show them locations of meeting and exhibit areas, food and beverage outlets, and other features of the property.

10. Check daily on each meeting and function room, exhibit area, and registration area to ensure that proper room setup, audiovisual equipment, supplies, and other servicing details have been taken care of in accordance with the customer's requirements.

11. Ensure that the time and location of each event is posted daily on reader boards, in elevators, and distributed as a daily events sheet to all departments; check to make sure that function signs are placed around appropriate doorways and that directional signs are properly placed.

12. Maintain close communication with the customer to coordinate any last-minute changes.

13. Contact convention officials at the end of the program to discuss their plans for future events and issue invitations to return.

14. Prepare a detailed critique at the end of the convention comparing forecasted room pick-ups and meeting/function guarantees with actual figures.

15. Schedule a post-convention briefing between the convention officials and property department heads to discuss the results of the convention on a department-by-department basis.

Source: HSMA International, *Career Tips in Hotel Sales and Marketing*.

Filing Systems   As this book is being written, the industry is in the middle of a transition between manual file maintenance and computerization. At the present time, the very large and the very small properties use computers to a greater extent

Exhibit 7.4   Type of Information Needed Concerning Client

1. The normal meeting period of the organization, including the days of the week preferred
2. Qualification as to whether there is any degree of flexibility in the selection of dates
3. Expected attendance in terms of number of people attending as well as the number of guestrooms required
4. Breakdown of types of rooms and suites required (number of single rooms, double rooms, twin-bedded rooms, family style accommodations, and suites)
5. Arrival and departure patterns; number of rooms to be occupied by specific nights prior to, during, and after the convention
6. The prospect's preferred policy concerning guestroom charges; preference for a rack rate or a flat rate setup
7. A day-by-day recap of the organization's meeting room requirements, including specific hours for each meeting, type of setup required, and any unusual needs for audiovisual presentations
8. A complete breakdown of all food and beverage functions
9. Hospitality suite requirements
10. Detailed exhibition requirements, including number of gross feet required for the exhibit, as well as unusual needs like water, steam, gas, or electricity
11. Previous convention locations
12. Sites that have been selected for future conventions on a tentative basis
13. Sites that have been selected for future conventions on a definite basis
14. Those individuals having authority to select the city or the general location for the meeting
15. When the selection of the city or general location normally occurs
16. Those individuals having authority to select the headquarters property for the meeting
17. The normal time period in which the selection of property headquarters is made
18. Whether an invitation is required from a local chapter or a local member; if this is a requisite, the property sales executive should then obtain the names and addresses of such contacts
19. Whether the organization follows a geographic rotation policy; if so, a determination of when the group is expected to return to the area in which the property is located
20. The name, title, and address of the person from whom this information was obtained, as well as the date the information was secured and the name of the sales executive receiving the information

than the medium-size properties. This is probably because the larger properties can afford the more sophisticated sales office computer systems, while the small properties can more readily adapt the more economical PC systems to serve their needs.

We will concentrate on manual setups and systems for two reasons: (1) the theories and principles behind the systems and procedures are more readily observable and (2) no matter how totally computerized the sales office may be, certain manual systems will always be needed for backup.

The key element in the entire filing system is the **master file**, also called the file jacket, master folder, or letter folder. In most cases, it actually is a 9-by 12-inch tab-cut manila folder kept in a special sequence in a file cabinet.

The initial physical arrangement is usually by broad market classifications: association (often subdivided by national, regional, state, and local groups through the use of color coding); corporate; tour and travel; and catering/banquet.

The individual files within each of these groupings are then arranged by one of the following methods: alphabetical; key word; or numerical. Each system has inherent advantages and disadvantages.

Alphabetical systems are easy to sort and locate, but they become cumbersome at larger properties having a large number of national accounts. For example, a substantial number of files will begin with the words "American" or "National." This means you must then use the second and even third word for proper alphabetizing.

Key word systems (in which files are arranged alphabetically according to the most important word of the organization's name) must often rely on a judgment call. For example, what is the key word for the "Hotel Sales & Marketing Association"? It could be any one of the first three words. But some properties, especially those whose accounts can be grouped mainly within very specific professions or specialized fields of interests, have found key word systems to be workable.

Numerical systems using a combination of numbers and letters (e.g., A-101 or C-402) can be quickly and efficiently located. However, they are not as easy to initially identify, especially if you do not have immediate access to the coding system.

There are two secondary categories that will either be incorporated within the system or maintained separately: hold files and neutralized files.

Hold or Pending Files. These files are set up for new accounts you are working on but that you have never booked. Once the first booking is made, the file will be integrated into its proper place within the association, corporate, tour and travel, or catering files section.

Neutralized Files. These files are also known as dead or canceled files and are the opposite of pending files. These are former accounts that you have lost for one reason or another. If lost business is deemed unsalvageable, the file should still be maintained in a separate area for later follow-up, especially should the property want to expand or upgrade.

Work Forms

Work forms provide a continuous method of obtaining and recording data and information vital for successful selling and servicing of a convention or meeting.

Forms are means of permanently recording the history of contacts with each client. They also aid in systematic follow-up for both selling and re-booking.

There are at least eight forms that should become an integral part of each file:

Front sheet. This is the basic form summarizing all the pertinent information necessary to properly sell to and service the account. It is usually attached to the inside front cover of the master file.

Call report. This form is the "Report of Interview" that details the account or sales executive's contacts with the client. It also contains information essential for follow-up action.

Proposal or letter of invitation. This item is sent to a prospect who shows interest in meeting with you for a specific event. The proposal outlines in general terms the facilities and services the facility can offer.

Contract or letter of agreement. This is sent to a client after the verbal confirmation of a specific booking. It sets forth specific details about dates, rooms, space, etc., and also serves as a legal document confirming the obligations of both buyer and seller. A separate form, which includes detailed rules and regulations, is usually prepared to cover any commercial exhibits.

Booking report. The booking report is a set of forms used mainly for internal distribution to appropriate departments. There are three varieties of this form: tentative booking, confirmed booking, and cancellation.

Follow-up correspondence. Generally, this includes copies of all correspondence exchanged during the time between the confirmation of the booking and the arrival of the group. The correspondence usually relates to adjustments in the room block, function space, and guarantees for meals and receptions. Maintaining this correspondence with groups that have booked several years in advance is very important.* It is also essential to have this documentation when the property account executive turns the bookings over to the convention service staff for follow-up.

Detailed requirements memorandum. This is an event-by-event listing of the customer's program needs, from arrival through departure. It is used internally and also with the customer during pre- and post-convention briefings.

Guest history. This is often maintained on a departmental basis. It is a recap of the group's activities and value. It compares projected or guaranteed figures with actual pickups and event attendance. It should also show departmental revenue, including the amount of public food and beverage usage during free time or non-scheduled events.**

There may be other types of information placed in the master files, depending on the size and type of property. For example, a lead or referral form is often used by chain or franchise properties to record information exchanged between the property and its national or regional sales office. Information is often exchanged between properties within the system.

Reference and Work Files

Because of the sheer size of the active files, quick reference systems can aid when you have to work with the files. These reference systems, usually maintained on 3- by 5-inch cards, include the following:

Master cards. These are kept alphabetically and usually contain the name of the group, address, phone number, and key contact.

---

*It has been said that in situations where the booking is more than two years in advance, in all probability one or both of the parties concerned will no longer be with their respective organizations. In this age of rapid career changes, the property's account executive might be sent to another property, while the association executive or corporate meeting planner may have been moved to another job within the organization but at a different location.
**This is not difficult to track because the majority of attendees will sign charges to their room accounts. Personal charges for dining room, lounge, room service, laundry, valet, and phone services can be extracted from the individual folios. You should also include a copy of the convention or meeting program because many organizations retain the same format year after year.

Geographic card. This is essentially the same as the master card, but it is maintained alphabetically by state or key feeder city groupings. It is especially useful when planning sales calls and sales blitzes. These cards are essential if the property sales staff is organized by geographic territory instead of by market segment.

Key-word file. This system is used when the master files are maintained alphabetically according to a key word. This reference file is kept in a regular alpha sequence according to the first word of the name of the group, with the key word underscored. This is basically a backup system to be used when the key word of the name of a group is not readily apparent.

Key contact file. This is another cross reference to the master files. In this case, a file is kept alphabetically by the last name of the key contact. The only other listing on this card is the full name of the association or company.

Trace file. This is also known as the "tickler" or the follow-up file. Its use can make or break the sales/marketing effort because ineffective or inoperable tracing systems result in a significant amount of lost business. File cards are maintained in chronological order, by dates within each month. For example, your last contact with a potential client indicated they would consider sites for their next annual sales meeting during the middle of next July. You would then insert a trace card in the file within the July grouping. The card should contain the name of the group and include space to record when the file was traced and by whom. The person working the tracing system (usually one of the secretarial staff) places the appropriate file on your desk for action, usually the day before.

Internal Records

There are a number of other records and files used for storing information for internal use. These include:

Function book. This is sometimes called the function diary, and it is a day-by-day, room-by-room blocking of meeting and function space on both a tentative and confirmed basis. There are two key rules that must be observed to prevent double bookings and misuse of the facilities: (a) only one function book is to be maintained and (b) one person must have control of entries.

Function setup or banquet order form. This is a document backing up each entry in the function book. Very often, it serves as the function contract between the property and the client.

Function change form. This form is used to record changes in the function book, such as a change in status from tentative to definite, changes in date, time, number of people, etc.

Rooms control record. This document is often maintained as a hanging calendar-style chart. Future room allocations and blocks are usually indicated by color coding on acetate, with the name of the groups also listed across the applicable dates. It serves as a combination room availability and future booking status report.

Daily events sheets. These are prepared for each day's group events. They generally contain the name of each group and the type, hours, and location of each group function. Sometimes they include additional information like the name of the person in charge and the number of persons expected for each function. These forms are generally prepared from the entries in the function book and then are distributed the evening preceding each day to all departments. They can be used for daily review meetings and postings to reader boards.

Weekly events sheets. These are compilations of future daily events sheets. Although the sheets are called "weekly," many properties prepare them on Thursday to cover the period between and including the second following Sunday. In effect, they cover a 10-day period with a weekend overlap. These forms also serve as forecasting guides for the operating departments because they pinpoint staffing requirements.

Information Records

This category is a catchall for records that do not readily fall into the other classifications.

Some properties maintain **reading files** that contain file copies of all pertinent correspondence originated by each member of the sales/marketing department. They are retained for weekly review by the head of the department.

General **information files** also may be kept on a need or use basis. They can include samples of advertising, press releases, special packages and promotions, special projects, mailing lists, reference source lists, etc.

At facilities where there is considerable correspondence for soliciting, booking, servicing, and following up accounts, a **form letter file** can be very valuable—especially now since the use of word processors allows these letters to be customized. Exhibits 7.5 through 7.10 show some of the more common standardized forms and records referred to in this chapter.

Computerization

The benefits to be gained from automating and computerizing the sales/marketing function are just now becoming evident. Most, if not all, the filing systems, records, and forms covered in this chapter can be readily converted to computerized systems. Even basic equipment like word processors can greatly increase the efficiency of the office by combining speed with accuracy.

Certain forms and procedures can be computerized very easily. These include the function book, guest history, time and territory management records concerning sales calls, correspondence, and trace or follow-up records.

The Foundation of the Hotel Sales & Marketing Association International and the Educational Institute of the American Hotel & Motel Association have jointly produced a publication written by Charles L. Eudy, *Automating Hotel/Motel Sales Functions: A How-To Manual on Computerizing the Sales Department* (see the Reference Section at the end of this book for

Exhibit 7.5 Front Sheet for an Association File

Trade Associations—Regional or Local

File Name_____

Executive and Title_____

Association Name_____

Street Address_____

City, State and Zip Code_____Phone_____

Additional Executive and Title_____Phone_____

City, State and Zip Code_____

Exhibit Manager and Title_____Phone_____

City, State and Zip Code_____

Size of Meeting_____to_____Persons.   Month(s) Preferred_____ _____ _____

Number of Rooms_____(S) _____(D) _____(T) _____(SU)   Number of Days_____

Number of Exhibits_____to_____   Size_____

Meeting Attendance_____to_____   Function Attendance_____to_____

Follow-Up Record

Year	Jan	Feb	Mar	Apr	May	June	July	Aug	Sept	Oct	Nov	Dec

Cities and Hotels Being Considered for Future Years:

19____ _____   19____ _____

19____ _____   19____ _____

19____ _____   19____ _____

19____ _____   19____ _____

19____ _____   19____ _____

Potential Source of Business Rating: ☐ Fair   ☐ Good   ☐ Excellent

Hotel Preference: ☐ Downtown   ☐ Airport   ☐ Resort   ☐ Commercial   ☐ Combination

☐ Inn   ☐ Motel   ☐ Other_____

Comments_____
_____
_____
_____

Exhibit 7.6   Front Sheet for a Corporate Account File

Corporate Account

File Name_____

Contact and Title_____

Company Name_____

Street Address_____

City, State and Zip Code_____Phone_____

Local Contact and Title_____Phone_____

Address_____

Additional Contact_____Phone_____

Potential Business: ☐ Sales Incentives ☐ Sales Meetings ☐ Conferences ☐ Conventions

☐ Trade Shows ☐ Employee Tours ☐ Individual Room Reservations

Food and Beverage Functions_____Other_____

Home Office_____

Follow-Up Record

Year	Jan	Feb	Mar	Apr	May	June	July	Aug	Sept	Oct	Nov	Dec

Potential Source of Business Rating: ☐ Fair   ☐ Good   ☐ Excellent

Hotel Preference: ☐ Downtown   ☐ Airport   ☐ Resort   ☐ Commercial   ☐ Combination

☐ Inn   ☐ Motel   ☐ Other_____

(1) Size of Meeting_____to_____Persons   Number Per Year_____

   Rooms Required_____(S) _____(D) _____(T) _____(SU)

   Number of Days_____ Months Preferred_____ _____ _____

(2) Size of Meeting_____to_____Persons   Number Per Year_____

   Rooms Required_____(S) _____(D) _____(T) _____(SU)

   Number of Days_____ Months Preferred_____ _____ _____

(3) Size of Meeting_____to_____Persons   Number Per Year_____

   Rooms Required_____(S) _____(D) _____(T) _____(SU)

   Number of Days_____ Months Preferred_____ _____ _____

(4) Size of Meeting_____to_____Persons   Number Per Year_____

   Rooms Required_____(S) _____(D) _____(T) _____(SU)

   Number of Days_____ Months Preferred_____ _____ _____

Comments_____

_____

_____

Exhibit 7.7 Call Report Form for Association Accounts

CONVENTION REPORT FORM

Date_____ Year_____ Salesman_____

Name of Organization_____

Address_____

Name and Title of Contact_____

Name and Title of Person Spoken With_____

Type Contact: ☐ Telephone ☐ In Person ☐ In Hotel ☐ In Client's Office

Normal Meeting Month_____ Attendance_____ Bedrooms_____

Number and Size of Exhibits_____

Future Definite Arrangements:

Date	City	Hotel Headquarters

Future Tentative Selection or Cities Being Considered (Indicate Which)

_____

_____

_____

- Who Selects City?_____

- Who Selects Hotel?_____

- Are Local Invitations Required?_____

When Will Decisions Be Made?_____

Has Group Ever Met In Our City? ☐ Yes ☐ No When_____

Future Possibilities: ☐ Excellent ☐ Good ☐ Fair ☐ Poor

Does Group Have Other Meetings For Which We Can Be Considered?_____
(Such as Board of Directors, State, District or Regional Meetings. If so, fill in separate sheets on these meetings.)

- (On reverse side list names & addresses of local or committee contacts, meeting requirements, additional information, etc.).

Exhibit 7.8   Call Report Form for Corporate Accounts

CORPORATE OR INDUSTRIAL REPORT FORM

Date_____Year_____   Salesman_____

Name of Firm_____

Address_____

Name and Title of Contact_____

Name and Title of Person Spoken With_____

Type Contact: ☐ Telephone   ☐ In Person   ☐ In Hotel   ☐ In Client's Office

Type Function (Sales Meeting, Training Meeting, Retirement Dinner, Etc.)_____

Expected Attendance_____ Bedroom Requirements_____

Date(s) of Function_____

How Often Is Function Held?_____

Who Selects City?_____

Who Selects Hotel?_____

When Will Decision on Future Functions Be Made?_____

Has Group Ever Used Our Hotel?_____

If So, How Did They Rate Our Services?   ☐ Excellent   ☐ Good   ☐ Fair   ☐ Poor
(If rating was less than "Good," give details on back of report.)

Future Possible Use of Our Hotel: ☐ Excellent   ☐ Good   ☐ Fair   ☐ Poor

Other Possible Needs for Hotel Facilities:

☐ Individual Bedroom Reservations

☐ Sales Meetings   ☐ Length of Service Award Dinners

☐ Management Meetings   ☐ Christmas Party

☐ Training Meetings   ☐ Bowling League Banquet

☐ Stockholders Meetings   ☐ Employee Club Activities

☐ Labor Negotiations Meetings   ☐ Other Functions

☐ Distributors Meetings   _____

☐ New Products Demonstrations   _____

☐ Retirement Dinners   _____

(Indicate proper contact(s) for events checked)

Exhibit 7.9   Function Contract Form

FUNCTION CONTRACT

File_____

Organization_____

Representative_____

Address_____

_____

_____Postal Code_____

Phone Bus: (_____)_____Home: (_____)_____

Bill to:_____

_____

_____Postal Code_____

Method of Payment: ☐ Cash   ☐ Cheque   ☐ Invoice

Deposit Received:_____

MENU: TIME:

Special Remarks:

Price Per Cover_____Room Rental_____

Audiovisual_____Flowers_____
All audiovisual equipment is rented and charged to you.

Other_____

Date_____

Event_____

Function Time: Location:

Registration _____   _____

Breakfast_____   _____

Break_____   _____

Break_____   _____

Break_____   _____

Meeting_____   _____

Reception_____   _____

Luncheon_____   _____

Dinner_____   _____

Meeting   Number Expected_____

Seating Plan_____

Head Table_____   Raised_____

Lectern_____   Podium_____

Blackboard_____   Easel_____

Flipchart_____   Screen_____

Audiovisual_____

PA_____   Telephone_____

Other_____

Ticket Collectors_____   Ticket Sellers_____

Checkroom_____

Bar_____

Bartender_____

Wine_____

Liqueurs_____

Meal Function_____# Expected_____

Dinner Dance_____

Seating Plan_____

Head Table_____   Raised_____

Lectern_____Podium_____PA_____

Cloths_____   Napkins_____

Centerpiece_____ Candles_____

Flowers_____

Music_____

Stages_____

Other_____

☐ Order Taken Date_____   ☐ Typed Date_____

The charge for your function will be for the guaranteed number or the actual number of people attending the function, whichever is higher. The guaranteed minimum of persons can be revised no later than 48 hours prior to your banquet.

Customer Signature

Distribution:
Customer (2)   Maitre D   Bev. Supervisor
Chef   Banquet Dept.   Accounting

Catering Manager

c.c.
Sales   Front Office   Room Serv.   Coffee Shop
Reservations   Housekeeping   Restaurant

Exhibit 7.10   Function Space Change Form

FUNCTION SPACE CHANGE   Date_____

Organization_____

Post As_____

	Type of Change
☐ Definite _____Date ☐ Revision #1_____Date	1. Day/Date 4. Room 7. Addition
☐ Tentative _____Date ☐ Revision #2_____Date	2. Time 5. # of PP 8. Deletion
☐ Revision #3_____Date	3. Function 6. Setup

ORIGINAL						CHANGE		
Day/Date	Time	Function	Room	# of PP	S/U	From	To	Type of Change

_____   _____
Originator/Approved By   Entered By/Date

the publisher's address). According to the author, computers can be used for eight major functions: (1) general and special correspondence, (2) managing group information, (3) managing guest history information, (4) market planning and forecasting, (5) prospecting, (6) sales and room management coordination, (7) decision support, and (8) sales support.

Because forecasting is a process of collecting and evaluating data, the use of a computer is ideal to take you from one forecast period to the next.

The following example illustrates how computers can help you in everyday direct selling situations.

Mary Smith is the general sales manager of the Center City Conference Hotel. She has just called on the meeting coordinator of the Mini-Creek Geological Society to book the group's next annual conference.

She used her computer's trace system to learn that the society will make its site-selection decision this month. The meeting coordinator will choose both the location and the property. She learns that the society's headquarters is in a city where she can make 20 to 25 other good calls. Thus, it is cost effective for her to visit the society.

She calls up her master file records on the organization and gets a printout of the group's prior meetings for the past five years. The society met at the Center City Conference Hotel four years ago, so she obtains a guest history record of its activities and performance.

Mary visits the group and meets with the meeting coordinator. She shows how her property can fill specific needs of the group's next meeting and eventually makes the sale.

While still in the customer's office, she accesses her computer back at the property through a telephone modem. The computer prepares a contract and other pertinent information that is then forwarded to the customer.

Back at the property's sales/marketing office, the booking is routed through the property's computer system to such operating departments as reservations, food and beverage, and housekeeping. Guestrooms are blocked, and meeting/function space is blocked in the function book.

Other aspects of the property's file system are also brought into play. The front sheet of the master file and other records are updated to reflect the booking, the trace cards are adjusted to remove the old date and replace it with a new follow-up date, preliminary function sheets are prepared and stored, and entries are made in the running record of future daily and weekly events sheets.

All of this, of course, would be done one way or another in a manual system. But with a computerized operation, a particular item can be entered on one form and then automatically entered on a number of other key records as well. It is done with the utmost speed and accuracy.

The future of computerization within the sales/marketing department appears very promising. Perhaps its greatest general benefit is that it will free sales executives from the drudgery of manual "pencil pushing" and allow them to spend more time creatively packaging and promoting the property as well as selling to and servicing the customer.

Departmental Checklist

The modern sales/marketing department can be viewed as the "management center for profit production."

Because of the many dimensions of this department, proper attention must be given to organization, staffing, administration, systems, procedures, and controls.

The questionnaire shown in Exhibit 7.11 can be used to evaluate the department's activities. This questionnaire is extensive, but it covers all the activities requisite to organizing to sell and service.

Chapter Summary

Understanding the concept of effective marketing is the first step toward organizing to sell and service. The sales executive must understand all departmental responsibilities and know the organizational structure of the department. Comprehensive job descriptions are particularly important in the organization process.

The heart of all marketing activity is found in the records and files systems, and detailed records about clients are essential. There are various types of filing systems, each having inherent advantages and disadvantages.

The sign of the future is computerization, and even small-scale equipment can increase the efficiency and effectiveness of the sales and marketing department significantly.

Exhibit 7.11   Sales/Marketing Department Activities Questionnaire

SALES FILES, RECORDS, AND OFFICE EQUIPMENT

1. Is the sales office an attractive "showplace" or is it makeshift, conveying a poor impression of the entire property?

2. Are files tightly controlled, signed in, and signed out in a log by salespersons? When a customer calls, is the individual salesperson at the caller's mercy because no record of previous calls can be located quickly?

3. Is there an up-to-date reading file circulated weekly for all to see, to learn from, and to avoid duplication of efforts?

4. Is the time and date stamped or written on mail inquiries, and are they entered in a lead distribution book, assigned to specific individuals, monitored and dispatched, resolved, answered within "X" hours, etc.?

5. Is equipment regularly serviced and maintained, and does everyone respect the equipment?

6. Is there an adequate inventory of all supplies, forms, stationery, and other materials necessary for the operation of the office?

7. Is there a system for the maintenance and security of account files, with a record of where the files are at all times, and with a log showing frequency of trace and follow-up (call reports) built in?

8. Is a monthly group sales summary done with a room nights "at a glance" chart to keep everyone aware of percentage comparisons with the marketing plan?

9. Are lost business reports submitted by all sales people, giving reasons the business was lost (e.g., rates, location, unavailability of dates, banquet pricing, etc.) so that trends can be spotted, and any problems can be solved by management?

10. Are the group résumés (instructions) sent out far enough in advance to all department heads to ensure proper servicing when groups arrive? Are these instructions complete and accurate?

11. Is repetitive paperwork handled on a word processor or do salespersons spend their time unproductively and inefficiently by writing letters that could be done on a machine or produced at night?

12. Is every file called on at least once annually?

13. Are files that should be deleted taking up valuable time and cabinet space?

14. Does every sales staff member have a forecast sheet readily available?

15. Does everyone understand that the group rooms control book (the rooms flowchart) must be reviewed daily and that only the director of sales (DOS) or a designated representative may make changes or entries in the book?

16. Are adequate supplies of routinely budgeted and updated brochures and other collateral materials always available?

SALES STAFF ADMINISTRATION

1. Does the DOS have the knowledge to inspire and lead subordinates?

2. Does the DOS praise subordinates for a job well done as quickly as he or she criticizes them for doing something badly?

3. Are salespersons thanked periodically for trying hard?

4. Is there a special individual who can get away with anything while others cannot?

5. Does everyone watch the clock?

6. Can salespersons see their boss every day for guidance or do questions go unanswered and problems remain unresolved?

7. Does everyone understand the chain of command so that they know how to communicate with the director of sales?

8. Is there a daily, short, sit-down sales meeting with the DOS and staff? Is there a more thorough weekly sales meeting with a set agenda? Does the weekly meeting include the front office manager and at least the resident manager (if not the GM) as well as the convention service and banquet managers?

9. Has a ratio of tentative to definite bookings been established for each staff member that will guarantee meeting goals and objectives?

10. Are creative ideas solicited from the entire staff to promote the property during off-season, valley occupancy periods?

Exhibit 7.11 *(continued)*

11. Does each salesperson have a quota of site inspections to ensure that customers and potential customers personally experience the product?

12. Do salespersons entertain potential customers on the premises as often as possible?

13. Is the sales office "covered" at all times, and does this coverage include the weekends and holidays? Is it done on a rotating basis?

14. Is the staff polled to find out if anyone might prefer to be off on Sunday and Monday instead of assuming that everyone must work Monday through Friday and rotate the weekends?

15. Are the hours of the sales office staggered to provide evening coverage for late-calling customers in other time zones?

16. When scheduling assignments, does the DOS realize that some staffers may be "morning people" while other may be "night people"?

17. When a staff member goes on vacation, will someone take over his or her work?

18. Does the boss take some of the unpleasant assignments, like covering the office on weekends?

19. Are all salespersons trained to set an example by picking up litter as they travel throughout the building and grounds? By helping out on the front desk occasionally during heavy check-in and check-out periods? By looking neat and well groomed at all times and by maintaining a business-like attitude?

20. When staff members make mistakes, are they shown the errors and taught to avoid doing the same thing again? Is the subject then closed?

21. Are salespersons motivated with incentives to sell more or upsell?

22. Is success clearly defined at regular intervals?

SALES STAFF TRAINING AND EDUCATION

1. Do new salespersons receive training and orientation? Or are they just sent to a phone and a desk and told to begin working?

2. Does everyone recognize the specific competition in the area? Is everyone familiar with full product analyses?

3. Does everyone on the sales staff (including clerical people) know the product internally and externally?

4. Does everyone get a chance to attend HSMA meetings, functions, and seminars?

5. Is there active participation not just in HSMA and EI but also in customer organizations and associations?

6. Does everyone get a chance to attend industry organization functions pertaining to the particular market segments with which they may be involved?

7. Are trade journals circulated throughout the office to keep everyone up-to-date and informed?

DEPARTMENTAL OPERATIONS, POLICIES, AND PROCEDURES

1. Does everyone on the sales staff have a thorough understanding of the marketing plan? The plan's goal? Its time frame?

2. Does everyone on the sales staff have a clear understanding of his or her own objectives and goals— day-by-day, week-to-week, and annually?

3. Does everyone submit a weekly call plan and include a list of assigned files to be traced and followed up?

4. Is a rough, six-month activity plan, including sales trips and trade shows, in effect and in line with a budget? Is there some flexibility in this plan?

5. Is everyone responsible for developing and maintaining certain key and destiny accounts?

6. Have sales guidelines been distributed and kept updated so that each salesperson is selling during periods when group business is needed most, instead of simply taking orders at reduced rates for periods when the property can easily sell out at rack rates?

7. Is a 90-day (or longer) forecast kept current at all times?

8. If the property is part of a chain, are referrals to sister properties a routine part of daily operations? Do sister properties refer calls routinely to your facility?

9. Are salespersons trained to periodically visit competing properties to keep up-to-date on changes in facilities, conditions, reader boards, events listings, etc.?

Exhibit 7.11 *(continued)*

DIRECT SELLING PROCEDURES

1. Is all outgoing sales correspondence thoroughly reviewed for typographical, grammatical, philosophical, image, and rate errors? Is the work neatly prepared?
2. Does everyone know how to correctly answer a telephone call?
3. Are all salespersons taught that travel agents are not "enemies" but rather another sales source for the property?
4. Are salespersons taught to find out where their groups have met before in order to determine what kind of qualitative factors may be involved with new groups?
5. Do salespersons give up or do they keep trying to close a deal with a customer? Are they persistent without being obnoxious?
6. Are salespersons taught to search for the customer's real needs? Are they trained to match features or benefits of the property with customer needs or requirements when selling?
7. Do salespersons know how to spot true buying signals when a customer gives them?
8. Are salespersons taught to run to customers who have the biggest complaints, not away from them? Do they try to solve customers' problems before doing anything else?
9. Is the department's philosophical attitude simply "Take it or leave it" or is it "Let's see if we can work together"?
10. Do salespersons try to help customers with their other, non-hotel problems such as limousine service, bus transfers, airline contact, stenographic services, etc.?
11. Are salespersons taught never to say "No" about a sold-out date to a customer but rather to try to sell another date?
12. Do salespersons ask for the business or do they forget to do that?
13. Has everyone been told never to turn down a piece of business without checking first with a superior?
14. Has everyone been told not to accept a piece of business without consulting with a superior or following other established guidelines?
15. Do salespersons thank the customer for having booked? Do they stay on top of booked business periodically to keep from losing it before it even arrives?
16. Does the person responsible for the incoming group run through the group's daily schedule 24 hours in advance? Does this person monitor the service staff personally to make certain servicing errors do not occur?
17. While groups are still meeting at the property are critiques held with the account decision maker(s) to correct any service shortfalls that would make the customer want to take its business to another property in the future?
18. Is every attempt made to book the group again before it checks out of the property?
19. Are key customers' birthdays remembered?
20. Are salespersons made to feel responsible for billing and payment arrangements before agreeing to accept any group payments? Or do salespersons book anything possible, regardless of whether the property is going to be paid?

SALES/ADVERTISING COORDINATION

1. Does the property's advertising reflect the sales department's thinking as well as that of the general manager?
2. Is the sales staff informed ahead of time about where and when ads are scheduled?
3. Does the property's advertising provide some method of feedback for the sales staff to follow up after the ads have been run?
4. Before ads are run for packages and special offers are the sales staff and reservationists advised?

SALES/OPERATIONS RELATIONSHIPS

1. Does everyone remember to consult the banquet director, with the customer present, concerning functions, food arrangements, menus, food prices, etc., after a room block has been secured? Are entries in the banquet diary made within established guidelines and with the full knowledge of the banquet manager beforehand?

Exhibit 7.11 *(continued)*

2. Are the property's future problems made known to salespersons to keep them forewarned? Is input solicited for resolving these problems?

3. Does the individual salesperson personally inspect the VIP suite or special room assignments for cleanliness, availability, and the little things that can often go wrong?

4. Is the DOS involved in the weekly forecast meeting so that he/she can make certain the salespersons keep on top of group client bookings?

5. Are comp rooms controlled by the DOS only?

6. Is there sufficient interaction among all departments in the property so that they all can work together more efficiently?

7. Is the sales staff kept informed of what the GM's plan and budget guidelines are? Do they know what pressures the GM may be under?

8. Does the sales staff eat in the employee dining room whenever possible to promote understanding and a better relationship among lower-level employees?

8 Communicating with the Customer

Chapter Objectives

1. To identify various sales tools available to a sales/marketing executive

2. To learn how to use five of these sales tools to promote a property's convention facilities

3. To learn how to effectively coordinate the joint use of these sales tools

To this point, we have covered several criteria used to evaluate a property's objectives and goals. We have discussed the following elements:

Who represents the convention and group business market, particularly associations and corporations.

What these markets offer the hospitality industry in terms of business potential.

Where these markets come from.

When these groups meet.

Why meetings are held, including the objectives and goals of those who prepare and program meetings and their role in the facility selection process.

The remaining factor, **how**, consists of bringing together the meeting planner and the property's sales/marketing executive. Essentially, this is a communication process that, when successful, results in a purchase that benefits both buyer and seller.

This chapter focuses on communication from the seller's perspective, developing for the reader a conceptual framework for cultivating and using communicative techniques to create an awareness of and need for the product.

Sales Tools

The hospitality industry uses a variety of communication channels or sales tools to sell or motivate. Each tool has advantages and disadvantages.

These are due not only to the inherent nature of the tool itself but also to the differing impact the tool may have on various market segments. These tools range from interpersonal communication media, such as personal calls and telephone calls, to mass media such as direct mail and radio/television advertising.

Exhibit 8.1 analyzes some of the more common sales tools, pointing out advantages and disadvantages with respect to securing convention and group business. The broad evaluation depicted in the exhibit is not absolute. The relative effectiveness of each tool also depends on such factors as the type and location of the property, the nature and promotional activities of the competition, the specific types of group business that form key target markets, and the overall history and reputation of the property.

Sales Tools Selection

There are several considerations to bear in mind when it comes to selecting sales tools, and they should be addressed when the action plans of the property's overall marketing plan are prepared. Tools should facilitate developing business from each targeted market segment.

For example, if the target segment is corporate training meetings, the objective might be to acquaint the market with a new training facility you have under construction. In this case, a significant amount of trade journal advertising would be appropriate before the facility is opened and before making sales calls in the key industrial areas. This could be followed by some public relations efforts, especially to generate publicity. You might want to consider an "opening ceremony," possibly held in conjunction with a site inspection by key corporate training directors.

On the other hand, your property may be trying to realign its market mix. You may want to change the property's image from that of a leisure-oriented facility to one concentrating on the smaller state and local association meetings. In this case, some initial advertising about image repositioning would be applicable. This could then be followed by a direct mail campaign to obtain an up-to-date prospect list, a mailing of the new convention brochure, and finally a concentrated program of sales calls.

If your property is significantly upgrading its facilities and services because of competition from new properties in the area, you might consider some additional advertising in the more consumer-oriented publications. You could emphasize the renovation and expansion of services because these would be of specific interest to potential attendees. New folders or brochures would be helpful in direct mail programs, especially if an already booked customer uses them in a promotional mailing to its membership.

These examples raise some interesting questions about how advertising and promotional funds should be allocated. How the budget should be split among the different sales tools can be determined by adding up all the costs of the different promotional tools. This can be calculated from all the action plans for all market segments. Some properties even add 10% to the advertising budget for contingencies.

The proportion of the total advertising and promotion budget that would be devoted to convention and group business is a simple mathematical calculation. It is found by dividing the total funds indicated in each of the

Exhibit 8.1 Sales Tools Analysis for Group Business

Type	Advantages	Disadvantages/Limitations
Personal Call	Personalized, two-way communications. Allows immediate "countering" of objections and affords direct negotiating opportunities. Allows one to use all "six senses." Booking can be made any time during the initial presentation.	Ever-increasing "on the road" costs. Time and effort "on the road." Sales people "off property."
Telephone Call	Same as for personal calls, though to a lesser degree. Cost-effective, especially for prospecting and for follow-ups. When tied into "fax" equipment, allows quick transmission of printed items. Especially suited to responding to customer-initiated inquiries.	Currently, does not allow for wide use of supporting visual and collateral materials. Not suited to persons who prefer to interact based on customer reactions.
Video Sales Presentation	Can showcase the property "in action." Easily hand delivered or mailed. Can be readily and economically duplicated for wide distribution.	High initial production costs, which can range from $1,000 to $5,000 a minute. Individual recipient must have playback equipment (VCRs).
Direct Mail	Can be specifically tailored to the specific recipient or group. Allows ready customizing of enclosure materials.	Increasingly higher costs of preparation and postage expenses. "Clutter." Meeting planners are deluged daily with what is often non-relevant mail. Delays. Impossible to determine when mailings, especially 3rd class bulk, will reach recipients.
Consumer Print Advertising	Mass approach to establishing visibility and image, which can be helpful, especially for the association market, in promoting attendance.	Reaches only a relatively few key decision-makers, so from a direct sales viewpoint, contains considerable "waste" circulation.
Trade Journal Advertising	A "segmented" advertising approach allowing tailored messages to the decision-makers of specific market potentials.	Short shelf life; often quickly read and tossed. "Clutter" . . . often several hundred of similar ads in the same publication. Not as easy to trace and track as personal calls and direct mail.
Broadcast (radio)	Message strengthened by voice, music, and sound effects. Can be targeted to reach certain markets at certain time periods.	Not particularly suited to soliciting the group market. Short life; heard and gone.

Exhibit 8.1 *(continued)*

Type	Advantages	Disadvantages/Limitations
Broadcast (TV)	Combines sound, sight, and motion. Highly effective in creating an overall image and visibility.	Relatively costly except for large chains and franchise systems. Short life; seen and gone. Only indirectly reaches the meeting maker.
Public Relations	A "soft sell" approach which can help build image and set the stage for positive recognition and acceptance of more direct selling methods.	Cannot stand on its own as a sales tool.
Display/Transit Advertising	(Not suited to the group business market. Certain forms of highway signage may have some functional use, such as directional, for attendees who drive.)	

convention and group business market action plans by the total promotional funds for *all* action plans.

Thus, these allocations are determined by the task basis budgeting method, rather than by assigning arbitrary, pre-determined percentages that have no relation to the cost of what the property is trying to accomplish. Task basis budgeting is discussed in Chapter 6.

A Coordinated Program

The actual use of sales tools often follows a specific sequence. It is rare that one particular tool is used alone. Virtually every property must rely on the combined, coordinated, and integrated use of multiple tools to gain maximum exposure and impact.

Personal Sales Calls

Although all forms of sales tools can be used in convention and group business solicitation and follow-up, there is a general ranking of their potential effectiveness. For most properties, personal calls receive top billing, primarily because large amounts of volume business can be generated through direct face-to-face dialogue with customers.

One sales call has the potential to develop thousands of room nights, food and beverage covers, and other income potentials. Over the course of several years, these sales could represent millions of dollars. It is rare that a customer would make such a commitment solely on the basis of looking at an ad, a brochure, or a form letter. This is not to imply that these other forms of customer communication do not have their value. Their effective use will be discussed later in this chapter. However, somewhere close to the actual decision-making point, buyer and seller must personally get together.

Key items associated with personal sales calls are the environment in which the meeting occurs, objectives that should be met during the visit, and the presentation itself.

Environment. In addition to making appointments to meet with potential customers, there are several other meeting situations that can be productive.

For example, you can create visibility and make contacts by either visiting or actually participating in customer conventions and trade shows. Alternatively, there are times when the customer initiates the contact. Frequently, a customer may already be at the property for other business and decide to drop in unannounced. Whatever the case, the sales executive must be astute enough to recognize the possibility of identifying potential customers and be able to act accordingly.

Sales Call Objectives. The particular type of sales call used is usually related to achieving a key objective. Objectives can include the following:

- To establish a positive image or ameliorate a negative one
- To create visibility for the property or the sales executive
- To identify business prospects on the basis of "suspects," especially for files and records maintenance purposes
- To discover customer needs
- To get the customer interested in the property and its facilities
- To obtain an advance commitment
- To close a sale and get a definite booking
- To rebook an account that could not be rebooked previously
- To salvage a cancellation

The Presentation. A naturally occurring dialogue should take place in any presentation. It is based largely on the main purpose of the call. The basic working technique in most sales presentations is to simply let the customer or potential buyer talk—but in terms of responses to a series of probing questions or statements. These can be posed around a specific structure. Exhibit 8.2 shows a hypothetical structure and the associated probing questions or statements that can be used.

Following Up. An important step in following up a sales call is to send the prospect additional information, brochures, or other literature. It can also involve scheduling another sales call to make a presentation before a small group or before a larger site selection committee. Or, it may consist of scheduling a customer or committee visit to the property.

Unfortunately, follow-up activities sometimes do not receive the priority they deserve, and this can result in lost business. The act of following up serves a dual selling function.

First, it gives the decision-maker a reason to make a favorable recommendation on the property's behalf, especially when presenting the property's case to a committee or board.

Second, it gives the customers a fairly good reading on how well the property will follow through and ensure the fulfillment of requirements and servicing details, especially if they have not dealt with the property before.

In addition to sending whatever information the customer needs, also

Exhibit 8.2   Presentation Structure Points and Sample Questions/Statements

Key Structure Point	Sample Question/Statement
1. Research the prospect.	1. "Now that each of your individual departments will be responsible for its own meetings, I'm sure you'll find our series of smaller multi-media conference rooms especially suited to your company's training needs."
2. Know your product—and relate it to prospect needs.	2. "You are using more outside presenters? Yes, well I imagine you might have greater need for facilities to reproduce handouts . . . they never seem to bring enough. We have high speed quick-print facilities on site, as well as several of the latest white boards which have built-in photocopy capability.
3. Know your history or prior relationship with the customer and organization.	3. "It seems we haven't been able to serve you in the past three years because you've grown so in membership. However, we just bought and are renovating the property across the street. Would our ability to now offer 400 rooms instead of 250 be helpful to you now?"
4. Seek out other leads within the company or association which can offer additional opportunities for your property or system—as well as potentially strengthen your own selling position.	4. "Who currently handles your incentive travel programs? We've just developed a series of special incentive packages in conjunction with several of our sister properties in the Islands, which could tie in nicely with your new 'Training for Better Sales' programs."
5. Seek out additional uses for your accommodations, facilities, and services.	5. "We're delighted that you've been using our facilities each year for your quarterly sales meetings. Since you also handle social activities for your company, you might be especially interested in the total remodeling program we've just started in the Grand Ballroom. It'll be completely finished in time for your annual Christmas Party."
6. Look for opportunities to extend the sale.	6. "I imagine you have quite a number of weary people after they finish your fantastic program of Skills Improvement Workshops. If they would like a little R & R, we can offer a total optional package which would include one or two extra days—at the same special group rates we're offering during your convention."
7. Keep control.	7. "You indicate you prefer not to meet in a large city in the summer—but aren't you concerned about getting the best available facilities and services at the most reasonable price? O.K., so the time of the year is not as critical to you as costs? Well, let me show you what we can offer your group during summer weekends. We can possibly save you up to 40% on both rooms and meals and still give you top service."
8. Stress benefits.	8. "Our small island resort location means that you can have complete control and optimum security for your special new-product testing."

Exhibit 8.2   *(continued)*

Key Structure Point	Sample Question/Statement
9. Positively counter objections.	9. "But is central location really that important? Isn't the total cost of your sales meeting critical to your budget? Our airport location can save you considerable surface transportation charges as well as saving valuable time. And we have our own 18-hole golf course right across the street."
10. Look for buying signals (especially those which may be more personal than professional).	10. Prospect: "Is September or October the better month for trout fishing on your Resort Conference Center lake?

send a short thank you note. This is particularly important when dealing with potential buyers for the first time.

In cases when a booking is not made, information about the reasons, dates for future contacts, and changes or additions to existing data on the account should be included on the call report. The information also should be entered on the appropriate system records in the sales office.

When a booking is made, the call report serves as the basis for recording the next steps to take between the sale and the arrival of the group. If the sales executive does not service the account, it is particularly important to let the customer know who will handle the account and when that person will be in touch.

Follow-up activities might include one or more of the following steps:

- Preparation of a new account or updating the master file, front sheet, master card file, and other sales office records

- Entering new "next available data" information and relevant trace data in the tickler file and trace card system

- Preparation and acceptance by both parties of a formal proposal and letter of agreement or contract

- Preparation and departmental distribution of booking report

- Function book entries to reserve meeting and exhibit space

- Preliminary room block

- Establishing contact dates between the account and the property for updating room blocks and other reserved space

Telephone Sales   Many sales executives are taking a second look at a more expanded use of the telephone, especially in light of its potential impact on time/staff management and cost-effective selling techniques.

Next to standing alongside another person, the phone affords the best means for communication between buyer and seller. It offers the opportunities for two-way, give-and-take communication, being able to counter objections, and focusing precisely on items of interest to the specific buyer. Realistically, however, most of the skills that can be used by the observant and flexible sales executive are lost or unavailable because of the absence of visual contact.

A very serious challenge presented by the telephone sales call is that more and more people are trying to use the call as a means of forcing a customer decision. This is not to imply that a sale cannot be finalized over the phone. Usually when this happens, however, much of the groundwork had already been laid through the coordinated use of other communication tools. The telephone then becomes the contact that solidifies the sale.

The telephone can be particularly helpful in other aspects of convention and group sales. It can be used in any of the following situations:

- To prospect for potential customers, particularly within a given geographic area or community where names and phone numbers can be obtained from Yellow Pages listings or other business directories

- To verify information and update records, especially between the support staffs of the buyer and seller

- To make or reschedule appointments

- To set the stage for a sales call by learning what specific items the customer wants to see or have mailed in advance

- To check back with the sales office (while making a presentation) for an update on the availability of facilities, accommodations, or alternative dates

- To follow up a personal visit

- To follow up responses generated by direct mail and media advertising

Technological advances are being constantly improved to enhance the feasibility of using the telephone as a primary selling tool. In the future, we can expect to use conference calls, linked facsimile transmission (FAX) techniques, computer links, and closed-circuit TV hookups.

Exhibits and Trade Shows

For some properties and chains, visibility at customer conventions and trade shows offers a substantial opportunity for personal contact with customers and potential clients.

There is a dual benefit here in that participation at a customer function can build recognition and visibility that can be helpful in the future for making appointments for sales calls, telephone selling, and other more direct forms of contact. This type of participation also offers the opportunity to talk to a large number of people within a relatively short time.

In an exhibit booth environment, the seller is usually confined to an 80-square-foot area, while potential contacts are free to wander about. Somehow, the potential customer must be attracted to your booth. Also, unlike a one-on-one sales call, there is a constant clamoring for attendees' attention from other booths in the area.

Thus, location becomes an important consideration if you are to maximize traffic to your booth. Try to locate in the heaviest traffic areas, which usually are the main aisles leading to either the adjoining function or the restrooms. Other good locations are near such congregating areas as coffee tables and bars.

Proximity to food and beverage areas can be helpful in attracting visitors, but avoid being alongside or directly opposite a service bar. If your booth is too close to the bar, the booth table may become a "waiter storage station"— filled with half-empty cups, glasses, ashtrays, soiled napkins, and trash.

Some conventions set up educational displays within the commercial exhibit area. If you can locate your booth within the traffic flow pattern to these displays, you can attract a large number of visitors.

Exhibit 8.3 lists ten general considerations relating to booth operation and management.

Although some people look at exhibitions as a "soft sell" approach to marketing, the possibility always exists of making direct bookings. However, the primary benefit of exhibiting at a customer convention (especially one composed of the meeting planners within a general organization or those representing a specific field or profession) is the access it gives you to a segmented portion of the overall convention and meetings market.

Direct Mail Advertising

Direct mail advertising involves sending any of the following items to potential customers: letters, postcards, folders, brochures, stuffers, reprints, and sample items. These materials are usually sent through the postal system.

Like personal calls, telephone sales, and presentations at customer meetings and trade shows, direct mail can be easily targeted and focused on specific individuals or groups that have similar profiles or needs. Direct mail is similar to other forms of one-on-one contact in that you generally know something about the buyer or prospect, and this knowledge allows you to tailor or personalize your presentation.

However, direct mail is not a system that merely entails sending a letter to a prospective customer. There is considerable difference between personal correspondence and the proper use of direct mail as an effective marketing tool.

Perhaps the best way of illustrating this point is to call your attention to the letter in Exhibit 8.4. This letter was sent some years ago to the office of the Hotel Sales Management Association and was addressed to the then executive director, Frank W. Berkman. Although the letter contains no grammatical or spelling errors and calls attention to enclosed material, it violates just about every fundamental marketing principle.

First, the letter was sent to the wrong person. It should have been addressed to the individual responsible for site selection.

Then, the letter was sent at the wrong time. It actually arrived two weeks after the time-and-place committee had met to make its selections for future conventions. It came from an area where the association does not have a local chapter. This is a basic requirement in this case for site consideration.

Next, the property was too small to house even half of the average number of convention attendees. And the site for the following year's convention had already been selected and publicly announced three years previously!

In general, the letter omitted the very first principle of common-sense selling: Do your homework first.

If one could summarize in a single sentence the major complaints from meeting planners about the direct mail they receive, it might be the following statement: "We receive too many mailings from too many properties that cannot accommodate or service us in any way."

Exhibit 8.3 Operating a Booth

1. This may be your first contact with a potential customer. Because impressions are critical, neatness counts—both in personal grooming and in the appearance of the booth. Take time to periodically "police" the area.

2. Make certain you have a sufficient supply of business cards. Have some method for storing the cards you receive in exchange. Use the back of the customer's card to jot down items about the client, especially anything to follow up.

3. Have a purpose in mind. Your potential customers are in the exhibit area to gather information about your facilities, accommodations, services, and other products that will be useful to them in their meeting management responsibilities. Emphasize specific developments at your property, especially those that are new, updated, expanded, and specifically related to the type of business represented by the customer.

4. Speak the customer's language. Highlight benefits that are applicable to the types of business potential customers represent. Have appropriate literature on hand.

5. Be selective in the type of literature you bring to the booth. In most cases, it should consist of "teaser" items rather than a bulky assortment of every printed piece you've ever produced.

6. Use common sense if you decide to distribute novelty items or other imprinted giveaway items. How many more key rings and calendars does the average meeting planner need?

7. Contests and drawings sometimes can be helpful in steering attendees your way. Of course, this depends on the quality and usefulness of the prizes. Most of these activities involve selecting a business card drawn from a box, so this can become a good method of initiating contacts and obtaining a large number of cards.

8. Make certain you pay attention to everyone approaching your booth, especially when a number of people come simultaneously from various directions. Talk with one and recognize and acknowledge the others.

9. Thank each person for visiting your booth. Ask if he or she would like additional materials. When the opportunity arises, try to schedule a follow-up appointment.

10. Most important, follow through when you get back to the office with a personalized letter when possible. Send out promised literature, schedule any appointments, and enter all pertinent information and data in the appropriate sales records and trace files.

Other complaints about direct mail relate to the following items:

- Poor timing, especially in relation to meetings that have already been placed

- The lack of response mechanisms, such as pre-paid business reply cards

- The lack of specific information that would help in offering solutions to the recipient's needs

- The sheer volume of mail generated by the widespread use of word-processors, particularly from properties that have not done their homework

Effective Direct Mail Advertising. There are a number of key differences between direct mail advertising and other forms of personalized contact.

First, there is both a time and space displacement between the buyer and seller. There is no direct contact that allows for dialogue and the use of nonverbal communication.

Exhibit 8.4   Letter

July 18, 19—

Dear Mr. Berkman:

We would very much like to invite the Hotel Sales Management Association to hold next year's convention at the new and luxurious XYZ Resort.

Located in the midst of the beautiful _____ Mountains, free from the distractions and pressures of the hectic urban scene, our 220 deluxe rooms, 4 spacious meeting rooms (largest accommodating 350 persons), and outstanding sports and recreational facilities will insure an ideal facility for your delegates and their families.

The enclosed brochure pictures and describes the variety of meeting and banqueting facilities available to your group. Our spring convention season runs from March 1 to May 15 and we look forward to the opportunity of serving your needs by hosting next year's HSMA Convention.

Source: Frank W. Berkman, Hotel Sales Management Association.

Second, there is such an information and communications "overload" that many direct mail pieces are probably not even read by the intended recipient. Some meeting planners report receiving 250 to 300 pieces of direct mail advertising each week from a variety of suppliers.

In the usual one-on-one personal selling situation, you and the customer can easily tune out the surrounding environment. However, a direct mail piece must compete with numerous distractions to gain attention before it can have any impact. Part of the problem is also caused by the internal screening process whereby the office staff opens, sorts, and distributes mail. So, while mail advertising is a form of direct communication, there is no assurance that its message will ever reach its intended audience.

There is an abundant supply of training material that relates to writing effective mailing pieces. Much of this material concerns such external factors as the overall attractiveness and appearance of both the letter and the envelope, the neatness and legibility of the message, and considerations of design, color, layout, graphics, and general copy approach.

These considerations are certainly important. Many direct mail pieces that actually contain useful or important messages end up being tossed away because they look sloppy, unappealing, and unreadable.

How can direct mail be made effective? To prepare effective and productive direct mail, one must begin by carefully defining the purposes and objectives one wishes to achieve.

Direct mail is a rather unique medium because it can be used to reach a large general audience, but it also can be narrowly beamed to reach a variety of specific demographic, psychographic, and geographic segments within that audience. Consider the Center City Conference Hotel example.

Center City Conference Hotel Example. The Center City Conference Hotel plans to add two concierge-level floors. They will be opened eight months from today.

Included within this special VIP complex are three meeting rooms, each seating up to 50 persons in a classroom style. They will contain the very latest state-of-the-art design, layout, and equipment.

One of the ways to call these features to the attention of potential users is through a direct mail program. This consists of three or four mailings in the form of progress reports. The overall purpose of the mailings is to "inform potential users of quality accommodations and meeting space that we are expanding and upgrading our facilities."

The general audiences would consist of both individual business travelers and association and corporate meeting planners. However, it would be a waste of time, money, and effort to send a series of mailings to *every* corporate travel manager and every meeting planner.

So, the next consideration would be the mailing list. In this situation, one would limit the list to those individuals who represent the following four entities:

1. Organizations from within a specific geographic area

2. Associations and groups that are not predominantly cost-conscious

3. Companies whose traveling executives represent a relatively affluent segment of the market

4. Specific departments wanting or requiring the latest in meeting facilities

The sources for compiling the mailing list must next be determined. There are several options available for developing the appropriate list:

1. *Your own resources*, such as sales files and records. For specific programs directed at specific markets, the general list must be "weeded" to contain only those names that fit the target profiles. Computerized records can be a great asset, provided the proper sorting information was initially incorporated in the program.

2. *Internally developed lists*, from names obtained from commercial directories of associations and of companies, association membership rosters, phone directories, city directories, and similar outside sources. In addition to the costs of purchasing these lists, there may be considerable time and labor involved in screening, sorting, and retrieving the pertinent listings from these sources.*

3. *Purchased lists*, from direct mail houses and list brokers. These are key outside sources and are often used when time and labor are significant factors. Computers allow greater choice in purchasing lists that are already broken down into key segments. For example, company lists are usually grouped by state, by dollar sales volume brackets, and by executive or departmental titles. Thus, in our case,

---

*Some organizations sell their membership lists, often on gummed labels. Other organizations require you to hold membership (either regular or allied) in order to have access to the lists. Still others prohibit commercial use of their rosters or membership lists.

the Center City Conference Hotel could rent or purchase a list of training directors in companies with an annual sales volume of $1 million and greater, headquartered in selected states.*

4. *Tailored lists,* from list brokers and direct mail houses. They are specifically tailored to fit the parameters given by the purchaser. For instance, the Center City Conference Hotel might want a list composed of meeting planners of the top 250 companies within a tri-state area that schedule board of directors meetings of 50 or fewer people during the spring months. If the property doesn't have the time, staff, or resources to compile such a list, it may call on a mail order house to do the research, screening, and compilation.

At the same time the list is being compiled, thought should be given to scheduling the mailing. This is particularly true when it involves a series of items sent out at pre-determined intervals. Scheduling actions should be done in coordination with the objectives of the mailing. This is illustrated in Exhibit 8.5, which shows how a direct mail campaign might be planned and implemented for the Center City Conference Hotel example described earlier. This planning guide could be expanded to include additional columns headed "Number of Pieces in Mailing," "Source of Names," "Cost or Budget," "Person Responsible," etc. These divisions are very similar to the format for the action plan portion of a marketing plan.

Maintaining Mailing Lists. Regardless of how the lists are obtained, the key to their effective use is making certain they are kept up-to-date. A "clean" list, one having very few returns, is essential for a strong direct mail program. Updating procedures include sending out questionnaires and reply cards. When they are used at the beginning of a direct mail campaign, they can significantly reduce the amount of wasted time and costs.

The Marketing Plan Approach. Up to this point, we have been working somewhat backward from what a property must do if it uses the marketing plan approach to developing and implementing its business promotion programs.

In a true marketing plan approach (as described in Chapter 6), a direct mail action plan must be developed. In the case of the Center City Conference Hotel example described earlier, the plan must have as its main objective increasing individual guestroom business from the upscale end of the individual business travel market. A similar plan would be aimed at increasing business from the upscale portion of the meetings market.

All methods of customer communications would be included in the action plans, including personal sales calls, media advertising, and publicity (e.g., feature stories in the customer trade press about the proposed addition).

An important point to remember is that no single medium of customer communication can do it alone. In order to be effective, advertising media and direct communications tools must be integrated. Each must be selected and used on the basis of its particular strengths.

---

*Rented lists are for one-time use and are not to be duplicated for follow-up mailings or other purposes. Purchased lists, which initially cost more, can be reused.

Exhibit 8.5 Actions/Objectives of a Direct Mail Campaign for the Center City Conference Hotel

Action	Objective
1. Initial mailings to selected lists of corporate passenger traffic managers, corporate and association meeting planners	1. To acquaint potential prospects with the plans for an upgraded addition to the property which could be of interest and use to those for whom they make travel and meeting arrangements
2. Follow-up letter with reply questionnaire one month later	2. To screen the list and delete those who show no interest or who could not utilize the new facility
3. Progress report #1 to screened list one month later	3. To continue to "whet the appetite" of those prospects who have indicated an interest in the facility
4. Progress report #2 to screened list 2 months later	4. To present additional details as the construction program continues
5. Final mailing to final prospect list one month prior to opening, with letter of invitation to special pre-opening reception and business reply card	5. To invite key prospects to a pre-opening "site inspection," as guests of the property

Direct mail, for example, may be used as the means of implementing the action step of a property's advertisement placed in a meeting planner trade magazine. This action step can be initiated in a number of ways:

- A coupon that is part of the ad and meant to be clipped and mailed directly to the advertiser
- A tip-in business reply card, inserted alongside the ad, that can be used to request additional information from the property
- A "bingo" card on which readers circle numbers corresponding to advertisements about which they want to receive more information (see Exhibit 8.6)

Direct mail is a valuable tool for soliciting a sale, and it is also ideal for sending additional information or for maintaining communication between buyer and seller both before and after the meeting.

Collateral Materials

Direct mail usually consists of a letter containing a message or a cover letter calling attention to enclosures in the envelope. Enclosure materials can include folders, brochures, reprints of newspaper or magazine articles, and other pictorial items.

These collateral materials are multipurpose sales tools. They can be distributed when making sales calls or made available at an exhibit booth. They can also be displayed internally in the sales office, at the registration desk, or in guestrooms. They can even be inserted in a trade magazine.

Another key promotional use of collateral materials like folders and brochures is distribution *by the customer*. Travel agents may include these items in their display racks or selectively distribute them to key customers.

Exhibit 8.6   A "Bingo" Card

Right: Front portion of a typical "bingo" card.

Simply fill out the attached postcard.

Circle the numbers which correspond to the advertisements and items mentioned in this issue.

|||| NO POSTAGE NECESSARY IF MAILED IN THE UNITED STATES

BUSINESS REPLY MAIL
FIRST CLASS PERMIT NO. 1217 BOULDER, COLORADO
POSTAGE WILL BE PAID BY ADDRESSEE

SUCCESSFUL
MEETINGS
P.O. BOX 4586
BOULDER, CO 80306

|||| NO POSTAGE NECESSARY IF MAILED IN THE UNITED STATES

BUSINESS REPLY MAIL
FIRST CLASS PERMIT NO. 1217 BOULDER, COLORADO
POSTAGE WILL BE PAID BY ADDRESSEE

SUCCESSFUL
MEETINGS
P.O. BOX 4586
BOULDER, CO 80306

Mail the card today! No postage is necessary!

SUCCESSFUL MEETINGS READER SERVICE CARD

Below: Back of the same "bingo" card. The questions are used to provide information to the publication for survey purposes.

Mail the card today! No postage is necessary!

SUCCESSFUL MEETINGS READER SERVICE CARD

SM 7/87-1

Name _____ Telephone ( ) _____

Title _____

Company _____

Address _____

City _____ State _____ Zip _____

PLEASE COMPLETE ALL ITEMS BELOW TO FACILITATE PROCESSING

I. Season(s) in which meetings are booked
1. ☐ Winter   4. ☐ Fall
2. ☐ Spring   5. ☐ All Seasons
3. ☐ Summer

II. Number of meetings (all types) planned each year
A. ☐ 1-3   C. ☐ 8-11
B. ☐ 4-7   D. ☐ 12 and over

III. Attendance of largest meeting
F. ☐ Less than 100
G. ☐ 101-200
H. ☐ 201-500
I. ☐ Over 500

IV. Do your responsibilities include:
L. ☐ Selection of Destination
M. ☐ Selection of Hotel/Resort

V. Reason for inquiry
R. ☐ Immediate need
S. ☐ Next 6 months
T. ☐ Future project

PLEASE SEND ME INFORMATION ABOUT CIRCLED ITEMS

Card Expires: October 31, 1987

```
  1   2   3   4   5   6   7   8   9  10  11  12  13  14  15  16  17  18  19  20  21  22  23  24  25  26  27  28  29  30
 31  32  33  34  35  36  37  38  39  40  41  42  43  44  45  46  47  48  49  50  51  52  53  54  55  56  57  58  59  60
 61  62  63  64  65  66  67  68  69  70  71  72  73  74  75  76  77  78  79  80  81  82  83  84  85  86  87  88  89  90
 91  92  93  94  95  96  97  98  99 100 101 102 103 104 105 106 107 108 109 110 111 112 113 114 115 116 117 118 119 120
121 122 123 124 125 126 127 128 129 130 131 132 133 134 135 136 137 138 139 140 141 142 143 144 145 146 147 148 149 150
151 152 153 154 155 156 157 158 159 160 161 162 163 164 165 166 167 168 169 170 171 172 173 174 175 176 177 178 179 180
181 182 183 184 185 186 187 188 189 190 191 192 193 194 195 196 197 198 199 200 201 202 203 204 205 206 207 208 209 210
211 212 213 214 215 216 217 218 219 220 221 222 223 224 225 226 227 228 229 230 231 232 233 234 235 236 237 238 239 240
241 242 243 244 245 246 247 248 249 250 251 252 253 254 255 256 257 258 259 260 261 262 263 264 265 266 267 268 269 270
271 272 273 274 275 276 277 278 279 280 281 282 283 284 285 286 287 288 289 290 291 292 293 294 295 296 297 298 299 300
301 302 303 304 305 306 307 308 309 310 311 312 313 314 315 316 317 318 319 320 321 322 323 324 325 326 327 328 329 330
```

Source: *Successful Meetings.*

Meeting planners frequently use properties' promotional brochures to promote attendance at the meeting. Often, the property will provide sufficient quantities of its regular promotional folder or supply folders that have space on the cover for a particular group to imprint its name, the event, and the event's time and place. The group sends these items to its membership along with the necessary registration forms.

Brochures and Folders. Folders and brochures are the most commonly used pictorial sales tools of the industry. The general distinction between them is that a folder is usually a four-page printed piece, while a brochure is a printed piece of six pages or more. Several considerations must be taken into account when preparing either.

The purpose of these items is to sell a product, service, or idea. They sell intangibles by describing the worth of the idea. Brochures and folders should be used when pictures can tell the story better than words.

The primary consideration in designing brochures and folders is their concept. For example, art, photographs, and words have to somehow fit together to convey an idea or sell the message. The first step in preparing them is to write down everything you want to convey. Next, determine what you can show. Then, try to find a way to represent the rest of the information in easy-to-read ways such as graphs, charts, or boxes. The next step is to look at the piece itself as a whole to determine how big it should be and how to use the space—i.e., how much space should be allocated for text and how much for art. Finally, cut and polish and then begin fitting the copy into the available space.

It is effective to use one large illustration on the cover instead of several smaller ones. Show activity, not just scenery. And, you should definitely show some benefit on the cover as well. The trick is to set your property apart from your competition, and one way of doing this is to avoid cliches, either written or visual.

If you are not certain about how to prepare folders or brochures, seek professional advice to maximize the effectiveness of these items.

Exhibits 8.7 through 8.9 show examples of various types of brochures.

The key to using collateral materials successfully is to view them from the customer's perspective. Pictorial brochures and folders, especially those directed at the convention and meetings market, are not just supporting sales tools for the property—they are also used by the buyer in two key ways.

First, if the meeting planner is sold on holding a meeting at your property, he or she may still have to gain the full support of a committee before the actual purchase decision is made. The materials you present for viewing by the committee must aid in this effort.

Second, the person actually in charge of the meeting program should be able to use the convention brochure as a preliminary planning guide. Therefore, an all-purpose "rack folder" aimed primarily at the leisure and commercial traveler is relatively useless in this case.

An effective convention brochure, folder, or similar pictorial collateral piece should contain at least the following information:

1. Detailed floor plans of meeting, exhibit, and food/beverage function areas.

Exhibit 8.7 Convention Brochures

This montage shows some of the variety of cover designs used for convention brochures.

Source: Lithographics, Altamonte Springs, Florida; Disneyland Hotel; and The Sagamore.

Exhibit 8.8   Convention Brochures

These 9" × 12" convention brochures are tabbed for the filing convenience of the recipient.

Source: Bill Bard Associates, Monticello, New York.

Exhibit 8.9 Convention Brochure

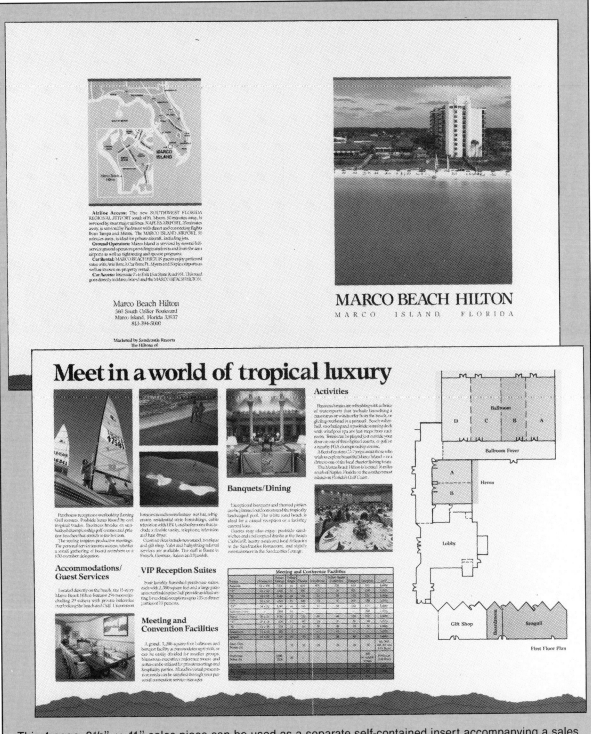

This 4-page, 8½" × 11" sales piece can be used as a separate self-contained insert accompanying a sales letter. It can also be inserted into a 9" × 12" folder (secured by a bottom fold-up flap), and together with other materials can be mailed or hand-carried as a sales kit when making calls.

Source: Lithographics, Altamonte Springs, Florida.

2. A room-capacity chart, showing dimensions (in both English and metric systems) and the maximum number of people each room can accommodate in the commonly used setup styles (i.e., classroom, auditorium, board of directors, etc.).

3. Photos of the various types of function rooms. These do not always have to include people. For example, a picture of an executive boardroom might not be able to highlight key distinctive features if they are hidden by people.

4. A list of available meeting room equipment, especially audiovisual.

5. Descriptions and appropriate pictures of other property features and facilities that will be of interest to both the meeting planner and the attendees.

Perhaps the best way of viewing effective meeting brochures, folders, or other pictorial material is to consider them an "on-paper, off-premises" site inspection. It is essential that their written and pictorial copy reflect those items that directly relate to the needs and wants of the convention buyer.

Media Advertising

The most common definition of advertising is "purchased time or space." This differentiates it from other means of communication, such as personal selling and publicity generated by public relations programs.

For our purposes, media advertising can be grouped into two major categories: print and broadcast. Print media include newspapers, consumer magazines, and special-market publications like those specifically directed at association executives, corporate officials, and others responsible for conventions and meetings. Broadcast media include radio and television stations.

There is a third form of advertising, perhaps not as extensively used as the first two: transit or display advertising. This includes outdoor billboards, signs on buildings and marquees, bus/train/taxi cards, display windows and signs at airports, and posters in lobbies and elevators. However, transit advertising has little use in communicating to the convention and meetings market. Thus, it will not be covered here.

The Role of Advertising. Simply stated, the role or purpose of advertising is to "tell and sell."

For certain types of markets, the "sell" aspect is very important. For example, many holiday and vacation packages are sold directly to the leisure market through ads in consumer magazines and in the travel sections of Sunday newspapers. Advertising in business newspapers, magazines, and airline in-flight publications might influence those business travelers who make their own hotel arrangements. And advertising in the food and entertainment sections of area newspapers and on local TV and radio stations can directly attract patrons of restaurants and lounges.

But when it comes to a "big ticket" item like a 750-person, 3-day convention, one must be realistic about the ability of a single ad (or even a series) to directly effect a volume purchase.

One would not expect a meeting planner to make an immediate financial commitment of hundreds of thousands of dollars solely on the basis of reading an advertisement. Instead, the planner will phone or write for additional information, ask for layouts and floor plans, make an appointment for a site inspection, and negotiate the price. But, in this case the advertisement has still fulfilled its primary role: it *told* the meeting planner something. By providing information, the ad opened the door for the direct communications and selling tools that ultimately led to a booking. Viewed in this manner, advertising is extremely important—even essential—to both the convention facilities buyer and seller.

Effective Advertising. John Wanamaker, founder of the famous Philadelphia department store bearing his name, once remarked that he knew half his advertising was wasted. The only problem was, he said, that he could never tell *which half*.

This statement is undoubtedly relevant today. The advertising challenge in the hospitality industry, especially as it relates to the convention and meetings market, is chiefly twofold: First, to reduce the percentage of ineffective, wasted advertising; and second, to get maximum benefit from advertising that obtains some type of return.

Several years ago, HSMAI officials wrote to some prominent association and corporate meeting planners, asking them what types of advertising "turn them off" and what types "turn them on."*

The negative responses included the following:

- Advertising that is too general, that doesn't say anything that any other property couldn't say

- Meaningless superlatives, such as "the finest of convention facilities," "the most modern meeting rooms," or "the friendliest staff"

- Copy that boasts about the property's features but does not stress benefits

- Advertising that is irrelevant (that doesn't "talk to me")

- Pictures that have nothing to do with conventions and meetings

- Boring, "so what" messages that leave the reader flat

The positive responses from the questionnaire focused on opposite reactions. Combining the positive responses with basic marketing principles, we can offer the following checklist to help you plan effective advertising:

1. *Have clear objectives and goals.* These must be readily apparent to the reader in order to:
   a. Convey a specific image or position

   b. Advise of an expansion or addition to facilities

   c. Promote a new service that would be of specific value to the reader

   d. Promote the visibility of a key staff member, especially if that person is new to the property but well known to the industry

   e. Stress a specific difference that can be of benefit to the user

---

*The questions used this exact phrasing.

2. *Relate to other promotional activities.* Because one of the main purposes of advertising is to create reader awareness, there should be some relationship between what you say in your advertising and what you say in direct mail or personal sales call follow-ups. (If you develop an annual marketing plan with supporting action plans, then the coordinated use of all promotional activities will be specifically keyed to each market segment and goal.)

3. *Reflect the image and tone of your property.* Do not overuse four-color graphics and overly sophisticated type styles, for example, if your message is supposed to convey an atmosphere of laid-back, carefree informality.

4. *Aim at specific markets.* If your facility is particularly suited to training meetings, your advertising should "talk to" training directors. Concentrate your advertising in the periodicals these directors read.

5. *Speak the language of the target market.* If you are advertising in a periodical read by trainers, selectively use the "buzz words" of the trade. Stress those facilities in which they would be most interested, such as in-house audiovisual production capabilities and closed-circuit TV.

6. *Motivate the reader by stressing benefits.* Focus on the convenience of your location, the diversity of your meeting rooms, and your recreational facilities.

7. *Offer solutions to customer problems.* Stress your ability to shoulder the details.

8. *Follow the basics of two-way communication.* Make it easy for the reader to respond by using complete telephone, telex, cable, and FAX numbers. Consider using coupons, business reply cards, and other direct response vehicles.

9. *Use attention-getting headlines.* These should have the "stopping power" to get the reader to read your advertisement.

The importance of following the steps outlined in the preceding checklist is apparent in the light of the following two statistics.

First, the average business executive is exposed to more than 1,000 sales messages each day. The average meeting planner probably receives another 400 to 500 messages during certain times of the year. A person can absorb and then recall the next day fewer than 1% of these.

Second, periodicals aimed specifically at the association and corporate meeting markets contain an average of 100 advertisements from properties, convention and visitor boards, and transportation companies. These are in addition to advertising from various other suppliers.

This advertising clutter makes it essential that you capture and hold the interest of the readers as they skim through the average publication looking for articles that interest them.

Media advertising is most important to the seller in developing visibility and creating acceptance of the product. From the buyer's perspective it is also important because it offers current information that is valuable in the decision-making process.

Advertising Agencies. Media advertising is expensive, and the money and effort can be wasted if the advertising is not done properly. Unlike in the case of some other forms of communications, it is wise to seek the advice and services of professionals, such as advertising agencies.

There are more than 1,000 agencies in North America that handle accounts in the hospitality industry. There are also a number of prominent agencies that were formed by persons having practical experience in the lodging field.

Chapter Summary

Effective business communication is the key element that brings together the meeting planner interested in conducting a conference and the lodging property sales/marketing executive hoping to sell his or her property's meeting facilities.

The sales/marketing executive can use various sales tools to sell or motivate. These tools range from personal sales calls and telephone calls to advertising and public relations, and each tool has inherent advantages and disadvantages. The selection of the proper tool will enhance a communication process that, if successful, will result in the sale of meeting facilities that will benefit both buyer and seller.

9 Servicing the Group— Before, During, and After the Meeting

Servicing the group begins immediately after an agreement is reached between the group holding the meeting and the property hosting the event. Servicing continues while the meeting is in progress and goes on for some time even after the meeting has concluded. This chapter describes the many aspects of servicing that must occur during these three phases.

The material is presented in three sections and is discussed from the perspective of the seller (i.e., the property), which differentiates it from the material discussed in Chapter 5, "Planning and Managing the Meeting: The Client's Perspective."

Section A: Servicing Before the Meeting
Section Objectives

1. To explain the importance of intra-property coordination
2. To explain why the convention service manager must contact the group's meeting planner
3. To identify the procedures required between the booking and the meeting date
4. To explain what the convention service manager must do in pre-conference meetings

Intra-Property Coordination: The Sales Executive and the Convention Service Manager

Servicing before the meeting consists of gathering and disseminating information. Through meetings, letters, and telephone calls with both the sales executive and the meeting planner, the convention service manager gathers necessary information about the group and its requirements. Then, the service manager disseminates that information to other departments at the property and to suppliers connected with the meeting.

Our major concern at this point is the service manager's interaction with the property's sales executive responsible for booking the meeting and with the group's meeting planner.

The Sales Executive

Normally, the property's sales department initiates contact with the convention service manager before the event is definitely booked at the property. All information that has been compiled concerning the event will be shared with the convention service manager.

The sales executive responsible for the booking should give the service manager copies of proposal letters, letters of agreement, and general correspondence with the planner. The service manager must know all items that have been promised to the group by the sales executive, including floor plan arrangements, menus, and other meeting requirements.

It is also helpful for the service manager to know certain personal characteristics about the meeting planner (e.g., work habits and character traits). This knowledge can prevent friction between the property's staff and the meeting planner.

This flow of information, however, is not one-way. The sales executive must be kept informed of developments during the early stages of the booking process, especially if there is any indication that the booking may not be finalized. For example, if for any reason the service manager believes the meeting planner may break the contract, he or she should contact the sales executive immediately to try to forestall such an event.

Obtaining Credit History. Early in the booking process, the sales executive should determine the convening organization's ability to pay its bills. An easy way to do this is to consult Dun & Bradstreet's *Reference Book*, which provides information about a company's estimated financial strength and composite credit appraisal. For organizations not listed in the *Reference Book*, the sales executive should ask the meeting planner to complete a standard credit application form like that shown in Exhibit 9.1. This form should contain the group's authorization for the release of credit information from credit reporting institutions. Without this release, the property cannot legally receive information from a credit reporting agency or a banking institution.

The sales executive should also determine who in the group will be authorized to make charges to the account before and during the event. Signature samples and complete identification must be obtained from these individuals.

Frequently, an exhibitor or some other affiliated member of the group will sponsor a dinner, cocktail party, or a similar event at a convention. In these cases, the sales executive must request the property's credit department to conduct a credit check on these sponsors.

Information about the client's deposits, credit limits, billings from other suppliers, payment policies, and other financial information should always be provided by the meeting planner in writing.

Obtaining Meeting History. The sales executive must ask the group to provide at least a three-year history of the group's meetings along with references from other properties where the group has met in the past. The group's meeting planner must sign a release to allow the property to contact former sites for information about the group.

Exhibit 9.1   Credit Application Form

CREDIT APPLICATION

This Credit Application Must Be Received 60 Days Prior to Your Function.

Name of function or tour _____

Type of function _____   Date of function _____

If tour group, estimated yearly business _____

Estimated amounts: Rooms _____ Food & Beverage _____ Other _____

Firm name _____   Phone _____

Address _____

Billing address if different from above _____

Special billing instructions _____

Type of business _____

Name of parent company if subsidiary _____

Address _____   Phone _____

Name of bank _____   Branch _____

Address _____   Phone _____

Type of account _____   Account # _____

References (other hotels where credit is established preferred):

Hotel name _____   Phone _____

Address _____

Date function held _____

Hotel name _____   Phone _____

Address _____

Date function held _____

Hotel name _____   Phone _____

Address _____

Date function held _____

Terms: Upon approval of credit, our organization agrees to pay a minimum 50% deposit of estimated charges 15 days prior to our function. Our organization also understands that our account must be paid within 10 days after the event. If this account is not paid 30 days after the function date, a 1½% monthly interest charge or the maximum permitted by law will be charged.

Signature _____ Title _____ Date _____

Disneyland Hotel P.O. Box 3441 Anaheim, California 92802 (714) 778-6600 (213) 636-3251

Source: Disneyland Hotel, Anaheim, California.

Traditionally, even competing properties have freely exchanged information about organizations and their meeting planners. This practice is based on common sense: if a property were to deny requests from other properties about the credit or meeting histories of past bookings, that

Exhibit 9.2   Meeting Inquiry Form

OPRYLAND HOTEL

To: _____

From: **Market Research Coordinator** _____

RE: _____

Date/Location _____

History Info:

_____
_____
_____
_____
_____
_____
_____
_____
_____
_____
_____
_____
_____
_____
_____

Singles _____   F/B _____

Doubles _____   _____

Suites _____   _____

Exhibits_____ #_____ S/up_____ T/down_____

Comments _____
_____
_____
_____
_____
_____

White—Original   Green—Director of Sales   Blue—Director of Marketing   Yellow—Marketing Research Coordinator
Form #3925

Source: Opryland Hotel, Nashville, Tennessee.

property would soon find itself without access to the same information about its own future business. Many properties have designed meeting history inquiry forms, such as that shown in Exhibit 9.2.

Convention Service Manager

The property's sales executive must introduce the convention service manager to the meeting planner, either in person or by letter. If this introduction is done by letter, the service manager should contact the meeting planner shortly after the letter is sent. The sales executive should state in the letter that the service manager will contact the meeting planner at a certain date and time.

The service manager should then arrange a meeting or even a series of meetings between the property's convention staff and the meeting planner to:

- determine in detail all the meeting and catering requirements, and
- communicate to the meeting planner an honest representation of the property's service capabilities.

The service manager should request programs, registration materials, and attendee packets from prior events. This material can contribute to the service manager's better understanding of the group and its meeting requirements.

Besides providing the property with important information about the group, these meetings serve another important purpose. By asking the meeting planner for information about the group's special needs, the service manager is perceived as a professional and thus enhances his or her property's image. This builds self-confidence in the meeting planner and may be important later when it comes time to rebook the group.

Pre-Conference Meetings

Depending upon the size, complexity, and lead time involved, the meeting planner and the convention service manager may meet several times before the event.

Some properties hold a formal pre-conference meeting immediately before the client arrives. Opryland Hotel in Nashville has a policy requiring a meeting only for groups booking more than 100 guestrooms.

One of the main reasons for a pre-conference meeting is to establish room rates and food and beverage prices for catered events. If the conference was booked a number of years prior to the actual date of the event, room rates and menu prices will not be finalized until the property management feels it can accurately forecast costs and the inflation rate. Room rates will usually not be established until at least one year before the event.

Because of the smaller profit margin in food and beverage functions, the property management must prepare an accurate forecast for these activities. Menu prices usually are not established until six months before the event.

Other considerations between the meeting planner and the convention service manager at these preliminary meetings might include:

- Check-in procedures
- Meeting room configurations
- Handling VIPs
- Setup and teardown times
- Audiovisual needs
- Table decorations
- Facility staffing considerations

- Union rules
- Fire codes
- Last-minute changes
- Leisure activity preferences
- The group's eating habits

It is very important that communication be maintained between the meeting planner and the property and between the service manager and the rest of the property's staff. The convention service manager can facilitate this process by providing the planner with copies of relevant correspondence about the event one week before the pre-conference briefing. This will give the meeting planner time to determine if there are any discrepancies between the items and services that were requested and what is being offered.

A good example of a systematic method of maintaining open communication between the meeting planner and the rest of the property's staff is the system used by the Amway Grand Plaza Hotel in Grand Rapids, Michigan.

The convention service manager there holds a "Gold Key" meeting with the meeting planner and all the hotel department heads 24 to 48 hours before a major convention or conference. At this meeting, the corporate or association executive in charge of the event is introduced to the property staff. He or she is then given a gold key pin to wear during the event. The pin identifies the person as the executive in charge of the event, someone who should be extended every possible courtesy the hotel has to offer.

Procedures and Documentation Between Booking and Meeting Date

When the contract and all other correspondence between the sales executive and the meeting planner have been reviewed by the service manager, the booking will be listed in the property's function book. An illustration of a function book is shown in Exhibit 9.3. At this time, all verbal commitments made on behalf of the property by the sales executive will also be reviewed and any special considerations regarding the meeting will be addressed.

After the service manager has made initial contact with the meeting planner, documentation of all communication with the planner or any representative from the organization should be placed in the group's file.

A property's convention sales department uses several different forms to communicate information internally to its various departments:

- Tentative booking sheet
- Definite booking sheet
- Change sheet
- Lost business report
- Master prospectus
- Function prospectus
- Requisition sheets

Exhibit 9.3 Function Book Entry

Director of Convention Services Don Ross makes an entry into the Caesars Palace function book as Director of Catering Anthony Gibson observes. (Photo courtesy of Caesars Palace, Las Vegas, Nevada.)

Tentative Booking Sheet

The tentative booking sheet is used to alert departments at the property of potential business. The form is circulated after a proposal letter has been sent to the group planning the meeting or convention. A pencil entry is usually made in the function book at this time. Exhibit 9.4 shows an example of a typical tentative booking sheet. The form is color-coded to distinguish it from the definite booking sheet.

Definite Booking Sheet

Except for its color and a few minor changes, the definite booking sheet is quite similar to the tentative booking sheet. Exhibit 9.5 shows a definite booking sheet. Note the names of recipients of the form printed on the lower right-hand side.

Exhibit 9.4 Tentative Booking Sheet

```
┌──────────────────────────────────────────────────────────────────────────┐
│                    TROPICANA RESORT & CASINO                                │
│                    TENTATIVE GROUP BOOKING                                  │
│                                                                            │
│ TOTAL NUMBER GUEST ROOMS (INCLUDING PARLORS)_____ TOTAL NUMBER PARLORS _____ │
│                                                                            │
│ GUEST ROOM RATES  SINGLES $_____ DOUBLES $_____ TRIPLES $_____ SUITES $ 1 Bdrm ____ │
│ ┌─────┬──────┬─────────┬──────────┬───────────┐          2 Bdrm _____       │
│ │ DAY │ DATE │ ARRIVALS │ TOTAL RMS │ DEPARTURES │                           │
│ ├─────┼──────┼─────────┼──────────┼───────────┤                           │
│ │     │      │         │          │           │  REQUESTED LOCATION _____  │
│ │     │      │         │          │           │  CATEGORY _____            │
│ │     │      │         │          │           │  ROOM NIGHTS _____         │
│ │     │      │         │          │           │  ROOM REVENUE _____        │
│ │     │      │         │          │           │                             │
│ └─────┴──────┴─────────┴──────────┴───────────┘                           │
│                                                                            │
│ ARRIVAL:  DAY:_____DATE_____ DEPARTURE: DAY _____ DATE _____   │
│ CUT-OFF DATE FOR ABOVE BLOCK OF ROOMS: _____           │
│ MULTI-HOTEL:                                                               │
│ PROCEDURE FOR HANDLING GUEST ROOM RESERVATIONS: _____       │
│ GAF: _____                                                             │
│ QUOTED RATES APPLICABLE_____DAYS PRIOR AND _____DAYS FOLLOWING CONV. ARR & CONV. DEP. │
│ ORGANIZATION NAME: _____               │
│ CONTACT_____ TITLE _____                │
│ ADDRESS_____ TELEPHONE _____                 │
│ CITY_____ STATE _____ ZIP _____                 │
│ COMPLIMENTARIES:                                                           │
│ FUNCTION SPACE OR PACKAGE DATA:                                            │
│                                                                            │
│                                                    DISTRIBUTION:           │
│                                                    HOTEL MANAGER           │
│                                                    CONVENTION/CATERING MANAGER │
│                                                    ACCOUNTS RECEIVABLE     │
│                                                    ROOM RESERVATIONS       │
│                                                    SALES FILE              │
│                                                    FRONT OFFICE MANAGER    │
│ DEFINITE DECISION EXPECTED BY:                                             │
│ BILLING INSTRUCTIONS:                                                      │
│                                                                            │
│ CONFIRMED BY: _____ APPROVED BY: _____              │
│ DATE _____                                                     │
│ 4/87 SSP                                                                   │
└──────────────────────────────────────────────────────────────────────────┘
```

Source: Tropicana Resort and Casino, Las Vegas, Nevada.

Change Sheet   Unexpected developments, overly high projections by the planner, and changes in policy can all cause a change in the format of the meeting or convention. When these occur, a change sheet is used to inform the departments at the property of these developments. Color-coding is again used to distinguish this form from the tentative and definite booking sheets. Exhibit 9.6 is an example of a change sheet.

Exhibit 9.5   Definite Booking Sheet

TROPICANA RESORT & CASINO

DEFINITE GROUP BOOKING

New ☐
Change from Tentative
to Definite ☐

TOTAL NUMBER GUEST ROOMS (INCLUDING PARLORS) _____ TOTAL NUMBER PARLORS_____

GUEST ROOM RATES   SINGLES $_____ DOUBLES $_____ TRIPLES $_____ SUITES $ 1 Bdrm _____

2 Bdrm _____

_____ _____

DAY	DATE	ARRIVALS	TOTAL RMS	DEPARTURES

REQUESTED LOCATION _____

CATEGORY _____

ROOM NIGHTS _____

ROOM REVENUE _____

% DOUBLE/DOUBLE _____

ARRIVAL: DAY _____   DATE _____   DEPARTURE: DAY _____   DATE _____

CUT–OFF DATE FOR ABOVE BLOCK OF ROOMS: _____

MULTI-HOTEL:
PROCEDURE FOR HANDLING GUEST ROOM RESERVATIONS: _____

QUOTED RATES APPLICABLE _____ DAYS PRIOR AND/OR _____ DAYS FOLLOWING CONV. ARR. & CONV. DEP.

ORGANIZATION NAME: _____

CONTACT _____   **TITLE** _____

ADDRESS _____   **TELEPHONE** _____

CITY _____   **STATE** _____   **ZIP** _____

COMPLIMENTARIES:

FUNCTION SPACE OR PACKAGE DATA:

BILLING INSTRUCTIONS:

DISTRIBUTION:
HOTEL MANAGER
CONVENTION/CATERING MANAGER
ACCOUNTS RECEIVABLE
ROOM RESERVATIONS
SALES FILE
FRONT OFFICE MANAGER

CONFIRMED BY: _____   APPROVED BY: _____

DATE: _____   3/87 SSP

Source: Tropicana Resort and Casino, Las Vegas, Nevada.

Lost Business Report

The lost business report is used by a property to communicate information on the status of a group (see Exhibit 9.7). This form may be initiated by the sales executive or the convention service manager. This form's main purpose is to inform all departments that a prior booking will not be handled by

Exhibit 9.6 Change Sheet

TROPICANA RESORT & CASINO
CHANGE ORDER

Definite Booking ( )

Tentative Booking ( )

Organization _____ Q-Name _____

Contact _____ Title _____

Address _____ Telephone _____

City/State _____

CHANGES:	FROM	TO
A. Group Arrival Date		
B. Group Departure Date		
C. Rates		
D. Number of Rooms		
E. Cut Off Date		
F. Arrival Pattern (Day of the Week)		
G. Meal Plan		
H. Other (specify)		

DAY	DATE	ARRIVALS	TOTAL RMS	DEPARTURES

Previous Room Nights _____

Corrected Room Nights _____

Previous Room Revenue _____

Corrected Room Revenue _____

Reason for Change:

DISTRIBUTION:
HOTEL MANAGER
CONVENTION/CATERING MANAGER
ACCOUNTS RECEIVABLE
ROOM RESERVATIONS
SALES FILE

Change Handled By _____ Approved By _____

Date of Change _____

3/87 SSP

Source: Tropicana Resort and Casino, Las Vegas, Nevada.

the property. However, it also serves several other functions:

- If the loss was due to the unavailability of certain dates because of other bookings, these bookings can be analyzed in relation to the

Exhibit 9.7 Lost Business Report

CAESARS PALACE
LOST BUSINESS REPORT
Convention Sales

TYPE OF BOOKING: ☐ DEFINITE *(attach copy of Confirmed Booking Form)*   DATE OF CONFIRMATION:_____

☐ TENTATIVE *(attach copy of Tentative Booking Form)*

☐ PROSPECTIVE 1st Option _____ 2nd Option _____

MARKET SEGMENT: ☐ Association ☐ Corp. Business ☐ Incentive ☐ Tour & Travel ☐ Other_____

ORGANIZATION: _____ GROUP NUMBER: _____

ADDRESS: _____ CITY: _____ STATE: ____ ZIP: ____

CONTACT/TITLE: _____ PHONE: (___) _____

GROUP REQUIREMENTS

MAIN ARRIVAL: _____ MAIN DEPARTURE: _____

NUMBER OF ROOMS: _____ NUMBER OF PARLORS: _____

MEETING ROOMS: _____

F & B FUNCTIONS: _____

EXHIBITS: _____

RECAP OF SOLICITATION: _____

REASON FOR BOOKING LOSS: _____

EFFORTS MADE TO SALVAGE BOOKING: _____

ESTIMATED CASINO REVENUE POTENTIAL: ☐ Excellent ☐ Good ☐ Fair ☐ Poor

ESTIMATED CALCULABLE REVENUE BOOKING LOSS: (Rooms, F&B, Meeting Space) _____

REPRESENTATIVE: _____ DATE: _____

REVIEWED BY: _____ DATE: _____
VICE PRESIDENT, CONVENTION SALES

Source: Caesars Palace, Las Vegas, Nevada.

lost business to determine if the property's booking policy is generating optimum revenue.

- If the loss was service related, steps can be taken to rectify the problem area in order to prevent a repetition.

- If the loss was somehow related to the condition of the property, top management can use this information to take corrective action.

The Master Prospectus

Based on discussions with the meeting planner, the convention service manager designs a complete schedule of the convention. This document is referred to by various terms. Summary sheet, "bible," résumé, and the specification sheet are all synonyms for the master prospectus.

The master prospectus is shared with a number of department heads within the property and with outside suppliers who are involved in the meeting. The following is a partial list of those who might receive this form:

Individuals and Departments within the Property

- General Manager
- Director of Sales and Marketing
- Food and Beverage Director
- Property Manager
- Comptroller
- Catering Director
- Front Office Manager
- Executive Housekeeper
- Reservations Manager
- Executive Chef
- Banquet Chef
- Room Service Manager
- Director of Security
- Head Banquet Captain
- Executive Steward
- Concierge

Outside Suppliers

- Exposition Contractor
- Decorator
- Bus Company
- Audiovisual Supplier
- Florist
- Convention and Visitors Bureau
- Photographer

The master prospectus lists everything requested by the meeting planner. Items should be arranged in a chronological order. Function room assignments will also appear on the prospectus.

The meeting planner should receive a copy of the master prospectus as soon as it is prepared and verify its accuracy. Without written verification of the meeting plans, important details may be overlooked. Many elements of the master prospectus will become an essential part of the contract.

It is extremely important that **all negotiations be completed prior to the signing of any contract or letter of agreement**. Hidden or overlooked charges will cause most meeting planners to become extremely upset and are a major reason for their refusal to rebook an event. Caesars Palace presents meeting planners with a seven-page booklet of terms and conditions that the meeting planner is asked to read. The planner then acknowledges understanding of the conditions by signing and returning a copy to the property's catering department. These conditions are shown in part in Exhibit 9.8.

Function Prospectus

The function prospectus is derived from the master prospectus. Every event of the meeting should have a separate sheet that lists in detail the requirements for that event. Information that is generally found in the function prospectus includes the following:

- Name of the sponsoring organization

- Name of the group's representative

- Date, day, and beginning and ending times of the event

- Location of the event

- Room setup style

- Equipment needed

- Cost of the room

- Billing information

- Food and beverage requirements

- Number guaranteed for the event

- Signatures of the client and the property's representative

- Diagram of the setup

- Setup and teardown times

The function prospectus is also known as the function sheet, banquet sheet, or event form.

Regardless of its name, the function prospectus serves as the main source of communication between the convention service manager or catering director and the supervisory personnel directly responsible for the setup, operation, and teardown of the event. These personnel include the head banquet houseman, banquet chef, chief steward, banquet beverage manager, and all other property personnel directly associated with the event.

Some properties use a different prospectus for each type of function. A function prospectus sheet is shown in Exhibit 9.9.

Exhibit 9.8 Terms and Conditions

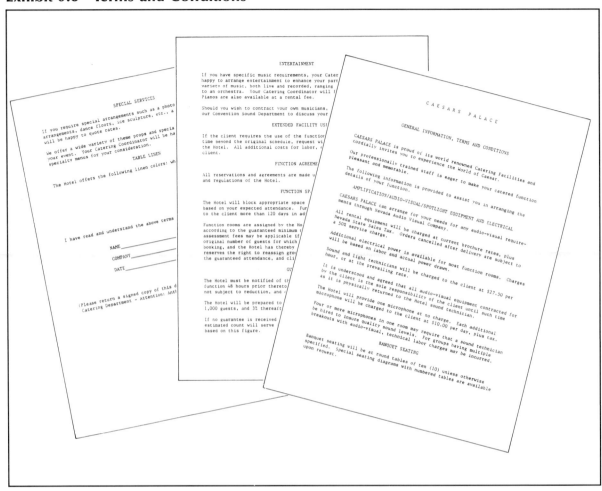

Source: Caeasars Palace, Las Vegas, Nevada.

Requisition Sheets and Reports

The catering department must requisition materials from the property's storage facilities for many functions. Strict accountability must be maintained for all materials used at banquets and meetings.

Various forms are available for requisitioning food, beverages, and equipment. Exhibit 9.10 is an example of a requisition form.

Familiarity with Facilities

The convention service manager must ensure that the meeting planner is thoroughly familiar with all the property's facilities and services.

Planners should be given detailed schematics of function rooms. These schematics must include all key elements necessary for the design of a meeting program:

- Floor loads
- Ceiling heights
- Locations of electrical outlets

Exhibit 9.9   Function Prospectus

TROPICANA HOTEL			PAGE: _____	
LAS VEGAS				
The Island of Las Vegas	**MEETING PROSPECTUS**		DATE: _____	

NAME OF ORGANIZATION:

| DAY: | EVENT: | | TIME | ROOM: |
| | | FROM: TO: | | |

| DATE: | POST AS: | | ROOM RENT: |

| PERSON IN CHARGE: | ADDRESS: | TELEPHONE: |

| NO. GUARANTEED: | NO. SET: | BILL TO: |

ARRANGEMENTS MADE BY:

ROOM SET UP

1. Conference _____   5. Hollow Square _____
2. Theater _____   6. Rounds _____
3. Schoolroom _____   7. T-Shape _____
4. U-Shape _____   8. Other _____
9. Head Table for _____
    Head Table on Riser _____ inch _____ X _____
10. Extra Table Inside/Outside Room
     With _____ Chairs

MISCELLANEOUS EQUIPMENT

11. Blackboard _____   19. Standing Lecturn _____
12. Corkboard _____   20. Table Lecturn _____
13. Flipchart _____   21. Pads/Pens _____
14. Easel _____   22. Water Glasses _____
15. Coatrack _____   23. Waste Basket _____
16. Telephone _____   24. Wood Pointer _____
17. Flag _____   25. Other _____
18. Smoking/No Smoking Signs _____

SOUND/AUDIO VISUAL

26. Lecturn Mike _____   30. 35mm Carousel _____   34. Extension Cord _____   38. Tapes Required _____
27. Standing Mike _____   31. Overhead Projector _____   35. Electric Pointer _____   39. VTR ½ ¾ _____
28. Table Mike _____   32. 16mm Projector _____   36. Cassette Recorder _____   40. Screen Front/Rear _____
29. Lavalier Mike _____   33. 8 mm Projector _____   37. Reel to Reel   41. Screen Size _____
                                                                                                                   Recorder _____
42. _____   AV By: _____

DIAGRAM/INFO	**CATERING**
	APPROVED FOR ORGANIZATION BY:
	_____
DATE: _____	APPROVED FOR TROPICANA BY:
	_____

Source: Tropicana Hotel, Las Vegas, Nevada.

- Placement of columns
- Locations of exits

The planner should have an opportunity to sample all food that will be served to the group. He or she should see the guestrooms and suites, visit the

Exhibit 9.10   Equipment Requisition Form

```
                          EQUIPMENT REQUISITION

    DAY: _____    DATE: _____   CONTRACT #: _____   GUESTS: ____

    NAME OF GUEST: _____

    TYPE OF FUNCTION:  Coffee Break      Breakfast     Lunch/Sit-Down    Lunch/Buffet   Other
                       Continental Breakfast   Dinner/Sit-Down   Dinner-Buffet   Reception

    LOCATION: _____  EQUIPMENT TO BE READY BY: _____
    *************************************************************************************
    CHINA                                    BEVERAGE SERVICE
    _____  Coffee Cups                    _____  Water Pitchers
    _____  Saucers                        _____  Tea Pots
    _____  B & B Plates                   _____  3-Oz. Creamers Stainless/Silver
    _____  Dessert Plates                 _____  Silver Coffee Pots
    _____  Salad Plates (Clear)           _____  5-Gal. Cambro Coffee Containers
    _____  Dinner plates (Base) White     GLASSWARE
    _____  Dinner Plates (Hot)            _____  1-Oz. Cordial (#8090)
    _____  Pink Base Plates               _____  9-Oz. Brandy Snifter
    SILVERWARE                               _____  4½-Oz. Champagne (#8077)
    _____  Soup Spoons                    _____  9-Oz. Tulip Champagne (#8476)
    _____  Cocktail Forks                 _____  5½-Oz. Juice Glass (#47011K)
    _____  Teaspoons                      _____  10½-Oz. Water Goblet (#3712)
    _____  Knives                         _____  Highball Glasses
    _____  Forks                          WINE SERVICE
    _____  Salad Forks                    _____  10-Oz. Standard Wine Glass (#8456)
    MISCELLANEOUS SERVING EQUIPMENT          _____  12½-Oz. Tall White Wine
    _____  Bus Pans                       _____  14-Oz. Bolla Grand (#8415)
    _____  Oval Aluminum Trays            _____  Wine Buckets  White/Silver
    _____  Tray Jacks                     FOOD ITEMS
    _____  4-Qt. Silver Chafer            _____  Creamers (Individual)
    _____  Silver Chafing Dish            _____  Half & Half
    _____  Sterno                         _____  Milk
    _____  Serving Spoons/Tongs           _____  Lemons  Bowls/Bucket
    _____  Ash Trays White/Clear          _____  Dinner Rolls
    _____  Candleabras                    _____  Butter  Wrapped/Gourmet
    _____  Small Glass Bowls              _____  Ice     Bustubs_____
    _____  Heat Lamps/Carving Boards              Garbage Cans_____
    _____  Glow Pans                      OTHER
    _____  Juice Jet Sprays               _____
    _____  Wooden Sald Bowl w/ Fork/Spoon _____
    _____  Copper Skillets                _____
    _____  Large Plastic Bowls            _____
                                             Equipment Prepared By: _____
                                             Received By: _____
```

Source: Caesars Palace, Las Vegas, Nevada.

entertainment lounges, eat in the restaurants, visit the property's health club, swim in the pool, and tour the property's shops. Only by experiencing first-hand all that the property has to offer can the planner adequately prepare for the meeting.

File Update Sheet

A file update sheet, such as that shown in Exhibit 9.11, is another important form of documentation. This sheet is usually attached directly to the group's master file. An entry is made on the form each time there is contact between the property and the meeting planner. The form should include sufficient space to record all pertinent information about the contact:

- Date and time of the conversation

- Brief description of the content of the discussion

- Names of the parties who engaged in the conversation

Personnel on both sides can change from the time a meeting was first placed on the books to the time it actually occurs. A file update sheet is an invaluable supplement to the contract when questions arise about matters that were discussed and decided upon by former representatives of either the client or the property.

Section B: Servicing During the Meeting
Section Objectives

1. To understand those elements associated with providing guestrooms and related amenities

2. To understand those elements associated with providing function rooms and concomitant meeting services

3. To learn how to set up press rooms

4. To learn how to provide service to VIPs

5. To learn how to arrange outside services

6. To learn how to deal with emergencies

Arranging activities and facilities directly concerned with the meeting itself and preparing for contingencies compose the broad group of enterprises known collectively as servicing during the meeting. Some of these items (e.g., guestroom reservation systems or function room layout) will by necessity be discussed and negotiated for well in advance of the meeting date. However, because they are directly related to the meeting itself, they more appropriately belong in this section.

Guestrooms and Amenities

The focus of a convention or conference is not limited to just the meeting facilities at a property. Delegates and attendees must be housed, fed, and entertained. In order for all aspects of the meeting to be considered a success, guestrooms and other guest amenities must meet the expectations of the group being served.

Reservation Systems Room reservations for groups may be handled in a variety of ways. The best method for your property depends on a number of factors: the size of the group, whether the convention is a city-wide event, whether the

Exhibit 9.11 File Update Sheet

FILE UPDATE	TELEPHONE NO.: ( )

Organization: ....

DATE	INFORMATION

FILEUPDT (MS/FM) (1/88)

attendance is mandatory or voluntary, and, of course, your property's existing policies and procedures.

Additional information about reservation procedures is contained in Chapter 5.

Reservations for Corporate Meetings. Because attendance at corporate meetings is usually mandatory and the names of attendees are known in advance, corporate meeting planners will often provide the property with a rooming list of those who will attend the meeting. Reservations are normally made directly by the property's sales executive or the convention service manager with the property's reservation department. From the property's perspective, corporate meetings are the easiest to process, and they usually have the smallest no-show factor because of their mandatory nature.

Reservations for Association Meetings Held at One Facility. Reservation procedures for association meetings are generally handled in one of two ways.

The preferred method requires greater involvement on the part of the association hosting the event. The sequential steps are as follows:

1. A convention packet is mailed to each association member. It includes a reservation form provided either by the facility or the association (see Exhibit 9.12). Addressees are asked to mail their responses with a deposit directly to the property.

2. The property collects the reservation forms and deposits. The property then performs a daily analysis of these reservations, both in terms of volume and patterns.

3. Using a master list provided by the association, the property sends confirmations to the association members.

A second reservations method for association conventions or conferences includes the following steps:

1. A convention packet is mailed to each association member. The packet contains a reservation form with directions to send the completed form with a deposit or credit card number directly to the property.

2. The property processes the reservations, sends confirmations to association members, and informs the association of the number of responses that have been received from its members.

3. Unless other arrangements have been made, the property releases any remaining rooms in the association's block to other individuals and groups at the cut-off date. Members of the association who contact the facility after the cut-off date may still receive a room, but there are no guarantees as there were before the cut-off date.

Reservations for City-Wide Conferences. For city-wide conferences or conventions, a city's convention and visitors bureau will often act as a housing liaison. Properties throughout the city will make commitments to the bureau for blocks of rooms for guests attending the conference.

The housing bureau sends reservation forms to the association, and these will be included in the convention packet mailed to the group's members. Exhibit 9.13 is an example of a typical reservation form.

After receiving these packages, association members can send their reservation forms back to the housing bureau, which will make hotel assignments according to the members' wishes. Space is usually provided on the form for an individual's second and third choices if the first is unavailable.

Exhibit 9.12   Reservation Form

Tear along dotted line. Moisten here, fold here, fold flap down and seal.

Welcome to the Opryland Hotel®

| Name of Group _____ |
| Dates of Function _____ |

(Please print or type)

Name _____

Title _____

Company Name _____

Address _____

City _____ State _____ Zip _____

Phone Office ( ) _____ Home ( ) _____

Sharing room with _____

Arrival Date _____ Departure Date _____

Room Selection

# OF ROOMS	ROOM TYPE	1 PERSON	2 PERSONS
_____	Conservatory	☐	☐
_____	King	☐	☐
_____	Standard	☐	☐

	SUITE TYPE	1 BEDROOM	2 BEDROOM
_____	Standard Parlor	☐	☐
_____	Jr. Suite		
_____	Colonnade	☐	☐
_____	Parthenon	☐	
_____	Centennial	☐	
_____	Conservatory	☐	

*There is a possibility your requested room type may not be available. If room type requested is not available, the next available room type will be assigned.

Reservations must be accompanied by one night's room deposit. Opryland Hotel accepts deposits made by check, MasterCard, VISA, Diners Club, Discover, Carte Blanche or American Express. (Refunds will be made only when cancellations are received at least 72 hours prior to scheduled arrival date.)

Rates are quoted for single or double occupancy. Children age and under and sharing room with adult are free. The rate for additional persons over age _____ is $ _____ per person.

Special Requests (subject to availability):

Rollaway Bed _____

Crib _____

Connecting Room _____

Handicapped Room _____

Other _____

Credit Card # _____

Expiration Date ____ / ____

Reservations received after _____ will be confirmed on a space available basis.

Rooms may not be available prior to 3 p.m. check-in time.

| Check-in 3 p.m. |
| Check-out 11 a.m. |

Arrival at hotel by Auto _____ Airport Shuttle _____ Flight # _____

Airline _____ Estimated time of arrival _____ a.m. _____ p.m.

If you need additional information, call our Reservations Department at 615/889-1000.

Source: Opryland Hotel, Nashville, Tennessee.

Exhibit 9.13   Reservation Form for City-Wide Conference

CONVENTION HOUSING
LOYAL ORDER OF MOOSE
56th ANNUAL MICHIGAN STATE CONVENTION
October 13-16, 1988 - Lansing, Michigan
HOTEL RESERVATION

Please indicate your FIRST, SECOND and THIRD preference in the space provided on the form at the right of the facility. Reservation requests MUST BE RECEIVED by the Convention/Visitors Bureau of Greater Lansing no later than September 12, 1988. Confirmation will be sent directly to you from your assigned hotel. The hotel's deposit and cancellation policies should appear on your confirmation. Please DO NOT SEND ROOM DEPOSITS TO THE CONVENTION/VISITORS BUREAU. Any changes in reservations must be made directly with the hotel after confirmation is received.

PLEASE MAIL FORM TO:

Convention/Visitors Bureau of
Greater Lansing
Suite 302, Civic Center
Lansing, Michigan 48933
517/487-6800

HOTEL SHOULD CONFIRM THIS RESERVATION TO:

Name_____

Address_____

City_____ State_____ Zip_____

Phone (days)_____
                 Area Code

HOTEL/RATES (not including tax)

1. *Midway ____Headquarters____
       (no rooms available)
2. Clarion_____
       Single $60.00/Double $70.00
3. Dillon Inn_____
       Single $36.00/Double $36.00
4. Holiday Inn_____
       Single $41.00/Double $46.00
5. Howard Johnson's_____
       Single $37.00/Double $45.00
6. Knights Inn-South_____
       Single $26.55/Double $31.50
7. Knights Inn-West_____
       Single $28.50/Double $35.00
8. Ramada Inn_____
       Single $38.00/Double $43.00
9. Red Roof Inn-West_____
       Single $29.95/Double $34.95
10. Regal 8 Inn_____
       Single $25.88/Double $30.88
11. Sheraton Inn_____
       Single $57.00/Double $57.00

Arrival Date_____Time_____

Departure Date_____

TYPE OF ROOM:

        Single: 1 person, 1 bed   _____
        Double: 2 persons, 1 bed   _____
        Twin: 2 persons, 2 beds _____
        Quad: 3-4 persons, 2 beds_____

NAME OF EACH PERSON OCCUPYING ROOM:

_____

_____

_____

_____

FOR GUARANTEED RESERVATIONS:

____CREDIT CARD - AX____MC____V____

_____
Card Number   Exp. Date

NOTE: One reservation form per room. This form may be duplicated if additional forms are needed.

The Convention/Visitors Bureau is not responsible for room rates.

SPECIAL REQUESTS:_____

Source: Convention/Visitors Bureau of Greater Lansing, Lansing, Michigan.

Housing bureaus normally require a six-month lead time to process a conference's reservation requirements. At any given time, a bureau may be handling the reservation requests for 20 or more conferences. While some housing bureaus still handle reservation requests manually, many use computers to reduce turnaround time.

Confirmation forms must be sent to all conference attendees. A copy of the confirmation form should also be sent to the property, with another copy retained by the bureau.

Room Assignments

The property should try to accommodate an attendee's wishes regarding room assignment. VIPs, of course, are given a much higher priority for room assignments. The meeting planner must prepare a VIP list and forward it to the convention service manager. If the list has not been received within a reasonable amount of time, the convention service manager must request it from the meeting planner.

The convention service manager should personally ensure that the proper rooms are blocked for all VIPs.

VIPs entitled to special treatment from the property usually include:

- Association executives
- Officers of the sponsoring corporation
- Board members
- The meeting planner
- The meeting planner's staff
- Famous entertainers
- Special guest speakers
- Major exhibitors

The VIP list should also identify those individuals who should be assigned suites and receive any other special treatment such as fruit baskets or flowers in the room.

No-Shows and Overbookings

The association convention or conference presents the greatest potential for no-shows, late arrivals, and early departures.

One solution to these problems is to require first **and** last night deposits. Another solution is for the convention service manager to request the no-show figure from the group's last conference. This figure (usually between 5% and 30%, with the average closer to 20%) becomes the maximum allowable overbooking figure.

Overbooking agreements should be made part of the conference contract.

Walking Guests. Situations may arise when it is necessary to walk guests. When this occurs with a convention group, it is imperative that the front desk give the convention service manager some latitude in determining who will be walked.

The meeting planner should be notified immediately when these occasions arise. If members of the meeting group's staff are to be walked, the planner may want to double up the staff members in guestrooms or even move the entire staff off the property.

If a conference delegate with a reservation is walked from the property, that person should be provided with a commensurate room at a nearby property and free transportation to and from the conference site.

Check-In/ Check-Out Procedures

It takes a receptionist about three minutes to register a single guest. If a property were to register 1,000 delegates on a single day at the rate of 1 delegate every 3 minutes, it would take 50 work hours to register the entire group.

If all delegates arrived at the property over a 5-hour period, 10 receptionists would have to be on duty to register the group. Furthermore, if 4 buses arrived from the airport simultaneously with a total of 200 passengers, a delegate arriving by taxi immediately after the buses would have to wait in line for an hour to register at the property.

The preceding scenario is why most conference facilities now pre-register guests whenever possible and maintain separate registration facilities for groups. Conscientious hotel companies have also instituted express check-out procedures for conference guests. Exhibit 9.14 is an example of a typical express check-out form.

The need for express check-outs becomes very apparent when morning departure flights of several major airlines all leave the local airport within 10 minutes of each other. Without an express check-out system, guests hoping to catch these flights will be stacked up several deep at the front desk.

Certain guidelines should be followed when setting up express check-out systems:

- Everyone concerned—front desk staff and guests—must know exactly how the system works.
- Billing must be accurate.
- The convention service manager must know if the group normally pays by cash or credit card. If a cash-paying group is involved, an express check-out system will not work.

Computerized Applications

Computers can aid properties in a number of areas:

- Speed up registrations
- Make room assignments
- Post charges
- Prepare guest folios

Point-of-sale systems have virtually eliminated errors in posting charges and the problem of late charges. These systems also provide management with timely accounting information by generating numerous management reports.

The price of such systems have made them economically feasible for all but the smallest operations.

Exhibit 9.14   Express Check-Out Form

THE SAGAMORE
AN OMNI CLASSIC RESORT
ON LAKE GEORGE, AT BOLTON LANDING, NEW YORK 12814

**OMNI'S
EXPRESS CHECK-OUT**

We hope your stay with us was enjoyable, and we look forward to serving you again soon.

For your convenience, enclosed please find a copy of your account. To avoid unnecessary delays upon your departure, we invite you to use our **Express Checkout Service.** We ask that you complete the requested information on the back of this envelope and leave it with our Concierge in the Main Hotel or with the Front Desk in the Reception Building.

Check out time is **12 noon**

May we remind you that late arrival or early departure causes forfeiture of deposit unless changes were made 14 days in advance of arrival date.

Please check me out of Room# _____

My room will be vacated at _____AM

CHECKOUT TIME IS 12 NOON
Any departures past our checkout hour will be at a charge of $75.00 up until 5 PM at which time a full days room rate will be charged.

Please indicate manner of payment:
☐American Express
☐Diners Club
☐MasterCard
☐Visa
☐Carte Blanche
Card Number _____
          Exp. Date _____

Name _____
Address _____
City _____ State ___ ZIP _____

Signature _____

Source: The Sagamore, Bolton Landing, New York.

One point to remember about computers, however, is that when the system malfunctions the property staff must know how to perform the computerized operations manually. Even the most sophisticated systems fail on occasion.

**No-Smoking
Rooms**

In the last five years, the concept of providing smoke-free guestrooms has evolved from being a novel amenity to a strategic marketing tool for many facilities accommodating conferences and conventions.

Guests are demanding their rights to breathe easier in a smoke-free environment. It is predicted that by the end of the century, a majority of the hotel rooms in this country will carry a no-smoking designation.

Hotels, resorts, and conference centers that wish to remain competitive are well advised to give delegates the opportunity to select no-smoking rooms on their reservation forms.

Smoking concerns related to function room activities are discussed in detail later in this chapter.

Function Rooms

The property must have both the necessary amount of space as well as the proper type of space to justify its selection for a meeting or conference.

Types of Function Rooms

There are three general types of meeting facility space found in most major convention properties:

1. *Exhibit hall space.* This is an area of immense size that offers exhibitors certain necessary facilities:

   - Loading docks
   - Freight receiving area
   - Dray storage
   - High floor load limit to support displays
   - All utilities (gas, water, electricity, etc.)
   - Proximity to other function areas
   - Food outlets
   - Restrooms
   - Telephones
   - Secure area for exhibitors and their displays

   See Exhibit 9.15 for a representative example of an exhibit hall.

2. *Ballroom space.* This consists of a multipurpose function room that is used for banquets, social events, and meetings. The main area is frequently capable of being divided into smaller areas by portable walls. Exhibit 9.16 is an illustration of a well-designed ballroom.

3. *Conference space.* Criteria for conference centers are found in Chapter 1. Exhibit 9.17 shows a typical executive conference room. Note the built-in projector screen at the rear of the room.

Meeting Room Schematics

Conference and convention brochures have become more sophisticated in recent years. This is because astute meeting planners base their selections of properties upon factual information about these properties.

If the brochure does not provide the following details about the meeting facilities, the convention service manager should have drawings of the meeting rooms that include this information:

- Location of exits
- Location of electrical outlets
- Location of microphone plugs

Exhibit 9.15 Centennial Exhibit Hall

Photo courtesy of Mesa Convention and Visitors Bureau, Mesa, Arizona.

- Light and sound control panels
- Location of water faucets and drains
- Dimensions of all rooms
- Floor load limits
- Maximum seating capacity by setup style for each meeting room
- Locations of any obstructions such as pillars in the room
- Dimensions and locations of all doors, windows, stairs, and elevators

Copies of all drawings should be made available to meeting planners. Exhibits 9.18 and 9.19 are two excellent examples of comprehensive meeting room drawings.

A few properties use scale-model furniture pieces laid out on a scale drawing to assist the meeting planner in arranging the configuration of the meeting rooms.

Meeting Room Assignments   Assigning specific functions to individual meeting rooms is a complex task that involves the convention service manager and the meeting planner. A host of variables that can disrupt the event must be taken into account when scheduling rooms.

Exhibit 9.16   Ballroom

The 18,000-square-foot Grand Ballroom in the Disneyland Hotel's Convention Center comfortably seats up to 1,750 guests theater style. The 1,200-square-foot center stage, which can be hydraulically raised or lowered in tiers, features electronically operated drop curtains, side curtains, large movie screen and AV and CCTV capabilities. (Photo courtesy of Disneyland Hotel, Anaheim, California.)

An important consideration is the need for breakout rooms (smaller meeting rooms used for workshops) after a general session. A major problem will occur if a sufficient number of these rooms are not available to meet the needs of the conference or convention.

Sometimes, a meeting planner purposely overestimates the number of attendees expected for all sessions of a conference. Consequently, the conference rooms that are reserved are much larger than necessary. This problem can be alleviated by ensuring that the contract specifies when and how adjustments can be made once the exact number of attendees is known. If the client continues to insist on an inordinate number or size of conference rooms, the convention service manager must then appeal to the client's sense of fairness and responsibility.

Another problem occurs when association delegates or conferees overwhelmingly choose one workshop over all others being offered. In this situation, 90 guests may head for a room that has a total capacity for only 75. At this point, the convention service manager must act fast. First, he or she must obtain permission from the meeting planner or a member of the planner's staff to move the workshop. Second, a room of adequate size must be allocated and set up for the group. All of this must be done within a matter of minutes if the conference is to proceed on schedule.

There are several other solutions to this problem of overcrowding:

Exhibit 9.17   Executive Conference Room

The Sam Davis Board Room in the Opryland Hotel features a fireplace and seating for 24 persons, with additional center and perimeter seating available. (Photo courtesy of Opryland Hotel, Nashville, Tennessee.)

- Take the group back into the room where the general session was held.

- Use public space if any is available.

- Transfer groups from other rooms that are underutilized.

- Offer popular sessions or workshops more than once during the meeting or convention.

Another problem that may occur is dissonance resulting from two or more groups meeting in the facility at the same time. Different groups may not always be compatible. Serious study groups may strongly object to being placed next to "badge and bottle" conferences or chapters of the Sweet Adelines. One convention service manager pointed out how he had inadvertently booked a Future Business Leaders of America contingent with a group of former substance abusers. Each group had reserved 400 rooms at the facility. When the service manager realized what had happened, he met with representatives of both groups two months in advance of their meetings and explained the situation. He agreed to separate the groups as much as possible, and both meetings proceeded without incident.

Exhibit 5.16   Meeting Room Drawings

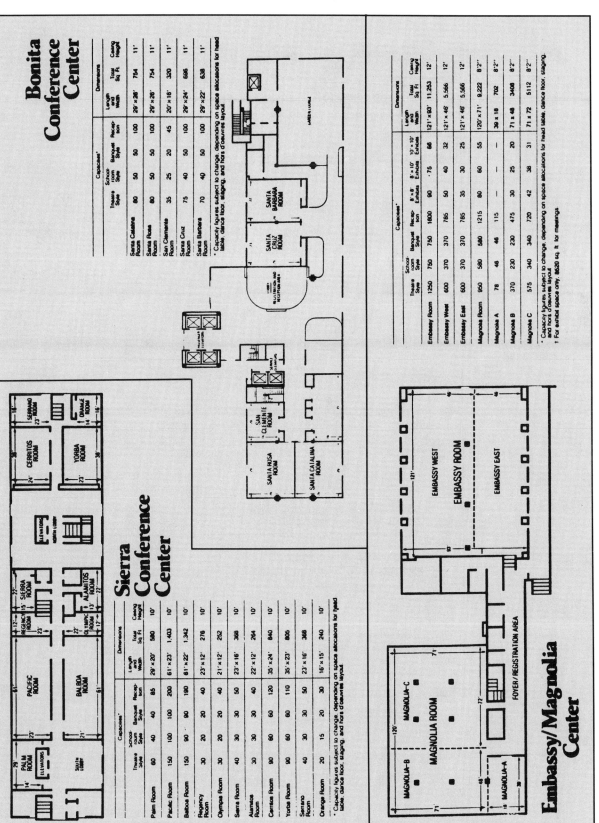

Bonita Conference Center

	Capacities*				Dimensions	
	Theatre Style	School-room Style	Banquet Style	Recep-tion	Length and Width	Total Sq. Ft.	Ceiling Height
Santa Catalina Room	80	50	50	100	29' × 26'	754	11'
Santa Rosa Room	80	50	50	100	29' × 26'	754	11'
San Clemente Room	35	25	20	45	20' × 16'	320	11'
Santa Cruz Room	75	40	50	100	29' × 24'	696	11'
Santa Barbara Room	70	40	50	100	29' × 22'	638	11'

* Capacity figures subject to change, depending on space allocations for head table, dance floor, staging, and hors d'oeuvres layout.

Sierra Conference Center

	Capacities*				Dimensions	
	Theatre Style	School-room Style	Banquet Style	Recep-tion	Length and Width	Total Sq. Ft.	Ceiling Height
Palm Room	60	40	40	65	29' × 20'	580	10'
Pacific Room	150	100	100	200	61' × 23'	1,403	10'
Balboa Room	150	90	90	190	61' × 22'	1,342	10'
Regency Room	30	20	20	40	23' × 12'	276	10'
Olympia Room	30	20	20	40	21' × 12'	252	10'
Sierra Room	40	30	30	50	23' × 16'	368	10'
Alamitos Room	30	30	30	40	22' × 12'	264	10'
Cerritos Room	90	60	60	120	35' × 24'	840	10'
Yorba Room	90	60	60	110	35' × 23'	805	10'
Serrano Room	40	30	30	50	23' × 16'	368	10'
Orange Room	20	15	15	20	16' × 15'	240	10'

* Capacity figures subject to change, depending on space allocations for head table, dance floor, staging, and hors d'oeuvres layout.

Embassy/Magnolia Center

	Capacities*						Dimensions	
	Theatre Style	School-room Style	Banquet Style	Recep-tion	8' × 8' Exhibits	8' × 10' Exhibits	10' × 10' Exhibits	Length and Width	Total Sq Ft	Ceiling Height
Embassy Room	1250	750	750	1800	90	75	66	121' × 93'	11,263	12'
Embassy West	600	370	370	785	50	40	32	121' × 46	5,566	12'
Embassy East	600	370	370	785	35	30	25	121' × 46'	5,566	12'
Magnolia Room	950	580	580	1215	80	60	55	120' × 71'	9,222	8'2"
Magnolia A	78	48	48	115	—	—	—	39 × 18	702	8'2"
Magnolia B	370	230	230	475	30	25	20	71 × 48	3408	8'2"
Magnolia C	575	340	340	720	42	38	31	71 × 72	5112	8'2"

* Capacity figures subject to change, depending on space allocations for head table, dance floor, staging, and hors d'oeuvres layout.
† For exhibit space only, 8620 sq. ft. for meetings.

Source: Disneyland Hotel, Anaheim, California.

Exhibit 9.19 Meeting Room Drawing

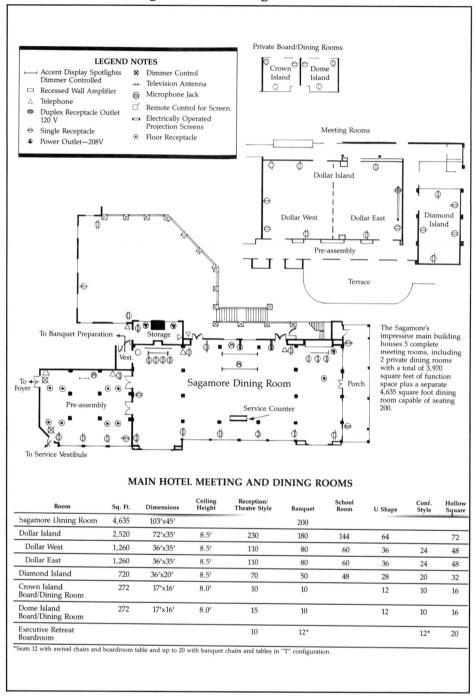

MAIN HOTEL MEETING AND DINING ROOMS

Room	Sq. Ft.	Dimensions	Ceiling Height	Reception/ Theatre Style	Banquet	School Room	U Shape	Conf. Style	Hollow Square
Sagamore Dining Room	4,635	103'x45'			200				
Dollar Island	2,520	72'x35'	8.5'	230	180	144	64		72
Dollar West	1,260	36'x35'	8.5'	110	80	60	36	24	48
Dollar East	1,260	36'x35'	8.5'	110	80	60	36	24	48
Diamond Island	720	36'x20'	8.5'	70	50	48	28	20	32
Crown Island Board/Dining Room	272	17'x16'	8.0'	10	10		12	10	16
Dome Island Board/Dining Room	272	17'x16'	8.0'	15	10		12	10	16
Executive Retreat Boardroom				10	12*			12*	20

*Seats 12 with swivel chairs and boardroom table and up to 20 with banquet chairs and tables in "T" configuration.

Source: The Sagamore, Bolton Landing, New York.

Because some meetings and conventions are booked as many as 10 years in advance, the problem of hosting incompatible groups is not as improbable as it may sound. Sometimes, groups will even stipulate in their contracts that there be no competitors at the property the same time they are conducting their meeting. Still, many things can happen between the time a contract is signed and the time the meeting finally takes place.

While incompatible groups meeting simultaneously pose a definite problem, the same also holds true for groups that are too compatible. For example, groups from the same industry or business can present similar problems for the convention service manager.

Regardless of the circumstances, unexpected situations require an immediate response from both the property and the meeting planner. In order to ensure a timely response, the service manager should ask for a list of representatives from the group who have authority to make decisions in the meeting planner's absence. These individuals should be introduced to the convention service manager before the event. Walkie-talkies or paging systems should also be provided to the planner and those members of the planner's staff who are authorized to make decisions about matters pertaining to the conference. Frequently, an experienced convention service manager will recognize potential problems like overcrowded break-out rooms early in the planning process—if he or she asks the right questions.

Meeting Room Capacity

A number of variables affect the capacity of a meeting room: room setup styles, the configuration of the room itself, audiovisual equipment needs, and special considerations such as registration tables and clothes racks, for example.

Important considerations also include the claims made by either the convention service manager or the sales executive. For example, exaggerated claims about a room's capacity will inevitably lead to a property executive's embarrassment and a ruined meeting when the "maximum capacity" actually shows up for an event. Honesty still remains the best policy when discussing room capacity.

Timetables: Setups and Teardowns

Another area where honesty should prevail is in estimating setup and teardown times for meeting rooms. Meeting planners who are given realistic timetables are often more than happy to make adjustments in their own scheduling if it becomes necessary.

If a convention service manager can schedule similar events for the group in the same space, valuable time and money can be saved in setups and teardowns.

Timetables can be destroyed very quickly if individual events run well past their scheduled finish times. For example, consider the case of a speaker who, although scheduled to finish his address at 6:00 p.m., drones on until 6:40 p.m. An open bar reception with hot canapes was scheduled to open at 6:15 p.m. In this situation, the convention service manager can offer the meeting planner two alternatives: serve the now overdone hors d'oeuvres or prepare fresh ones that the group will have to pay for. The point to remember is that the meeting planner and not the convention service manager is responsible for the speaker.

Timetable problems like the one just described can be avoided if events are scheduled in some type of logical sequence with sufficient free time built in between them to allow for contingencies. The meeting planner should be familiar with a speaker's reputation for adhering to schedules. The planner must also be aware of the overall meeting schedule. If everything is beginning to run behind, he or she must be able to adjust accordingly.

When events end ahead of schedule, the resourceful convention service manager can often help the beleaguered meeting planner. For example, when an event ends much earlier than expected, the service manager may be able to set up a bar or provide guides to direct attendees to nearby public facilities.

Meeting Room Charges

Meeting room charges are based on several factors, including the number of guestrooms used by the group, the type and number of food functions held, and other revenue for the property that can be directly attributed to the group's presence.

When a group has rented a number of guestrooms in a hotel or resort and booked several food functions, there is typically no charge for the use of meeting rooms. On the other hand, if a group has no need for either guestrooms or food functions, the meeting room rent is normally quite high. In conference centers, the norm is a complete package plan that includes lodging, meals, conference space, and the specialized services normally associated with conference centers.

A convention service manager must know the costs of setting up, servicing, tearing down, and cleaning the meeting space. Knowing these costs gives the service manager a greater latitude during the negotiation process.

There is also the hidden cost of losing a lucrative piece of meeting business because there is another function already booked into a property's meeting rooms. A pragmatic service manager will not commit meeting space to a marginally profitable group like a one-half-day seminar (which has no need for rooms or food functions) until all other possibilities for business on that date have been exhausted. Typically, the property's director of marketing will develop guidelines for committing space for different types of functions. The director of marketing approves any exceptions to these guidelines, thereby ensuring the profitable use of lodging and function space.

Release Dates for Meeting Facilities

Even when a facility hosts a major conference or convention, all the meeting space that the property has available may not be needed by the conference group. Once the final meeting agenda is established, there should be a clause in the contract stipulating that any unused meeting space will revert to the facility and can be sold to other groups so long as there is no conflict of interest between the groups.

Furniture and Linens

Chairs, tables, platforms, lecterns, and linens are standard furnishings available at all convention facilities. At conference centers, the standard furnishings are more specialized.

The convention service manager should have a complete list of all in-house furnishings, including the quantity of each item. Because furniture receives heavy use, an inventory should be taken monthly to maintain an accurate list.

Chairs. Rigid but comfortable chairs are the norm for banquet and meeting facilities and are available in an assortment of colors, fabrics, and styles. Most chairs are stackable and built for rugged use. The standard dimensions of a banquet chair are 17 inches high at the seat, and 18 inches wide by 18 inches deep. Banquet chairs with arms are approximately three inches wider than the armless type. Criteria for selecting banquet chairs should include comfort, strength, durability, color, and design. Folding chairs are very uncomfortable. Avoid purchasing or using them except in an emergency.

Tables. Banquet and meeting tables are available in an assortment of styles and sizes. The most widely used table is the rectangular type. This table comes in standard lengths of either 6 or 8 feet, with a standard height of just under 30 inches and are either 24 or 30 inches wide. However, many properties stock tables with an 18-inch width for schoolroom setups. When delegates are seated on both sides of a table, a 30-inch-wide table should be used.

Another popular style is the round table. Round banquet tables come in 4-, 5-, and 6-foot diameters. Four-foot tables will comfortably seat four to six people and are used primarily at cocktail parties. The 5-foot table is the most popular size for food functions and will seat 8 to 10 people. The 6-footer will seat from 10 to 12 people. Other specialty tables include serpentines, half rounds, and quarter rounds. These types are used primarily as buffet tables, punch tables, as well as for other special purposes.

Platforms. Platforms are designed to elevate and accentuate a key portion of the meeting or banquet area. A platform may be called a riser, stage, podium, rostrum, or dais. Typically, a head table, speaker, band, or group of panelists occupy space on a platform. Heights of a riser will vary from 6 to 32 inches with lengths from 4 to 8 feet and widths from 4 to 6 feet. Platforms should be carpeted and placed flush against a rear wall if possible. Step units should be illuminated at all times, and a railing and bannister should be installed on the taller models if possible. To make it look more attractive, a riser should have a facing or a skirting around the bottom.

Lecterns. Two models are almost always present at conference facilities: the table lectern and the floor or standing lectern. At many properties, the traditional lectern has evolved into a central command center for the speaker. Lights, sound, audiovisual equipment, and even the height of the lectern can be controlled from switches on the lectern.

Linens. Napkins, tablecloths, and skirting are included in this category.

On rectangular tables, the tablecloths should be centered with the crease turned up. The hem of the cloth should just touch the front edge of a seat in all instances. Skirting is added to head tables, display tables, and tables arranged in a schoolroom setting. Pins are sometimes replaced by plastic and Velcro fasteners.

Linens add warmth and color to a meeting room, but there is one instance where their use should be avoided. Cloths should not cover tables used as writing surfaces because the cloths tend to get dirty, slip, and become wrinkled. In these situations, they are more of a nuisance than an asset.

The most convenient and durable linens are made from a blend of polyester and cotton that has had a permanent press treatment. For banquets, extra tablecloths or padding are sometimes placed on the table's surface to deaden sound.

Basic Setups   How tables and chairs are arranged plays a very important role in the success or failure of a meeting. Each setup style has a purpose and certain advantages and disadvantages associated with it. Each configuration or setup style is intended to facilitate the intended goals of the meeting. There are three basic arrangements for meetings:

Auditorium or Theater Style. This arrangement calls for chairs to be set up in rows facing the speaker or stage. A center aisle or side aisles are provided if the seating capacity warrants them. Never put more than 12 persons in one contiguous row of seats. Aisle width can range from 4 feet for smaller groups to 6 feet for groups of more than 200 persons. When setting up the room, it is easiest to set the aisle seats first. Chairs should never be placed so that they touch adjacent seating. A space of 1 to 3 inches should be left between all seats. A minimum of 30 inches should be left from the back of one chair to the front of the chair behind it. Never put the front row closer than 6 to 8 feet in front of the speaker, and never place a row closer than 7 feet to the rear wall.

While theater-style seating can accommodate large groups, it does have numerous disadvantages. Attendees cannot take notes (unless there are folding tablet arms), and they tend to feel uncomfortable and crowded. Sight lines are bad for the members in the rear unless these sections of the audience have been placed on risers. There are a number of variations of the theater-style format. Exhibit 9.20 illustrates the semicircular and V-shape formats as well as the straight theater style.

Schoolroom Style. Schoolroom style is a favorite with both large and small workshops. A space of 30 to 36 inches should be left between tables. Participants should never be placed closer than 30 inches to one another. Aisles should be from 4 feet in width for groups of fewer than 100 persons to 6 feet in width for groups of more than 200 persons. Leave at least 6 feet of space between the speaker and the first row and at least 8 feet in the rear of the room. A major disadvantage is the amount of space used by this setup. Exhibit 9.21 illustrates various arrangements of the schoolroom style.

Conference Style. The purpose of a conference style setup is to facilitate a flow of discussion among participating members. The most popular arrangements include the following, which are shown in Exhibit 9.22:

- U-shape. This style allows all participants to see and hear each other. Its main disadvantage is that it takes up an inordinate amount of space. Participants can be seated on the interior of the "U," but 30-inch tables should be used.

- T-shape. This style has a distinguishable head table from which a single leg of tables extends. This leg is usually made up of double tables.

- Hollow square. This style creates a feeling of equality among the participants. A major disadvantage is that it is difficult to use audiovisual equipment. No matter where audiovisual equipment is placed, some members will be forced to turn their seats around.

- Board of directors. This is a popular arrangement for smaller groups. It is merely a single column of double tables. A variation called the oval arrangement uses half round tables at each end. A minimum of 24 to 30 inches should be left between all participants this and in the previously mentioned seating styles.

Exhibit 9.20   Variations in Auditorium or Theater-Style Seating

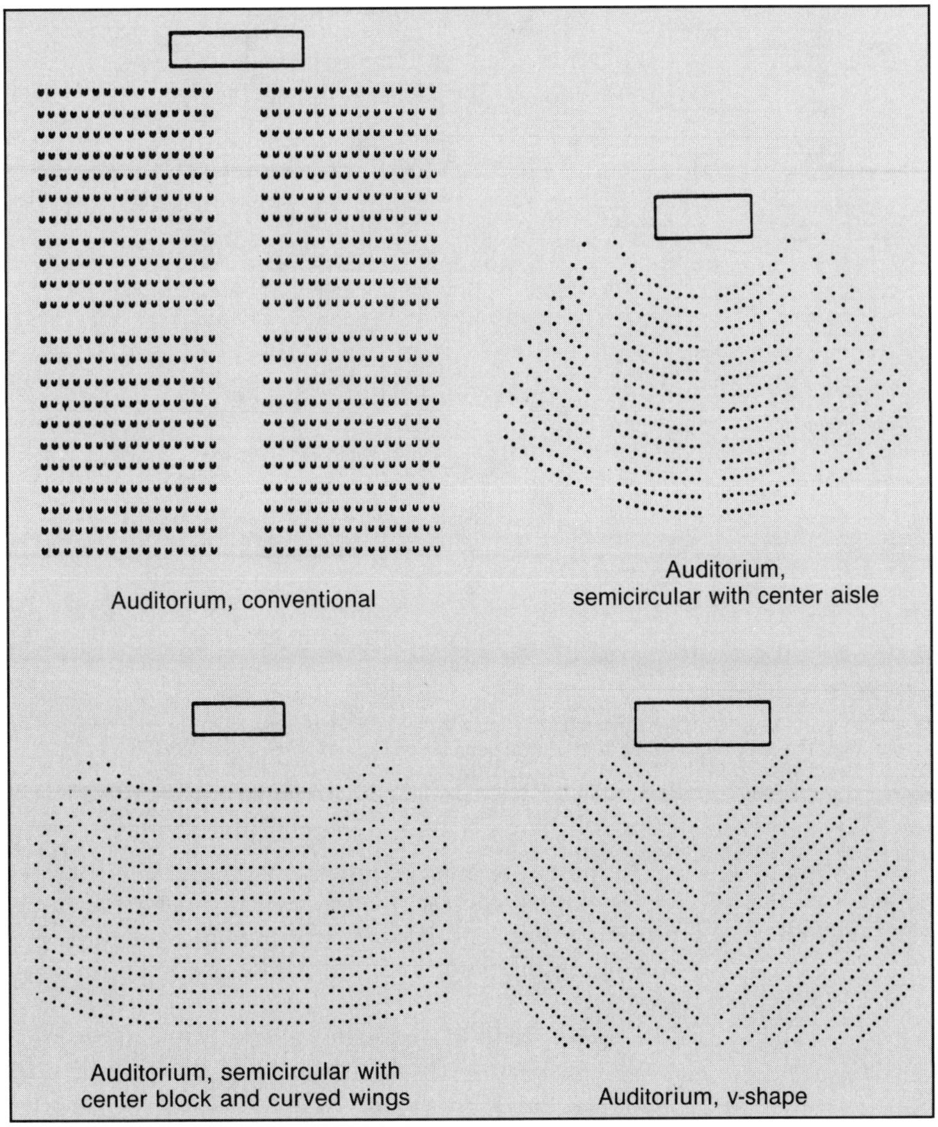

Auditorium, conventional

Auditorium, semicircular with center aisle

Auditorium, semicircular with center block and curved wings

Auditorium, v-shape

Source: Reprinted with permission from Convention Liaison Council, *The Convention Liaison Council Manual,* 4th ed. (Washington, D.C., 1985), p. 40.

• Round tables or banquet style. This is the most popular style, and it uses the 5-foot round table that seats 8 to 10 persons comfortably. A minimum distance of 4 feet should be left between the tables.

Press Rooms

When dignitaries or newsmakers of any sort attend a meeting or conference, a convention service manager will often face demands from media representatives for space to prepare press releases and to file their stories.

Exhibit 9.21   Various Arrangements of Schoolroom-Style Seating

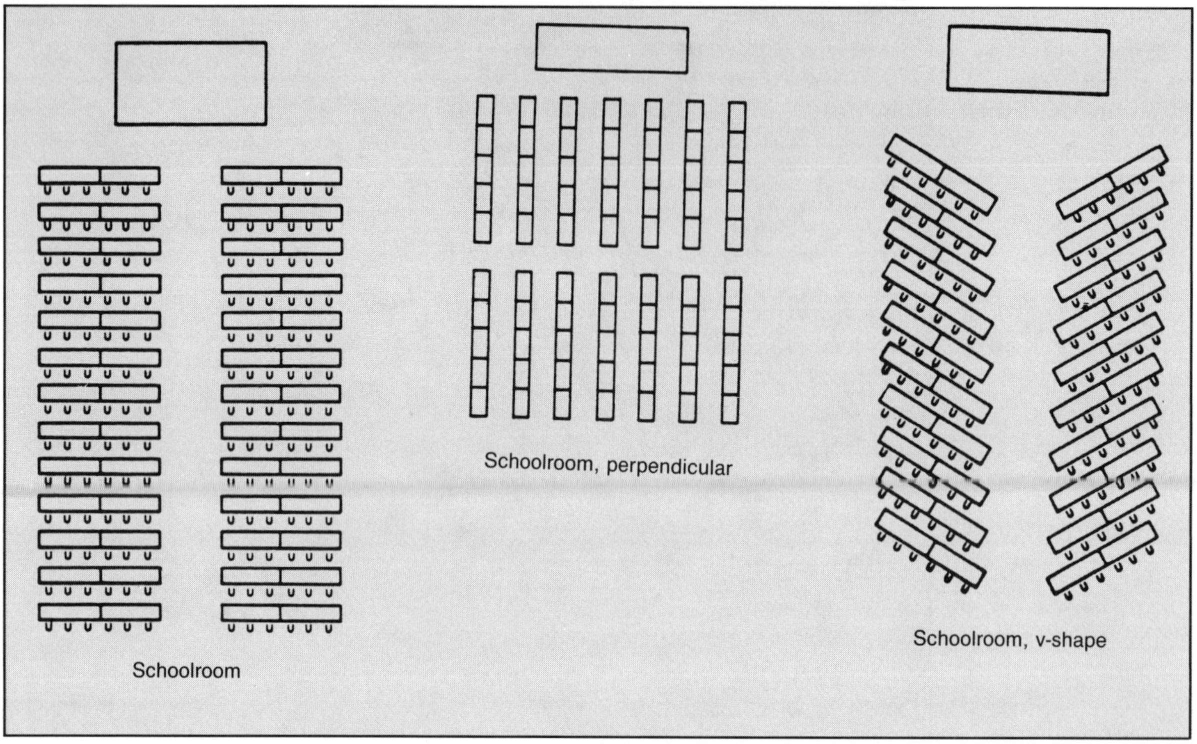

Schoolroom, perpendicular

Schoolroom

Schoolroom, v-shape

Source: Reprinted with permission from Convention Liaison Council, *The Convention Liaison Council Manual*, 4th ed. (Washington, D.C., 1985), p. 41.

One of the main requirements of any press room is a sufficient number of telephones, each with a separate line. The telephones should be placed on a solid writing surface where the media representatives can make notes while talking on the phones. Sound baffles between the telephones are a welcome plus.

Other items of importance in a press room are pens, pencils, tablets, typewriters, comfortable seating, and a refreshment table with light snacks, coffee, and soft drinks. A relative degree of isolation and quiet is also a prerequisite for most press rooms.

Attending to the needs of the members of the news media may reap the convention service manager some additional rewards in the form of favorable reviews for the property in ensuing news articles.

Handling VIPs

VIPs or distinguished guests may make special demands upon the convention service manager. Entertainers and guest speakers may ask that certain liquors or special foods be made available in their guestrooms. Guest speakers may also need preparation areas where they can review their audiovisual presentations and practice their remarks in private. As to accommodations, the distinguished guest usually expects to be housed in one of the property's better suites.

Exhibit 9.22 Various Arrangements of Conference-Style Seating

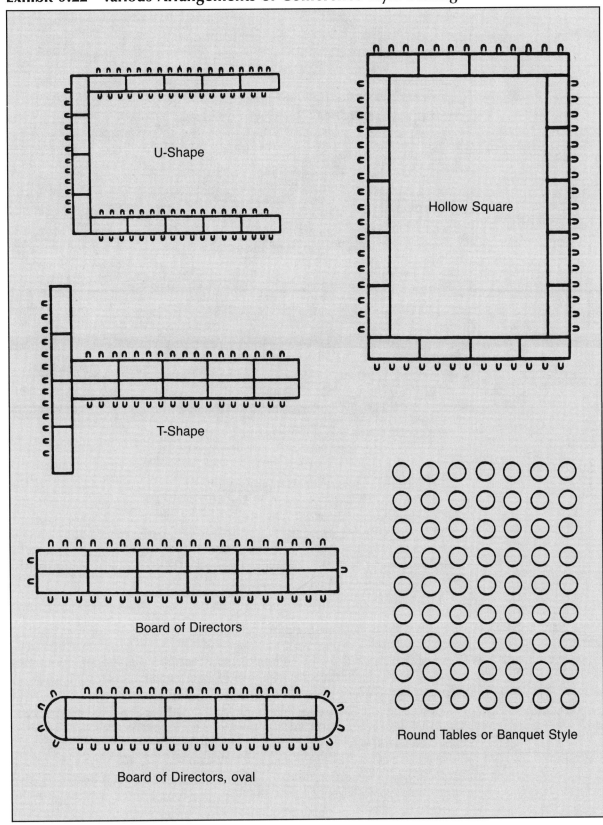

Source: Reprinted with permission from Convention Liaison Council, *The Convention Liaison Council Manual,* 4th ed. (Washington, D.C., 1985), pp. 40-41.

Exhibit 9.23 Centerpiece Design

Photo courtesy of Centerpieces Plus, Las Vegas, Nevada.

When the VIP is a government leader or a foreign head of state, the service manager will often share in the responsibility of planning for and supervising additional security personnel.

Whatever the situation, the logistics of handling the special guest should be planned for well in advance by the meeting planner and the convention service manager. Once the plans are finalized, VIP considerations should be a part of the final contract.

Outside Services: Florists, Designers, Others

In order to meet the usual requests of most meeting planners, many conference facilities will maintain an inventory of stock centerpieces for banquets. A property may also keep a standard inventory of theme party decorations.

However, when a meeting planner needs something above the ordinary for a special banquet or social event, the services of an outside specialist are needed. A good convention service manager must be able to recommend qualified outside specialists who are dependable and who can provide quality items.

Outside services may be provided by lighting and sound designers, florists or centerpiece design firms that can produce unique designs like the

Exhibit 9.24 Table Setting for Theme Party

Photo courtesy of Tropicana Resort and Casino, Las Vegas, Nevada.

example in Exhibit 9.23, or even a special events design firm that specializes in extravagant theme parties such as those pictured in Exhibits 9.24 and 9.25.

Meeting Room Housekeeping

All meeting rooms should be cleaned immediately after a function. Nothing is as unappetizing to a prospective client as viewing a meeting room that contains the dredges from the previous night's cocktail party still on display. Furthermore, stains that are allowed to set in the carpeting or other furnishings become almost impossible to remove the next day.

A major problem is the care of portable bars. Far too often, these units are not cleaned properly after an event. Garnishes left on the bar in receptacles become an open invitation to insects and vermin. Ice bins left uncleaned become giant petri dishes for mold. Spilled soda under the bar turns the unit into a portable breeding ground for roaches.

Chair fabric also suffers from abuse. Porters rarely take the time to clean up spills on the chairs.

Exhibit 9.25 Black-and-White Theme Party

Photo courtesy of Tropicana Resort and Casino, Las Vegas, Nevada.

A third area of concern involves meeting and banquet tables. Frequently, tables are not lifted when they are moved but are instead heaved across the room like cordwood. With this treatment, table tops splinter and chip easily, rendering them useless and unsightly without a tablecloth. Unfortunately, a tablecloth is neither needed nor desired when the table is used as a desk top for workshops.

Finally, the meeting room furnishings should also be cleaned, broken down, and stored—unless the next event in the room is to be a repetition of the preceding one.

Periodically, all meeting room equipment should be inventoried and those items in need of repair should be attended to by the engineering department. A monthly inspection is recommended for meeting facilities that are used very frequently.

Service Control Forms

A standardized function sheet for each separate function during the conference is an absolute necessity. The function sheet minimizes communication problems among the property's conference staff and ensures that set-ups and teardowns will be done correctly and on time.

A master schedule of the day's events should also be drawn up to give the staff a complete listing of all that is needed by the various groups meeting at the property.

Smoking and Other Concerns

Smoking has become an acute social issue that can be handled in one of two ways at meetings:

- The group allows its meeting planner to unilaterally permit or forbid smoking.

- The group votes on whether to allow smoking at all.

If smoking is allowed, two alternatives are available:

- Space is provided for both smokers and non-smokers.

- Smoking is permitted in all rooms, with no space provided for non-smokers.

The convention service manager must convey the appropriate decision to the attendees at the meeting.

If smoking is allowed, normally one-half of the room is designated as the smoking section. Traditionally, that half is the section of the audience on the speaker's left or the stage left (audience right) section of the room.

If smoking is not allowed at a meeting, that message can be transmitted in the following ways:

- Ashtrays are not distributed inside the meeting room.

- The speaker or moderator in charge of the event asks attendees not to smoke.

- "No Smoking" signs are posted by the property on the doors of the meeting room and inside the room.

- Property staff, with support from the meeting planner, are instructed to politely inform violators of the rules and see to it that smoking materials are extinguished.

Other concerns usually involve the installation of honor bars and the availability of movies intended for adult or mature audiences. In the first case, the convention service manager should remove these bars from rooms used by groups like Alcoholics Anonymous or Weight Watchers. If the bars cannot be removed, they should be locked. In those instances where movies with adult themes might be offensive to certain groups, the cable access boxes in the guestrooms should be disconnected.

In most cases, these concerns become actual problems when changes are made after the contract or letter of agreement has been signed. The key element in dealing with these situations is that the meeting planner and the convention service manager remain flexible.

Role of Computers at Meetings

Computers are being used more frequently in meetings. At large meetings and conferences, computer projection equipment allows the entire audience to view computer-generated graphics. On the other hand, at small meetings there may be computer terminals at every seat.

But computers are expensive. Even properties that normally maintain a complete selection of their own audiovisual equipment may not carry computers because of their high initial cost. Planners can have their computer needs met by computer stores that offer rental equipment. These stores usually provide an expert to deliver and set up the equipment for a nominal fee.

Emergencies

Even the most carefully planned and skillfully executed meeting or conference can be seriously disrupted when the unexpected occurs. Emergencies test the mettle and leadership abilities of both the meeting planner and the convention service manager.

The convention service manager should have a comprehensive emergency plan that covers such contingencies as medical emergencies, fire, arson, theft, bomb threats, demonstrations and picketing, violence, and strikes. This plan must do three things:

- Describe the types of situations that could occur
- Outline procedures for dealing with each situation
- Delineate who is responsible for performing required actions

Medical Emergencies

Medical emergencies usually result from the stress of meeting attendees being in unfamiliar surroundings, changes in their diet, increased liquor consumption, lack of sleep, and dozens of other interruptions to their daily routines.

Common problems include fatigue, choking, food poisoning, heart attacks, suicide attempts, drug overdoses, acute alcohol intoxication, ulcer attacks, allergic reactions, and asthma attacks.

The convention service manager should have made arrangements with local physicians, dentists, ambulance services, and nearby hospitals for incoming convention groups.

The service manager should provide the meeting planner with the names and telephone numbers of physicians, dentists, emergency treatment centers, emotional crisis centers, and ambulance firms so that these may be printed in the convention program. A separate brochure on medical facilities in the city should be included in the convention packet given to each attendee.

An excellent proactive stance is to have all management employees and every security staff member at the property trained in cardio-pulmonary resuscitation (CPR) techniques and Red Cross first aid techniques. Furthermore, all food servers should be trained in the Heimlich Maneuver, and all bartenders and cocktail servers should know how to recognize intoxication and prevent the overconsumption of alcoholic beverages by conferees. Seminars such as the Educational Institute's "Serving Alcohol with Care" should be a requirement for all beverage servers.

The meeting planner should have a list of all personnel at the property who are trained in life-saving techniques. The planner and all conferees should also be instructed to telephone the house operator in an emergency so that proper help can be dispatched to the scene.

A medical problem of grave consequence to any convention or meeting is food poisoning. The specter of food poisoning arises when one or more guests report being ill following a banquet meal.

In these situations, the convention service manager must react decisively without appearing to panic. If many people are ill, the property's security division and the local public health department should be notified. Security personnel can keep count of the number of people becoming ill and indicate whether there is a trend or these are just isolated cases.

The convention service manager should recognize the scope of the problem and react accordingly. It is important that while the service manager must act responsibly, he or she cannot appear to be overly sympathetic with the client; this could be construed later as an admission of responsibility.

Fire   The checklist in Exhibit 9.26, developed by the National Fire Protection Association, can be used by meeting planners and convention service managers alike to provide protection against the threat of fire.

In addition to complying with the fire safety checklist, the convention service manager should conduct a fire safety inspection tour of the premises with the meeting planner. A brochure on fire safety procedures should be included in every meeting attendee's convention packet.

Arson   Fires that are suspicious in origin present the convention service manager with a true dilemma: when should the meeting planner be notified?

Every situation is different, but the service manager must realize that sometimes there is a fine line between being informative and engaging in scare tactics. The important point is that the client should not be frightened when there is no cause for it.

Theft   When theft is suspected, the convention service manager must first notify the property's security division. The service manager would contact the group's meeting planner only when members of the group were affected. Although the property staff should extend sympathy to any victim, **no one on the staff should in any way imply that the loss is the fault or responsibility of the property or its employees.**

The meeting planner should be made aware of how the property responds to reported thefts.

All attendees should be warned to guard their valuables. Coatracks in the back of meeting rooms should have warning signs attached to them stating that the property will not be responsible for valuables left unattended.

Exhibit 9.26 Fire Safety Checklist

	Check (✓) when done
1. A fire alarm system is present to alert guests of a fire.	☐
2. The meeting planner recognizes the sound of the fire alarm.	☐
3. Exit doors and routes to them are indicated by illuminated "Exit" signs.	☐
4. Emergency lighting exists for exitways and stairs.	☐
5. There are no obstructions in corridors, exit doorways, exit stairs, and other exit routes.	☐
6. Exit doors are not locked or secured in any manner that would preclude their quick use.	☐
7. Doors to exit stairs close and latch automatically after use and remain closed.	☐
8. Instructions are prominently displayed in each guestroom, giving details about the fire alarm system and indicating locations of the nearest exits.	☐
9. Guestroom doors are self-closing and do not have transoms or louvers that might permit penetration of smoke into the rooms.	☐
10. There is a sign in each elevator lobby station indicating that the elevator is not to be used during a fire.	☐
11. There are signs posted at the main entrance to meeting and function rooms specifying the maximum number of occupants allowed.	☐
12. Meeting rooms have sufficient exits to allow the occupants to leave readily, based on the following ratio: more than 1,000, 4 exits; 300–1,000, 3 exits; 50–299, 2 exits.	☐
13. Exits are sufficiently remote from each other so that occupants are able to use alternatives if one exit becomes unusable in an emergency.	☐
14. Corridors, stairways, and aisles are free of temporary or permanent storage including laundry, chairs, tables, room service trays, and trash.	☐
15. Folding partitions or air walls are arranged so as not to obstruct access to required exits.	☐
16. Exhibit areas are provided with automatic extinguishing systems (sprinkler), and if not, alternative arrangements are provided to compensate for lack of such sprinklers.	☐
17. Adequate services and facilities are available in exhibit areas for removal of packing and other combustible materials before the exhibit opens and that no such materials are allowed to accumulate on the premises during the exhibition.	☐
18. The layout of booths, stands, and exhibits will not impede or block exits and exit routes.	☐
19. A fire watch is maintained in exhibit areas when setting up the exhibit, during the exhibit, and during the exhibit breakdown to spot fire hazards and detect fires, and that the fire department is to be called if an emergency occurs.	☐
20. There are a number of approved receptacles for the disposal of smoking materials in meeting rooms and exhibit facilities.	☐

Source: National Fire Protection Association.

Also, a brochure in the convention packet warning conferees not to leave valuables on their seats or anywhere in the room during breaks is advisable.

All policies regarding thefts should be explained thoroughly to the meeting planner, and the planner should be asked to sign a "hold harmless" agreement to that effect.

Physical Assaults

Learning that a guest has been physically assaulted on the premises is, in many ways, a hotelier's worst nightmare come true. Yet it does happen, even at those properties with the best security systems.

Sufficient reference materials are available to document existing case law and liability aspects in this area. Still, the point should be made that it is important to indicate reasonable security risks to clients in advance.

If an assault does occur, the first priority is to give the victim proper first aid. Medical help must be summoned even if the victim protests that he or she is all right. It is always possible that the victim is in shock and unaware of the extent of the injuries caused by the assault.

Second, security and the police must be summoned to the scene. Witnesses must be asked to remain until statements can be obtained and given to the police.

Third, the meeting planner and other convention executives should be notified of an assault against one of their members.

Finally, it is very important for the property to do everything possible to cooperate with the police investigation, to give aid and comfort to the victim, to report the incident to top management, and to make a full report to the property's attorney.

Properties located in downtown areas of major cities may have a special problem with homeless persons. During periods of inclement weather, these individuals may infiltrate the property seeking shelter. In these situations, it is advisable for a security team consisting of at least two members to check all guestrooms and function rooms. Particular care should be given to checking under stages and tables.

Bomb Threats

Although most bomb threats are hoaxes designed to disrupt the activities of either the property or the convening group, responsible management must respond as though they were actual life-threatening occurrences.

When a threat is received (usually by telephone) and the caller has identified the convention area as the site of the device, the convention service manager must immediately notify the police and ask all convention attendees to leave the area. If possible, a public address system in the convention area should be used to simultaneously warn people in all the public areas of the property.

To avoid panic, specific reference about a bomb must never be made. Instead, the public should be instructed to evacuate the property immediately by the nearest exit for "security reasons."

The meeting planner must be told of the reason for the evacuation as soon as possible so the attendees can be informed once they are safely outside the facility.

Explosive devices are usually left in public restrooms or in stairwells. These areas should be the first places to be inspected by security. If it has been determined that an explosive device has been left on a specific floor of a multi-story building, the floor above the device should be evacuated before any of the lower floors.

Doors and windows should be opened by property personnel prior to evacuating the building to lessen the compression of any blast. Security should be posted at all exits to the building to prevent any looting while the building is evacuated.

Finally, no one should be allowed to re-enter the building until civil authorities have inspected the entire facility and pronounced it safe.

Demonstrations and Picketing

The presence of certain associations and corporations may attract protest groups that want to use the meeting site as a forum to present their opposing views. The convention service manager should query the meeting planner about the likelihood of such an occurrence.

If the planner feels there is a probability of a demonstration at the meeting or convention, civil authorities must be forewarned. It may also be necessary to hire security professionals to augment the property's own security force. This will ensure that any planned demonstrations do not get out of hand.

The service manager should counsel the meeting planner to avoid any escalation of the situation by refraining from direct confrontation with the dissidents. Every effort must be made to minimize hostilities. Television coverage of riots at the property are not the kind of publicity the public relations department hopes for.

Depending on the particular situation, the convention service manager might suggest that convention executives meet with the dissidents' leaders in a controlled environment, such as an unused meeting room at the property (provided with the compliments of the property). If this proposal is accepted by both parties, an unpleasant situation might be defused and the property stands to win the admiration and respect of both groups.

If a peaceful accord cannot be reached, the service manager should assist the meeting planner in making certain that confrontation between the attendees and the demonstrators is avoided as much as possible. The service manager should suggest alternate entrances to and exits from the property or provide sufficient security escorts to minimize any direct confrontation. If all else fails, the property's attorney should seek a court injunction to eliminate or minimize the presence of the dissidents in front of the property.

Strikes

Imagine a situation where the local labor union calls a strike 24 hours before the arrival of a large group at a property!

In most cases, contracts between labor and management specify that wildcat strikes are not permissible. Such strikes are usually grounds for termination of employees taking part in them.

Labor usually agrees to give advance notice of a proposed strike, so the convention service manager would have sufficient time to notify the incoming group and help the meeting planner make other arrangements if necessary. Meeting planners have the right to know when union contracts expire.

Sometimes, however, strikes can cause problems in unexpected areas. A case in point involved a very famous entertainer who, as a matter of principle, refuses to cross any picket line. He had been scheduled to speak to a group at a property where a strike was taking place. The convention service manager knew this individual's pro-labor stance but also recognized his importance to the convention. The entertainer was to have spoken at the end of a banquet, so the service manager managed to transfer the entire banquet activity to a nearby property where the entertainer agreed to speak. Attendees were transported to and from the other property, and the event went off as planned.

Acts of God

Severe weather can seriously affect a meeting or convention. Freak snowstorms, hurricanes, and even flooding can destroy a meeting planner's schedule.

At its worst, a sudden, violent storm can cause loss of life and tremendous property destruction. While such losses cannot be prevented entirely, adequate planning for these events can help minimize losses.

Again, the convention service manager is responsible for preparing an emergency plan for such contingencies. The details of this plan must be shared with the meeting planner so that if a disaster is imminent all guests can be directed to the safest places available before the calamity strikes.

Less disastrous weather problems like unexpected snowstorms can delay the departure of the attendees. A convention service manager can save the day by planning "blizzard parties" to entertain stranded guests.

This author remembers a freak snowstorm that happened during the last week in April one year. It resulted in the property's complete isolation for four days. Snowdrifts extended as high as the property's second story. During the storm, convention rooms were turned into bingo parlors, bridge halls, and poker dens. The cocktail lounge "expanded" its hours of operation. When the snowplows finally arrived, many of the guests said they had never had so much fun on an impromptu vacation before.

Construction or Renovation

Normally, extensive construction or renovation projects would not be scheduled at a time that would disrupt a major conference. Unfortunately, because of the lag between the time a conference is booked and the time it is finally executed, construction projects may be required. And, emergencies can easily arise that necessitate this type of activity.

The convention service manager must remember that ultimately it requires more energy to cancel a conference than it does to execute the event around the construction. Nevertheless, honesty is always a prerequisite in these situations. Tell the meeting planner what is taking place. Very often, the planner may see the problem in a different light or have a better solution to the problem than the service manager might have.

Miscellaneous Activities

There are any number of unforeseen problems that can develop and threaten the success of even the most carefully planned meeting or conference. It is impossible to describe and plan for every contingency.

In dealing with the unexpected, meeting planners and convention service managers must take each situation seriously, but they cannot lose their perspectives. Whenever possible, the service manager must exercise leadership and be perceived as having complete control of the situation. When appropriate, one way of doing this is to try to inject a note of optimism into unpleasant situations. It does not hurt the convention service manager's reputation to let the client know how he or she was able to work around a threatening situation. This reassures the client, indicating that the property has the group's best interests in mind.

Section C: Servicing After the Meeting
Section Objectives

1. To learn how to set up the master account

2. To learn how to collect other charges

3. To understand how gratuities are determined and distributed

4. To understand the elements of post-conference logistics

5. To understand the elements of the final evaluation meeting

Many top convention service managers agree that the work involved in post-meeting servicing is just as important as that before and during the meeting.

Servicing after the meeting includes such activities as preparing accurate billing, distributing gratuities, arranging for post-convention logistics, and conducting the final evaluation meeting.

All these activities are important because they give the participants an opportunity to plan for the future. The importance of repeat business has been stressed throughout this text, and successful servicing after the meeting will help ensure repeat business.

Billing Procedures

Months prior to the convention, representatives from the property and the convening group should have met and established the policies and procedures that will be used in the billing process.

Typically, the group will be asked to forward a deposit prior to the event. At the beginning of the conference, another payment will often be made by the organization. This is followed by another payment immediately after the event. The final payment is made after all disputes about charges have been resolved.

This pattern will vary depending upon the credit and meeting history of the group. A solid corporation that has held numerous meetings at the property and has consistently paid its bills on time and in full may not be required to submit deposits. However, political fundraising groups, volunteer organizations, and student groups frequently are asked to settle their accounts prior to the event.

Master Account

A master account is usually established for most groups. This is an accounts receivable account that contains all the organization's accrued charges.

The property and the organization must establish well in advance of the meeting exactly what charges will be paid by the organization and what charges are the responsibilities of the attendees.

There may be more than one master account folio for a group. For example, exhibitors and other affiliates of the convention organization may want to host one of the activities of the convention such as a cocktail party or a dinner. These charges would be posted in a separate account folio.

The convention contract should explicitly state who is authorized to charge to the master account and exactly what constitutes an allowable charge.

The personal charges of VIP guests frequently cause problems. When the convening organization tells the VIP that the group will pay for his or her charges, it should be made clear at that time whether this includes such incidental charges as long distance telephone calls, small purchases from the property's gift shops, or bar charges.

To prevent these problems, the convention service manager must follow up and see to it that all those involved are informed of what can and cannot be charged to the master account.

Another way to prevent such incidents is to have the meeting planner sign a document stipulating what can and cannot be charged to the master account. A copy of this document is kept at the front desk and shown to anyone who protests a charge.

Generally, corporate meetings will pay for their attendees' guestrooms and food charges. Attendees at association meetings pay all their own expenses, which may or may not be reimbursed by the association.

Disputed Charges   Occasionally, the meeting planner will dispute charges accrued to the master account. There may be a number of reasons for disputed charges, but poor or improper service is definitely one of the leading causes of disagreement.

A dispute may also arise over the number of guests served at a banquet or cocktail party. To avoid such disputes, it is wise to have representatives from both the sponsoring group and the catering department stationed at the door of the food and beverage function. The group representative should verify the function charge and initial the bill and all supporting vouchers so that neither side has to rely on memory when the final reconciliation of the total account takes place. A daily reconciliation of the group's charges should also be made, and this information and all supporting vouchers should be given to the meeting planner at the beginning of each day.

Other Charges

There are other charges that must be considered. Primary among these are supplier charges and individual accounts.

Supplier Charges   The property may or may not be responsible for paying bills from outside suppliers. This is a negotiable item in the contract.

If the property does agree to make these payments, it is very important that both parties understand what constitutes an approved charge. There should also be a clause in the conference contract stipulating that if the property agrees to pay any disputed charges from third party suppliers, the property will be reimbursed for the payment by the planner. The planner then will be responsible for collecting any unwarranted payments made by the property.

Individual Accounts   Individual attendees at a convention are expected to settle their accounts when checking out of the property. As mentioned earlier, these charges will vary depending upon the type of event that was held.

The property must ensure that everyone involved understands the billing arrangement. When convention material is sent to prospective attendees, the convention service manager should insist that a full explanation of the property's credit and payment requirements be included in the pre-convention mailings. Attendees should also be told which credit cards the property accepts, direct billing requirements, and the property's policy for cashing personal checks.

Gratuities

There is a tendency to get away from providing gratuities as such at the conclusion of a convention or conference, but the practice still persists. Both meeting planners and convention service managers must understand the protocol involved in giving and receiving gratuities.

Gratuities fall into three categories:

1. *Service charges that are automatically added to the bill.* These charges may result from a standing property policy on group billing or a labor union collective bargaining agreement. In Las Vegas, the current union contract specifies that all banquets will have a 17% service charge added to the bill. Food servers working the function receive 86% of that amount and banquet captains receive the remaining 14%. Service charges may also be added to room charges to cover tips to housekeepers, bell staff, and desk clerks.

2. *Discretionary tipping to hourly wage personnel.* If the property has a policy of levying a service charge to groups meeting at the property, discretionary tipping would be limited to those individuals who have performed beyond the normal scope of their jobs. The following is a guide for tipping hourly wage personnel at a property. Rates vary by city and area of the country.

   • Food servers—15% of the check

   • Bell staff—$1 per bag

   • Housekeepers—$1 per person per day (or more if there have been special requests or if a party was held in the room)

   • Bartenders and cocktail servers—$1 minimum or 15% of the tab

   • Valet parking attendants—$2 or more if they had to service the car or perform other special services

3. *Discretionary tipping to supervisory staff.* The property may have a strict policy prohibiting this practice. If this is the case, the convention service manager should discreetly refuse the meeting planner's gift, thank the planner, and explain that it is a house policy to refuse such gifts.

Both parties must know who at the property should receive a gratuity. At the post-convention meeting, the meeting planner should name those employees who provided exceptional service. At the same time, the convention service manager must identify those persons who might have done extra work for the group; these persons might not always be known to the meeting planner.

With this information, the convention service manager can help the meeting planner prepare a list of employees who should receive gratuities and suggest what percentage should be given to each. Normally, the manager would provide only guidelines concerning the range of gratuities. It is difficult to quote exact amounts.

Cash is normally placed in an envelope containing the names of both the convening group and the employee. The envelope should be personally presented to the employee who then signs for it. Both the meeting planner and the service manager should be aware of the amount given to each employee.

The convention service manager should discourage the meeting planner from giving any gratuities in advance. These appear to be bribes designed only to reward the anticipation of good service.

But gratuities are only one form of recognition and appreciation. A party for the property's employees, a gift for the convention manager's spouse, and a letter to the property's general manager are other ways the meeting planner can say, "Thanks for a job well done."

One final word about gratuities. Neither the convention service manager nor the property should ever expect a gratuity as a matter of principle. In fact, it is always better to assume there will be none.

Post-Conference Logistics

Rental Equipment

The property staff may be expected to assist the meeting planner in returning any rented equipment used for the meeting or convention.

If the property agrees to help the planner, the convention service manager should confirm the pickup time and have an inventory list available to verify that everything has been returned.

Material to be returned should be stored in a secure area immediately after the function has ended. Unattended recorders, projectors, and microphones can disappear if left in empty meeting rooms. If the supplier cannot pick up the equipment immediately, the convention service manager should ensure that all materials are kept secure until they can be retrieved.

Before the equipment is turned over, the supplier should verify in writing that all items have been returned in safe condition.

Signage

Many expensive special signs can be reused by the meeting planner at the group's next event. The convention service manager should instruct the house crew to collect all signs and ensure that they are returned to the planner.

Planners appreciate such gestures of concern by the convention service staff.

Return Shipments

If the property is asked to provide return shipment of convention materials, the meeting planner should provide proper shipping instructions.

Charges for such shipments can be applied directly to the master account. Again, there should be a complete understanding between the property and the organization on what is expected.

Final Evaluation Meeting

The post-convention evaluation is an opportunity for all the principals involved to discuss the relative success of the activity and to resolve any questions about the billing for services rendered.

All the principals should be present for this final meeting. The list would include representatives from the convening organization, representatives from the property, and outside suppliers.

Personnel from the property might include the following:

- Convention Service Manager
- Catering Director
- Food and Beverage Director
- Property Manager
- Director of Security
- Front Office Manager
- Reservations Manager
- Sales Executive

Evaluations   Every meeting should be considered a learning experience for all parties involved. The property should make a serious effort to determine how service might be improved for future events similar to the recently concluded meeting or convention.

Property's Input. Property staff members should meet by themselves prior to the final meeting with executives from the meeting group to discuss candidly the problems experienced with the meeting. A decision must be made prior to the final meeting with the planner about whether or not to pursue future bookings with this group. This decision must be based on a careful analysis of several factors:

- Comparison of projected revenue with what was actually realized
- Comparison of the number of rooms blocked with those that were actually used
- The size of the no-show factor
- Whether actual revenue from the property's public outlets met projections
- Whether the property had sufficient staff to handle the group's demands
- The number of early departures
- The number of overstays
- The nature of problems with outside suppliers
- Conflicts between exhibitors and the sponsoring group

All these items must be addressed, and a determination must be made whether the property should seek to rebook this particular piece of business. If a group does not match the property's marketing objectives, there is a high probability that neither the group nor the property were satisfied with the results. A property cannot expect to satisfy the needs of all groups nor should it try.

At the meeting with the group's executives, the property should be honest in its appraisal of the group and the property's contribution to the meeting.

Property reports should be shared with the meeting planner to apprise the planner of problems that developed. If the property is candid, the meeting planner can better evaluate the property's contributions and also better prepare for future meetings. Property reports that might aid the meeting planner include the following:

- Room pickup

- Percentage of singles, doubles, and suites used

- Number of overstays, understays, late arrivals, and no-shows

- Restaurant, room service, and lounge usage

- Peak demand times for various property facilities

- Banquet attendance figures

Each member of the property staff attending the meeting should also report on problems he or she has experienced and offer possible solutions. These reports should be written, and copies should be provided to the meeting planner.

Meeting Planner's Evaluation. The meeting planner should be encouraged to offer constructive criticism of the property's efforts during the convention. Many properties use a checklist to aid the planner in evaluating how the property provided service. Exhibit 9.27 is an example of an evaluation form the meeting planner can complete. Also included in the exhibit is a form by which individual attendees can provide input about the meeting.

The meeting planner must review the group's master account during this final evaluation. Any disputes about charges should be negotiated at this time. If an agreement cannot be reached on the entire bill, the property should persuade the planner to at least pay the undisputed charges so that some payment is not held up over a few small disputed amounts.

Evaluations from Suppliers. Suppliers should attend the post-convention meeting if their contributions to the meeting are viewed as significant. Suppliers that might be included are the following:

- Audiovisual supply firms

- Convention bureaus

- Drayage companies

- Exposition service contractors

Exhibit 9.27   Meeting Planner's Evaluation

Attendee's Evaluation
(Con't)

The Meeting Site

Overall
Location
Guest rooms
Hotel services
Comments

Overall, how would you rate the (name of meeting)?
Why?

Are you able to apply insights of the keynote speaker to y
☐ Yes   ☐ No   Why?

How valuable were the discussion groups to your particula
☐ Very valuable   ☐ Somewhat valuable   ☐ Not
Why?

Do you plan to attend a future (name of meeting)?   ☐ Ye
Additional comments

Attendee's Evaluation

*U*sing an evaluation questionnaire is a good way to find o
thought of your meeting. Try to be specific in your questions
questionnaire giving examples of how questions can be geare
response.

Design a questionnaire that's simple to complete and tab
registration desk on the last day.

The Program

Overall
Opening Session
Guest speaker (list separately if more than 1)
Audio/Visual materials
Workshops (list separately)
Question and answer session
Handout materials
Comments

Social Program

Overall
Receptions (list separately if more than 1)
Entertainment (list separately)
Banquets (list separately)
Refreshment breaks
Recreational activities
Comments

*Y*our evaluation of the meeting, the facility, and other aspects of the event is just as important as your
attendees'. Use this worksheet to note your thoughts, point out problems, highlight changes that should be
made in the future, and offer positive comments. Each meeting presents new challenges, problems, rewards -
and by learning from them, you'll plan a better meeting next time.

Meeting _____ Hotel/City _____ Dates _____

What is your overall feeling about the meeting? Was it successful or not and why?

Registration: Goal of attendance met/Peaks and valleys of mail-in-registration/Percentage to total of on-site
registration/No-show factor/Registration Fee sufficient to cover costs (if applicable)

Announcements of Program: Timely/Informative/Clearly written

Hotel: Service/Cleanliness/Food/Appearance/Location

Meeting Space: Sufficient/Setup/Appearance

Sleeping rooms: Sufficient rooms reserved/Early arrivals-late departures covered/Appearance of rooms

Administration: Sufficient support staff/Division of duties

Other Comments:

Source: Sheraton Corporation, *The Sheraton Meeting and Conference Workbook* (Boston, Mass., 1988).

- Florists
- Ground transportation companies
- Photographers
- Security firms
- Tour operators

Gifts and Thank You Letters. The property staff should send out thank you letters to the meeting planner and other conference executives within 24 hours after the group's departure from the property.

Small tokens of appreciation for the business are often presented at the post-convention evaluation. A memento that has the property's logo affixed to the gift is a subtle reminder that may result in future business.

However, caution should be exercised in the presentation of a gift. The gift's value should never be so great so as to imply that the property is offering a bribe for future business.

Rebooking the Group. Finally, if everything has gone relatively well, the post-convention meeting is an excellent time for the account executive to step forward and make a pitch for future business. A number of groups use the post-convention evaluation as an opportunity to begin negotiations for the organization's next meeting or convention.

Chapter Summary

Servicing a group meeting is a complex set of activities that must be conducted at distinct times.

It is totally inaccurate to think of servicing as efforts or procedures that take place only after the meeting group is in place at the property. Servicing occurs before, during, and after the meeting.

Before the meeting, convention service managers must be concerned with establishing and maintaining a flow of communication among themselves, meeting planners, and other individuals and departments at the convention property.

Servicing during the meeting consists of a wide array of activities ranging from setting up guestrooms and function rooms to handling emergencies.

Servicing after the meeting centers on such things as paying bills, returning equipment, and evaluating the success or failure of the meeting.

To merely state that good servicing is an essential part of meeting management grossly understates its importance. Convention service managers must thoroughly understand not only how servicing is done but also when it is to be performed.

10 Catered Functions and Special Events

Chapter Objectives

1. To learn how to provide efficient banquet service

2. To learn about food preparation systems

3. To learn how banquet rooms are reserved

4. To learn the categories of food functions

5. To learn the categories of beverage functions

For most convention hotels, banquet functions are second only to the sale of guestrooms in generating revenue. In this light, studies have shown that a major determinant in the selection of a meeting site is the perceived quality of the food service offered there. Industry experts note that "food service delivery often determines whether a planner uses a facility a second time."[1]

The standards by which catering departments are judged are dynamic, not static. The tastes of the American public are in a state of flux. For example, the current preoccupation with "healthy" food is recognized as being a trend rather than a fad. Light and fresh foods are "in" and are likely to remain popular for the indefinite future.

This chapter concentrates on those aspects of food and beverage functions that are usually part of any large meeting or conference.

Simplifying Banquet Service

One of the most important aspects of banquet service is finding ways to simplify it. Several factors are involved.[2]

The best place to start is simplifying servers' tasks. Because you may have to rely on some part-time help, it is important that you acquaint these employees with your service system and all instructions in a minimum amount of time. You will have to brief these personnel on the facility, the building, the managers, and the particular function they will be serving.

Exhibit 10.1 Typical Banquet Service Rules

1. All servers must carry a clean napkin or side towel at all times.
2. All food must enter the room on a tray with a cart unless otherwise specified.
3. Containers of liquids (hot or cold) must be on trays and spouts should face inward.
4. When placing plates in front of guests, servers must place them so the property logo is at the top and the entree is facing the guest. This requires careful plating in the kitchen.
5. Used plates, glasses, and flatware must be left on properly stacked trays and covered with a napkin. They must be removed as soon as possible.
6. Leftover foods must be placed on a tray and set under the cart.
7. Servers should always pick up glasses by the base, flatware by the handle, and plates by the rim.
8. Serve all plated food from the right, using the right hand. Serve anything that is actually passed by the guests from the left.
9. Serve all beverages from the right, using the right hand.
10. Serve the head table first.
11. Serve women guests first.
12. Clear all dishes and glasses from the right, using the right hand.
13. Do not stack dishes or scrape plates in front of guests.
14. Place appetizers on the tables before service begins, unless they are hot items that must be served after the guests are seated or cold items to be served chilled.
15. Set salads on tables unless they are served as a separate course.
16. Clear the empty appetizer plates or bowls.
17. Serve the main course.
18. Serve coffee and/or wine.
19. Refill water glasses as needed.
20. Replace ashtrays if needed.
21. Clear entree plates, bread and butter plates, butter, rolls, salt and pepper shakers, and any flatware not needed for dessert.
22. Serve the dessert.
23. Serve more coffee if needed.
24. Clear dessert plates, empty wine glasses, empty coffee cups, and remove napkins. If a meeting follows food service, leave water glasses, partially filled coffee cups, and ashtrays on the tables.

Source: Anthony M. Rey and Ferdinand Wieland, *Managing Service in Food and Beverage Operations* (East Lansing, Michigan: The Educational Institute, 1985), pp. 262–263.

Then, you will have to explain their duties at the function: what they will serve, the timing, and where all service stations will be located. Because part-time help usually arrives at the property shortly before the function begins, you will not have a large amount of time in which to accomplish this briefing.

A rule of thumb is to assign ten part-timers to one experienced supervisor and two or three regular employees. It is usually a good idea to have everyone perform the same task at the same time.

Usually, part-time servers' tasks are limited to pre-setting non-perishables, serving and clearing courses, serving beverages, and cleaning tables at the conclusion of the event.

Service can be further simplified if as many items as possible can be

Exhibit 10.2 After-Banquet Duties Checklist

Check (✓) when done

Banquet Service Staff

Clear all tables of china, glass, silverware, and ashtrays. ☐

Remove all linens. ☐

Straighten legs on all tables. ☐

Rearrange all chairs around tables neatly. ☐

Store salt and pepper shakers, sugar bowls, ashtrays, water pitchers, etc. ☐

Clear all remaining carts and lock them. ☐

Remove candles and any melted wax from candelabras and return to storage. ☐

Pour several pitchers of water into garbage cans in kitchen to prevent possible fire hazard. ☐

Check out with supervisor on duty. ☐

Banquet Supervisor

Supervise the banquet service staff. ☐

Turn off public-address system. ☐

Collect microphones and cords and return to proper storage area(s). ☐

Collect projectors and other audiovisual equipment and return to storage. ☐

Search area for valuable items left behind. ☐

Check cloakroom and restroom areas. ☐

Secure any items found and turn into Lost and Found the following day. ☐

Inspect for fire hazards. ☐

Turn off lights. ☐

Lock all doors. (If a band is moving out, alert front desk personnel.) ☐

Leave written information regarding any maintenance problems or items helpful to the supervisor who will open the room the next day. ☐

Leave written information on the banquet manager's desk regarding any guest complaints or serious employee relations problems. ☐

Lock, secure, and turn off lights and air conditioning units in all other banquet rooms. ☐

Source: Rey and Wieland, *Managing Service*, p. 264.

pre-set and extra courses are eliminated. The decision to pre-set food items must be made on the basis of their perishability at room temperature. Water, bread, and condiments can usually be pre-set without problems. However, some food items can become warm and dried out if allowed to sit too long.

Banquet managers must develop rules for serving guests at banquets. Exhibit 10.1 contains a list of basic banquet service rules used at one property.

Upon completion of service, the banquet supervisor for the specific function must perform several after-banquet tasks. Exhibit 10.2 contains a checklist for after-banquet duties.

Simplifying banquet service depends primarily upon good planning and efficient organization. It is essential that a written plan be assembled that takes into account all the details associated with a banquet. Examples of such plans are shown in Exhibits 10.3 and 10.4.

Exhibit 10.3   Written Plan: Meal Requirements

Aetna Life & Casualty
Meal Requirements

Function: Dinner

Location: Morgan – Downstairs
(Evelley – Backup)

Day: Friday

Date: July 29

Time: 8:00 p.m.

Attendance: 61 persons

Room to be Ready By: 7:30 p.m.

Billing: Master Account

Price: $10.00 surcharge per person, plus 7% tax, plus 17% gratuity

Menu

Terrine of Lobster and Crawfish
Spinach and Orange Salad
Veal Loin En Croute
Bouquetlere of Fresh Vegetables
  (Cauliflower and Broccoli Fleurettes, Baby Carrots)
Dinner Rolls, Whipped Butter
Cold Souffle Marie Brizzard
Coffee, Brewed Decaf, Tea

With the appetizer and salad, serve Chateau Chevre Sauvignon Blanc, 1982 at $24.00 per bottle. With the entree, serve Grgich Hills Zinfandel, 1981 at $28.00 per bottle.

Setup

Seating will be at table of 4 persons each. Cover tables with jade linen, white napkins. Floral bud vases on each table.

Service Requirements: One waiter for every 8 guests. Cordial orders should be taken following the dessert and coffee service.

Wine service should not be excessive—glasses should be poured to 2/3 full, not to the rim. (To be discussed further.)

Entertainment: Peter Smith has confirmed a Classical Guitarist to perform throughout the evening.

Audio/visual Requirements: n/a

Source: The Sagamore, Bolton Landing, New York.

Setting Up the Banquet

Using the number of special functions scheduled each day as a basis, the banquet manager must schedule employees to set up and tear down the rooms, as well as perform all the front-of-house service and related tasks.[3] Exhibit 10.5 is a sample schedule of special function room activities for each day.

Procedures for setting up each banquet room will vary with the needs of the function scheduled to be held there. The following is a partial list of activities involved in setting up banquet rooms:

1.   Place runways, carpets, and pianos.

Exhibit 10.4   Written Plan: Meal Requirements

Aetna Life & Casualty
Meal Requirements

Function: Continental Breakfast

Day: Saturday

Time: 7:00 a.m.

Room to be Ready By: 6:30 a.m.

Price: $7.50 plus 7% tax, plus 17% gratuity

Location: Diamond Island

Date: July 30

Attendance: 15 persons

Billing: Master Account

Menu

Assorted Chilled Juices (Orange, Grapefruit)
Fresh Fruit Platter (Strawberries, Seedless Grapes, Sliced Pineapple, Melon, Kiwi)
Assorted Breakfast Breads and Miniature Pastries
Butter, Jams
Coffee, Brewed Decaf, Tea

Setup

Display all coffee service materials on a skirted table station. Service should be left set up in the room throughout the afternoon for self-service.

Service Requirements: Replenishments will be called in to Room Service as needed.

Other Requirements: n/a

Audio/visual Requirements: n/a

Source: The Sagamore, Bolton Landing, New York.

2. Place dinner tables, meeting tables, and head tables.

3. Place chairs, sofas, and other seats.

4. Place bars, buffets, and cake tables.

5. Place the registration, gift, and display tables.

6. Place the movie screen, projector table, projectors, and extension cords; include spare bulbs for projectors.

7. Place chalkboards, chartboards, easels, etc.

8. Place lecterns and flags.

9. Place linens, ashtrays, sugar bowls, salt and pepper shakers, etc.

10. Place candle holders, fountains, flowers, cakes, etc.

11. Place table numbers on each table, if necessary.

12. Place and test microphones, speakers, and related equipment.

Exhibit 10.5   Special Function Room Activities

DATE	TIME	FUNCTION	# PERSONS	ROOM	BEO/FILE NUMBER*	GROUP
Tues. 3/22/XX	9:00 AM–6:00 PM	Refreshments LH/RS	300/400	Cotillion	1576 C-236	Texaco, USA
	12:30 AM–3:00 PM	Buff. Lunch LH/RS	375/400	Green	1577 C-236	Texaco, USA
	11:30 AM–1:30 PM	Lunch JC	60/70	Le Palais	1194 B-144C	Rotary
	7:00 PM–8:00 PM	Reception LH/RS	350/400	Cotillion P.F. and Foyer	1578 C-236	Texaco, USA
	8:00 PM–11:00 PM	Dinner LH/RS	350/400	Superstar	1578 C-236	Texaco, USA
Wed. 3/23/XX	4:30 PM–5:30 PM	Rec/Mtg. CS/JC	65	Derbyshire	1585 B-200B	R.I.C.H. Dept. Heads
	7:00 PM–8:00 PM	Reception JC	50	Green	1249 B-200	Intertel
Thurs. 3/24/XX	10:00 AM–2:00 PM	Mtg/Lunch RS	25/30	Derbyshire	G-69	Government Information Mgmnt. Assn.
Fri. 3/25/XX	8:45 AM–5:00 PM	Coffee JP/RS	250	Cotillion	1181 C-300	Nuclear Medicine
	9:00 PM–1:00 AM	Reception JP/RS	300	Green	1184 C-300	Nuclear Medicine

*BEO = Banquet Event Order

Source: Rey and Wieland, *Managing Service*, p. 259.

Prior to opening the banquet room, the banquet service manager, captain, or other official assigned to the function must perform specific tasks to ensure that the room setup is complete. Exhibit 10.6 is a checklist of typical pre-opening duties. At the pre-conference meeting, the property's convention service manager must check with the group's meeting planner to ensure that no changes have occurred in guest counts, seating arrangements, or timing of the event.

Food Preparation Systems

The banquet kitchen may be a separate area used to prepare meals for special functions; however, it is often a mini-kitchen located close to the banquet rooms. In some mini-kitchens the staff merely portions banquet food that has been moved in bulk from preparation areas. In other facilities, equipment like that used to heat food before it is plated, as well as the plates themselves, is available in the banquet kitchen.

Roll-in refrigerators are frequently used to store salads and other refrigerated foods that production employees prepare in advance of actual banquet service needs. Coffee urns and ice-making machines are also found in banquet serving kitchens, and dishwashing facilities are sometimes located adjacent to banquet halls.

A banquet kitchen moves most food preparation tasks close to the point of service, which provides significant advantages for banquet operations. For example, less time and equipment are needed to transport food, the variety of menu items that can be effectively served increases, food quality may improve, and labor may be reduced.

Exhibit 10.6 Sample Checklist of Pre-Opening Duties

	Check (✔) when done
Obtain a copy of the function order to familiarize yourself with the client's requirements.	☐
Check room for the proper number of tables and chairs, table numbers, etc.	☐
Check room to ensure that the proper equipment is in place, such as microphones, spotlights, easels, projectors, flags, and other miscellaneous items requested on function order.	☐
Check room to ensure that the proper items are in place, such as linens (proper color), lace cloths, candelabras, cakes, flowers, etc.	☐
Check room for proper cleanliness, light level, air conditioning, heating, unusual noise.	☐
Check room for potential safety hazards, such as damaged chairs, tables, sofas; tripping hazards, such as carpets, extension cords, microphone cords; or the unsafe use of candles in connection with flower arrangements or other combustible decor.	☐
Check the restroom facilities to ensure they are operational and clean.	☐
Assign staff to specific stations/tables in the room.	☐
Assign cart numbers to staff.	☐
Make sure all employees are on time, in proper uniform, and familiar with their assignments.	☐
Hold a meeting with the staff and discuss the plan of action as well as pertinent safety matters.	☐
Check to see that the cloakroom attendant, if any, is present and aware of his/her specific duties.	☐
Greet the host, introduce yourself, and discuss such matters as the final objectives of the function, the timing of it, and the specific course of action.	☐
Other duties:_____	☐

Source: Rey and Wieland, *Managing Service*, p. 261.

Some properties use conveyor assembly lines to portion banquet meals, but most use a manual plating and setup process. Exhibit 10.7 shows one arrangement of people, equipment, supplies, and food products that can be used to plate and set up banquet meals.

As shown in this exhibit, one person carves and places the entrée on plates and then passes (or slides) them along the table to a second employee who portions a vegetable. A third employee portions the potato dish and slides the plates across the table to a fourth employee who adds the sauce to the meat. A fifth employee puts plate covers on the dishes and places them in a rack or onto a mobile cart. With this system, five employees can portion food for 300 persons in about 45 minutes.

Portion-control tools help maintain consistency in the size of menu items served to guests. Employees should use a scale when learning to portion the correct amount (weight) of the main entrée on each plate and when randomly checking the accuracy of portions as plating continues. Portion-control tools include slicers, portion scoops, slotted spoons, and ladles.

Of course, the staff must practice basic sanitation principles to ensure that guests receive high-quality, safe food. Other aspects of plating quality include ensuring a clean presentation, deciding to use hot or cold plates, and using attractive garnishes.

The chef or his/her representative should be a member of the banquet planning team because no one knows better what can go wrong in banquet food

Exhibit 10.7   Possible Setup for Plating Banquet Meals

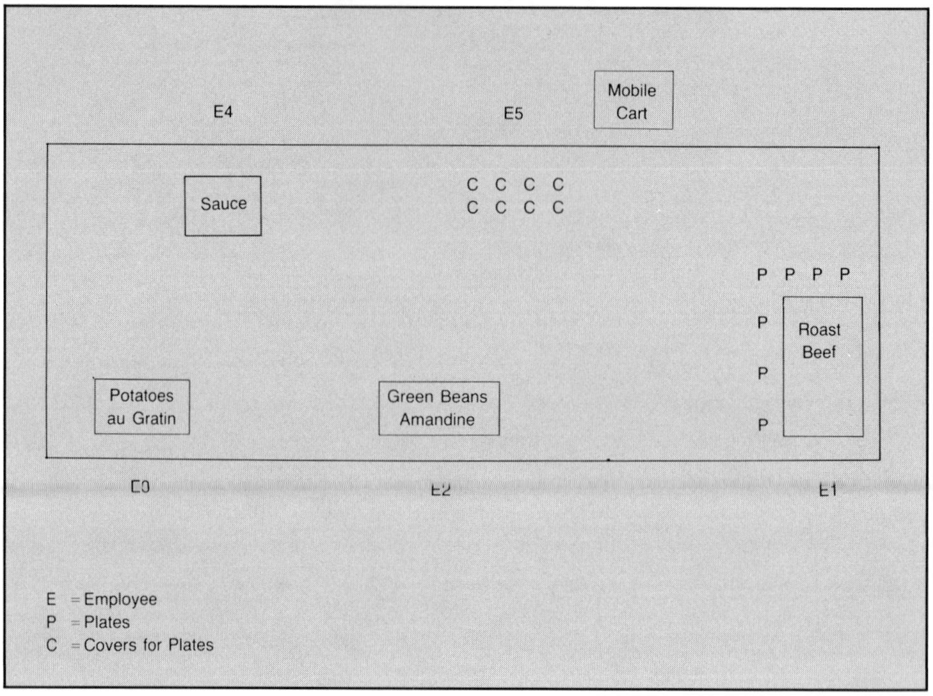

E = Employee
P = Plates
C = Covers for Plates

Source: Rey and Wieland, *Managing Service*, p. 262.

production. When banquet menus are being created, consultations with the chef and other food production staff members will help prevent operating problems later. When considering changes in established banquet menus, it is very important to involve the chef. Experienced catering representatives share the chef's concerns about selling such delicate items as veal cutlets, rare roast beef, Yorkshire Pudding, and flaming desserts to large groups. Such hard-to-prepare items as roast duckling or rack of lamb do not lend themselves to preparation in large quantities. Also, some products may not meet acceptable levels of quality or freshness during certain times of the year. You should also consider the chef's concerns as you plan buffets. While stews, casseroles, and items in sauces may maintain their quality on buffet lines, what about such items as a seafood mousse, most plain, hot vegetables, or individual cuts of broiled meats without sauces?

The important point to remember is that dissatisfied guests will blame the property—not the meeting planner. Do not allow the meeting planner to talk you into serving anything you should not, even if it means the property will lose the business.

Reserving Banquet Rooms

The space reserved for a banquet is very important to both the facility and the guests. The facility views this space as a product to be sold. Unused space represents lost profits. As a convention service manager, what should you do if a client wants to use a specific room that could seat 50 guests for a party of only 20? Obviously, if the client is booking the event two years in

Exhibit 10.8   Sample Sheet from Daily Function Room Diary

Date: May 12, 19XX

	ROOM	7:00 a.m.–11:00 a.m.	11:00 a.m.–4:00 p.m.	4:00 p.m.–Midnight
Grand Ballroom	ROOM A	Group: **AFSIA** By: **PF** Function: **Breakfast Mtng.** File # **107-C** Max: **50**	**Womens Club** By: **AS** **Luncheon (Request this room)** **109-F** Max: **70**	By: Max:
	ROOM B	Group: By: Function: File # Max:	By: Max:	By: Max:
	ROOM C	Group: By: Function: File # Max:	By: Max:	By: Max:
CARIBOU		Group: **Lions Club** By: **DP** Function: **Breakfast Mtng.** File # **1001-D** Max: **300**	By: Max:	By: Max:
ESSEX		Group: By: Function: File # Max:	By: Max:	**Acme Book Co.** By: **JN** **Awards Dinner/Dance** **1007-F** Max: **350**

Source: Rey and Wieland, *Managing Service*, p. 256.

advance, you would try to convince him or her of the benefits of a smaller room so that you might be able to use the larger room more profitably for a larger future booking. However, if the client is booking a party that will occur within two weeks, you might be more likely to satisfy the guest's request. (Most properties set a minimum number of covers for each banquet room, but if a client requests a larger room that is not booked, often it will be released.)

Catering executives use a daily function room diary to determine if space is available for a particular banquet. They also use the diary to reserve the room after they sell an event so that no one else will commit it for another function. (See Exhibit 10.8 for a sample sheet from a daily function room diary.)

The daily function room diary lists all the function space a property has available for sale and divides it into various intervals throughout the day for the sale of different events. The diary varies, according to the size of the operation and the number of available function rooms. Some properties require less information in their daily function room diaries than others do.

Catering executives may make a tentative entry in the diary to hold space for a potential client until the client has made a definite commitment for a particular room on a particular day.

When the catering executive confirms an entry, the diary's coordinator will officially enter the event into the appropriate time slot. An actual copy of the guest-signed confirmation letter or a function room diary entry form may serve as official authorization for the event. Again, remember that properties vary their procedures considerably according to what best suits their needs.

At larger properties, one person is responsible for maintaining the daily function room diary. This individual must notify sales and/or catering executives of any duplicate bookings, conflicts, or overdue holds on space in the diary.

Most properties will permit clients to hold space on a tentative basis for up to two weeks. These understandings, however, should be in writing. Never trust oral agreements. Draft a proposal letter outlining your decisions and understandings for the client. Written agreements help eliminate communication problems that could adversely affect the success of the event. At the conclusion of the period, the coordinator should update the diary regarding the spaces on hold. Because the daily function room diary controls the flow of business through public function rooms, good judgment must be used when entries are made in it to maximize the catering department's revenues.

From the guest's standpoint, selection of the banquet room is very important because the atmosphere it provides must complement the event and its size must accommodate the number of people expected. A tour of the property, particularly at a busy time when rooms under consideration are set for another special event, can often influence the client's final decision to contract with the property.

In making banquet room assignments, the following factors should be considered:

1. Is space available for all the support services, entertainment, and other equipment? Besides space for a specific number of guests, it may be necessary to provide space for head tables, portable bars, buffet tables, entertainment bandstands, dance floors, and other items.

2. Does the event require the seating of guests? The room may easily accommodate many more people for a stand-up reception than a sit-down banquet. (A rule of thumb is 10 square feet per person if guests sit, 9 square feet if they stand.)

3. Are any events planned for the space immediately before and/or after the special function under consideration? For example, if you must tear down a room that held a meeting with exhibits before you can set up the next activity, you will need much more time to prepare the room for the next function than if the room were set up for a theater-style meeting or a stand-up reception.

4. What type of function is planned in rooms adjacent to the room being considered for assignment? Many after-dinner programs have been spoiled by a loud rock band performing on the other side of a "soundproof" wall.

5. What municipal codes and ordinances affect room assignments? Fire or other codes may limit the number of people that can occupy a room. Moreover, you must never block fire escape doors.

6. Is the room easily accessible to both the guests and the service staff? Rooms accessible only by stairs might be undesirable; you should use them only when no other appropriate space is available.

7. What are the sizes of the tables, chairs, and other equipment that you plan to use for the event? While this may seem like a minor

point, tables or chairs that are just a few inches larger than others can significantly reduce the number of guests that you can accommodate. For example, placed theater style, 900 chairs which are just two inches wider than necessary will require 25 square feet more than their smaller counterparts.

8. If a reception is scheduled to be served outdoors, have the convention service manager and meeting planner provided for indoor backup space in case of inclement weather?

Categories of Food Functions

Food functions include, but are not limited to, breakfasts, luncheons, and dinners. All are usually held in the property's banquet facilities. Other related food and beverage functions include such activities as refreshment breaks, receptions and cocktail parties, midnight suppers, theme parties, dances, theatrical presentations, and other special events.

Breakfasts

Banquet Breakfasts

Banquet breakfasts have undergone a significant change in recent years. The mainstays of the typical American breakfast—steak, eggs, bacon, and corn flakes in heavy cream—are in less demand and are being replaced by granola, yogurt, skim milk, and fresh fruit. Gone are the days when canned fruit in heavy syrup was the accepted breakfast fruit, and a cold prune Danish was the standard breakfast pastry.

Today, canned fruit has been replaced by a made-to-order crepe stuffed with fresh sliced strawberries drizzled with a dash of Cointreau. Frequently, hot oversized muffins are substituted for a cold Danish.

A major benefit for the meeting planner from this shift in breakfast preferences has been savings in costs and time. As Michael Ross, director of catering standards for Marriott Hotels and Resorts, explains, "A breakfast of this type can be pre-set. Attendees can eat whenever they come in. And since everyone doesn't have to sit down all at once, it cuts down on service costs."[4]

Unfortunately, one area that has not changed at many properties is the level of service found at "early riser" breakfasts. Many catering departments have traditionally delegated the responsibilities of these early morning functions to room service departments without bothering to educate the staff on how to service group functions. Servers who are used to serving one or two guests in their rooms are suddenly thrown into situations where they are expected to wait on 20 people simultaneously.

Compounding the problem is the usual absence of a manager on the premises before 7:00 or 8:00 a.m. Breakfasts, especially early breakfasts, get short shrift from catering managers in too many instances.

Continental Breakfasts

Variations on the old theme of coffee, juice, and Danish are becoming increasingly popular. Many groups (especially corporate groups) want added touches, such as mimosa cocktails, Virgin Marys, exotic coffees, French pastries, and fresh fruit in season. Accents like these can turn breakfast into an event to be savored rather than one to be endured. These specialty items can also have a positive effect (from the hotelier's point of view) on the size of the check.

A continental breakfast may either be a conventional sit-down function or be presented as a stand-up buffet outside the meeting room.

If the breakfast is presented as a stand-up buffet, the presentation should be set up away from exits, traffic lanes, and other areas where a congregation of people is likely to create congestion.

For a breakfast buffet, make certain that all pastries are half-sized so that attendees will not have to use knives or forks while standing. It is also a good idea to use two tables—one for food and the other for beverage service. This will help eliminate congestion. A rule of thumb is to provide one food server for every 100 persons. If the group is larger than 100, you should seriously consider setting up another buffet area to eliminate congestion. And service tables should be set up so that guests can move down both sides of the buffet. A separate buffet area is required for each additional 100 persons.

Be sure to provide trash cans for paper products and trays for dirty plates and cups. Few sights are as unattractive as finding a half-eaten roll beside the fresh pastries. A few small cocktail tables with ashtrays and one or two chairs placed strategically around the area will preserve your carpet and give the early arrivals a place to sit. Placing numerous copies of one or two morning newspapers near those tables will also be appreciated by your guests.

It is important that the breakfast should not only begin on time but also end promptly to ensure that all members of the group are able to go to their first meeting on time. A typical continental breakfast lasts about one hour.

Buffets offer a number of advantages. They are fast, provide a high level of service, do not require highly skilled services, and offer guests a number of choices. Labor costs can be reduced if a large number of guests will be served.

Traditional Breakfast Buffet

For a traditional breakfast buffet, you might include two or three types of breakfast meats, three to six varieties of pastries, two styles of eggs, one potato dish, and several selections of cereals, juice, and fresh fruits.

You might also take into consideration the desires of health-conscious guests by providing sufficient quantities of foods that appeal to them.

Conventional Breakfasts

Conventional sit-down breakfasts make greater demands on the property's staff than other types. More food servers are needed if a plated breakfast is requested. For a typical plated breakfast, one food server for every 20 guests is sufficient.

Full English-style breakfast buffets with a separate area where waffles, crepes, or eggs are cooked to order are popular with many groups. Exhibit 10.9 shows an attractive breakfast buffet presentation, and Exhibit 10.10 shows a breakfast crepe-making area. This style of presentation will help reduce labor costs, but it raises the house's food costs. Breakfast buffets usually carry a higher price than plated affairs.

In some instances, the group may require a head table and audiovisual equipment at the breakfast. These special considerations, together with a

Exhibit 10.9   Breakfast Buffet Presentation

Photo courtesy of Marriott Corporation.

buffet presentation, will significantly lower the capacity of the room. The convention service manager must consider these variables when selecting an appropriate meeting room.

On rare occasions, the group may request liquor service at breakfast. Usually, such service is limited to Bloody Marys, screwdrivers, mimosas (champagne and orange juice), and champagne.

Refreshment Breaks

The concept of the refreshment break has changed considerably in the past few years. In the past, the refreshment break was strictly a useful interruption in the meeting program. These breaks were simply opportunities for conferees to visit the restrooms, obtain soft drinks, and eat cold snacks. A typical break was usually held in the public hallway outside the meeting area and seemingly far removed from the nearest restroom or public telephone.

Today, the astute meeting planner and convention service manager realize that the refreshment break should not be an interruption of the program, but an integral part of the meeting itself. As Lisa Melucci, senior associate editor for *Meeting News*, writes, "The refreshments you decide to offer, and the setting in which they're served, should be carefully planned to work with—not against—the goals of the meeting."[5] Different groups have different needs and wants, and these differences extend to even meeting places and refreshment breaks.

Exhibit 10.10   Breakfast Crepe-Making Area

Photo courtesy of Marriott Corporation.

For example, an incentive group may want a refreshment break that more closely resembles a theme party than a conventional coffee break:

At the Registry Resort in Scottsdale, Arizona, a "recovery room" coffee break is popular the morning after a late night of entertainment. Chris Carpenter, director of conference services, says she creates a Red Cross Station atmosphere by dressing the attendants in nurses' uniforms and [surgical] scrub suits, hanging the Red Cross flag, and serving tomato juice and other drinks from intravenous bottles.[6]

Other popular concepts for breaks are sports themes, western themes, and breaks that feature a local attraction or atmosphere in the theme.

In recent years, the location of the refreshment break has become a major consideration. Meeting planners and catering directors agree that the traditional locations—in the hall outside the meeting or in the rear of the meeting room—are in many instances the worst places for the refreshment break.

If the meeting planner wants to provide an atmosphere that facilitates communication between the participants on the topics discussed during the meeting, then a refreshment area in a room adjacent to the meeting room is probably best. A private room rather than a public hallway tends to promote conversation, especially if the topics are sensitive. To further facilitate communication, tables and chairs should be provided so participants can break into groups of two, three, and four or more.

At the Scottsdale Conference Resort in Scottsdale, Arizona, a lounge is adjacent to a section of meeting rooms. One area of the lounge is designed as a series of "conversation pits" that accommodate from two to six persons. This area was specifically designed to encourage discussion among the meeting participants during refreshment breaks. The resort also has several outdoor patios with tables and chairs adjacent to the meeting rooms. This outdoor setting serves to revitalize many conferees. Interior settings, no matter how attractive, cannot replace a moment of sun, a breath of fresh air, and a chance to stretch as effective ways to refresh attendees.

Logistics of Breaks

Breaks normally last from 15 to 30 minutes. You must consider the time it takes the group to move from the meeting hall to the refreshment area (and restrooms) and back again. Lack of attention to this time aspect is one of the major reasons many meeting planners never seem able to keep their programs on schedule.

Because it is impossible to predict if the program will end on time, the catering department must be prepared for the break from 20 minutes before to 30 minutes after the expected time. The refreshments must also be able to be "held" for that period. Obviously, a refreshment break is not the time to suggest serving souffles!

There should be at least one server for every 100 participants at a standard refreshment break. Of course, the number of personnel needed will vary depending on the style of service and the complexity of the menu.

Adequate preparation is a must for breaks. If there is an inadequate supply of refreshments, it is almost impossible to get more from the kitchen within the time frame of the break. Thus, you must be familiar with such serving formulas as getting almost 20 cups of coffee from each gallon brewed.

When serving groups larger than 50 persons, it is wise to place condiments (lemons, sugar, cream, etc.) and the silverware on a separate table. This will help prevent congestion around the coffee urn. If you serve groups larger than 100 persons, a separate serving area should be used for each 100 persons to prevent congestion. When serving large groups, it is wise to open the serving areas at the rear of the facility first to draw people into the room and avoid "traffic jams" at the entrance to the room.

Menus for Refreshment Breaks

At mid-morning breaks, the beverage of choice is still coffee. Ice water and decaffeinated coffee should also be made available. All coffee urns should be clearly marked. More than half of all beverages consumed in the morning will be hot. One exception is when the meeting facilities are hot and stuffy. In this case, the meeting planner and convention service manager should jointly consider increasing the order of iced tea and soft drinks.

During the afternoon, popular beverage selections include soft drinks, iced teas, and other iced beverages. In fact, fully two-thirds of all beverage selections will be cold drinks in the afternoon.

Most meeting planners avoid serving any type of alcoholic beverages at breaks. After the lights are dimmed and the projector starts, half the audience will be asleep after even one glass of wine. However, one group that may consider alcoholic beverages at refreshment breaks is the incentive travel group.

When selecting foods, meeting planners have learned from experience to avoid including heavy, filling items on the menu. Like alcohol, heavy foods will impair the audience's level of concentration. Red meats, sandwiches, and cheeses should be avoided. "Light" and "healthy" are the key words when selecting refreshment menu items. Providing a protein shake called a "smoothie" is a fashionable refreshment break alternative that is becoming very popular at more and more properties. This type of break is usually followed by an interval of group flexing and stretching exercises taught by qualified aerobics instructors.

Before suggesting such an alternative, however, the convention service manager and the meeting planner must understand the composition of the group. An aerobics break with protein shakes being substituted for more conventional fare is not likely to be accepted by an older, more conservative group.

One exception to this trend toward healthy foods is in the area of afternoon breaks. Build-it-yourself ice cream sundae bars or chocolate fondue breaks are very popular with many diverse groups. These exceptions are examples of the inconsistency in American tastes referred to earlier in the chapter. Many of us feel we deserve a reward or treat for eating broiled halibut and spinach salad at lunch.

Banquet Luncheons

With so much attention given to providing innovative refreshment breaks, exotic evening theme parties, and receptions, some meeting planners and convention service managers tend to overlook the banquet luncheon. Unfortunately, the main preoccupation with luncheons has been efficiency— how to get the guests in and out again in the shortest possible time.

While the time factor may be a major consideration, the meeting planner should not view the luncheon as a waste of time or an interruption to the program. It should be considered an integral part of the program.

Certainly, the catering department staff should devote as much time and effort to the luncheon program as they do to any other revenue-producing activity in their department.

There has been a trend recently for some meeting planners to schedule marathon morning sessions that contain the entire day's activities but include no breaks. At noon, they dismiss the group for the day so that the members can enjoy the recreational activities available in the area. The planners then reconvene the group for a cocktail reception in the late afternoon. This means that unless the property can introduce innovative food and beverage alternatives to the group, potential revenue from mid-morning breaks and luncheons may be lost to outside competitors.

Sensing these lost opportunities, some properties and resorts have taken a proactive stance in trying to recover this business. The Greenbrier's estate provides afternoon hikers with a "Valley View Picnic Lunch" that consists of a "very civilized" meal of smoked Cornish game hen with sauce Cumberland, knob celery salad, and fresh pasta salad. This is followed by California grapes, saga cheese, and a pecan tart.[7]

**Styles of
Service at
Banquet
Luncheons**

Banquets may be served as either a plated sit-down affair or a buffet. The choice depends upon a number of variables.

If the length of the luncheon is a major concern for the planner, the catering director should suggest a plated sit-down luncheon. This approach ensures that everyone in the group will begin and finish the meal at approximately the same time.

There are other ways to shorten the dining time at a sit-down luncheon. Offering three or fewer courses will speed up the affair. Using a cold appetizer or salad instead of a hot soup means that the banquet staff can pre-plate the item before the conferees arrive at the table; this can reduce serving time by 15 minutes. Placing the entrée, vegetables, and bread on one plate will also save time. Finally, eliminating dessert will speed up the luncheon and enhance the attendees' attention span during the luncheon speaker's presentation.

The composition of the group often dictates whether the luncheon should be served as a buffet or a sit-down. A Fortune 500 company's board of directors would probably prefer being served, while middle-level management from the same company attending a training meeting may prefer the buffet.

The menu also determines whether the meal should be presented as a sit-down or a buffet. Many food items simply cannot be held properly on a buffet table. For example, sauces may break down or curdle, and some entrées dry out quickly. Frequently, food items are added to a menu with little consideration given to their holding characteristics. In general, large pieces of food retain heat or cold longer than small pieces and cold foods hold longer than hot foods.

Popular luncheon buffet trends include salad or deli buffets. Many groups enjoy the opportunity to choose from several alternatives at lunch while still eating "light."

Finally, if expense is a major consideration with the meeting planner, a buffet may not be the best choice for the group. Because the property cannot portion-control a serving from a buffet, it will normally carry a higher price.

**Banquet
Luncheon
Menus**

The current trend toward light cuisine is continued at most banquet luncheons. Fish and chicken are the entrées of choice with many meeting planners. Formal luncheons offering heavy sauces, rich desserts, and alcoholic beverages spell trouble to most planners and have therefore declined in popularity. And meaningful work just cannot be accomplished after an hour-long open bar.

This does not mean that an extra sale at lunch cannot be suggested to the meeting planner. A four-ounce glass of Chardonnay with grilled swordfish will not negatively affect the majority of participants. It may even provide a welcome complement to the meal. Similarly, a six-ounce serving of Black Forest cake may be inappropriate, but the suggestion of a three-ounce serving of crème brûlée may be just the accent needed to end the meal.

Not every group will conform to the prevailing trends mentioned above. Incentive groups, for example, may very well want the full treatment, including an hour-long open bar at lunch. The catering department at Loews Ventana Resort in Tucson, Arizona, provides a six-course gourmet wine-tasting luncheon with a wine expert to direct the tasting.[8]

Banquet Dinners

The evening meal has experienced the least amount of change in recent years. Dinners are often seen as rewards for all the work that was accomplished during the morning and afternoon meetings and for eating so sensibly at breakfast and lunch.

In fact, many groups demand greater creativity from properties' catering departments for their evening meals. If a catering department wants to remain competitive, it can no longer force standardized menus on meeting planners. The "what you see is what you get" attitude on the part of the catering department is a certain formula for disaster.

At the same time, a property cannot be competitive by offering a double standard of service to its guests. That is, a property should not feel that it can provide lower service standards because it is serving a group. Allowing a 1-to-20 server-to-guest ratio in a banquet room while holding to a 1-to-8 ratio in the dining room is a prime example of such a double standard.

This shortsighted attitude also prevents many catering managers from recognizing additional sales opportunities in their departments. For example, one such opportunity that is typically neglected is wine sales to banquets. Many property caterers believe wine sales cannot be promoted to groups for their evening banquets because meeting planners do not want to pay the additional price.

However, planners' attitudes may in fact be based on what the catering department offers the planners. The wine selection in many catering departments does not match the sophistication of the group members.

If price is a factor, the planner might be persuaded to allow the catering department to sell good wine by the bottle or by the glass to persons attending the event. This is a case where the same consideration should be given to the promotion of wine at a banquet as is done in the property restaurant. An enterprising catering department could feature a wine display or have a special wine list on the tables showing the wines available by either the glass or the bottle. A sommelier or wine steward (working on a commission) could visit banquet tables, and the tables themselves could be set with wine glasses as a psychological inducement.

A similar procedure can be used with after-dinner cordials and cognacs. A cordial cart could be used instead of relying on the attendees to get up and walk to the opposite end of the banquet room where the cash bar is located. The guests will appreciate the extra service, and the house is virtually assured of extra sales and the servers extra gratuities. The important point here is that what works in the dining room often works just as well in the property's banquet facilities.

Styles of Service at Banquet Dinners

While buffets are used quite often at dinners, there is a greater demand for sit-down plated dinners at the evening meal than at other meal periods. Again, the composition of the group is the key factor in determining styles of service.

Even when buffets are used at night, most groups expect to receive greater service than at the daytime meals. It is quite common to see a chef carving a steamship round at the end of the dinner buffet line. Desserts may be on a separate buffet table to prevent traffic congestion or the group may want desserts and beverages served at the tables.

Regardless of the style of service used, there should be a correlation between the service level and the price of the function. Groups expect (and rightly so) to receive the proper value for their investment.

Providing Kosher Service

Many conferences and meetings require kosher catering and banquet operations.

Kosher, a term that means "fit or proper," applies to foods that meet the requirements of Jewish dietary laws.[9] These laws are very strict, allow no deviations, and dictate how food is to be purchased, prepared, and served.

The material in this section is explanatory only. Because kosher laws are technical and complex, the supervision of a mashgiach (a trained supervisor) is required. The food service operation offering kosher food must ensure that all aspects of the function are in accordance with kosher dietary laws.

Meat, Fish, and Poultry

Meat from those animals that have split hooves and chew their cud may be eaten. Although pigs have split hooves, they do not chew their cud; that is why pork may not be eaten. Specifically, those animals that may be eaten include cattle, sheep, goats, and deer.

Only those fish that actually swim and have easily removable scales and fins may be eaten. Shellfish and mollusks are forbidden, thus eliminating lobster, crab, clams, oysters, shrimp, and mussels from a banquet menu.

Fish does not have to be koshered and may be used in its entirety. It requires no salting after cleaning. Fish dishes may be combined with dairy foods, but must not be combined with meat dishes. Fish may, however, be eaten separately at a meat meal as an appetizer (separate forks should be set).

Only domestic birds, such as chicken, duck, goose, turkey, and Cornish hen, may be eaten. Neither birds of prey, nor scavenger birds, nor those used for hunting are permitted.

Finally, only specific portions of permitted animals and food may be consumed. For example, there are certain nerves, veins, and fats that may not be eaten and must be removed.

Fruits and Vegetables

There are no prohibitions against eating anything that grows on the land. Thus, all fruits, vegetables, and edible grasses (e.g., oats and wheat) are permitted by kosher law.

Fruits and vegetables may be combined with either dairy or meat dishes.

Rituals Involved in the Preparation of Kosher Food

Rituals of preparation generally apply to the slaughter of animals and how they must be treated immediately after slaughter **before** being prepared for eating.

Meat and poultry for any kosher food production must be slaughtered and koshered by an authorized "shocket." The kosher process is very detailed and must be followed meticulously. Meat may not be frozen for future use unless it has first been koshered. Only meat from the forequarters may be eaten; the hindquarters may be used only if certain textured fat and all the veins have first been removed.

Meat used for broiling does not have to be koshered if it is used within 72 hours of slaughter. Livers need not be koshered and may be frozen for preparation later. However, when livers are ready to be processed, they must be completely thawed, washed, sliced, broiled, sprinkled with salt while broiling, rinsed, and prepared for eating.

Other Regulations Governing Kosher Food

No meat and meat products may be cooked with any dairy product or dairy derivatives. For example, you may not serve chicken à la king or creamed chipped beef at a kosher function.

Dairy food may not be served at a meal where meat is being served. Thus, butter may not be served at a steak dinner. Further, coffee may not be served with cream; however, a non-dairy substitute may be used.

The pots and pans in which meats have been cooked and the dishes upon which they are served may only be used for meat products. The same is true of pots, pans, and dishes used for dairy food preparation and service. It is important to note that if these utensils are used incorrectly, they must be discarded. Drinking glassware does not have to be changed as service moves from meat to dairy products; however, glass dishes used for service of hot food require a separation of meat and dairy items.

Since it is not permissible to mix meat and milk, separate sets of utensils become necessary. Most kosher caterers prepare only meat dishes and eliminate the need to maintain two sets of utensils. Some properties with extensive kosher business maintain two separate kitchens, one for the preparation of meat and one for dairy products.

Kosher regulations prohibit the cooking of kosher food in non-kosher equipment; similarly, kosher food may not be served in non-kosher serving utensils. Therefore, utensils used in hot food preparation and subsequent service must be used for kosher purposes only.

Utensils, equipment, and flatware can be made kosher even if they were previously used for handling non-kosher items. Techniques include immersing them in boiling water, passing them through a flame, or putting them into the soil. However, these techniques must be performed with a mashgiach (a trained supervisor) or rabbi in attendance.

Utensils made of porcelain, enamel, and earthenware cannot be made kosher because they are porous and absorbent. Solid flatware made of a single piece can be made kosher; items made with a plastic or bone handle or with uncleanable crevices or grooves cannot.

When Kosher Rules Apply

Kosher laws are never relaxed. In fact, they become even more rigid during the eight days of Passover. During Passover, for example, unleavened bread is the only bread that may be eaten. Also, the separate cooking and serving of meat and dairy products is done with special pots, pans, and china set aside for use only during Passover. Specific utensils are also used for Passover and are stored for the remainder of the year.

In general, kosher catering is not seasonal, but that depends to some degree on the scheduling of community activities. Usually, there are no catered kosher functions during Jewish holidays or during brief periods that are designated as times of mourning. Cooking is prohibited on the Jewish Sabbath (from sunset on Friday until after sunset on Saturday). Therefore, most kosher functions are not routinely scheduled for Saturday evenings during the summer months since the Sabbath ends late in the evening.

Alternatives for Kosher Catering at a Property

Properties make various provisions for kosher catering. For example, as mentioned previously, some properties maintain separate kosher kitchens in which personnel from the property prepare the food. In contrast, other properties contract with an external kosher caterer who does catering exclusively for kosher functions at the property. Still other properties rent their kitchen facilities to one or more kosher caterers. The subcontracting of facilities for kosher events is frequently justifiable due to the extensive amount of thorough cleaning required to render utensils and equipment items kosher.

Sometimes, kosher food is ordered only as needed for a specific function; no separate storage areas for meat are then required. In contrast, dry products may be stored in a central storeroom as long as they do not come into direct contact with non-kosher products.

Theme Parties

Theme parties range from simple affairs that require no special decorations (the theme may be limited to the menu) to elaborate events that cost hundreds of thousands of dollars.

Most major convention properties keep in stock decorations for two or three different parties. However, when a meeting planner wants more than the standard selection, the services of a special events design firm are usually required.

Entertainment that complements the theme is usually requested by the planner. This might include Mariachi bands for a Mexican theme party or swing-era, big band music for a black-and-white (art deco) party. Similarly, a "Hooray for Hollywood" party might feature a 1930s film, or a "Broadway Babies" party might include a stage presentation or a musical revue.

The attendees may even be encouraged to "dress the part" with costume rental made available through an outside supplier.

This segment of the meeting industry has grown so much in recent years that the International Special Events Society (ISES), an association of specialized suppliers, has been formed to meet the needs of party suppliers. Exhibits 10.11 and 10.12 show examples of an art deco theme party setup.

Late Suppers

A late supper for a group represents a potential extra sale that many convention service managers fail to suggest to meeting planners.

When a group is engaged in late meetings like collective bargaining sessions, a late snack is almost mandatory. But when the group is at a social function like the theater or a sports event, this opportunity is unfortunately often ignored.

Fondues, cold pheasant, champagne, cordials, and cognac are ideal ways for the group to have a communal "night cap" before retiring for the evening.

Exhibit 10.11   An Art Deco Bandstand for a Theme Party.

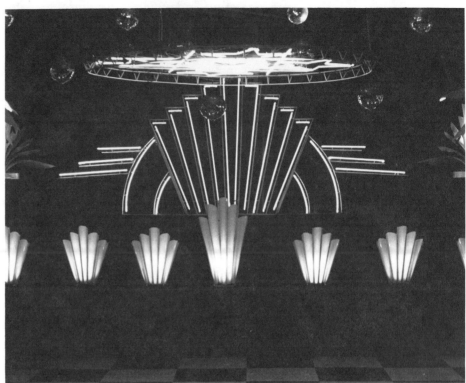

Photo courtesy of Sam Salde Design, Las Vegas, Nevada.

Receptions

Receptions have increased in sophistication and importance in recent years. Until recently, the food served at most receptions was of dubious quality and was relegated to serving as a dietary "sponge" for the liquor that was consumed.

Now, most of the emphasis is placed on the quality of food served at these functions. This was evident in a catering survey recently conducted by Marriott:

> For receptions, food items carved or prepared in the banquet room were cited as most popular by 80% of the catering directors. Foods that work well include shrimp scampi, fettucini, carved beef, crepes and pizza prepared in the room. Regional specialties, like seafood in Florida or barbecue cooked out West, are most often found at receptions rather than meal functions.[10]

The style of service for a reception can vary. One method that is regaining popularity is the use of food servers in formal dress to distribute cocktails and hors d'oeuvres to the group.

When buffet tables and service bars are used and guests help themselves, it is wise to stagger the opening of the tables and bars to keep the guests from congregating near the entrance of the room.

While many receptions are stand-up affairs, it is necessary to provide some tables for ashtrays, dirty plates, and glasses and a few chairs for the

Exhibit 10.12   Cocktail Lounge

An art deco cocktail lounge that is completely portable and can be set up in any property ballroom that has a standard loading dock. (Photo courtesy of Sam Salde Design, Las Vegas, Nevada.)

disabled or elderly. However, because many receptions last only one hour, the number of chairs may be kept to a minimum.

Entertainment may also be a part of the affair. Strolling musicians, magicians, and mime artists are often used at receptions. Large musical groups, however, tend to overpower most receptions.

Finally, receptions should not always be confined to the meeting rooms. Other possible locations include poolside, in the lobby, on the roof, or anywhere safety and common sense suggest.

Categories of Beverage Functions

At receptions or in hospitality suites, beverage functions can be divided into two major categories: hosted and non-hosted bars.

Hosted bars are those cocktail receptions that are paid for by the sponsoring association or corporation. Attendees are not expected to pay for their own drinks. Non-hosted bars or C.O.D. bars are cash bars. Attendees are expected to pay as they go.

The use of cash bars is on the rise. Many meeting planners are offering to pick up the food tab at cocktail functions, but they are reluctant to do the same for the liquor bill. Mainly, this is due to the price tag and the legal considerations inherent in serving alcohol.

Hosted Bars

A sponsor of a hosted bar has several options concerning how the event should be charged.

One option is to pay *by the drink*. This can result in the highest average check for a sponsored function. However, the sponsor only pays for the actual drinks consumed by the group.

Another option for charges is based on the number of people at the function, the length of the event, and the types of liquor consumed. The catering department charges the sponsor on a *per person basis*. A flat fee is charged regardless of whether a person in the group consumes a soft drink or a mixed drink.

A third method of charging a sponsor is on a *per bottle basis*. The sponsor pays only for those bottles opened. Usually, the charge is somewhat less than that run up on the by-the-drink method. Normally, any opened bottle, no matter how much has been consumed, is charged to the sponsor. However, in those states where it is legal, some properties will only charge for what was actually consumed and will take back partially filled bottles.

A problem that sometimes arises with hosted bars is that a representative of the sponsoring organization is not available at the predetermined time to close the bar, and many of the patrons are demanding that it remain open. In this situation, the convention service manager can give the complainers a final drink and then close the bar. A second way to solve this problem is to send the patrons to another bar on premises where a check can be opened for them. The charges could then be billed to the master account but this should have pre-approval of the meeting planner.

Cash Bars

Service at cash bars may be handled in one of two ways: the bartender can dispense the drinks and collect the money through the *cash system* or there can be a separate table where coupons are sold and then redeemed for drinks at the bar.

Whenever possible, the *coupon method* is preferred over the cash method. This system allows for faster service because the bartender does not have to handle cash and provide change. It also increases speed of service so fewer bartenders are needed. Finally, the coupon method provides good control, making errors or theft easier to detect.

But coupon bars also have some disadvantages. Attendees may not realize they must purchase tickets or coupons for bar service, and there may not be a sufficient number of cashiers selling coupons. Attendees sometimes overestimate the number of coupons they must purchase, and they can become confused by having to mentally compute different coupon prices for different beverages.

If coupon bars are used, planners should simplify the system by minimizing the different kinds of tickets sold (perhaps color coding them to match different beverages) and posting a sufficient number of signs around the room explaining the coupon system.

Liquor and Liability
Properties must exercise as much control over the consumption of alcoholic beverages at party bars as they do at the public lounges in the property. The property and the meeting planner can both be held responsible for injuries caused to third parties by intoxicated patrons under state dram shop laws and common law precedents. The property should *never* allow a hosted bar where the patrons are allowed to serve themselves. This once common practice can easily result in damaging lawsuits and is an irresponsible and unethical practice.

Additional information about liquor liability can be found in several Educational Institute products: *Understanding Hotel/Motel Law*, a textbook by Jack P. Jefferies; "Serving Alcohol with Care," a videotape; and the "Serving Alcohol with Care" training seminar.

Expected Beverage Consumption
At hosted bars, the rule of thumb for beverage consumption is to expect approximately 2.5 drinks per person per hour for the first hour. This average will, of course, vary with the composition of the group. For example, all-male groups tend to drink more, while all-female groups tend to consume less.

At cash bars, the average rate of consumption of alcoholic beverages is 1.5 drinks per hour for the first hour. Again, this figure will vary depending on the composition of the group.

Banquet Bar Setup
Exhibit 10.13 shows a typical banquet bar. Each unit has a soda dispenser, ice well, and a rack for bottles (called a speed rail). As long as an electrical outlet is available for this equipment, banquet bartenders can have the same capacity and flexibility as their counterparts in the cocktail lounge.

The types of liquor and other beverages available at the bar are determined by the meeting planner. Liquor may be either *well* (generic varieties normally offered at a lower price) or *premium* or *call* (brand name liquors offered at a higher price). More beer and wine are consumed at party bars, and the astute catering director will ensure that popular and quality products are available. Soft drinks (including diet types), water, and juices should be made available to guests at party bars—not only for mixes but also for those who do not wish to consume alcohol. Non-alcoholic beers should also be on hand, along with a full selection of bar fruits. A "class" property will also provide the guests with glassware, garnishes, and cream-based and blended drinks. (However, under no circumstances should glassware be used at poolside functions.)

Backup carbon dioxide and soda canisters should be stored close by, and canisters and gauges should always be checked prior to use.

After a banquet bar has been torn down, it should be completely cleaned and the manager in charge should always inventory all items not used to ensure proper controls have been exercised. There are special devices available to measure partially filled liquor bottles.

A complaint frequently made by meeting planners is that their group had to wait an inordinate amount of time for service at a reception during the previous year's convention. A convention service manager can solve the problem of slow service in one of several ways.

Some service managers have had success placing one large bar in the middle of the reception room instead of several smaller ones spread throughout the room. On the other hand, if a theme party is planned, a self-serve bar

Exhibit 10.13   Typical Banquet Bar Setup.

can be set up (e.g., a Margarita fountain at a fiesta party). Finally, the most popular drinks can be pre-made.

Sometimes, just getting the group into the reception room can be a problem. This can be solved by placing bars at the back of the room. These should be opened first.

In any event, both the meeting planner and the convention service manager can alleviate many problems by analyzing ahead of time those problems encountered in the past.

Room Setup and Audiovisual Considerations at Food and Beverage Functions

Convention service managers and catering directors must know the capabilities of their banquet service facilities. They must also know how the needs of meeting planners will affect the capabilities of the facilities. For example, special requests for certain types of services can have a significant impact on room capacity, kitchen production, and setup and teardown times.

A given banquet facility may have a capacity of 500 persons for a sit-down dinner. However, when a head table, buffet line, audiovisual equipment, risers, reception table, and coat racks are brought into the room, the facility may be able to accommodate only 400 persons for a function.

Exhibit 10.14   Banquet Contract

CONFIRMATION
(STANDARD FUNCTION CONTRACT)

GS 10755 REV 10-79

DATE _____

HOTEL DU PONT Wilmington, Delaware 19899 656-8121

TENTATIVE ☐   DEFINITE ☐

NAME OF PATRON

CHARGE TO

ADDRESS

ADDRESS

FUNCTION   PHONE NO.

ROOM(S) ENGAGED

TIME   FROM   TO   SERVING TIME

GUARANTEE   SET FOR   PRICE PER PERSON

PLEASE NOTE: FINAL ARRANGEMENTS REQUIRED TWO WEEKS BEFORE DATE OF FUNCTION.

MENU

OTHER SERVICES

_____ deposit required to reserve facilities. Refundable if Patron cancels function in writing at least 90 days prior to date.
Total estimated cost

FOR HOTEL DU PONT

FOR YOUR SIGNATURE
(please approve within 30 days and return one copy with your deposit)

NOTE: This agreement includes the terms listed on the reverse side of this form.

1.   The Patron hires and the Hotel agrees to furnish the services herein set forth in accordance to the terms hereof.

2.   The Hotel reserves the right to require additional payments or full payment at any time prior to the scheduled date of the function.

3.   Patron agrees to advise the Hotel at least 48 hours in advance of the function of the definite number of guests. This figure will be used as the guaranteed minimum. Hotel shall not be responsible for service or accommodations to more than 5% increase over minimum guaranteed attendance.

4.   Unless the Hotel is provided with satisfactory credit references for Patron and explicitly waives its right to advance payment, seventy-five percent (75%) of the total estimated cost for the function must be paid by Patron at least two weeks prior to the date of the function and the remainder must be paid within thirty (30) days after the function. The Hotel reserves the right to cancel this agreement and the function to which it pertains within ten (10) days prior to the function if the required advance payment is not received. Furthermore, in the event of any failure to make any payment due the Hotel, the Patron hereby agrees to be personally liable for such payment.

5.   No food or beverage of any kind can be permitted to be brought into the Hotel by the Patron or any of the Patron's guests or invitees.

6.   Patron assumes responsibility for any and all damages caused by it or any of its guests, invitees, or other persons attending the function, whether in rooms reserved or in any other part of the Hotel.

7.   Patron shall not put up any displays within the Hotel without the permission of the Hotel.

8.   Patron agrees not to enter into any contracts for music or other forms of entertainment or other service or accommodation in connection with this function, without prior consent of the Hotel.

9.   In the event that the Hotel, at request of Patron, furnishes any food, beverages, or any other services not provided for in this contract, Patron agrees to pay Hotel the charges thereof.

10.   In the event this agreement is signed in the name of a corporation, partnership, association, club, or society, the person signing represents to the Hotel that he has full authority to sign such contract, and that in the event that he is not so authorized, he will be personally liable for the faithful performance of this contract.

Source: Rey and Wieland, *Managing Service*, p. 270.

The convention service manager's primary task is to facilitate the communication process between the meeting planner and the property so that the latter can meet and even possibly exceed the planner's needs.

Banquet Contracts

After the catering executive and client have agreed on the exact terms of the special function, they should confirm the terms in a contract. Exhibit 10.14 is a contract that one property uses. Every detail that the two parties have discussed and agreed upon should be written on the contract. The client should also be alerted to the requirement of a guaranteed number of guests.

Chapter Summary

Food and beverage functions are an integral part of most meetings and conferences, and the degree to which these functions are successfully carried out will determine whether a meeting planner will use the meeting property in the future.

Convention service managers must have some understanding of the details involved in setting up food preparation systems as well as how to simplify banquet service. Adherence to carefully prepared checklists greatly simplifies these tasks.

There are different categories of both food and beverage service, and a thorough understanding of their characteristics and requirements will ensure a successful conference.

Notes

1. Leo M. Renaghan and Michael Z. Kay, "What Meeting Planners Want: The Conjoint-Analysis Approach," *The Cornell Hotel and Restaurant Administration Quarterly*, Vol. 28, No. 1 (May 1987), p. 76.

2. Material in this section is adapted from Kanode Associates, *Operations Manual for Convention Centers* (Phoenix, Arizona, 1985), pp. 2–4.

3. Material in this section is adapted from Anthony M. Rey and Ferdinand Wieland, *Managing Service in Food and Beverage Operations* (East Lansing, Michigan: The Educational Institute, 1985), pp. 258–260. The material in "Food Preparation Systems" is adapted from that found on pp. 61–62 of the same text, and the material in "Reserving Banquet Rooms" is adapted from that on p. 255.

4. Gayle Ehrenman, "Big Breakfasts Bow Out As Lighter Food Trend Continues," *Meeting News*, April 1987, p. 18.

5. Lisa Melucci, "Good-Bye Seminar Danish; Hello Chocolate Fondue," *Meeting News*, December 1987, p. 44.

6. Susan Hatch, "Coffee, Tea, or a Little Bit of Fun?" *Successful Meetings*, December 1987, pp. 122–123.

7. Lisa Melucci, "Keep Attendees Awake at Luncheons by Serving Lighter, Healthier Fare," *Meeting News*, March 1988, p. 57.

8. Ibid., p. 56.

9. Adapted from Rey and Wieland, *Managing Service*, Appendix B, pp. 383–385.

10. "Marriott Catering Survey Identifies Latest Trends in Food and Beverage," *Meeting News*, April 1987, p. 19.

11 Meeting Technology

Chapter Objectives:

1. To become familiar with audiovisual aids used in the meeting environment

2. To become familiar with staging and lighting used in the meeting environment

3. To become familiar with ancillary items of meeting technology

4. To become familiar with the reasons for and against ownership of audiovisual equipment

The term "audiovisual" is too restrictive to adequately describe the technology used to assist or enhance meeting presentations. This does not mean that all the traditional AV tools have been replaced by sophisticated electronic equipment. Rather, computers and videotape machines are now being used to complement chalkboards and flipcharts. This is evident from the variety of meeting room aids shown in Exhibit 11.1.

Numerous technological innovations are being used as meeting facilitators. For example, developments in computer technology have made radical changes in the meeting environment, and keypad response systems allow for greater audience interaction. Still, not all meeting room innovations are high-tech.

Remarkable accomplishments have taken place in the low-tech area as well. Improved delivery systems and methods of operation have made the jobs of the meeting planner and convention service manager much easier.

This chapter will examine a variety of both new and old audiovisual devices and will also explore many subjects indirectly related to audio and visual presentations.

Projectors and Screens

Projection systems have been an invaluable aid for presenting educational or motivational material to groups.

Exhibit 11.1 Meeting Facility Setup

Meeting facility with classroom-style setup, incorporating the following AV equipment: from right to left, flipchart, projector screen, carousel slide projector, lectern with microphone, color TV monitor, and videotape recorder (behind lectern). (Photo courtesy of Marriott Corporation.)

Convention service personnel must learn the proper use of different projectors and their optimum operating conditions. The equipment can be owned by the group conducting the meeting, rented from an outside supplier, or owned by the property hosting the meeting. In any case, the convention service manager may have to assist in the setup, operation, or repair of the equipment.

Overhead Projectors

The overhead projector, a mainstay of the classroom environment, is a relatively simple device that projects transparent images onto a screen or a blank wall surface.

The operator can also write on clear acetate sheets or on a continuous sheet of acetate mounted on a roller and project this material onto a screen. Special felt-tipped pens must be used for writing on the transparencies, and these pens come with different tip widths and in a variety of colors.

The overhead is the easiest projector to operate. Controls usually consist of an on-off switch and a means to focus the image. The projector may also have a two-position switch or a dimmer to control the lamp's intensity.

Although the projector lamp will last longer if the less intense setting is used, most operators prefer to operate the machine at its brightest setting.

Many speakers like to use the overhead projector for the following reasons:

- It is simple to operate.

- Transparencies can be constructed rather quickly by photocopying printed matter.

- Writing on acetate is not as messy as writing on a chalkboard.

- Speakers do not have to erase the transparency when it is filled; they can easily replace it with an empty acetate or advance the acetate if it is on a roller.

- Speakers can face the audience while using the overhead projector.

- Speakers can stand in one place rather than have to move back and forth as is the case when using a chalkboard.

Audiences, on the other hand, are ambivalent about overhead projectors. From their standpoint, the following three problems detract from the projector's usefulness:

1. The noise from the built-in fan (used to cool the lamp) can be very distracting.

2. Transparencies made from printed matter can be completely illegible to viewers in the rear if the writing is not enlarged.

3. Transparencies can be either overpowering (too many words) or dull and uninspiring (typewritten material).

There is one major feature of an overhead projector that appeals to both the audience and the speaker: it can be used in a lighted room. This feature has endeared the overhead projector to many training directors.

Speakers interested in using the overhead projector can improve their presentations significantly by practicing a few basic rules:

1. Limit the projector's use to groups of fewer than 60 participants.

2. Never leave the projector running if it is not needed. A visual image left on the screen will distract the audience from what the speaker is saying.

3. Have the acetates mounted on frames to make them easier to handle.

4. Have transparencies produced by a professional. A professional AV firm can produce color transparencies. Light images on a darker background are easier for the audience to view.

5. Photocopying colored material and then making a transparency of it almost never works. The result is usually illegible.

6. Cover those areas of the transparency that are not being discussed. An audience tends to read the material on the screen rather than listen to what the speaker is saying.

7. Do not turn your back to the audience as you discuss the transparency. Maintain eye contact with your audience.

8. Transparencies can become exciting visual aids if you have the right equipment to produce them. Computer software programs and laser printers can produce excellent transparencies that have all the earmarks of having been produced by a commercial firm.

9. Check out the visibility of your transparencies by viewing them from the last row in the room prior to the presentation. If they are illegible, either have them enlarged or get a larger screen and move the projector farther out into the audience.

10. When using a pointer with transparencies, point to items on the screen—not on the transparency. A pen moving across the transparency is very distracting.

11. Ambient light can reduce the quality of the projected image. If there is too much light, dim the room lights or get a higher wattage projector.

12. Rehearse with your visual aids.

13. Project your transparency onto the screen and give the audience enough time to read it before you speak. However, do not merely repeat each item word for word; explain and discuss.

14. Each transparency should contain just one thought. If possible, limit the number of words on a transparency to between 15 and 20.

Two recent innovations in overhead projector technology have increased the projector's popularity.

One advancement has been the introduction of a briefcase model. This device can be collapsed and carried like a standard briefcase.

The other major innovation has been the development of a special attachment to the projector screen that allows a computer image to be shown. Images on the computer's cathode ray tube (CRT) can be projected onto the screen. The device consists of a liquid crystal display with an interface card and a hand-held remote control. It will work with any IBM PC or Apple computer and any standard overhead projector. The system is marketed by Kodak under the name Kodak Data Show and by Telex Communications under the name MagnaByte Systems. However, be certain the device has a fan for cooling; overheating causes the image to darken.

Slide Projectors

The slide projector most commonly used for presentations at meetings is the 35mm projector and is usually called a carousel projector. It takes a standard 2- by 2-inch slide. The film in the slide has a height-to-width ratio of 2:3 and produces an image on the screen that is one-third wider than its height.

The Kodak Ektagraphic slide projector (models AF-2 and the newer AT-3) is the most common type in use.

A carousel tray that holds a maximum of 80 slides fits on top of the projector. Although a 140-slot tray has been developed to replace the 80-slot type, the new tray is not recommended because older slides that may have frayed edges will jam the machine. It is better to use two 80-slot trays and manually change the trays or to use two separate projectors.

Controls for the projector are fairly simple to use. The instrument can be operated from either the machine itself or from a remote control device. There are two types of remote control systems: a wired remote and a wireless type. Both can advance and reverse the slide tray and focus the slides. Obviously, the wireless remote gives the speaker greater flexibility. In any case, the speaker should have an assistant stationed near the machine as a trouble-shooter during the presentation.

Most slide projectors can also be connected to an audio-sync tape recorder. These recorders will advance the slide trays by a silent electronic cue contained on a tape while providing music and/or narrative accompaniment.

Most slide projectors are equipped with a 4-to-6-inch zoom lens. However, larger lenses can be obtained for projecting over longer distances. These special lenses are very expensive. Special, faster lenses are also available that produce more light on the screen, making for a brighter picture. The speed of any lens is measured in f-stops; the smaller the f-stop number, the faster and brighter the lens.

Slide projectors normally use a quartz-halogen lamp, but special projectors containing a xenon lamp can greatly increase the brilliance of the image on the screen, especially when projecting over great distances. However, the xenon lamp is filled with a high pressure gas and can be extremely dangerous if used by an inexperienced operator.

The type of lens and lamp used in a slide projector is determined by the size of the projection screen and the distance or "throw" from the projector to the screen.

Operating the Slide Projector. Although the standard carousel slide projector is relatively simple to control, the operator should be aware of a few basic rules:

- Timing is important when presenting slides. First, flash a slide and give the audience time to absorb the scene or read the material; then discuss what is on the screen.

- Do not leave a slide on the screen after you have moved to another topic. Either turn the projector off or insert a shutter (blank) slide.

- When you have finished with the slide portion of the presentation, turn off only the light and let the fan run until the air from the projector is cool. Turning off the fan may cause a very expensive lamp to overheat and pop like a flashbulb.

- There is no single, all-encompassing rule governing the number of slides to show an audience over a given period of time. However, certain guidelines exist. For workshops and technical sessions, a single slide can be shown for several minutes. The same slide might even be used a number of times to stress an important point. For motivational seminars, using the same slide for even a minute would be boring to the audience. A suggested guideline for motivational seminars would be three slides per minute.

- Place the projector on a stand to elevate the projected image over the heads of the participants. Skirting on the stand will enhance the setting of the meeting room.

Slide Preparation. When preparing slides, there are a number of considerations that must be addressed:*

---

*For additional information about preparing artwork for slides, consult *Legibility—Artwork to Screen, No. S-24,* a pamphlet published by Eastman Kodak Company.

- Avoid using white letters on a black background. White or light letters on a dark colored background other than black are easier to read.

- Limit the words on a single slide to 20.

- Artwork should be rectangular, and the standard size is 6 inches high by 9 inches wide.

- Characters should be a minimum of 1/8-inch high.

- A space the height of a capital letter should separate lines of copy.

- Eliminate needless details. Too many lines, numbers, and words on a slide can confuse the audience.

- Bar charts or pie graphs are better than line graphs.

- Use upper and lower case letters rather than all capital letters.

- Make duplicates of slides that you will show more than once in the presentation rather than trying to return to the original slide in the tray.

- A kit is available from Polaroid Corporation that allows a presenter to take pictures (using Polaroid's instant slide film) and develop the film at once. A speaker can take pictures of a group's reception and show the slides to the group during an after-dinner speech the same night.

Other Types of Slide Projectors. Variations of the standard 2- by 2-inch slide projector are available.

The lantern projector has a slide format that measures $3^1/_4$ inches by 4 inches. Slides must be changed manually, and the projector lacks other modern features.

Another type used frequently by meeting planners is the self-contained rear-projection unit. The screen resembles a small television screen (12 inches). The units may have a cassette tape recorder built in to advance the slides by electronic impulses timed to an audio presentation. These units are used in individualized instruction programs, product demonstrations, and as rehearsal instruments for speakers.

On the leading edge of projector technology are holographic projectors that can create a realistic three-dimensional image in space without the use of a screen. These projectors are expensive, but the technology has been available for a number of years. Sophisticated special effects companies usually rent or lease such equipment.

Overall, slide projectors remain the preferred AV instrument of most speakers and will likely remain so in the years ahead. Used properly, a slide presentation increases audience involvement to a degree that is not possible with an overhead projector or other less sophisticated audiovisual aids.

Film Projectors

Many meeting planners consider film projectors to be an endangered species in the AV world. These projectors have been replaced by the more user-friendly videotape recorder.

However, on some occasions, a meeting planner will have to use a film projector. A wise convention service manager will know where to find one if it is not available in the property's inventory of AV equipment.

The standard film size for educational and industrial films is 16mm (the width of the film). The ratio of the film's height to width is 3:4. On rare occasions, the convention service manager may be asked to provide an 8mm or a super 8mm projector.

If, however, you purchase or rent a 16mm projector, be sure to obtain one with an automatic threading mechanism or a manual channel threading mechanism rather than a totally manual system. A manual threading system is almost always guaranteed to cause the operator problems at inopportune times.

Sound is recorded on motion picture film by one of two methods: optical soundtracks or magnetic soundtracks. Magnetic soundtrack recordings are quite rare, so it is wise to purchase the projector with an optical sound head.

Built-in speakers provide poor quality sound reproduction. Auxiliary speakers should be used, and the speakers should be placed high off the ground and behind the projection screen for clarity and realism. It is distracting for a viewer to watch an individual on the screen in front but have to listen to that person's voice coming from the rear of the auditorium.

Finally, there are several considerations the operator should be aware of when using a motion picture projector:

- Carry a roll of splice tape and a splicer to fix the film when it breaks.

- On every projector there is a film cutter (usually near the front). This device is invaluable if the film becomes mangled as you try to thread the machine.

- NEVER attempt to rewind the film if the meeting is still in progress.

- If you are working with an unfamiliar projector, practice operating it well in advance of the meeting. Read the directions and follow the diagram printed on the inside cover before trying to operate the unit.

- Finally, suggest to meeting planners that they transfer their favorite films to videotape as soon as possible.

Filmstrip Projectors

A filmstrip is a series of still pictures contained on a 35mm strip. The filmstrip can be accompanied by sound. Audio cassettes can advance the film by silent electronic cues in the same manner as in audio-sync slide shows.

Because of its limited projection distance, the filmstrip projector is used as a teaching aid in workshops. It has few other uses.

Opaque Projectors

Noisy, cumbersome, and a source of constant frustration in its operation, the opaque projector has become an anachronism among projectors.

It is designed to project an opaque object onto a screen in a completely darkened room (no ambient light) from a distance of about 10 feet. This is usually done very poorly. In addition, the large fan that cools the lamp in the machine will usually blow away individual sheets of paper that are to be projected.

Usually, it is more advantageous to pass the object throughout the audience than to try to use an opaque projector to show it.

Final Notes on Projectors and Their Operation

Regardless of the type of projector used, a few common rules of operation and maintenance apply to all:

- Keep track of the hours of operation of each lamp and replace the lamp **before** it is likely to burn out during a presentation.

- Give the operator an extra lamp in case the other burns out before its expiration life. Some new projectors have housings for spare lamps built into the machine.

- When replacing lamps, **do not touch the glass surface of the lamp with your bare hand**. Oils from your hand will form hot spots on the lamp, causing it to burst when turned on. At the very least, these spots will significantly reduce the rated life of the lamp. Always wrap the new lamp in a lint-free tissue when replacing a burned-out lamp.

- **Never replace a lamp while the projector is still plugged into the outlet**. This is a common safety practice applicable to any situation involving electrical devices.

- After you have just replaced a bulb, turn on the projector away from any bystanders. The bulb may burst the first time power is applied to it. Modern lamps like quartz-halogen and especially xenon tend to explode.

Projector Screens

Projector screens come in a variety of sizes, surfaces, and shapes. The incorrect type of screen can ruin an entire visual presentation.

There are three types of screen surfaces that are commonly used: matte white, glass-beaded, and lenticular. Each type has advantages and disadvantages.

Matte White Surface. This is the most common type found in meeting rooms. The surface is a flat white and is the dullest of the three types. Hence, ambient light must be held to an absolute minimum for the screen to be effective. A major advantage of the matte white surface is that it provides an even reflection over a wide viewing angle. This lack of distortion makes it a must in wide, shallow meeting rooms.

Glass-Beaded Surface. Although the glass-beaded surface produces an extremely bright image (approximately three times brighter than the matte white surface), the viewing angle is much narrower than the matte white. The audience should be seated within 30 degrees of the projection axis.

Lenticular Surface. The lenticular screen is an excellent compromise choice. The surface is very bright even in considerable ambient light, and the viewing angle is much larger than that of the glass-beaded screen. The major disadvantage of the lenticular screen is its relatively small size. Maximum size is approximately 6 by 6 feet.

Fixed and Portable Screens. A fixed projection screen can either be mounted on the wall or from the ceiling. Ideally, every meeting room should have at least one ceiling-mounted, motor-driven screen.

There are three types of portable screens: tripod, saddle screen, and fastfold screen.

A tripod has a pull-up surface and ranges in size up to 8 feet high. The screen is supported by a rod and can be set up by one person. A major disadvantage to tripod and saddle screens is that in many viewing situations they must be placed on a riser or a table.

A saddle screen is similar to the tripod screen. A saddle screen is bulky, cumbersome, and has a tendency to tip and buckle. It must be used with caution.

The fastfold screen is mounted on a folding aluminum frame. This screen can be hung from a ceiling, or legs can be attached to the frame.

Screen Sizes. Most portable screens are never larger than 12 feet square. However, permanent screens can be many times that size. Care should be taken to select the right screen size. The size of the facility and distance to the back row of the audience are important variables. A simple rule of thumb to employ is the 2-by-6 rule. This means the screen width should be one-half the distance to the first row of seats and one-sixth the distance from the screen to the final row of seats.

In a level room, the bottom of the screen should never be closer to the floor than five feet. The average height of a seated person is 4 feet 6 inches, and with the bottom of the screen at least 5 feet off the ground, sight lines are fairly unobstructed.

Boards and Flipcharts

Chalkboards and flipcharts are certainly at the low-tech end of the audiovisual spectrum. However, they do have their place in the meeting room environment.

Chalkboard

Teachers may love chalkboards, but they are messy. Their purpose is better served by the whiteboard. About the only relatively recent innovation in chalkboards has been in the change of their color from black to green.

If the speaker insists on a chalkboard, provide an assortment of different colored chalk in order to enliven the presentation.

Whiteboard

The whiteboard is a vast improvement over the chalkboard. It uses a dry-erase marker instead of chalk as the writing instrument. The whiteboard is cleaner and certainly more convenient.

Markers come in a variety of colors, which means the speaker can stress different points with different colors (a nice touch). The only negative characteristics associated with the markers are their offensive odor and their indelibility if applied to a porous surface or clothing.

When a whiteboard is permanently installed in a meeting room, it can also serve as an impromptu projector screen for a small group. Additionally, two whiteboards mounted on vertical tracks give the speaker the freedom to continue a presentation when one board is filled without having to erase the filled board. The speaker merely has to move one board down and continue on the second board.

Some whiteboards are marked like graph paper, thus helping the instructor to write in a straight line.

Electronic Whiteboards

An additional technological improvement is the electronic whiteboard. Presenters at meetings are usually frustrated because attendees spend most of their time taking notes and not enough time listening to the presenter. Until now, there was no other way for attendees to take notes.

Panasonic's Panofax is an electronic whiteboard that reproduces everything written on or taped to it. The board measures 4 feet high by 8 feet in width. When a copy of material on the board is required, the operator pushes a button and an arm slides across to photocopy everything on the board. An 8 1/2- by 11-inch sheet is produced that can be photocopied in sufficient quantity for everyone at the meeting.

Another innovation in board technology is the Gemini Blackboard. This device has the capacity to send material written on it to another board thousands of miles away. The transmission of the message is done over telephone lines. This device is extremely important in teleconferencing sessions.

Flipcharts and Easels

The flipchart has been an audiovisual meeting fixture for years. Best used for groups fewer than 50 persons (as are whiteboards and chalkboards), the flipchart is appropriate for training meetings. This is especially true when the presenter must record ideas from the audience during a brainstorming session.

The paper pad, which normally measures 27 by 34 inches, is mounted on an easel that has a solid flat back and may have telescoping legs so that it can be set on either the floor or a table. The flipchart easel differs markedly from an ordinary easel that is used to hold signs. Because the latter does not give the writer a stable surface, care must be taken to provide the right type of easel.

Writing on the flipchart is usually done with ink markers that come in an assortment of colors. Paper can either be purchased with a completely blank surface or a graph surface that cannot be seen by the audience.

Electronic Video Equipment

The use of video equipment in the meeting room has revolutionized the meeting environment. Video presentations range from the simple playback of recorded tapes to the use of cameras and playback systems for sales training and other role-playing exercises.

Some groups, especially corporate groups, now videotape an entire event. The edited tape can then be used as an educational or motivational tool for members of the organization who were unable to attend the meeting.

The main problem with video equipment (or any other rapidly developing technology) is compatibility among different systems and equipment. The meeting planner and the convention service staff must be aware of any incompatibilities if the event is to proceed without mishaps.

Videotape Recorders (VTR)

Convention service managers must be aware of the different video formats of videotape recorders. None of the current formats are compatible with any of the others. This problem resulted when a number of video manufacturers introduced their own patented equipment, and no attempt was made to limit the equipment to a single format.

A standard format is only now slowly being established in the United States, largely as a result of the buying patterns of the American public. An increasing number of consumers seem to prefer video recorders that have the VHS 1/2-inch tape format, but several other formats are still in use.

There are currently five video formats in the United States today:

1. The **VHS** format uses 1/2-inch tape. Tapes are manufactured by a number of suppliers. However, care should be taken to purchase only those tapes that carry the VHS insignia that appears on the narrow end of the box. Most name brands, like BASF, Fuji, and Scotch, carry this insignia. VHS tapes can be recorded at different speeds, and most recorders and cameras have three speed settings for recording. Standard play (SP) is the fastest operating speed and results in the best picture quality; long play (LP) and extended play (EP) are slower speeds that produce reduced picture and sound quality. Exhibit 11.2 lists the major types of VHS video cassettes and their recording times by the three different speed settings.

   As already mentioned, the VHS format is becoming the most popular with meeting planners because the majority of the American public who own VTRs have equipment that uses this format. This allows many meeting attendees the opportunity to take the recordings home and play them back on their own recorders. However, a recent refinement of VHS, which has improved picture quality, is called **S-VHS**. S-VHS machines will play back both VHS and S-VHS tapes, but VHS machines will not play back tapes recorded on S-VHS machines. Speculation is that VHS will be phased out in the future in favor of the more flexible, higher quality S-VHS machines.

2. The **Beta** format, developed and popularized by Sony Corp., has lost a considerable amount of acceptance by the general public in recent years. Yet, there are still a number of meeting speakers who request playback equipment in this format. As in the case of the VHS format, the Beta tape can be recorded and played back at a number of speeds. Tapes can also be purchased in a variety of lengths. Exhibit 11.3 lists the maximum recording times for the various types of Beta tapes.

   In the not-too-distant future, the availability of Beta playback equipment will become a real concern. Thus, speakers should be encouraged to have their Beta format tapes transferred to VHS tapes. The procedure for copying tapes is relatively simple. Two recorders (one VHS and the other Beta) and a set of "dubbing cables" are required. The cables can be purchased at any electronic supply store.

3. The **U-Matic** or **Industrial** format uses a 3/4-inch tape and is used extensively for educational tapes. The format generates a better

Exhibit 11.2   Types and Recording Times of VHS Video Cassettes

Types of VHS Cassettes	SP Mode	LP Mode	EP Mode
T-160	160 min.	320 min.	480 min.
T-120	120 min.	240 min.	360 min.
T-90	90 min.	180 min.	270 min.
T-60	60 min.	120 min.	180 min.
T-30	30 min.	60 min.	90 min.

quality picture than the 1/2-inch format of the standard VHS or Beta types. Although this format is also being replaced by the 1/2-inch VHS format for the same reasons cited previously, many corporate video producers will continue to use the U-Matic format. Thus, it is likely there will continue to be a need for equipment to play back 3/4-inch tapes.

4. **Broadcast Video** uses a 1- or 2-inch tape and is used almost exclusively by television stations and major production houses. There is almost never any requirement for this type of equipment in a meeting environment.

5. Sony has developed another format recently, called the **Video 8.** The cassettes are slightly larger than a standard audio cassette. Tapes are available in various playback lengths. It is extremely doubtful that this format will be used to any degree in the meeting room environment for presentations to groups. However, one possible future use might be in the area of exhibits, where space is an important consideration. MPO Videotronics has developed a compact 7-inch monitor with an 8mm player/recorder deck that weighs only 14.8 pounds. This unit has freeze frame, two-speed playback, and visual search features. Conceivably, such a device could be of use in product demonstrations or even in training programs. However, the continued viability of the 8mm format is very much in question.

Another variable must be mentioned concerning videotapes. That is the standard that varies according to where the tape was manufactured. Tapes made in the United States, most of Central America and the Caribbean, and some countries in South America are of the National Television Standards Committee (NTSC) standard. On the other hand, tapes made throughout most of Europe, in Australia, Africa, and Asia adhere to the Phase Alternating Line (PAL) standard. Tapes made in France, the Middle East, and the Soviet Union are made according to the Sequential Colour à Memoire (SECAM) standard. Unfortunately, these standards are not compatible. So, if a speaker from a foreign country plans to use a foreign videotape in his or her presentation, arrangements must be made for either compatible equipment to be present or to have the tape recorded on an NTSC standard tape.

Exhibit 11.3 Types and Recording Times of Beta Video Cassettes

Type of Cassette	B-1	B-II	B-III
L-830	N/A	200 min.	200 min.
L-750	90 min.	180 min.	270 min.
L-500	60 min.	120 min.	180 min.
L-250	30 min.	60 min.	90 min.
L-125	15 min.	30 min.	45 min.

If a property plans to purchase videotape recorders for its meeting room AV requirements, four key questions should be addressed:

1. What is the purpose of the equipment? Will it be used just for playback purposes or is there a need to record with it?

2. Will the equipment be used infrequently or will it receive hard and steady use?

3. Is it necessary to have equipment in more than one format available? Can a Beta or U-Matic machine be rented from an outside source should a request for such a device occur?

4. Who will operate the recorder? Will the operator be a skilled technician or will it be operated by the speaker?

Generally, the price of a recorder varies in proportion to the number of features included in it. It is senseless for the property to pay for features that are not needed by the group using the device. Most groups do not need 21-day, 8-event programming features for recording. However, they do appreciate a remote control device so that the speaker can turn the machine on and off or freeze a frame for closer inspection by the group. In order to have the capability of stopping the action, the machine must also be equipped with a quad-head playback system.

Equipment reliability should also figure in the purchase decision. Frequency of repair data for VTRs are available from consumer magazines like *Consumer Reports*.

Operating instructions should be complete and easy to understand. Some machines are very confusing to use even for the experienced operator. Finally, the remote control aspects of the unit should be user friendly.

Televisions, Monitors, and Projectors

Three devices are used to reproduce video images: television receivers, monitors, and projectors.

Television receivers are the most common types available and the cheapest to rent or own. Outwardly, monitors are similar to receivers, but they have a few major differences. Monitors have no tuners, have separate jacks for audio and video reception, and produce a higher resolution picture. Many monitors have no audio reproduction capabilities. Monitors are also more expensive than ordinary televisions.

Monitors and receivers vary in screen size. Screen size is measured diagonally. The smallest size that should be considered for a meeting room environment is 19 inches. Screen size can range up to 50 inches, but 19- or 25-inch screens are the norm. A suggested guideline is one 19-inch screen for every 20 persons or one 25-inch screen for every 40 persons, depending on sightlines and the configuration of the meeting room.

It is also important to note that a single videotape recorder can have its signal split among several monitors or receivers. These can then be spread throughout the meeting room.

When you have to deal with a large audience, you might also consider using a video projector. Instead of placing four, eight, or more monitors throughout the audience, you can project the video image on a screen having a width of between 6 and 40 feet.

Two types of video projectors are available. Self-contained units have a projector built into a base and come with an attached screen. Because of their bulky size, these "portable" units are not actually as portable as they seem. They also suffer from another limitation. The viewing angle of their screens is limited to approximately 30 degrees from the projection axis. This makes a wide and shallow seating arrangement impossible.

Another type of video projection unit is a detached system. It has a projector that may be mounted on the ceiling or placed on a stand, and the image is projected onto a wall screen. This type of system can also be adapted to serve as a rear-screen as well as a front-screen projection system. Detached video projectors can project images from 6 to 40 feet in width, depending on the type and model used.

There are major manufacturers of projection screens that can help the convention service manager avoid "ceiling clutter" caused by video projectors hanging from a meeting room ceiling. One company manufactures a device that stores the projector in the ceiling when it is not in use. When the unit is needed, it descends either by remote control or a wall-mounted switch.

Video projectors can also be used for computer projection as well as videotape playback. Computer projection has become very important to meeting managers involved with technical training or management meetings. For example, an electronic spreadsheet can be projected onto a meeting room screen and discussed by the participants.

Television sound systems have become more sophisticated in recent years. A number of models now feature stereo sound. However, if your television receivers do not have adequate speakers, you should consider patching the audio output into the facility's public address system.

Cameras and Meeting Recordings

Video cameras or "camcorders" are manufactured with a seemingly endless number of formats and features. All record sound as well as video.

The most popular formats are the standard VHS, VHS-C (a smaller cassette that fits into a special adapter for playback on a VHS recorder), and 8mm. The standard VHS camcorders are heavier than the other models, but they are generally considered to produce a higher quality picture and are recommended over the other formats.

Desirable features in a camcorder include an electronic viewfinder, a motorized zoom lens, low light sensitivity, a high-speed shutter, seamless editing (allowing a nearly invisible transition from one scene to the next), fade control for audio or video (or both), and a directional microphone. All these features are important to the meeting planner.

Consumer Reports or some other consumer magazine should be consulted when a decision has been made to purchase a camcorder.

The standard VHS camera is perfectly acceptable for recording role-playing exercises and other events where studio quality recording is not necessary. However, if meeting planners require high picture quality and high fidelity sound, they should contact one of the many production companies specializing in this area.

Some specialized conference resorts have an in-house recording capacity. The Scottsdale Conference Resort in Arizona maintains an 8-person AV team that can produce a studio quality tape of an organization's meeting from the conferees' arrival at the airport to their departure several days later. The property has one of the most complete recording studios in any hotel or conference center in the country. Exhibit 11.4 is a view of the recording studio at the Scottsdale Conference Resort.

Videotaping a conference or convention may be a source of revenue for some associations. Attendees or members who were unable to attend the convention may want to purchase videotapes of keynote speakers, workshops, or other events. When recording is planned, it is extremely important for the meeting planner to hire a professional production company.

Closed Circuit Television (CCTV)

Another innovation in video to assist the meeting planner is closed circuit television (CCTV). Using cable, CCTV systems can transmit special meeting-related programming into attendees' guestrooms.

Instructional films and tapes, motivational messages, or even agendas can be transmitted into the rooms. Attendees can learn of last-minute changes to the meeting agenda merely by turning on the television sets in their guestrooms.

Video-conferences

The technology for videoconferencing has been available for more than a decade, and not too many years ago the process was expected to toll the death knell for hotels and conference centers. Traditional meetings were expected to vanish, especially those convened by corporations. Meetings required by the corporate home office were to take place electronically. Thus, there would be no further need for expensive air travel, guestrooms, and meals.

However, many properties took a proactive stance. Their management reasoned that because the parties on each end of the videoconference line would still need a facility from which to broadcast, they could provide that service. It would be better to pick up some revenue from teleconferencing meetings than to lose all the business to a new technology.

But telecommunication systems were expensive to install and maintain. For many smaller properties, renting a local earth station would be more cost effective than to install all the equipment in-house.

Fortunately, the threat never completely materialized. Many companies and corporations felt that the benefits derived from immediate human contact far outweighed the added costs of transportation and accommodations.

This is not to say that current trends could not again change. Another fuel crisis, a worsening economy, or another negative shift in business

Exhibit 11.4   Recording Studio

State-of-the-art audio and video recording studio located at the Scottsdale Conference Resort.
(Photo courtesy of Scottsdale Conference Resort.)

deductions for travel and entertainment could resurrect the videoconferencing concept.

In the meantime, the idea has not disappeared entirely. Almost every major convention center maintains an earth station and the capability for participating in teleconferences. However, few centers maintain the equipment necessary for originating teleconferences. There are three basic modes of teleconferencing:

1. Audio only is simply people talking to people—teleconferencing's most basic form. This type of teleconferencing is most suitable when the company's budget is a major consideration.

2. Audiographic teleconferencing combines audio interaction with visual support in specially designed conference rooms. Participants can write or draw on blackboards or easels, exchange documents, and even show slides, viewgraphs, and still pictures of people or objects. Audiographic teleconferences are best suited to interactive planning sessions, briefings, remote speeches, and project status reviews.

3. Videoconferencing is the most sophisticated form of teleconferencing. It is full-motion, face-to-face interaction among meeting participants in remote locations.

Audio Equipment

Although we tend to emphasize the visual element of communication, we should never forget that at meetings the spoken word is the primary means of communication.

Sir Laurence Olivier, the famous actor, once complained that amplification of the human voice has been responsible for the deadening of the human ear. Whether his conjecture is true or not, we must realize that the unaided human voice is only sufficient for the smallest of groups and electronic projection is needed in the majority of meetings.

Microphones

Microphones represent the first step in the amplification process. There are four general types (classified according to usage) used in the meeting environment: hand microphones, lavaliere, wireless, and stationary.

Hand Microphones. Hand microphones are carried by the speaker or performer. Because they are handled so much, they must be very rugged and insensitive to physical shock.

Some years ago, this author saw a performer swinging her microphone like a policeman twirling a nightstick. At one point, the head of the microphone made contact with the floor, but the microphone continued to function and the performer was able to finish her song—a dramatic testimonial to the abuse that hand microphones must withstand.

Hand microphones must also be small and slim enough to be handled easily and should not be obtrusive when held by the speaker. They must also be fairly insensitive to explosive breath "pops" from the speaker. Above all, they must have good sound quality.

Most hand microphones are omni-directional in their pick-up range. Omni-directional microphones will pick up sounds in a 360-degree pattern. This also means they may pick up unwanted sounds from all directions.

Hand microphones can also be mounted on stands, freeing the performer's or speaker's hands.

Lavaliere Microphones. Lavaliere or neck microphones are small, unobtrusive microphones that are usually hung on a neck cord close to the chest, leaving the speaker's hands free for demonstrations and gestures. This microphone is used extensively by many meeting speakers.

The lavaliere microphone usually has an omni-directional pick-up pattern, and its small size makes it easy to conceal under a tie or a blouse. Its sound quality is generally not as good as the hand microphones, which are preferred by most vocalists.

Wireless Microphones. Whether they are the hand-held or the lavaliere variety, wireless microphones give the speaker almost complete freedom of movement within the meeting room environment.

All wireless microphones work according to a basic FM transmitter principle. The speaker wears or holds a medium-size microphone. This microphone is connected to a small pocket transmitter whose transmitting antenna is either worn around the speaker's waist or pinned on the speaker's trousers or skirt. Some microphones have the transmitter built into the microphone and the antenna sticks out of the base of the microphone.

Many speakers hesitate to use wireless microphones because of interference problems with the signal. Metal in the walls, electric motors, or passing radio broadcasts from citizen's band radios (CBs) can interrupt the signal. Furthermore, the transmitters are powered by batteries that can wear down during a long presentation. This can cause disastrous results.

A technician should always be present when a speaker uses a wireless microphone or when more than two microphones are being used simultaneously.

Stationary Microphones. Stationary microphones fall into two categories: desk microphones and stand or lectern microphones.

Lectern microphones should be mounted on an adjustable metal gooseneck extension that can be adjusted to the height of the speaker. Ideally, *all* microphones should be placed 8 to 10 inches in front of and just below the level of the speaker's mouth.

Some speakers will request that a hand-held microphone be attached to the lectern so that the speaker can remove it to break free and move around.

If a speaker fears sound failure from one microphone, a second should be attached to the first with a clip. In this way, the speaker has to direct his or her address in only one direction.

A group may request that microphones be placed on stands in the audience for question-and-answer sessions. However, care should be taken not to block aisles with the microphones and thus violate fire and safety codes. Signs should be hung over the microphone areas in a large audience to direct conferees to the closest available microphone.

Desk microphones are used extensively for panel discussions. While it is possible for panelists to share microphones (no more than two persons to one microphone), it is preferable to provide each panelist with a separate microphone.

Desk microphone placement is relatively simple. It is wise to set the desk microphone off to one side of the speaker rather than directly in front where it might obscure the speaker's face. When speakers are sitting directly opposite each other across a desk, each speaker should be "miked" separately. When more than one desk microphone is used, be sure that all are of the same type and model. A variety of microphone types will tend to distract the audience.

Purchasing Microphones. The convention service manager must first determine the purpose of the microphone. Unfortunately, there is not one generic type that can perform all functions equally.

If ambient noise is a problem, then a uni-directional or cardioid microphone is preferable. A uni-directional or cardioid (heart shaped) pattern picks up the sound from just one direction. This helps to cut down on unwanted sounds, but a speaker should be warned that the microphone is uni-directional.

If a microphone is to be used outside, a wind screen should be provided to cut down on wind noise.

Speakers   There are two types of speaker systems: built-in sound systems and portable speaker systems.

     Built-in systems are adequate for ordinary speech, but they may not be adequate for music or taped presentations. Built-in systems are usually ceiling mounted.

     A meeting planner's first concern about a built-in public address system is whether sound transmission can be limited to a particular meeting room or area. The ability to control sound is as important as the ability to control lighting in the meeting room.

     Public address systems are rarely adequate for music presentations or film and videotape shows. When presenting a movie or videotape, you should try to ensure a sense of realism by having the sound come from the same direction as the picture. This cannot be accomplished with most public address systems.

     When using a portable speaker system, you should raise the speakers off the floor and suspend them as close to the ceiling as possible. This will minimize the difference between the sound levels and the back and the front of the room. Entertainers may request that special monitor speakers be added on stage so that they can hear themselves.

Amplifiers and Mixers   All speaker systems require an amplifier to boost the signal strength from the microphone, turntable, or tape recorder to the speakers.

     Ceiling-mounted public address systems have their own amplification system, usually mounted in an adjacent storage area.

     The services of a professional audio technician are required when multiple microphones are used, when there is musical entertainment, or when the proceedings are to be recorded.

     A mixer balances sound input from different sources so that the audience's attention is directed toward the right source. The mixer board consists of a series of controls that raise or lower the volume of each input source. These controls are known as "pots." The mixer board is always located in the audience so that the technician operating it can hear the sound as the audience hears it.

Tape Recorders and Other Playback Systems   Reel-to-reel tape recorder systems have been replaced almost entirely by cassette recorders. Standard cassettes come in a variety of lengths with the most popular being the C-60 (30 minutes of playing time on each side) and the C-90 (45 minutes of playing time on each side).

     Cassette tapes come in different modes, from relatively inexpensive tapes that are only suited for recording the spoken voice to expensive metal tapes that can give concert quality sound reproduction.

     Digital tape and digital recording and playback systems are recent innovations. Although outwardly they resemble the more conventional systems, these newer systems break each note down to a digital reading process. This process is then reproduced and the listener enjoys an amazingly accurate reproduction of the original live performance.

     On rare occasions, a phonograph or one of the newer compact disc players will be requested by the meeting planner.

Recording the Event
Because workshops at a convention usually run concurrently, it is impossible for an attendee to attend all scheduled events. Thus, audio tapes are an excellent way for a person to review other sessions, and they are less complex to make than video recordings.

If an organization can show that its members have bought substantial numbers of tapes in the past, some companies will record meeting events for little or no charge to the organization.

The single biggest mistake when taping an event is failing to provide microphones for the audience during question-and-answer periods. Another mistake occurs when the speaker forgets to repeat a question so that it can be recorded adequately and also heard by all audience members. Correcting both mistakes will ensure a more professional recording.

When taping for profit is done, it is very important to have all the presenters sign a waiver giving their permission to be recorded. Equally important is effective promotion of the tapes. This should take place prior to the convention, during the convention, and after the convention.

Multi-Image Modules

Although it is based on many of the principles of the old 35mm slide show, the multi-image program combines a number of slide projectors (sometimes 20 or more) with a pre-recorded, synchronized tape presentation. It is usually run by a computer program that automatically performs all cues.

Dissolve units that allow the gradual transition from one picture to another are used in multi-image programs. In addition, multiple screens are frequently used (often rear-screen) to totally capture the audience's attention.

Multi-image programs are excellent motivational tools for sales groups, or they can be used to introduce the convention group to the host city.

There are a number of companies that develop generic modules on a variety of business-related topics (e.g., sales training, motivational topics, creativity in the workplace, etc.) that can be customized to the needs of a particular group. This is done by introducing key identity slides into the module.

Meeting planners and convention service managers who would like more information about the companies that provide this service and the products themselves should write to the Association for Multi-Image International, Inc., 8019 North Hines Ave., Suite 401, Tampa, FL 33614.

If a group meeting at a property wants to use more than one of these shows, the convention service manager should suggest that all shows use the same type and quantity of equipment.

Films

Films and videotapes about business-related topics are in abundance. *Successful Meetings* magazine publishes an annual review of new films and tapes in its April issue.

Control Booths and Studios

Control booths for conference rooms are becoming more elaborate as more and more properties add on specially designed meeting rooms for serious training and development meetings. Exhibits 11.5 and 11.6 show the newly developed conference room facilities and the control booth at Mesa's Centennial Hall.

From the control booth it is possible to orchestrate the entire meeting event from the time the curtain goes up to the finale. This level of sophistication is changing the meeting room environment and the look of the convention property.

Staging

A stage is that area in a meeting room occupied by the presenters of a meeting. Frequently, a meeting room stage is a raised platform at one end of the meeting room. In some instances, a proscenium arch separates the stage from the audience area.

For our purposes, staging is defined as the design and setup of this area to achieve maximum audience visibility, to obtain the best acoustical arrangement, and to direct the audience's focus to the presentation. This is accomplished through the use of creative lighting, proper arrangement of audiovisual displays, effective sound design, and the best arrangement of stage furniture, decor, and props.

Staging can range from the extremely simple (the placement of a lectern in front of theater-style seating for 10) to the complex (a full stage including scenery, props, theatrical lighting, and special effects).

To properly set the stage for an event, the convention service manager must obtain from the meeting planner a detailed description of the session and what it is intended to accomplish. When contemplating the staging needs of a session, you should answer the following seven questions:

1. Is a platform needed by the speaker? Will there be a need for members of the audience to reach the platform and will the speaker need to reach the audience?

2. What are the room setup requirements? What effect will these have on the staging requirements?

3. Will AV equipment and displays be used? Is it necessary for the speaker to see the displays?

4. Will there be a head table on the stage?

5. What are the sound and lighting requirements for the presentation?

6. What are the decor and scenery requirements?

7. Has everything been done to ensure the safety and comfort of all parties involved (the speaker and the audience)? Make certain everything has been done to eliminate the possibility of the speaker tripping or falling off the stage.

Exhibit 11.5   Auditorium

Classroom-style auditorium with a seating capacity of 100 persons at Mesa's Centennial Hall.
(Photo courtesy of Mesa Convention and Visitors Bureau, Mesa, Arizona.)

When referring to a stage area, designers and speakers often use the following theatrical terminology to define the parts of the stage:

- **Downstage** is that area of the stage that is closest to the audience.

- **Upstage** is the area of the stage that is closest to the rear wall of the stage area.

- **Stage right** is that area on the speaker's right when facing the audience.

- **Stage left** is that area on the speaker's left when facing the audience.

- **Center stage** is just that—the center of the stage.

- The **apron** is the area of the stage that extends into the audience beyond the proscenium arch.

- The **proscenium arch** is the wall that separates a stage from the audience area in a permanent stage arrangement.

- The **wings** are the areas off to the right and left of the stage where performers wait to go onstage and where scenery and equipment are stored. These areas are masked with curtains called "tormentors" that prevent the audience from seeing this backstage area.

- **Ramps** or **runways** are platforms that extend into the audience for the transit of speakers, models, or entertainers.

- **Flyspace** is that area above the stage where scenery is stored on a counterweight system.

The above terms are further combined to indicate movement around a stage by an actor or a speaker. These combinations include the terms downright, downleft, upright, upleft, upcenter, and downcenter.

Exhibit 11.6   Control Booth

Control booth featuring Mel Ruska, events coordinator, at the lighting and audio controls for the auditorium shown in Exhibit 11.5. (Photo courtesy of Mesa Convention and Visitors Bureau, Mesa, Arizona.)

Theatrical Lighting

In many ballrooms and meeting facilities (especially those with a permanent stage), lighting fixtures are present that differ markedly from ordinary household lighting. While the convention service manager is not expected to carry the credentials of a professional scenic or lighting designer, he or she should be aware of the basic types and uses of theatrical lighting equipment.

Profile Spots

Profile spots, also known as ellipsoidal spots or lekolites, are designed to light the downstage portion of a stage (that area of the stage nearest the audience). They are also sometimes used to project light patterns onto the background.

These lanterns are mounted in the ceiling of the audience area, range from 500 to 1,000 watts, and are normally of a quartz-halogen variety.

Color filters can be placed in front of these lamps to bathe the stage area in different colored lights. For a natural effect, two lanterns are used on one area of the stage. The light coming from one lantern uses a light yellow filter while the light coming from the other lamp will have a soft blue filter to represent shadows and thus give the speaker's face a three-dimensional form. This pattern of lighting will be repeated across the downstage area of the stage.

The most appropriate angle for these lanterns is 45 degrees above the speaker's face and 45 degrees to the right and left of the speaker's face as he or she faces the audience. This 45-degree angle tends to reveal the face most naturally.

Profile spots have shutters in the lantern that can adjust the shape of the light being thrown onto the stage. With the shutters fully extended, the light pattern is a circle, but the shutters can square off the pattern so that distracting spill light does not fall onto the audience or the proscenium wall. Exhibit 11.7 shows profile spots hung from pipes in a meeting room ceiling. Note the color filter frames on the lanterns and the shutters on the instrument in the corner of the ceiling.

Because of the harshness of the light produced by the profile spot, it should not normally be used from a position on the stage itself. It is designed to be used from the audience.

Fresnel Spots

Fresnel spots cast a soft-edged beam and are used on the stage to light the upstage acting areas. The color filter pattern established by the profile spots is repeated with the Fresnel spots.

The beam is adjustable in spread by the relative movement of the lamp and the lens. The beam shape can be controlled somewhat by the use of exterior shutters called "barn doors." Different types of stepped lenses in the instrument can produce light that has either a harder or softer edge to the pattern.

Like the profile spot, the Fresnel spot comes in a range of wattages and lens sizes.

Floodlights

Floodlights are available in a variety of shapes and sizes. These lights are designed to light objects rather than people. They are often used to light a backdrop known as a cyclorama that serves as a neutral background for the speaker.

Floodlights do not normally have lenses, but they do have frames for attaching colored filters. The floodlight's main purpose is to project a diffused, even light over the object.

Follow Spots

Follow spots are instruments used for giving special visibility to a speaker or performer on the stage.

The follow spot resembles a cannon and requires a technician to operate it. The focus of the lamp can be adjusted from a hard edged circle of light to a delicate softly focused moving light that the audience is hardly aware of. Colored filters can also be used with follow spots.

Because the follow spot is usually located at the rear of the auditorium, the light must be extremely brilliant. Most follow spots use a xenon lamp or are direct current carbon arc lamps. A follow spot is shown in Exhibit 11.8.

Special Effects Lighting

This type of lighting can serve a number of applications. Lighting can create a mood as well as provide illumination.

For example, a group may want a dance after dinner. Equipment such as ballroom globes, strobe lights, and laser lighting adds a festive and fantasy atmosphere to the proceedings. Exhibit 11.9 shows a number of ballroom globes and strobe spots designed for use at a dance.

Special effects lighting can also be used with kinetic objects like fountains to create visual centerpieces for banquets and receptions. Exhibit 11.10 is an example of a "Dancing Waters" display.

Lighting Controls

The heart of every stage lighting installation is the control system. Dimmer controls in the system balance the stage lighting to achieve the desired pictorial effect. All control boards, from the simplest to the most complex, provide this application with varying degrees of sophistication.

Exhibit 11.7   Profile Spots Mounted in a Meeting Room Ceiling

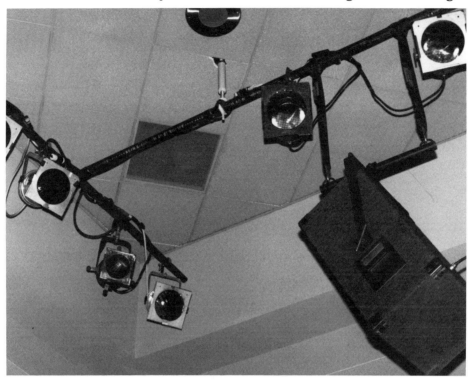

Photo courtesy of Tropicana Resort and Casino, Las Vegas, Nevada.

Meeting Room Furniture, Fixtures, and Accessories

Such formerly mundane and low-tech objects as pointers and lecterns have taken on high-tech characteristics.

The old wooden pointer has been replaced by hand-held laser pointers that can project a red dot onto the screen from 100 feet away.

Lecterns now have controls to adjust the lighting level of the room and turn AV equipment on and off. They can contain personal sized fans to cool the speaker, built-in teleprompters, and even controls to lower and raise the height of the lectern to fit the speaker. There are also timers that light up in yellow when it is time for a speaker to summarize and red when time is up. The devices also display the speaker's remaining time in hours, minutes, and seconds.

There are now "8-hour chairs" that are designed by engineers to give the attendee maximum seating comfort during long presentations.

Signs and Printing

Convention service departments should be prepared for the inevitable last-minute request from the planner for signs that were overlooked in the planning stages.

For larger signs, a set of colored markers and a supply of different colored construction paper should always be kept on hand.

Exhibit 11.8   Follow Spot

Photo courtesy of Tropicana Resort and Casino, Las Vegas, Nevada.

For smaller signs, handouts, and banners, the best equipment is a personal computer with a graphics program, a painting program, and a laser printer. This equipment, coupled with a heavy duty photocopier that can reduce and enlarge images and collate, can save the day for the meeting planner who has last minute sign and printing needs.

A meeting facility may also have an electronic reader board installed in the pre-function area to direct conferees to their room assignments. An electronic reader board is shown in Exhibit 11.11.

Computers and Computer Accessories

The computer plays many roles in the meeting environment. Computers are used by the convention service staff to allocate and keep track of function space. They are used by the meeting planning staff to register convention attendees, and they are used inside meetings to demonstrate and to teach.

The Use of Computers by the Convention Service Department

The traditional role that computers have played in the convention service departments of properties has been mainly in the area of accounting. Computers have been used to keep track of payables and receivables by the convention service department.

Elsewhere in the property, the computer has been used in reservations, guest accounting, and point-of-sale systems. But little thought has been given

Exhibit 11.9   Ballroom Globe and Strobe Lights

Photo courtesy of Tropicana Resort and Casino, Las Vegas, Nevada.

to the development of computer applications to meet the needs of the convention service department.

Now, software has become available to help the convention service manager answer questions immediately regarding space availability and prices. For example, an automated function book is available that integrates all elements of the meeting except room accommodations.

The Use of Computers by the Convening Organization

Meeting planners use computers to perform a number of functions. Two of these have a direct impact on the convention service department: automated on-site convention registration systems and computer classroom workshops.

Providing computer service to meeting planners has not been a high priority item for most properties. When a meeting planner demands computer assistance, computer rental specialists are called on to provide the necessary equipment and expertise. The property's convention service manager

Exhibit 11.10   Light Show

A computerized water and light show located at one end of a banquet room. (Photo courtesy of Tropicana Resort and Casino, Las Vegas, Nevada.)

should be able to provide the planner with a listing of reputable local computer services and should discourage planners from bringing their own equipment if at all possible. Computers are damaged very easily in transit.

Some meeting facilities do have computers available for workshops, but these are specialized properties like the Infomart in Dallas that offers 30 meeting rooms and 2 new computer-equipped classrooms and teleconferencing capabilities. Infomart is actually a supermarket, a permanent exhibit for computer and other technical products.

There is a similar facility in Santa Clara, California, called Techmart, which adjoins the 502-room Doubletree Hotel and the Santa Clara Convention Center.

If a property does play host to a computer workshop, the convention service staff should be aware of certain special demands that will be made on the facility:

- Computers use electricity, a great amount of it. The old workshop arrangement of tables around the perimeter of the room (where the electrical outlets are located) is no longer acceptable to many workshop instructors. Now that computer projection has become an integral part of computer workshops, instructors are demanding a traditional classroom-style setup. This means the property must be ready and able to provide sufficient electricity to the middle of the room.

Exhibit 11.11   Electronic Reader Board in a Pre-Function Area

Photo courtesy of Tropicana Resort and Casino, Las Vegas, Nevada.

- Computers must be kept cool. Be certain your meeting facilities can keep the computers and their operators comfortable.

- Computers take up space. Allot 100 square feet for each computer and operator.

- Printers clacking away are noisy. Make sure the adjacent rooms are not going to be occupied by groups requiring quiet.

Telephone Systems and Two-Way Radios

Meeting planners for large complex conventions will require a system whereby they can communicate immediately with fellow staff members and with the members of the property's convention service staff.

Telephone service can include the following features:

- Hotlines or telephones that ring at another location when the calling party picks up the telephone. No dialing is needed.
- Cellular telephones that have many of the characteristics of two-way radios.
- Pager systems by which the caller dials a telephone number and a remote pager notifies the wearer. Some systems beep when the number is rung. Dual pagers have two different numbers, and the pager has two different beeps so that the wearer knows which number to call. Voice pagers function like a one-way radio: the wearer can receive messages but cannot transmit. Finally, there are digital pagers that display a short message on a liquid crystal display.

Two-way radios or walkie-talkies can create a communication link with several individuals who are on the same frequency. The main problem with walkie-talkies is that they may suffer from signal interference from metal objects and electric motors. Their batteries also have to be recharged every evening if they are used heavily.

Language Interpretation Systems

Most properties do not maintain a permanent language interpretation system in their meeting facilities—unless the property has a reputation for hosting numerous international conferences. However, most major convention facilities will maintain a list of reputable interpreters and will know where to lease the audio system needed for language interpretation.

There are two primary approaches to language interpretation: simultaneous interpretation and consecutive interpretation.

In simultaneous interpretation, the interpreters are enclosed in a separate soundproof area. They listen to the lecture in progress over headsets and simultaneously interpret and broadcast their interpretations to the participants who wear headphones tuned to the interpreter's channel.

In consecutive interpretation, the apparatus is the same, but the interpreters only broadcast during pauses in the lecturer's delivery.

Whether the approach is simultaneous or consecutive, two interpreters must be present for each language being interpreted to ensure an uninterrupted program.

Operation of Technical Equipment

Qualified Operators   If the property maintains its own AV equipment, it should provide a technician to monitor and operate all but the most elementary AV equipment. This policy will ensure that the AV equipment is operated properly and that any failures can be repaired immediately. It will also help limit the property's liability by minimizing the risks to members of the organization who could be harmed while operating the equipment.

Union Technicians If the property or the outside AV equipment contractor has a union shop, the meeting planner should be told this at the beginning of the planning process. Minimum labor fees stipulated in the collective bargaining contract should be explained in detail to the meeting planner. The planner should also be notified of any union rules or regulations that involve the operation of any AV equipment.

Ownership of Audiovisual Equipment

There are three alternatives open to the convention service department when deciding whether or not to invest in meeting room technology.

First, the facility may opt to own all of the AV equipment and other meeting room technology. There are advantages and disadvantages to this option.

Advantages include the following:

- The property earns the revenue gained from the rental of technical equipment instead of turning the profits over to an outside contractor.

- The property can purchase equipment that is best suited for its meeting-room environment instead of having to rely on an outside contractor whose equipment may not fit the property's needs.

- By owning and maintaining the equipment, the property has greater control over its quality. This is the argument used by the Scottsdale Conference Resort and many other conference centers.

- There may be a lack of suppliers in the area, or certain equipment may be difficult to rent. Resorts often must maintain their own complete line of equipment.

Disadvantages to owning all of the technical equipment include the following:

- Maintaining an inventory of AV equipment is a costly process. Costs include not only expenditures for capital improvements but also for labor to operate and maintain the equipment.

- Certain technical items may either be so costly or may become obsolete so soon that carrying them on the inventory is cost prohibitive.

- Certain items are asked for so infrequently that the property could never hope to recover its investment in the items.

- Because the property owns the equipment, it will incur the loss if any of the items are lost or stolen.

- The property is more likely to be held liable if the equipment malfunctions and injures a guest.

- Because this equipment is quite expensive, it is particularly vulnerable to theft. Thus, elaborate security and storage provisions are required to protect it.

The second option is a compromise. The property owns only those items that are used regularly. This equipment usually includes boards, easels, a few microphones, permanent projector screens, and perhaps an overhead projector and a slide projector with stands or carts.

By carrying only what is used frequently, the property eliminates most of the negative aspects of owning AV equipment that were listed above. However, it will still lose revenue to an outside contractor, and it still does not have control over most of the equipment.

The third option is to own no technical equipment but to entrust all the planner's needs to an outside contractor. Many properties prefer this arrangement because they see no lost revenue from not owning the equipment themselves. They are also blessed with an AV contractor who is competent.

There are now six major properties in Las Vegas that have a special contract with Greyhound Exposition Services for AV equipment. Under this contract, Greyhound owns and services all the equipment, but the equipment is stored on the properties' premises. This ensures that when an item is needed at the last minute, there is no delay in getting that item to the meeting room. The convention service department of the property can requisition any of Greyhound's equipment on the spot.

The Future of Meeting Technology

As meeting technology becomes more sophisticated, the dependence of the meeting planner and the convention service manager on that technology will grow. Yesterday, managers could not think of what to do with the computer; today, computers have become indispensable to the operation.

The use of video in the meeting room environment will continue to grow exponentially. Indications of this trend are found in numerous articles about the use of interactive video or meeting and trade show networks.

Visitors Television Network (VTV) is a convention news network that will tape each day's activities at a trade show and play back the day's taping in a "Good Morning, America" format that evening over the delegates' guestroom televisions. Exhibitors buy commercial time on the show and have reported an increase in booth customers.

Live projection is another video technique that is being used to stimulate audiences. A television camera focuses on a speaker or members of the audience during a presentation and those live images are projected onto a large screen by means of a video projector. This allows the audience to see close-ups of the presentation and develop an interactive feeling between themselves and the presenter.

Where is all this leading? It simply means that the meeting environment is going to continue to become more sophisticated because of improvements in audiovisual technology. As a result, both meeting planners and convention service personnel will find it increasingly important to stay abreast of developments in AV technology.

Chapter Summary

We have grown up in a highly technological environment. This is an environment that has seen the development of radical new forms of communication during the last half century.

Educators now caution us to use a multi-media approach when trying to inform, educate, or even entertain an audience. The old, one-channel approach (the speaker-at-the-lectern syndrome) no longer works because the audience expects more. To effectively communicate with an audience today, a presenter must try to stimulate as many of the sensory channels of the individuals in the audience as possible.

The public has become desensitized. Meeting planners have recognized this and have taken a proactive stance. They know that in order to reach their audiences they must give them what they want. Part of the meeting's message does come from the media being used.

In turn, meeting planners demand from convention service managers the technology necessary to help them reach their audiences. If the service manager cannot meet these demands, the organization can, and will, go elsewhere. Competition will not allow the individual convention service manager to survive with a "Take it or leave it" attitude.

12 Ancillary Conference and Convention Activities

Chapter Objectives

1. To understand why trade shows and exhibits are important activities at many conferences and conventions

2. To learn the types of trade shows and exhibits

3. To learn the principals involved in trade shows and exhibits

4. To understand why tours, entertainment, and recreation are important activities at many conferences and conventions

5. To learn how to plan and conduct tours, entertainment, and recreational activities at conferences and conventions

The activities of attendees at a conference or convention often extend beyond meetings and banquets. Ancillary activities include, but are not limited to, exhibits and trade shows, tours, recreation and entertainment, and various activities for guests, spouses, and other family members traveling with the conferee.

The adjective "ancillary" in the title of this chapter may be a misnomer, for these additional activities are not really considered to be subordinate to the meeting and banquet activities in many instances. In fact, they can be very important to the success of the convention.

At many association conventions, for example, the leisure activities planned for the conventioneers and their accompanying spouses can be a primary motivating reason for attending the convention in the first place. And for some association conventions, a trade show or exhibit may be the attendee's sole reason for attending the event.

Exhibits and Trade Shows

A trade show is normally defined as a gathering of commercial purveyors whose products and services are related to a specific trade or profession.

The primary purpose of a trade show is to create in the attendees an awareness of, or interest in, the products or services on display. It is hoped they will ultimately be motivated to buy those products or services.

Trade shows may be sponsored by the exhibitors themselves, by an association representing members in that trade or profession, by a private company whose business purpose is to host trade shows, or by some other third party such as government. Most true trade shows are not open to the general public.

Consumers' shows or retail trade shows, on the other hand, are open to the general public. At these shows, only one category of merchandise may be represented (such as a camper show) or there may be a number of different items for sale.

An exhibit or exposition is distinguished from a trade show by its non-commercial aspect. Normally, an exhibition is presented for the cultural or educational benefit of the attendees, and there are no products or services for sale that are directly related to the exhibit. Flower shows, art shows, and craft displays at fairs are all examples of exhibitions.

Objectives of Trade Shows and Exhibits

The trade show or exhibit may be a major source of revenue to the association sponsoring the convention. In many instances, the revenue received from the rental of booth space is second only to the annual membership fees as a source of income to the association.

Beyond revenue considerations, the trade show and its exhibitors should be viewed as a major educational resource that can be used to help meet the goals of the association. An exhibition represents a chance for attendees to be introduced to products and services that will enhance the operation of their trades or businesses. Attendees can compare and contrast similar products and services at an exhibition to discover those products or services best suited to their needs.

To the exhibitor, the trade show is an opportunity to come into direct contact with prospective customers in a cost-effective manner. It is also a chance for the exhibitor to view new products of competitors. Finally, it gives exhibitors the chance to establish a dialogue with the users of their products in order to determine what further refinements they want.

Layouts Used in Trade Shows and Exhibits

There are three types of exhibit layouts used by trade shows. The needs of the exhibitor are the major determinants in the selection of a particular type of exhibit layout.

Area Exhibits. In area exhibits, exhibitors are assigned specific areas on the trade show floor. This layout is normally used for those exhibitions in which the size of the product precludes the use of a normal booth. For example, exhibitions featuring earth-moving equipment, aircraft, or large manufacturing implements would probably use an area exhibit layout.

The height of area exhibits often extends beyond the normal limitations placed on booth exhibits. The exhibit may be two or more stories in height.

Booth Exhibits. The booth exhibit is the most common type of exhibit layout used at trade shows and exhibitions.

There are four generally recognized categories of booths at most expositions:[1]

1. The **standard booth** is composed of one or more standard units in a straight line and may include an aisle on one side of the booth. A unit is normally a space that is 10 feet wide by 10 feet deep, but this size can vary. For some trade shows, the unit space may be as small as 8 by 8 feet. However, the generally accepted practice is to maintain the 10-foot width because many exhibitors have permanent exhibit modules that are 10 feet wide.

   The standard booth is usually constructed of piping and draping that separate it from its neighbors. A decorator or exposition service contractor generally installs piping and draping for the entire trade show and all exhibitors normally receive the same color draping.

   The standard height of the rear of a booth is 8 feet, and exhibitors are normally expected not to exceed that height so as not to detract from any booth directly behind the rear of the first booth.

   The side panels separating the booths usually have a maximum height of 3 feet. Exhibitors are expected to place anything in their booth that is taller than 4 feet and within 10 feet of a neighboring booth in the rear 5 feet of their booth. The intent here is to give every exhibitor a reasonable sight line from the aisle.

   All utility services (i.e., electricity, water, sewer, telephone, etc.) are normally installed in the rear of a standard booth.

2. A **peninsula booth** consists of four or more units of space that are back to back. It has an aisle on three sides.

   Peninsula booths are usually permitted a maximum height of 12 feet. The additional height does not interfere with other exhibits because there are no exhibitors facing the back wall of a peninsula booth.

   The wall adjacent to a neighboring booth is expected to have a finished surface and cannot display copy or other advertising that would detract from the neighboring booth.

   Other rules that were mentioned about standard booths also apply to peninsula booths.

3. The **island booth** is so named because it is defined as a block of space with an aisle on all four sides.

   The normal maximum height of an island booth is 12 feet. Because an island booth is surrounded on all four sides by aisles, there are no other restrictions concerning layout other than the 12-foot height restriction already mentioned.

4. A **perimeter wall booth** is a standard booth located on the outer perimeter wall of the exposition floor plan.

   A major difference between the standard booth and the perimeter wall booth is the maximum allowable height of the display area in the rear of the booth. Exhibit materials up to 12 feet are allowed in perimeter wall booths, whereas the maximum height in standard booths is 8 feet. All other rules pertaining to standard booths apply to perimeter wall booths as well.

Exhibitors are charged either by the square foot, by the unit, or by size and location within the hall for booth space.

Table-Top Exhibits. This type of layout is used when there is a limited amount of exhibit space, very few exhibitors, or when the products featured in the show are relatively small (e.g., perfumes or jewelry).

The table tops are rectangular and are either 6 or 8 feet long. The tables are also usually skirted. Setup charges for this type of exhibit are normally less than those for booth exhibits.

Facility Specifications for Trade Shows and Exhibits

Putting on a trade show or exhibition is an immense and complex task. Few properties possess the necessary space and design features in their meeting rooms to successfully host a trade show of any magnitude.

Space is a primary consideration when choosing a site for a trade show. A typical show consisting of 100 10-foot by 10-foot booths and a standard 10-foot aisle will require approximately 20,000 square feet of space. A good rule of thumb in estimating the amount of space required is to multiply the number of booths by the area (square feet) in each booth and then double that amount. This will determine the total gross square footage needed for the booths and the aisles.

Many exhibit booths need hookups for electricity, water, sewer, telephone lines, and, on occasion, natural gas. Conventions like consumer electronic shows may demand an inordinate amount of power for the booths. An ordinary meeting room simply does not have this capability.

Floor load is another major consideration with many expositions and trade shows. A typical trade show floor will support loads as heavy as 300 pounds per square foot, whereas a second-story meeting room floor at a typical property may not support loads greater than 50 pounds per square foot.

A third consideration is ceiling height. Minimum ceiling height for a trade show hall is generally considered to be 30 feet from the show floor, but heights of 40 to 50 feet are recommended. An adequate ceiling height reduces noise levels, helps provide adequate ventilation, and increases the versatility of the hall by providing space for oversize exhibits.

Adequate storage space for exhibit materials prior to setup and for holding the shipping cases during the show is an essential element of a well-designed exhibit hall.

The exhibit hall should also be in close proximity to food outlets, regular meeting rooms, and restrooms.

If the exhibit facility is a city convention center, it is very important that it be located within walking distance of convention hotels. An inadequate number of guestrooms nearby can create problems for any convention center.

Most meeting planners and exposition managers agree that the ideal arrangement is to have all facilities (meeting rooms, banquet facilities, exposition hall, and guestrooms) under one roof. This arrangement virtually guarantees higher attendance at meetings, banquets, and trade shows. Few conferees enjoy having to hail a cab and driving across town to the convention center to attend trade show events.

In recent years, a number of large exposition hotels have been constructed to capitalize on the preferred arrangement of having all facilities under one roof. Properties such as Bally's and the Las Vegas Hilton in Las Vegas, Loew's Anatole in Dallas, and the Hyatt Regency in Chicago are examples of this approach.

Principals Involved in Trade Shows and Exhibits

One of the primary reasons that a trade show is much more complex than an ordinary meeting or banquet is the number of different parties involved in the show's production.

At an initial meeting for a typical conference, the planner and the property's convention service manager might possibly be the only parties involved. At a trade show, however, there are dozens of participants, each with his or her own needs and expectations.

In this section, we will examine the role that each of the principals plays in the production of a trade show.

Sponsoring Association or Corporation

Trade shows are usually sponsored by a convening organization that considers the show to be an integral part of its meeting and a major source of revenue.

The convening organization is usually a trade or professional association, but other types of associations and even individual corporations may host a trade show.

The sponsoring organization usually leases space from a convention hall or property for the show and in turn markets that space to exhibitors at a price guaranteeing the sponsor a healthy profit margin.

A sponsoring organization may run the show from in-house, using its own management to organize, plan, and operate the show. On the other hand, it may hire an outside show manager to run the show.

A rule of thumb often used to determine whether or not to operate the show from inside the sponsoring organization is to first determine if the duties of running a trade show every year require the services of at least one full-time manager. If it is found that only a part-time manager is needed, then the sponsoring organization will generally hire an outside firm.

When an outside firm is chosen to run the show, an agreement is reached between the sponsoring organization and the exposition management firm concerning the duties of each organization and the remuneration to the exposition management company.

On occasion, the convening association or corporation may not be the sponsoring organization of a trade show. The show may be owned by an entirely different entity that uses the name of the convening organization in exchange for a fee paid to that organization.

Show Managers

Whether working in-house or coming from the outside, management talent is required to guarantee a successful show. The duties and responsibilities of a show manager are numerous and varied.

First, the show manager must select a site for the show. This requires a keen knowledge of the specific show's requirements, and it also requires the ability to negotiate a fair contract for both parties, the sponsoring organization and the property or convention center.

Second, once the site is selected, the show manager must then market the show to potential exhibitors.

The manager must first conduct research to develop a profile of attendees to the convention. Demographic, geographic, and psychographic data must be compiled on the attendees in order to attract new exhibitors and to maintain existing ones.

Next, a list of prospective exhibitors must be generated, and reasonable criteria must be established for granting space to these exhibitors. If a trade show arbitrarily bars certain exhibitors from the show, it exposes itself to restraint of trade litigation.

Another aspect of marketing the show is developing an exhibit prospectus. The prospectus contains information to aid the potential exhibitor in deciding whether or not to participate in the show. It contains all the basic information about the event: times, dates, sponsor, profile of the membership, method used in assigning booths, prices, exhibitor registration and housing information, official contractors, exhibitor instructions, rules, and regulations. Then, direct mailings containing the prospectus and a sales letter must be sent. This is followed up by telemarketing and personal sales calls to assure a successful show.

Fourth, the show manager must maintain an open line of communication with the exhibitors. He or she must answer all correspondence and immediately respond to all inquiries regarding booth rentals. The manager also must respond to all questions from exhibitors about the operation of the show.

Fifth, the manager must prepare an application form and a fair, valid, and binding contract to be signed by all exhibitors. This contract or exhibit space rental agreement must contain the following items:

- All rules and regulations of the event
- A full accounting of all fees and charges
- Spaces for the exhibitor to list choices for booth space
- Spaces for the name, address, and telephone number of the exhibitor
- Obligations of the sponsoring organization

Sixth, an official exposition service contractor must be selected. This contractor will be in charge of designing the layout of the booths, decorating the hall, and setting up booths. In addition, the contractor normally will be the official drayage company that stores the exhibitors' materials and transports those materials to and from the trade show site.

Seventh, the show manager must hire a security firm to protect the show from theft and vandalism.

Eighth, the show manager must arrange for adequate insurance to protect himself or herself and the sponsoring organization. He or she must also urge individual exhibitors to properly insure their own operations. And the manager must insert the proper "hold harmless" clauses into the contracts with the site and with the exhibitors to limit his or her and the sponsoring organization's indemnity.

Ninth, the show manager must prepare a directory of the trade show for the convenience of the attendees. The costs of printing the directories are often offset by selling advertising space in them to exhibitors. Some show managers have even begun producing "electronic directories," evening television shows featuring the highlights of that day's happenings on the trade show floor. These shows are broadcast every evening during the run of the show over the in-house cable system in the properties. Again, advertising space is sold to exhibitors on these video programs.

Finally, the show manager must oversee the mounting and operation of the show from move-in to move-out and must be prepared to enforce all established rules and regulations. The manager must also be prepared to administer all aspects of the show for the mutual benefit of all participants. A show manager's day is filled with 1,001 minor and major crises that require the manager to render decisions on the basis of extremely limited information in most instances.

Exhibitors

Most exhibitors use trade shows to qualify leads, gather information about competitors, and, most of all, sell their products and services.

An exhibitor may attend a hundred or more trade shows each year and must justify attending each one. Each show must produce readily identifiable results, or the exhibitor's attendance cannot be justified. The problem is that trade show exhibitors are currently faced with a leveling off in show attendance, while at the same time there seem to be more exhibitors seeking out the same number of show attendees.[2]

The property views exhibitors as important sources of business. Exhibitors are often major sponsors of receptions, banquets, hospitality suites, guest or spouse programs, and underwriters of other convention expenses.

Next to being selected as the headquarters property for a convention, the designation of a facility as the exhibitors' hotel is the most sought-after prize in a city-wide convention. That property will be the site of numerous food and beverage functions hosted by the exhibitors. Meeting planners and show managers will often dangle that plum in front of the property's account executives in order to win valuable concessions in the negotiating process.

Astute show managers also frequently hold special receptions for exhibitors to show their appreciation for the exhibitors' participation.

Finally, exhibitors mainly want honesty and fair treatment from the site and the show management. Discrimination and a "take it or leave it" attitude will not endear either side to the other. Exhibitors should be notified of all charges and the policies of either the show management or the site prior to and not during or after the show.

Convention Bureaus and Convention Centers

Effective convention bureaus and state-of-the-art convention centers are indispensable if a city wants to make a bid for city-wide trade shows and conventions.

Even when attendees at a convention can be comfortably housed in one property, the space demands of the trade show itself may require it to be housed at the city's convention center.

The introduction of the convention bureau brings additional complexity to the show, but the hotelier should never forget that it is extremely short-sighted to view the convention bureau as a competitor. Convention bureaus and city convention centers are assets to properties in the municipality. A convention center serves as a magnet, attracting those organizations that would not normally consider an area as a possible site.

Hotels

As has been previously mentioned, certain properties can play host to trade shows as well as regular meetings. These exposition properties offer the convention a level of convenience that cannot be equaled when attendees, meetings, and shows are spread throughout a city. This is a major competitive advantage for these types of properties.

Even if a trade show cannot be hosted at your property, you will benefit from the show by providing guestroom accommodations to the attendees and exhibitors, by hosting related meetings and banquets, and by providing food, beverages, and entertainment to the group through the restaurants, lounges, and other entertainment and recreation facilities located at your property.

Trade Unions

Unions that are directly and indirectly involved with trade shows represent another principal element to deal with.

Hotel or convention center personnel may be unionized. Unions may also represent employees of drayage companies and exposition service companies.

It is extremely important for all other groups to become acquainted with the policies of the unions involved with the trade show. Ignoring policies established through a collective bargaining agreement can result in work stoppages, strikes, and court injunctions brought against the offender.

It is also extremely important for exhibitors and show management to be aware of the union's policies regarding wages, overtime, reporting pay, etc. These charges are very important to the show management when move-in dates and times are established.

Exposition Service Contractor

A key element in the success of any trade show is the exposition contractor, also known as the decorator.

Traditionally, hotels and convention centers provided only an empty hall for the exposition or trade show. It was the job of the exposition service contractor to build the booths, paint signs, and carpet the exhibit hall floor. Today, the role of the exposition service contractor has expanded significantly. Now, exposition service contractors are asked to design the layout of the booths, design custom booths, provide drayage service, rent audiovisual equipment, rent furniture, provide plumbing and electrical service, provide hosts and hostesses for booths, and even provide security service.

Because of the increase in services offered by exposition service contractors over the past decade, the meetings and convention industry has enjoyed a corresponding increase in sales. The Las Vegas division of a leading contractor has experienced more than a ten-fold increase in business in this period. Exposition contractors can literally do it all for their clients, from the initial floor design to the final move-out.

Typically, a show manager will select one exposition service contractor to be the "official contractor" for the entire show. Usually, a contractor is selected after providing recommendations from the convention service manager at the intended site. Convention service managers tend to steer their clients to firms in which they have gained confidence from past experience.

The show management negotiates a contract with the exposition service contractor for the design of the floor layout, the laying of aisle carpet, and the installation of piping and draping in the booths. The show management might be charged for providing a table for each booth, hiring security personnel for the entire hall, contracting for clean-up crews for the public areas in the hall, and producing any required directional signs or signs advertising the entire trade show.

The contractor's name, address, telephone number, and contact name are sent to prospective exhibitors in the exhibitor prospectus. When the show management receives completed applications from exhibitors, it sends these names to the official service contractor who then sends the exhibitor an exhibitor's kit.

The exhibitor's kit contains information about the services offered by the service contractor as well as the necessary forms to request those services. Exhibits 12.1, 12.2, and 12.3 are sample letters and forms.

It should be noted that the exhibitor is not necessarily forced to use the services of the official service contractor. To force an exhibitor to do so may result in charges of restraint of trade by the exhibitor. In fact, many exhibitors sign annual exclusive agreements with certain exposition service contractors for all their trade show needs. To require an exhibitor to use another exposition service contractor would impose an undue economic hardship.

Other Principals

When a full-service exposition service contractor is not present, the show management must depend on the services of a number of individual specialized service companies, including the following:

- Florists
- Security firms
- Modeling agencies
- Janitorial companies
- Design firms
- Furniture rental companies
- Drayage companies
- Photographers
- Printing companies

Clearly, enlisting the help of separate companies makes for a more complex operation, and all trends seem to be pointing toward the "one-stop shopping" convenience offered by large exposition service contractors.

The Convention Service Manager's Role

When a property hosts a trade show or exhibit, the work of the convention service manager increases exponentially. The service manager now deals with not only a meeting planner but also a show manager, a service contractor, numerous exhibitors, and a number of outside firms hired by either the show management or the exhibitors.

Exhibit 12.1   Cover Letter from an Exhibitor's Kit

WELCOME EXHIBITORS!

We are pleased to have been selected by Show Management as your Official Service Contractor to assist you in making sure your show participation is successful.

This Exhibitor Kit contains information and order forms on the wide variety of services offered by Greyhound Exposition Services. Please review the pages carefully. If we are to serve you efficiently, it is most important that you fill out these forms and return them to us promptly.

To qualify for discount prices, full payment must be included with your orders and be received at least one week prior to show opening. Orders without payment will be invoiced at "Floor Order" rates as listed on the enclosed forms. Please note that the sum of your orders can be paid with one check instead of including a separate check for each order.

For your convenience, we are enclosing a credit card form and we accept Visa, MasterCard and American Express credit cards as well as your check.

Any additional costs incurred for orders or services placed at showsite, including labor and material handling, are due and payable upon presentation of the invoice at showsite. YOUR SHOWSITE REPRESENTATIVE MUST BE MADE AWARE OF THIS PAYMENT POLICY, AND HAVE A MEANS OF PAYMENT, WHICH MAY BE MADE BY CASH, CHECK OR CREDIT CARD AUTHORIZATION.

We realize that exhibiting in a convention can be complicated. If you need assistance or additional information, please contact our Tel-A-Com Service Division. In addition, our service desk staff will be available throughout the show to assist you.

We look forward to serving you.

GREYHOUND EXPOSITION SERVICES

1624 Mojave Road   •   Las Vegas, Nevada 89104   •   (702) 457-5075

Source: Greyhound Exposition Services, Las Vegas, Nevada.

Trade shows make special demands upon both facilities and the people in charge of them. Certain shows require electrical and plumbing facilities in the booths. Other shows demand extremely high security to protect the products on display. Exhibits may contain materials that are explosive, volatile, or poisonous. Some computer shows demand that the ambient temperature be kept low, causing an increased demand on air conditioning systems. In

Exhibit 12.2 Furniture Brochure from an Exhibitor's Kit

Source: Greyhound Exposition Services, Las Vegas, Nevada.

short, trade shows increase the demand on the property's facilities and services. However, it should never be forgotten that trade shows can also be a major source of revenue.

Planning the Event

When planning the show with representatives of the show management, the convention service manager will need to furnish show management the following information:

Exhibit 12.3   Order Form for Booth Cleaners for Exhibitors

GES Greyhound Exposition Services

Keep Yellow Copy, Mail White To:
Greyhound Exposition Services
P.O. Drawer 42669
Las Vegas, Nevada 89116
(702) 457-5075

BOOTH CLEANING

BOOTH NO.

EVENT OR SHOW _____

COMPANY NAME _____

STREET ADDRESS _____

CITY _____ STATE _____ ZIP _____

DATE _____ PHONE ( ) _____ P.O. #_____

ORDERED BY _____ / _____
                    (SIGNATURE)   (PLEASE PRINT NAME)

Please note: Greyhound Exposition is the exclusive cleaning contractor. No other cleaning services will be allowed on the floor.

VACUUMING OF RUGS, WASHING AND WAXING OF FLOOR TILE, SWEEPING OF BOOTHS, EMPTYING OF WASTEBASKETS, ASHTRAYS OR SMOKERS ARE NOT INCLUDED IN YOUR SPACE RENTAL FOR THIS CONVENTION.

PLEASE FILL OUT YOUR REQUIREMENTS (minimum 100 sq. ft.) and return to Greyhound Exposition Services. All work is performed each evening after close of show.

We will require the following:	Daily Rate	Daily	One Time Only	
☐ Vacuum, Empty Wastebaskets/Ashtrays ..	.12 sq. ft.	☐	☐_____ (date)	
_____sq. ft. @ $_____ x _____ Days	=			$_____
☐ Tile Cleaning	.17 sq. ft.	☐	☐_____ (date)	
_____sq. ft. @ $_____ x _____ Days	=			$_____
☐ Shampoo Carpet.	.25 sq. ft.	☐	☐_____ (date)	
_____sq. ft. @ $_____ x _____ Days	=			$_____

☐ Periodical Porter Service (price based on total area of booth):

Square Footage	One-Day Service	Duration of Show	
0 - 500 sq. ft.	☐ $25.00	☐ $ 65.00	
501 - 1500 sq. ft.	☐ $35.00	☐ $ 95.00	
1501 - up sq. ft.	☐ $45.00	☐ $125.00	$_____

Date Required

☐ Porter and/or miscellaneous services during show hours. . . $12.00 per hour straight time (2 hr. daily minimum) $_____

$18.00 per hour overtime   (2 hr. daily minimum) $_____

Specify dates, times and services for any additional porter services: _____

_____

_____

_____

IMPORTANT: FULL PAYMENT MUST BE INCLUDED WITH YOUR ORDER.

PAYMENT POLICY: All invoices must be settled at our Service Desk prior to the closing of the Show. For your convenience, MasterCard, American Express and Visa credit cards will be accepted. No credits will be issued after the closing date of the Show. To eliminate any misunderstanding regarding the invoice for this service, please bring any complaints to our immediate attention. Adjustments cannot be made unless deficiencies are reported (1) hour before Show opening following the night when service was to have been performed.

J586-12LVC

ADVANCE

PAYMENT

ENCLOSED $_____
(U.S. Funds)

Source: Greyhound Exposition Services, Las Vegas, Nevada.

- Complete schematics of the exhibit hall, with electrical and plumbing outlets pinpointed, floor loads designated, and ceiling heights given.

- Suggested layouts, such as the one shown in Exhibit 12.4. These layouts are merely offered as suggestions to give show management an idea concerning the capacity of the hall.

Exhibit 12.4   Suggested Format for an Exhibit Booth Layout

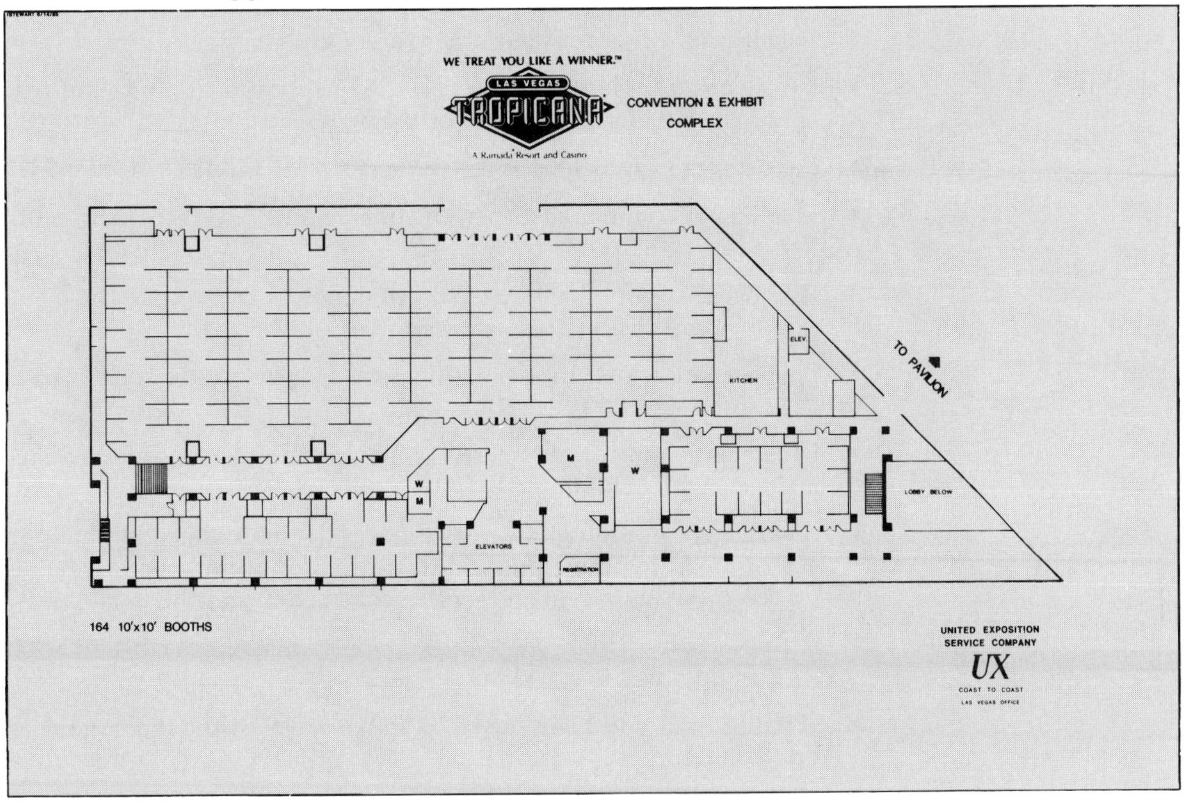

Source: Tropicana Resort and Casino, Las Vegas, Nevada.

- All policies and procedures that must be followed by the exhibitors, the service contractor, show management, and all other personnel associated with the show.

The Property's Fee

The most typical type of fee levied for an exhibit area is a flat charge. On occasion, a property will charge by the booth, but this method links the property's profits to the show management's efforts to attract exhibitors—efforts over which the property has very little control.

Rules and Regulations Pertaining to the Exhibit Hall

Every property that offers exposition space as part of its services should provide show managers, exhibitors, and service contractors a complete list of its policies. These policies should include or address:

- Well-defined move-in and move-out schedules

- A complete list of materials that are prohibited in the exhibit hall (e.g., dangerous chemicals, explosives, highly volatile materials, firearms, etc.)

- Offensive displays (e.g., nude models and obscene writings)

- A determination of who will pay for damages to the exhibit hall, the loading dock, and public areas adjacent to the exhibit hall

- Policies regarding the operation of machinery or the display of wild animals at exhibit booths

- Policies regarding fire and other safety codes

- Hold-harmless clauses protecting the property from litigation from either the show management or the exhibitors

- Policies regarding charges for the services of property personnel

- Policies concerning the dispensing of alcoholic beverages from exhibitor booths

- Any state, county, or municipal ordinances that apply to the operation of exhibits and trade shows

- Policies concerning the operation of hospitality suites sponsored by the exhibitors

- Credit policies of the property as they pertain to the show management and the exhibitors

- A statement outlining the areas that will be maintained by the property staff during the show and those areas that must be maintained by the show management, service contractor, and the exhibitors

- A final clean-up policy outlining the responsibilities of the various entities involved in the show

- Penalties that will be imposed by the property if the regulations are not followed

All participants in the show should be given a copy of the property's policies and should sign a document stating they have read, understood, and will obey all policies and will accept the outlined penalties if the regulations are disobeyed.

Associations Representing the Trade Show Industry

There are several associations that are directly related to the trade show and exhibit industry.

The International Exhibitors Association (IEA) is a professional association of exhibit managers. This Annandale, Virginia, association presently includes 1,400 members.

Another exhibitors' association is the Health Care Exhibitors Association (HCEA) that is based in Atlanta, Georgia.

Representing show managers is the National Association of Exposition Managers (NAEM), a professional association that is headquartered in Aurora, Ohio. NAEM currently has 2,700 members.

Associations representing the exposition sites include the following: the American Hotel & Motel Association (AH&MA), a trade association with headquarters in Washington, D.C.; the International Association of Auditorium Managers (IAAM), a professional association in Chicago; the International Association of Convention and Visitor Bureaus (IACVB), a trade association located in Savoy, Illinois; and the International Association of Conference Centers located in Fenton, Missouri.

Associations representing suppliers to the trade show industry include the Exhibit Designers and Producers Association (ED&PA) based in

Milwaukee, and the Exposition Service Contractors Association (ESCA) in Los Angeles.

The Convention Liaison Council (CLC) is a coalition of organizations that represent various facets of the meeting industry. This organization has been very active in helping to establish guidelines for the exposition industry.

Tours, Entertainment, and Recreation

Recreation and socializing have been successful activities at conventions for years. Studies show that attendees are more alert and have a more positive attitude when some "playtime" is mixed in with the work. The astute meeting planner and the knowledgeable convention service manager should recognize the need for organized recreational activities at meetings and conventions.

Planning Activities for Conferees

When planning a social and recreational program, the convention service manager should first be aware of activities available at the property and in the immediate area. But the key is not to merely recite a list of standard activities like a banquet menu list. First, the convention service manager should ask the meeting planner for information about the lifestyles of the attendees. The meeting planner should be able to provide information about activities that have been particularly successful at past meetings.

Once the convention service manager knows the attitudes, likes, and dislikes of the group, he or she can make thoughtful suggestions about activities for the attendees' leisure time.

Activities on Premises

There has been a prevailing trend in the type of recreational amenities offered at resorts and conference centers. There has been a movement away from the "wild" and a return to the more "mild" forms of recreation.

Sports like hang-gliding, horseback riding, go-carts, snowmobiling, skating, and other potentially injurious sports have been de-emphasized because of the liability exposure of the resort or property. These activities have been replaced by other activities considered to be less hazardous to the guest (and litigious to the property).

Participative Team Sports

Corporations prefer to have their employees participate in team sports because it is thought the cooperative attitudes inherent in these activities are transferable to the workplace. Many psychologists believe team sports promote team-building on the job, raise the enthusiasm of the staff, and foster a collective competitive attitude.

Activities that promote team accomplishments and downplay personal achievements are the most valued. Sports like volleyball or water volleyball are preferred. To a lesser degree, sports like slowpitch softball and basketball seem to work reasonably well. The traditional games of golf and tennis can work very well provided they are cast in the correct format.

With golf, the convention service manager must first determine the range of the abilities of the group's members. He or she must separate those golfers who have handicaps from those who do not and plan a separate event for the former.

If the field of players is large, the convention service manager should think about a "shotgun tournament" in which a foursome starts at each hole simultaneously.

If players with high handicaps have to be placed with those who have low handicaps, a team event like "best ball scramble" (in which everyone in a foursome drives off the tee) should be chosen. The team then selects the best drive of the four shots, and all four players hit their second shots from the points where they landed. Play is continued in this way until someone sinks the ball in the hole. Then, the shots the team played are totaled. Handicaps can also be used to level the playing field.

Another way to level the field is to use the Callaway Handicap System. Under this system, a player's handicap is determined after a round of golf. The scores of the player's worst rounds (through hole 16) are deducted from his or her actual score—based on a formula of the player's actual score.

In tennis, a round-robin tournament, in which doubles partners split after each round to overcome the pairing of weak or strong players, readily lends itself to a full-participation event for all players.

Other team events might include baseball, softball, volleyball, or even obstacle course races.

Spectator Sports Events

With enough lead time, the meeting planner can take a group to nearby professional or amateur sporting events. Baseball, basketball, football, or even boxing contests are memorable breaks in the meeting agenda.

Obtaining a block of seats takes considerable time and effort by the planner. If the group's activities are not paid for by a sponsor, getting a block of tickets becomes more difficult. The meeting planner should be encouraged to try for a reserved block that has a cutoff date. This way, the organization will not bear the responsibility of paying for unused seats. The unsold tickets revert to the house for resale if they are not purchased by members of the group by a certain time.

The same tactic can be used in arranging for reserved seating for cultural events.

Cultural Events

While one meeting group may prefer a boxing match, another might like a Broadway show, a night at the symphony, or an opera. Most symphonies and other cultural organizations announce their seasons and begin season ticket sales up to a year in advance, thus the need again for advance planning.

For really large meeting groups, it may be possible to arrange a special "command performance." If the group providing the entertainment is amateur or semi-professional in nature, they may welcome the opportunity for the extra revenue that a special performance might bring. That extra show may spell the difference to the group between profit and loss for the season.

Tours

In most communities, there are enough historic landmarks and attractions to justify the establishment of at least one professional tour company.

The convention service manager should know the name of the tour organization, the sights or attractions featured on the tour, and the price of the tour. Most tour companies charge on a per-head basis.

Many communities have attractions that are unique to their area. One example is the jeep tours around Scottsdale and Phoenix, Arizona. Conventioneers are taken out into the desert in jeeps driven by guides dressed in western costumes who are acquainted with the flora and fauna of the area. Shooting contests take place (under the watchful eye of the host), and Western barbecues are even arranged for the conventioneers.

In Las Vegas, attendees are taken on bus tours of the homes of famous entertainers, the Liberace Museum, and Hoover Dam.

Guest Activities

Activities that used to be termed "wives' programs" have taken on a bright new look and emphasis. Today, a convention service manager would not dare suggest a trip to the local shopping mall or a cosmetics demonstration as potential activities on the guest program.

The demographics and lifestyles of guests accompanying conventioneers to meetings have changed significantly during the past 10 years. Today, those guests may just as easily be men as women, and there are likely to be just as many "significant others" present as there are spouses. Children may also be in attendance.

The sophistication of the audience is also likely to be much greater. Financial seminars on personal investments have replaced the beautician seminars popular a decade ago.

Planning Guest Activity Programs

When helping the meeting planner construct the guest activity program, the wise convention service manager will ask the planner for a list of those events that have been especially successful in the past.

The idea here is not to merely repeat past successes (for the guest will soon become bored if this year's activities are a repetition of past events) but to determine what types of activities the typical guests are fond of. Any information that the meeting planner can furnish regarding demographics or lifestyles of the typical guests is extremely useful in the planning process.

Another consideration when planning guest activities is to avoid trying to do too much. A guest program that brings the attendees back to the property 20 minutes before the evening reception is not indicative of careful planning. Make certain all guest activities end at least two hours before any scheduled social function.

The Purpose of Guest Programs

For many conventioneers, their association's annual convention may also be their annual vacation. If associations hope to attract these delegates, particular attention must be given to keeping the delegates' guests entertained and happy. If they are not kept amused, chances are quite high the attendees themselves will not return next year.

Types of Guest Activities

While attention should always be directed toward meeting the needs and wants of any group, there are some suggested activities that the meeting planner should be familiar with:

- Culinary demonstrations are popular with a variety of people, and they offer the property's chefs an excellent forum from which to demonstrate their skills.

- A wine-tasting program is usually an enjoyable activity.

- Seminars on investment techniques are quite popular.

- Programs on the occult or parapsychology are usually a hit.

- Motivational speakers or name entertainers can provide the audience with a memorable experience.

- Weight-loss seminars, aerobics classes, and quitting smoking seminars are popular.

- Traditional tours like shopping trips can work if they are not overdone.

Budgeting for a Guest Program

Like any other activity at a convention, a guest program can be expensive. If the elements of a meeting are not funded by a single sponsor (like a corporation), the costs to the attendees can get out of hand.

One potential solution to this financing problem is to ask major exhibitors to underwrite the costs of the guest programs. Pointing out that attendees may stay home if they are unable to bring guests may encourage exhibitors to underwrite these programs.

Children's Activities

A children's program demands special attention from the meeting planner.

When offering such a program, the planner's first task is to divide the group on the basis of age. Twelve-year-olds will certainly not be interested in the activities planned for three-year-olds or even nine-year-olds. The following divisions are recommended:

- Group one: ages 3 and 4

- Group two: ages 5 and 6

- Group three: ages 7 and 8

- Group four: ages 9, 10, and 11

- Group five: ages 12, 13, and 14

- Group six: ages 15 and up

There should be at least one supervisor for every 6 children in group one, 10 children in group two, 15 children in group three, and 25 children in groups four, five, and six.

When dealing with children, the planner should keep several points in mind. First, children love games, recreational activities, and performers (especially magicians and mime artists). Second, children in groups one, two, and three dislike having to sit still for long periods of time and care little for activities that may remind them of schoolwork. Third, children in groups four, five, and six feel they are too sophisticated for "children's activities." Finally, there is usually little interaction between the sexes in groups three, four, and five.

The meeting planner should make certain that dangerous sports or other recreational activities are strictly avoided when dealing with children. Care should be taken to ensure that the backgrounds of all supervisors are checked thoroughly and that the staff is bondable. The organization should also carry special liability insurance when dealing with children.

It is best to consult an expert for suggestions when the need arises to deal with children of any age group. The local public school system can generally recommend competent resources.

Chapter Summary

While the heart of a conference or convention may be a meeting or a banquet, activities like exhibits and trade shows, tours, recreation and entertainment, and activities for guests and family members cannot be overlooked.

Exhibits and trade shows are designed to interest attendees in the products or services on display. In many instances, these activities are major sources of revenue for the organizations sponsoring them.

There are three types of exhibit layouts used in trade shows, and meeting planners and convention service managers must be aware of the physical requirements and facility specifications for the show. Very often, an exposition service contractor is the key element in the success of any trade show.

Recreation and social activities are important convention elements. The effective convention service manager should know how to plan these events and build them into the convention or conference.

Notes

1. Regina M. McGee and the Convention Liaison Council Editorial Committee, *The Convention Liaison Council Manual* (Washington, D.C.: Convention Liaison Council, 1985), pp. 49–56.

2. "Trade-Show Statistics Indicate More Exhibitors Sharing Same Audience." *Successful Meetings*, July 1987, p. 37.

Appendix
Sample Convention Contract

This will confirm the arrangements made by

_____ and _____

concerning the _____

forthcoming meeting/convention.

The _____ hereafter referred to as
the "Association" and _____ Hotel
hereafter referred to as the "Facility" agree that:

   1. The association hereby engages the facility
and its staff for a meeting/convention and the facility
agrees to furnish same on the following terms: (By
mutual agreement in writing, these rates, as well as
the rates set forth in paragraph 1 (f), hereof may be
revised or otherwise changed.)

   (a) Scheduled dates and days of meet-
ing/convention from _____ to _____

   (b) Start exhibit setup _____ a.m./p.m.

   (c) The rates to be charged by the facility for
sleeping rooms are as follows:

Single room from $ to $ or Flat rate
Double room from $ to $ or Flat rate
Twin room from $ to $ or Flat rate
Suites from $ to $ or Flat rate
Other from $ to $ or Flat rate

   (d) The association presently estimates the
number of rooms required to be as follows:
No. of Singles:
_____ minimum and _____ maximum
No. of Doubles:
_____ minimum and _____ maximum
No. of Twins:
_____ minimum and _____ maximum
No. of Suites:
_____ minimum and _____ maximum
No. of Other (Specified):
_____ minimum and _____ maximum
(Include here any penalty clause.)
NOTE: If room is from X to Y dollars (paragraph
c) then specify at **each rate.**

   It is anticipated that __of those attending may
wish to have an earlier check-in. The dates for early
check-in are _____, in which case
the facility will provide rooms therefore at convention
rates specified. The same rates will apply for _____
days following the convention/meeting.

   The facility guarantees it will provide at least the
maximum number of rooms set forth in paragraph
(d) and the association agrees to provide occupancy
for the minimum number of rooms specified.

   The association agrees to keep the facility informed periodically of registrations received in advance so that more exact estimates can be made as
to room requirements. It is agreed that periodic
changes in the above estimates (d) may be made
from time to time prior to the meeting/convention,

but in no case shall the minimum or maximum
number set forth in this agreement be changed except by written agreement. The association and facility shall agree in advance on a mutually satisfactory
review schedule of convention developments and
specify when and how rooms may be released by
either party. (Review dates and times should be specified in this letter of agreement.) After the agreed upon
cut-off date(s) the association and facility will be held
responsible to meet the final agreement.

   Facility agrees to refer all requests for suites (if
all are held) and/or public rooms to association for
approval before assignment if the applicant is identified with the association or industry it serves.

   The association shall/shall not request room deposits of convention delegates.

   The facility agrees to provide the association with
a final occupancy report showing number of rooms
occupied each day of the convention period.

   (e) It may also be incorporated in this contract
an agreement by the facility to improve, remodel, or
create certain rooms or areas or add services prior
to the event covered by this contract. The specifics
of the changes in the facility should be spelled out
in this contract and failure to meet the requirements
by a specified date would be cause for cancellation
of the agreement by the association without penalty.
Reasonable and adequate notification of the association should be required of any remodeling which
would result in a change in the number of suites or
public space available.

   (f) Anticipated meeting room requirements:
Room Reserved: From Date and Hour to
                       Date and Hour:

_____   _____

_____   _____

Type of Function   Rental Charge (if any):
Anticipated:

_____   _____

_____   _____

   A tentative schedule of meeting rooms required
will be submitted to the facility at least _____ months
in advance of the meeting/convention. A firm and
detailed schedule of meeting rooms required will be
furnished the facility not later than _____ months
before the meeting/convention. Unless otherwise
specified in this agreement, public space as outlined
above shall be reserved for the association unless
released in writing. (If total facility is being booked the
language should state "all public space shall be reserved for the association without charge," or with
charges as specified for use at the discretion of the
association. If the association is utilizing only a part
of the facility, the above room schedule should be
completed.)

   (g) Anticipated exhibit space required: The facility agrees to reserve _____ rooms for use as

exhibit space. Cost for space shall be _____ (if any). Services to be provided in exhibit hall by facility include:

(Here specify such items as cleaning, extra lighting, carpeting, advance storage, security, number of microphones available, audiovisual equipment available, operator rates, power supply, or other items agreed upon.)

_____
_____
_____
_____

The facility warrants that the following union regulations prevail in the exhibit hall and will promptly notify the association of any change. Current conditions are: (Outline union requirements in exposition hall.)

_____
_____
_____
_____

(h) Special equipment needs of the association. (description and rates):

_____
_____
_____
_____

(i) A guarantee of the number of persons attending each food or beverage function will be given to the facility at least _____ hours in advance of the function. The facility agrees to set for _____ percent over the guarantee. The above food functions (package) shall be provided at a per-person cost of $_____. Beverage/liquor by drink and/or bottle shall be provided at a cost of $_____. Such prices are subject to review up to six months prior to the event.

If a meal function is to be added to the package, the price applied shall be the same as that included in the above package for a like meal.

(j) The following complimentary accommodations will be furnished by the facility to the association. Descriptions of rooms and suites, dates of availability and numbers:

_____
_____
_____

(k) The facility will give the association notice of any construction or remodeling to be performed in the facility which might interfere with the event. In such event, facility must provide equal alternate space within the facility under contract.

2. The facility and association agree that the following procedure shall be followed with regard to gratuities:

_____
_____
_____

(**NOTE:**—specific individuals, amount or percent and procedure may be spelled out.)

3. It is agreed by the parties that the foregoing sets forth the essential features of the agreement between the parties and that **specific details** as to registration, rooming of persons attending, handling of material, special services, collection of tickets, accounting, master account charges, promotion publicity and other matters will be worked out in writing to the satisfaction of both parties prior to or during the meeting/convention and generally following the procedures set forth in the **Convention Liaison Manual** published by the Convention Liaison Council, 1575 Eye Street, N.W., Washington, D.C.

4. This agreement will bind both the association and the facility and except as above provided in paragraph 1 (e), may be canceled by either party only upon the giving of written notice at least _____ (years) (months) (days) prior to the dates of the meeting/convention or no later than _____ (specific date). It is further provided that there shall be no right of termination for the sole purpose of holding the same meeting/convention in some other city or facility.

5. The facility and the association **each** agree to carry adequate liability and other insurance protecting itself against any claims arising from any activities conducted in the facility during the meeting/convention.

6. The performance of this agreement by either party is subject to acts of God, war, government regulation, disaster, strikes, civil disorder, curtailment of transportation facilities, or other emergency making it inadvisable, illegal or impossible to provide the facilities or to hold the meeting/convention. It is provided that this agreement may be terminated for any one or more of such reasons by written notice from one party to the other.

7. Any controversy or claim arising out of or relating to this contract, or the breach thereof, shall be settled by arbitration in accordance with the rules of the American Arbitration Association, and judgment upon the award rendered by the Arbitrator(s) may be entered in any Court having jurisdiction thereof.

_____ Association

By _____ Chief Elected Officer (title)

_____ Chief Paid Executive (title)

Accepted: _____

_____ Hotel (Motel)

By _____ General Manager

_____ Sales Manager

Glossary

Guestroom Accommodations

ADJOINING ROOMS

Guestrooms side by side without a connecting door between them. In other words, rooms can be adjoining without being connecting.

CABANA

A guestroom adjacent to pool area, with or without sleeping facilities.

CONNECTING ROOMS

Two or more guestrooms with private connecting doors permitting access between rooms without having to go into the corridor.

DOUBLE

A guestroom assigned to two people.

EFFICIENCY

A guestroom containing some type of kitchen facility.

HANDICAP ROOM

A guestroom with special features designed for handicapped guests.

HOSPITALITY

A room used for entertaining (e.g., a cocktail party); usually a function room or parlor.

JUNIOR SUITE

A large guestroom with a bed and a sitting area. Bedroom may be separated from sitting area. (Also called a "mini-suite.")

KING BED

A bed approximately 78 inches by 80 inches.

LANAI

A guestroom with a balcony or patio, overlooking water or a garden.

QUAD

A guestroom assigned to four people; may have two or more beds.

QUEEN BED

A bed approximately 60 inches by 80 inches.

SAMPLE

A display room for showing merchandise; with or without sleeping facilities.

SINGLE

A guestroom assigned to one person.

SINGLE BED

A bed approximately 36 inches by 75 inches.

STUDIO

A guestroom having one or two couches that convert into beds.

SUITE

A parlor connected to one or more guestrooms.

TWIN

A guestroom with two twin beds.

TWIN BED

A bed approximately 39 inches by 75 inches.

Guestroom Reservations

BLOCK

An agreed-upon number of guestrooms reserved for members of a group planning to stay at a property.

BOOK

To sell or reserve rooms ahead of time.

CANCELLATION

A reservation voided by a guest.

CANCELLATION HOUR

A specific time after which a property may release for sale all unclaimed non-guaranteed reservations, according to property policy.

CANCELLATION NUMBER

A number issued to a guest who properly cancels a reservation, proving that a cancellation was received.

COMMERCIAL RATE

A special rate agreed upon by a company and the property for frequent guests. (Also called "corporate rate.")

COMPLIMENTARY (COMP)

A term indicating that a room is occupied, but the guest is not charged for its use.

CONFIRMED RESERVATION

An oral or written confirmation by the property that a reservation has been accepted. Written confirmations are preferred.

DAY RATE

A special room rate for less than an overnight stay.

DEPARTURE DATE

The date when a majority of meeting attendees check out of the property.

FAMILY RATE

A special room rate for parents and children in the same guestroom.

FLAT RATE

A specific room rate for a group agreed upon by the property and group in advance. (Also called "run-of-the-house rate.")

GOVERNMENT RATE

A special room rate made available at some properties for government employees.

GUARANTEED RESERVATION

A reservation that is held until check-out time of the day following the day of arrival. Payment is guaranteed and will be paid by a company or organization even though the guest may not arrive—unless the cancellation procedure in effect at each property is adhered to.

HOUSING BUREAU

A local convention bureau which (for certain convention groups) acts as a housing bureau and assigns rooms at various participating properties in the city or area.

NO-SHOW

A confirmed reservation that has not been fulfilled or canceled by the guest.

PRE-REGISTRATION

A process by which guest registration information is completed before the guest's arrival; room assignment may be included. Some properties have a pre-registration desk or rack near the front desk.

RACK RATE

The current rate charged for each accommodation as established by the property's management.

WALKING THE GUEST

Helping a guest with a confirmed reservation to find other accommodations when no rooms are available.

Guestroom Occupancy

CHECK-IN

The procedures for a guest's arrival and registration.

CHECK-OUT

The procedures for a guest's departure and settling his or her account.

EARLY ARRIVAL

A guest who arrives at the property before the date of his or her reservation.

LATE ARRIVAL

A guest holding a reservation who plans to arrive after the property's designated cancellation hour and so notifies the property.

LATE CHECK-OUT

A term indicating that a guest is being allowed to check out later than the property's standard checkout time.

OVERBOOKING

Accepting reservations that exceed available rooms.

OVERSTAY

A guest who remains at the property after his or her stated departure date.

ROOM NIGHT

One guestroom occupied for one night.

SELF CHECK-OUT

A computerized system, usually located in the property's lobby, that allows the guest to review his or her folio and settle the account to the same credit card used at check-in.

SELF REGISTRATION

A computerized system that automatically registers a guest and issues a key, based on the guest's reservation and credit card information.

UNDERSTAY

A guest who checks out before his or her stated departure date.

Banquets and Functions

A LA CARTE

A meal with each item priced separately on the menu.

BANQUET

A formal, ceremonial dinner for a select group.

BUFFET

An assortment of foods offered on a table in self-service fashion.

CASH BAR

A private room bar setup where guests pay for drinks individually. (Also known as a "C.O.D. Bar" or "A La Carte Bar.")

CONTINENTAL BREAKFAST

A small morning meal that usually includes a beverage, rolls, butter, and jam or marmalade.

CORKAGE

A charge placed on alcoholic beverages brought into the property but purchased elsewhere.

COVERS

The actual number of meals served at a food function.

FRENCH SERVICE

A system in which each food item is individually served on a plate at the table by a waiter.

GUARANTEE

Prior to a function, the figure given by a meeting planner to the property for the number of persons to be served.

HEAD COUNT

The actual number of persons attending a function.

HOST BAR

A private room bar setup where drinks are prepaid by a sponsor. (Also known as an "open bar.")

LUNCHEON

A light noonday meal.

PAID BAR

A private room bar setup where all drinks are prepaid. Tickets for drinks are sometimes used.

PLATED BUFFET

Food placed on a buffet table that is selected and served by a waiter.

RECEPTION

A stand-up social event with food and beverages.

REFRESHMENT BREAK

A period between sessions during which coffee or other refreshments are served.

TABLE D'HOTE

A full-course meal with limited choice at a fixed price.

THEME PARTY

An event at which food, entertainment, and decorations all relate to a central theme.

Negotiations and Arrangements

COMMITMENT

An agreement between the property and the buyer to reserve function and guestroom space.

CONVENTION SERVICE MANAGER

A member of the property staff who is responsible for all aspects of an event.

CUT-OFF DATE

The designated date when the buyer must release unreserved function or guestroom space.

LETTER OF AGREEMENT

A document listing services, space, and products that becomes binding when signed by both parties.

PRE-CONFERENCE (PRE-CON) MEETING

A meeting between planner and property department heads to review requirements and details of an event.

PROPOSAL

The first letter sent by the property outlining the understanding between the buyer and the property.

ROOMING LIST

A list of guests to occupy reserved accommodations submitted by the buyer in advance.

SHOULDER

In the hospitality industry, the period between peak and low seasons.

Types of Meetings

BREAK-OUT SESSIONS

Small groups formed from larger sessions for the purpose of discussing specific subjects.

CLINIC

A workshop-type session in which the staff provides small groups with training in one particular subject.

COLLOQUIUM

A program in which the participants determine the content. Leaders construct the program around the most frequent problems. Usually has equal emphasis on instruction and discussion.

CONCURRENT SESSIONS

Sessions scheduled at the same time.

CONGRESS

The most commonly used European designation for a convention.

CONVENTION

Usually, general sessions and committee meetings convened for a common purpose; the traditional form of annual meeting.

FORUM

A panel discussion by experts in a given field which provides opportunity for audience participation; hosted by a moderator.

INSTITUTE

General sessions and group discussions of several facets of a subject; usually a substitute for formal education where the staff provides most of the training resources.

LECTURE

A formal presentation by an expert; sometimes followed by a question-and-answer period.

PLENARY SESSION

A general assembly for all participants.

SEMINAR

A group sharing experiences in a particular field under the guidance of an expert discussion leader.

SYMPOSIUM

A panel discussion by experts in a given field before a large audience; some audience participation but less than that of a forum.

WORKSHOP

A general session involving participants who train each other to gain new knowledge, skills, or insights into problems.

Meeting Rooms

DAIS

A raised platform on which the head table is placed.

FLOOR OR STANDING LECTERN

A full-size reading desk that rests on the floor. (Sometimes mistakenly called a "floor podium.")

PODIUM

A raised platform or stage upon which the speaker stands. (Sometimes called a "rostrum.")

SETUP AND TEARDOWN TIME

The time needed before and after a function to arrange and rearrange the facility.

TABLE LECTERN

A raised reading desk that holds the speaker's papers and that rests on a table. (Sometimes mistakenly called a "table podium.")

Exhibits

BOOTH

The specific area assigned by the property to the exhibitor under the terms of the contract.

BOOTH AREA

The amount of floor space occupied by the exhibitor.

CONSUMER SHOW

An exhibition that is open to the general public.

CONTRACTOR

A company or organization that supplies services or materials.

CORNER BOOTH

Exhibit space with aisles on two sides.

DRAYAGE

The transportation of material from point of arrival to exhibit area.

EXHIBIT BOOTH

An individual display area designed to show products or services.

EXHIBIT MANAGER

The person in charge of an exhibit booth or the show management person in charge of an entire exhibit area.

EXHIBITION

An event at which products and services are shown.

EXHIBITOR

The company or organization sponsoring an exhibit booth.

FLOOR LOAD

The maximum weight per square foot that the exhibit floor can safely accommodate.

GROSS SQUARE FEET

The total amount of space in an exhibit hall.

ISLAND BOOTH

Four or more exhibit spaces with aisles on all four sides.

LOADING DOCK

The area where exhibit shipments are received.

MODULAR EXHIBIT

An exhibit containing interchangeable components.

NET SQUARE FEET

The actual amount of salable exhibit space.

OUTSIDE EXHIBIT

A booth located outdoors.

PENINSULA BOOTH

Two or more exhibit areas back to back with an aisle on three sides.

PERIMETER BOOTH

An exhibit area located on an outside wall.

PIPE AND DRAPE

Tubing with drapes that separate exhibit booths.

SHOW MANAGER

The individual in charge of all aspects of an exhibition.

TABLE TOP DISPLAY

A portable display that can be placed on top of a table.

Index

The
Educational Institute
Board of Trustees

The Educational Institute of the American Hotel & Motel Association is fortunate to have both industry and academic leaders, as well as allied members, on its Board of Trustees. Individually and collectively, the following persons play leading roles in supporting the Institute and determining the direction of its programs.

Caroline A. Cooper, CHA
Department Chair
Hospitality/Tourism
Johnson & Wales University
Providence, Rhode Island

Arnold J. Hewes
Executive Vice President
Minnesota Hotel & Lodging Association
St. Paul, Minnesota

Edouard P.O. Dandrieux, CHA
Director
H.I.M., Hotel Institute Montreux
Montreux, Switzerland

Howard P. "Bud" James, CHA
Hotel Consultant
Steamboat, Colorado

Robert S. DeMone, CHA
President, Chairman & CEO
Canadian Pacific Hotels & Resorts
Toronto, Ontario
Canada

Richard M. Kelleher, CHA
President & CEO
Guest Quarters Suite Hotels
Boston, Massachusetts

Ronald A. Evans, CHA
President & CEO
Best Western International, Inc.
Phoenix, Arizona

Donald J. Landry, CHA
President
Manor Care Hotel Division
Silver Spring, Maryland

Robert C. Hazard, Jr., CHA
Chairman & CEO
Choice Hotels International, Inc.
Silver Spring, Maryland

Bryan D. Langton, CBE
Chairman & CEO
Holiday Inn Worldwide
Atlanta, Georgia

Lawrence B. Magnan, CHA
President & CEO
Select Asset Management
Mercer Island, Washington

Gene Rupnik, CHA
General Manager/Partner
Days Inn
Springfield, Illinois

Jerry R. Manion, CHA
Executive Vice President - Operations
Motel 6
Dallas, Texas

Charlotte St. Martin
Executive Vice President
Operations & Marketing
Loews Hotels
New York, New York

John A. Norlander, CHA
President
Radisson Hotel Corporation
Minneapolis, Minnesota

William J. Sheehan, CHA
Vice Chairman
Omni Hotels
Hampton, New Hampshire

Michael B. Peceri, CHA
Chairman
Marquis Hotels & Resorts
Fort Meyers, Florida

William R. Tiefel
President
Marriott Lodging Group
Washington, D.C.

Philip Pistilli, CHA
Chairman
Raphael Hotel Group
Kansas City, Missouri

Paul E. Wise, CHA
Director
Hotel, Restaurant
   & Institutional Management
University of Delaware
Newark, Delaware

The
Educational Institute Fellows

Respected experts dedicated to the advancement of hospitality education

Scott W. Anderson, CHA
President & CEO
Callaway Gardens Resort, Inc.
Pine Mountain, Georgia

W. Anthony Farris, CHA
President & CEO
Rank Hotels N.A.
Dallas, Texas

Edward W. Rabin
Executive Vice President
Hyatt Hotels Corporation
Chicago, Illinois

Michael J. Beckley, CHA
President
Commonwealth
    Hospitality. Ltd.
Etobicoke, Ontario
Canada

Creighton Holden, CHA
President, Hotel Division
Encore Marketing
    International
Columbia, South Carolina

John L. Sharpe, CHA
Executive Vice President
Four Seasons Hotels
    & Resorts
Toronto, Ontario
Canada

Stephen W. Brener, CHA
President
Brener Associates, Inc.
New York, New York

Michael W. Jalbert
Vice President
National Sales & Marketing
    Non-Commercial Accounts
Pepsi-Cola Company
Somers, New York

Melinda Bush, CHA
Executive Vice President,
    Publisher
Hotel & Travel Index
Hotel & Travel Index/
    ABC Int'l. Ed.
Secaucus, New Jersey

Allen J. Ostroff
Senior Vice President
The Prudential Realty Group
Newark, New Jersey